The Roman Bazaar

It has long been held by historians that trade and markets in the Roman Empire resembled those found later in early modern Europe. Using the concept of the bazaar, however, Peter Bang argues that the development spawned by Roman hegemony proves clear similarities with large, pre-colonial or tributary empires such as the Ottoman, the Mughal in India and the Ming/Ch'ing in China. By comparing Roman market formation particularly with conditions in the Mughal Empire, Bang changes our comparative horizons and situates the ongoing debate over the Roman economy firmly within wider discussions about world history and the 'great divergence' between East and West. The broad scope of this book takes in a wide range of topics, from communal networks and family connections to imperial cultures of consumption, and will therefore be of great interest to scholars and students of ancient history and pre-industrial economics.

PETER FIBIGER BANG is an Associate Professor at the University of Copenhagen.

T0300548

CAMBRIDGE CLASSICAL STUDIES

THE ROMAN BAZAAR

A Comparative Study of Trade and Markets in a Tributary Empire

PETER FIBIGER BANG

CAMBRIDGE
UNIVERSITY PRESS

CAMBRIDGE UNIVERSITY PRESS
Cambridge, New York, Melbourne, Madrid, Cape Town,
Singapore, São Paulo, Delhi, Tokyo, Mexico City

Cambridge University Press
The Edinburgh Building, Cambridge CB2 8RU, UK

Published in the United States of America by Cambridge University Press, New York

www.cambridge.org
Information on this title: www.cambridge.org/9780521300704

First published 2008
First paperback edition 2011

A catalogue record for this publication is available from the British Library

Library of Congress Cataloguing in Publication data
Bang, Peter F. (Peter Fibiger)
The Roman bazaar / Peter Fibiger Bang.
p. cm. – (Cambridge classical studies)
Includes bibliographical references.
ISBN 978-0-521-85532-7 (hardback)
1. Bazaars (Markets) – Italy – Rome – History. 2. Rome (Italy) – Commerce – History.
3. Rome (Italy) – Economic conditions. I. Title. II. Series.
HF5474.I82R663 2008
381'.1 – dc22 2008031924

ISBN 978-0-521-85532-7 Hardback
ISBN 978-0-521-30070-4 Paperback

Some valuing those of their own side or mind,
Still make themselves the measure of mankind:
Fondly we think we honour merit then,
When we but praise ourselves in other men.

Alexander Pope, *An Essay on Criticism*

CONTENTS

FIGURES AND TABLES

Frontispiece   The bazaar in the old town of Damascus one day in the spring 2001.

Figures

Where no source is indicated, the graphics and photographs are the author's own.

Tables

A NOTE ABOUT ABBREVIATIONS

A few minor and unproblematic deviations apart, in referring to ancient sources I use the standard abbreviations of the *Oxford Latin Dictionary*, Liddell and Scott's *Greek–English Lexicon*, 9th edn. and J. Oates *et al.*, *Checklist of Greek, Latin, Demotic and Coptic Papyri, Ostraca and Tablets.*

PREFACE

"Habent sua fata libelli" the Roman writer remarked in days of old. This is just as true of scholarship as of literature. Over the years I have been met with extensive generosity, support, patience and liberal-minded curiosity from many people and institutions.

I am delighted to offer my heartfelt thanks to all of these at the completion of this study. It originated as a PhD submitted at the Faculty of Classics in Cambridge in 2003. The Danish Research Agency financed the three preceding years of work in Cambridge, for which Corpus Christi College provided a wonderful setting, both for me and my family. Fondation Idella, Knud Højgaards Fond, Corpus Christi College and the Faculty of Classics generously gave supplementary funding. In Denmark, Erik Christiansen and Uffe Østergård helped me lay the foundations to the research I conducted in Cambridge and have been unwavering in their support. In Leicester, David Mattingly tolerated a polemical visitor and provoked me to conceive the first ideas for a comparative study of the Roman Empire. Sarah Scott encouraged me to think of Cambridge. In 2001, The Danish Institute in Damascus and its then director, Peder Mortensen, made a research trip to Syria and the ruins of Palmyra an unforgettable experience. I owe particular thanks to Joyce Reynolds, who has been such a kind friend, as well as Dorothy Thompson and Michael Sharp for discussing matters of epigraphy and papyrology with me. Richard Duncan-Jones and Muzaffar Alam gave me kind advice on different occasions. Michael Crawford kindly let me have a preview of the new edition of the text for the *Asian Customs Law*, still in preparation.

Richard Saller generously invited me to Chicago, supervised my research for a term, did much more than one could reasonably expect and introduced me to Walter Scheidel, who has continued to offer friendship and inspirational discussions over the years. Keith Hopkins volunteered to supervise my second year and made it one of intellectual play and expanding horizons. Chris Bayly took a kind interest in the project from very early on, gave me invaluable guidance on Indian history and has grown into a trusted colleague and collaborator. Vincent Gabrielsen and my other colleagues in the Saxo Institute at the University of Copenhagen had faith in me, took me on as lecturer before the completion of my research and encouraged my work in every aspect. However, with that also came new obligations and new projects. Karl Erik Frandsen, the former director of the Institute, gave me the period of peace and quiet which enabled me to return to Cambridge for a second round in the first half of 2007 and to start turning the thesis into a book. This time Robin Osborne kindly extended hospitality as well as stimulating discussions at King's, while the Danish Research Council gave financial support. Dick Whittaker and Greg Woolf originally examined the thesis, offered penetrating observations and made the defence an occasion which I remember with joy. The comments of two anonymous readers, as well as my lecturership committee, further helped me to improve the manuscript and the argument.

Above all, however, my thanks go to Peter Garnsey who first took me on at Cambridge. I can hardly believe almost ten years have passed. Enjoying the privilege of his inspirational guidance, firm support, loyal friendship, tolerant patience and incisive comments has not only benefited my work immensely, it has also set an example to which I can only ever aspire in my own teaching.

On the domestic front, I owe an enormous debt of gratitude to my parents, who taught me to go my own ways, and to my in-laws; they have supported me in every way possible over the years. Ultimately, however, it was my family, Helena, Julian and Mette, who made it all possible by agreeing to follow me out on "foreign adventures", by tolerating my whims and by giving loving support in times of agonising doubts. It is to them that I dedicate this work. I wish it were perfect, they would deserve nothing less, but this is the best I could do.

Copenhagen, autumn 2007

KEY DATES AND TERMS IN MUGHAL HISTORY

1526:	Battle of Panipat, foundation of Mughal rule in northern India.
1526–30:	Babur, first Mughal emperor.
1530–56:	Humayum, reign interrupted by exile from 1540 until victorious return shortly before his death.
1556–1605:	Akbar.

Conquest and cooptation of the Rajputs, conquest of Gujarat and Bengal.

1571–85:	seat of government transferred from Agra to Fatehpur Sikri, a newly erected capital and palace complex, which was again abandoned after only a few years of use.
1605–27:	Jahangir.
1627–57:	Shah Jahan.

Expansion into the Deccan.

c. 1632–43 Taj Mahal:	construction of the mausoleum to the favourite wife of Shah Jahan, Mumtaz Mahal.
1639–48:	construction of the Red Fort of Delhi which was henceforth elevated to serve as the imperial capital under the name: Shajahanabad.
1650–56:	construction of the Jami' Masjid mosque in Shajahanabad/Delhi.
1658–1707:	Aurangzeb (Alamgir).
1685–87:	Annexation of the tributary sultanates of Bijapur and Golconda in the Deccan.

Last third of the century: insurgency of the Hindu Marathas drags down the Mughals in a fruitless war of attrition.

Gradual weakening and disintegration of Mughal rule follows in the decades after the death of Aurangzeb.

1707–12:	Bahadur Shah.
1712–13:	Jahandar Shah.
1713–19:	Farrukhsiyar.
1719–48:	Muhammed Shah.
1739:	occupation of Shajahanabad (Delhi) by the Persian ruler Nadir Shah. The Mughal capital is plundered and the famous Peacock Throne carried away to Persia. End of effective Mughal power.
1837–57:	Bahadur Shah 2 (deposed after the Great Indian Mutiny).

Mansabdar is the Mughal term for the individual members of the imperial aristocracy. The *mansab* refer to the ranks which the nobles were awarded by the emperor.

Jagirdar is occasionally used instead of *Mansabdar*. However, here the emphasis is on the revenue assigments, *jagirs*, which the nobles received in return for serving the emperor.

Zamindar is used to denote local landowning elites across the Mughal Empire and as such covers a broad spectrum of wealth, statuses and influence.

ROMAN WEIGHTS, MEASURES AND COINS

The principal grain measures

1 modius = *c.* 6.55 kg or *c.* 8.62 l
1 medimnos = *c.* 40 kg or 52.53 l
1 artaba = *c.* 30.2 kg or *c.* 39 l; in late antiquity 21.5 kg or 29 l

Liquid measures

1 metrete 39.39 l
1 kotyle *c.* 0.25 l
1 monochoron *c.* 7 l
1 sextarius = *c.* 1 pint (16 sextarii to a modius)

Square measures

1 iugerum = *c.* 2,500 m square
1 aroura = *c.* 2,760 m square

Coins

1 denarius (silver) = 4 sesterces (HS, bronze) = 16 asses
1 aureus (gold coin) = 25 denarii = 100 sesterces

myriad denarii: in late antiquity, the silver contents of the denarii dwindled to almost nothing and its value correspondingly collapsed. Hence we now find the notion of myriad denarii (10,000 denarii)

solidus: in the same period a new gold coin, the solidus, from the time of Constantine struck at 72 to the pound, became the new backbone of the Roman imperial coinage.

1 drachma = 6 obols (in Egypt 7 obols)
1 mina = 100 drachmai
1 talent = 60 minai = 6,000 drachmai

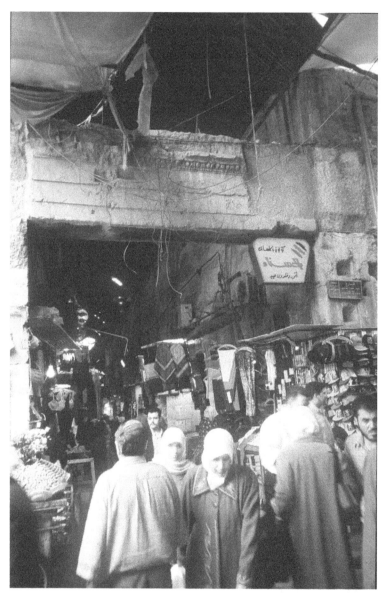

Frontispiece: The bazaar in the old town of Damascus one day in spring, 2001. Between the old Roman Via Recta and the Umayyad Mosque, itself built on the site of the former Temple of Jove, it is occasionally possible to catch a glimpse of how the bazaar has emerged from the ruins of the Greco-Roman city.

PROLEGOMENA

Alles "Factische" sei selbst "schon Theorie".
Goethe, Maximen und Reflexionen, no. 575

L'histoire comparée ... elle consiste à faire tout son devoir d'historien: ne pas se laisser emprisonner dans des cadres conventionels.
Paul Veyne, Comment on écrit l'histoire, p. 155

Roman Bazaar may seem a curious title. Bazaar, the Persian word for market, belongs to India and the Middle East on the Western mental map. It is a symbol of the Orient, a commercial universe at the same time exotic and tempting, and dangerously chaotic and impenetrable.[1] In a study of Roman markets and trade, the term at first appears misplaced and out of context. Nonetheless, the juxtaposition of East and (Roman)West is deliberate. It aims to challenge our preconceived notions and well-established intellectual barriers. The study of Roman trade needs this badly. The nature of Roman commercial life has been debated with varying intensity since the Enlightenment. The subject has become "falsely" familiar to the scholarly community; positions are well known and deeply entrenched, arguments repetitive and circular, the outcome a stalemate. A clear symptom of this is the continued vitality of the century-old debate between "primitivists" and "modernists".[2] There is an urgent need for a change in perspective. By examining Roman trade through the lens of the bazaar, the sense of familiarity will, it is hoped, disappear, or at least be considerably lessened, and thus allow the object to appear in a different, mildly alienating light, revealing new aspects of its existence. The bazaar will emerge in this study as not so much an exotic thing of the East,

---

[1] Kim, the character immortalised by Rudyard Kipling in his novel of the same name, always finds in the bazaar a refuge beyond the reach of his Western existence.

[2] Whittaker 1995; Bang 1997a; Davies 1998; Schiavone 2000; Mattingly and Salmon 2001; Morris 2002.

I

an Oriental "artefact", as the form of trade characteristic of the pre-modern high cultures of the agrarian world. The bazaar is not incompatible with a Roman setting, far from it; in Damascus it is still possible to observe how the two co-exist, the one organically built into the other, in the narrow alleys leading from the old *Via Recta* to the Umayyad Mosque, the former temple of Jove (see Frontispiece).

Evidently, part of the problem of ancient economic history is the poor and fragmented state of the evidence. Compared to historians of European trade and capitalism from the Middle Ages through to the industrial revolution, the situation of the ancient historian is deplorable. Nothing like the copious merchant archives, company records, toll registers and lists published by brokers of prices current in the bourses – the bread and butter of European trade history – exists from Roman antiquity. The ancient historian has to make do with much less and must be willing and able to combine the testimony of very different kinds of sources. He or she cannot afford to ignore the evidence of any one group of material. Papyri, *ostraca*, wax tablets, Roman law, the classical literature, inscriptions and archaeological evidence must all be consulted and made to contribute to the final image. No single group of sources can set the analysis on a firm footing. Inscriptions mentioning merchants, for instance, provide very little detailed information and are in any case relatively few in number, leaving large tracts of the Empire completely in the dark. Archaeology has produced abundant evidence of transport of goods around the Mediterranean, but mainly through finds of potsherds in field surveys and excavations. This tells us of transport of oil and wine in clay containers and trade in pottery. Perishable containers and goods are, on the other hand, often invisible. The huge number of grain ships bringing supplies from Egypt and Africa to Rome have left hardly any trace in the archaeological record, whereas the probably smaller number of ships sailing with cargoes of oil and wine dominate the wreck evidence.[3] Cloth, an important commodity in pre-industrial trade, is also largely unaccounted for by archaeology. Though clearly of great worth, the distribution patterns revealed

[3] Cf. Parker 1992.

by archaeology cannot easily substitute for our missing trade statistics.[4]

The general inadequacies of the evidence accentuate the role of conceptualisation in historical research. Too often historians forget that the sources are not identical with history; they are only the fragmentary remains, the traces of the past world which we seek to re-create in our writings. Sources are, in other words, not self-explanatory. They must be interpreted in order to bring us to the ancient reality. This has, in fact, always been acknowledged by most practitioners of the historical profession. But it would be fair to say that, with some very honourable exceptions, the discipline has neglected the development of interpretative tools. The way that history was institutionalised as a discipline across universities in Europe and America in the nineteenth and early twentieth centuries focused on promoting the detailed examination and critical scrutiny of sources. How to combine the observations into a coherent whole was, on the other hand, seen as a function of the personal inclinations of the individual scholar. Romanticist historians claimed to be artists, working on the basis of their personal intuition and "divine" inspiration.[5] Scholars of a more positivist bent agreed. They tended to regard the "art" of interpreting the evidence as a subjective activity, not really part of the proper "scientific" pursuit of history, which should simply stick to the sources. The latter was no solution; ultimately it was simply a way of giving up on writing history.[6]

The historian of Hellenism, Droysen, followed by Max Weber in the next generation, offered an alternative to this submission to subjectivism. Intuition might be of service to historians dealing with problems and occurrences of which they had immediate experience. However, as soon as they had to deal with questions beyond their personal horizon, their experience stopped being of any use to them. Indeed it might often lead them to make false judgements and introduce anachronistic features to their analysis – the

[4] Whittaker 1989.   [5] Meyer 1910.

[6] As the "founder" of the modern historical profession in Denmark, Kristian Erslev quite possibly did, cf. Tandrup 1979. A small booklet (Erslev 1911), making a sharp distinction between the critical scrutiny of sources and the subjective art of interpretation, has continued to provoke intense debate among Danish historians right up to the present day. See Finley 1985b, chapter 4 for a general treatment of the question.

cardinal sin of the professional historian. Such concerns are particularly pertinent with regard to phenomena either far removed in time and place from the historian, or such as cannot readily be seen from the observation of individual examples but only appear from the statistical study of large masses of evidence. Both conditions apply in the study of ancient economies. The response of Droysen and Weber was to pay close attention to the formation of concepts – our analytical tools – or theory. By broadening and refining his conceptual and theoretical repertoire, the historian acquires a method for improving and making explicit the assumptions that he brings to bear on the source material. Theory and conceptual analysis are a means by which the historian controls and compensates for his "deficient" experience.[7]

One example must suffice for demonstration. In common parlance market trade is always the same. Careful theoretical examination of markets, however, reveals that they may operate in very different ways according to circumstances. The bazaar, for instance, possesses a number of characteristics, which produce a distinct pattern of trade very different from that of modern, capitalist markets, as we shall see more fully explained in Chapter 3. For the moment, a basic definition in ideal-typical terms will do. As a form of trade, the bazaar has taken shape from the many irregularities characteristic of pre-industrial peasant societies. Compared to modern markets, the bazaar is distinguished by high uncertainty of information and relative unpredictability of supply and demand. This makes the prices of commodities in the bazaar fairly volatile. As a consequence, the integration of markets is often low and fragile; it is simply difficult for traders to obtain sufficiently reliable and stable information on which effectively to respond to developments in other markets. Considerable fragmentation of markets prevails. From a modern perspective where trade has focused on overcoming these obstacles to commercial integration by creating a more transparent and predictable environment, this condition has often been mistaken for a seeming chaos and lack of organisation. Most merchants operating in a bazaar environment are

---

[7] Droysen 1977, esp. 217–219 and 285–393; Weber 1922: 146–290; Finley 1985b, chapter 4; Veyne 1976b.

small and household-based. However, they were and are not passive victims of uncertainty. Instead they tend to pursue strategies which do not aim to eradicate the general conditions of uncertainty, but rather reproduce them as part of the solution. One such strategy, as observed by Clifford Geertz, is clientelisation. Merchants in the bazaar seek to cultivate personal and lasting relations of exchange with particular business partners. This serves to shelter them against the all-pervasive risks and uncertainties of the bazaar, but on the basis of specially trusted and favoured relations. The market as a generalised sphere of exchange is not available, or only in a very limited way, to the bazaar merchant. His is not a level playing field. Better opportunies might, for instance, be available in a different market. However, if the merchant lacks his network of personal alliances, he may not be able to make use of those opportunities and will therefore prefer to remain in the market he knows. Fragmentation of the market is not simply an imperfection; quite the reverse, it is reproduced by the way the bazaar functions.[8]

Described in this way, the bazaar as a model of markets is bound to be of particular interest to the student of pre industrial trade. It provides an attractive formula by which to treat the many irregularities characteristic of a world based on slow-moving animal and weather-bound sea transport. Yet, even here is it possible to make distinctions. In this study, the bazaar is used as a concept to describe markets in complex agrarian societies before the development of (early) modern capitalism with its links to mercantilist privileges and later liberal programmes of laissez-faire economics. These policies helped to strengthen the position of the middleman, often a man of dubious reputation and status in aristocratically dominated societies, and saw a development towards more stable and integrated markets during the seventeenth to nineteenth centuries within the European-led, for lack of a better word, world-system.[9]

Theoretical and conceptual reflection enables the historian to cultivate his analytical imagination and increases his capacity

---

[8] Geertz 1979 is the best theoretical description of the bazaar.

[9] Cf. Wallerstein 1974a. Steensgaard 1973a and Persson 1999 on the link between European commercial policies, institutional innovations and the gradual improvement in the integration of markets; Bang 2006, for further discussion.

for perceiving historical differences.[10] Traditionally historians have described Greco-Roman antiquity with concepts taken from the "Western" historical experience. For a long period classics was seen as the epitome of civilisation and constituted the backbone of elite education in Europe and America. As this position was lost in the cluster of processes normally referred to as modernisation, a gap began to open up in people's minds between the European present and the Greco-Roman past. Increasingly Greco-Roman culture has come to be seen as a foreign place and the experience of modernity as a correspondingly inadequate guide to the ancient past. This has set classicists and ancient historians free to explore the less familiar aspects of the ancient world. They have in particular sought inspiration from anthropology. This discipline, having developed a rich theoretical tradition, has proven a virtual gold-mine for ancient historians in search of organising concepts. Indeed, the anthropological work of Clifford Geertz greatly informs the use in this study of the bazaar as an ideal-type. But the relevance of anthropological research for ancient history also has very real limits. Anthropologists have traditionally either focused on so-called primitive societies or studied traditional, most commonly peasant, communities in isolation from the outside world.[11] This is a problem for the student of an urbanised high culture, which depended on its ability to break the isolation of the individual peasant villages and claim a part of agricultural production for the consumption of urban dwellers and specialists. The isolated units of anthropology are too simple for the ancient reality.[12] Economics might offer another possible theoretical avenue to the student of Roman trade. In particular, development economics, dealing with societies where agriculture still holds a very prominent position, has something to offer. But much has already changed in the third world. It does not represent a pristine version

---

[10] Bloch 1967: 44–81; Veyne 1971; Finley 1985b.

[11] A local emphasis, failing to take proper account of intercity/long-distance trade, is a particular weakness of Geertz' early work (1963) on the bazaar. The 1979 treatment is more aware of links between markets, but the attention is still pointed towards local links.

[12] Finley 1975: Chapter 6. Horden and Purcell 2000 struggle with this problem; they have difficulties combining their micro-analytical approach with a clear understanding of wider processes such as state formation; see Bang 2004.

PROLEGOMENA

of pre-industrial society. In addition, economics as a discipline is more orientated towards the future than the past. Its objectives are different from those of history. Both anthropology and economics offer valuable insights to the ancient economic historian. This study draws on some of these. But neither of the two disciplines has focused its attention on the problems most relevant to the student of the ancient world – a pre-industrial high culture. The ancient historian is thrust back on himself or herself to develop an adequate theoretical framework more thoroughly grounded in a historical experience relevant to his/her own subject. This brings us back to Weber's project. His ambition was to ground the social sciences securely in historical experience. Theories developed in relation to the modern world had to be complemented by concepts developed to deal with pre-industrial conditions – a historical sociology. Weber's tool was comparative history.[13] By studying other societies which resemble the Roman world more closely, ancient historians acquire a more secure basis for their own interpretations. Comparative history provides them with the historical experience they lack.

The number of relevant historical parallels to the Roman Empire is relatively limited. Pre-industrial history does not present us with many giant, multiethnic agrarian empires sufficiently well known to warrant closer comparison. The last point bears emphasis. Pre-Columbian empires in the Americas, such as the Inca and Aztec, though smaller, might for instance be considered potential candidates for comparison. But our knowledge of these polities is considerably less than of Rome. The sources are fewer and scholarship much less copious. The same goes for a number of ancient and medieval imperial formations.[14] Anyhow, this is not to say that these are not interesting cases.[15] But from a pragmatic perspective, the best candidates for comparison would seem to be found in the context of sixteenth- to eighteenth-century Asia. Ottoman, Ming/Ch'ing and Mughal history all offer attractive comparisons.

[13] Weber 1972. See Skocpol 1979; Skocpol and Sommers 1980 on the analytical qualities of comparative history.
[14] The volume edited by Alcock, D'Altroy, Morrison and Sinopoli (2001), while interesting, did reveal the huge discrepancies in the density of information between the Roman Empire and many potential comparisons.
[15] See Scheidel 2008 for an interesting attempt to compare Rome and Han China.

These empires have size, dense documentary record and extensive historiography speaking in their favour.

But the choice is not merely a matter of expediency. The early modern timeframe means that all three imperial societies were, in turn, confronted with expansive, European capitalism. This has caused Mughal, Ottoman and Chinese historians to debate to what extent trade and markets in these empires resembled or differed from European (see Chapter 1). The challenge facing these historiographies has in many ways been the same as that confronting the Roman historian: to find a way to account for vibrant commercial networks and considerable exchange without denying the existence of significant differences to the emerging forms of modern capitalism, in other words to avoid the Scylla of primitivism and the Charybdis of modernism.[16] The historian of Roman trade can surely learn from these efforts. This study draws on the experience from all three empires, but Mughal India has been singled out for more detailed comparison. This choice is not wholly arbitrary. The character and shape of the historiography of the Mughal Empire is such as to be particularly helpful in suggesting solutions to the problems which have occupied historians of the Roman economy and trade – as will appear from the following chapters. Suffice it here to note the availability of an extensive literature on trade in the Indian Ocean and the prominent position claimed by a model, positing a close link between state taxation and commercialisation, in explaining economic developments in the Mughal Empire, much as in Hopkins' influential interpretation of Roman economic history.

A Roman–Mughal comparison may seem to militate against the instincts of traditional historical research. It disregards both the unity of time and of space. Trans-epochal as well as cross-cultural comparisons are often viewed with suspicion.[17] This is in many cases unwarranted. Neither cultures nor epochs are "sacred" boundary markers. They are analytical, not arbitrary, I hasten to add, constructs, useful generalisations designed to throw light on specific aspects of reality. Such categories must be designed and

---

[16] Bang et al. 1999; See Bang and Bayly 2003 for some preliminary comparisons.
[17] Even Tilly 1984. Bloch 1967: 44–81 is more nuanced.

adjusted to serve the historical inquiry. From an economic point of view, imperial capitals like Rome and Agra – giant cities of the pre-industrial world with population figures reaching into the hundreds of thousands and financed by an enormous expenditure of imperial tribute – clearly have much more in common than each of them has with a contemporary smallish peasant village within their respective cultural orbits in, say, Anatolia or Bengal. "L'unité de lieu n'est que désordre. Seule l'unité de problème fait centre", as Marc Bloch once remarked.[18] This approach does not exclude recognising differences. The production of calicoes in Bengal during the Mughal era represents one of the most extensive pre-industrial examples of cloth production. A significant, though far from the biggest, part of production went to foreign exports.[19] Roman products such as wine and glass did find their way out of the Empire, but the Roman economy was without a similarly large export trade. In that respect, India, in spite of having often enjoyed a reputation for being the quintessential traditional society, would seem to be not less commercialised than the Roman world, rather the opposite. This makes Mughal India a useful upper benchmark for discussions of Roman trade and markets. Categories, in effect, must be handled pragmatically and tailored to fit our analytical needs.

This takes us to the problem of trespassing. Only rarely can comparative historians aspire to be experts in more than one field. Therefore they must depend, to a large extent, on the work of colleagues in other areas of research. Inevitably, they are bound to make some mistakes, just as their understanding of parts of the "foreign" material undoubtedly will leave much to be desired. None of this should be seen as vitiating the endeavour. It bears emphasis that the aim is not to produce a comprehensive and detailed account of Mughal India. Not every detail or nuance is important to the comparative historian. Emphasis must be placed on the aspects which can help to elucidate the problems in which he/she is interested. The same goes for scholarly disagreements. No historiography is ever fixed. New generations tend to produce new, competing versions of the past. Any historical question of

---

[18] Bloch 1934: 81. McNeill 1986: 35 and 84; Aymard 1990.   [19] Prakash 1998.

more than moderate interest is bound to be contested. In practice it is not possible, nor is it desirable, to account for every conflicting view in the interpretation of the comparative example. In general, I have chosen what seemed to be the better-argued case, even if controversial, and restricted myself to indicating only some of the major fault lines in scholarly debates on the Mughal Empire. The aim, it should be remembered, has been to use Mughal history to develop concepts for Roman history.[20]

Remaining to be explained are a few matters of terminology and chronology. The term "tributary" empire may require clarification. *Tributum* designates in Latin the taxes owed by the provinces to the Roman imperial state. During the 1970s and early 1980s the term gained currency among Marxist scholars to describe the predominance of the political power to tax in mobilising the agricultural surplus of peasant producers. This distinguishes a tributary empire from the modern colonial empires of the eighteenth and nineteenth centuries. The latter treated their dependencies much more with a view to commercial exploitation. Provinces provided the Romans with tax revenue; colonies served more as suppliers of raw products and consumers of metropolitan exports.[21] Chris Wickham gave the concept a well-directed twist, when he suggested it be used to distinguish centralised, imperial surplus extraction from rent claimed by local, decentralised and independent feudal lords.[22] It is in this sense that the term has been adopted in the present study, though in an undogmatic way and without subscribing to the broader Marxist framework. In general "tributary" seems preferable to the empty and less precise phrase "traditional" empire. Occasionally "tributary" has been used interchangeably with "agrarian" or "universal" empire. The term "universal" may help to clarify further the notion of empire used here. It is generally reserved for vast extensive hegemonic polities that manage to dominate and absorb most states within their orbits. This sets a tributary empire apart from the early modern absolutist monarchies which developed on the basis of European feudalism and formed part of a pluralistic

---

[20] Paludan 1995: 197–203 is the best available discussion of this problem. See further Goldstone 1991: xxvii and 50–60.

[21] See Hobsbawm 1987, chapter 3 for a treatment of colonial empires.

[22] Wickham 1985; Wolf 1982; Amin 1973.

state system maintained not by a clear hegemon, but by a balance of power.[23] Another terminological "mannerism" employed here is the concept "agrarianate society". The term was coined by the innovative comparative historian of Islam, Marshall Hodgson, who used it to emphasise that literary high culture and cities co-existed with peasant agriculture in the pre-industrial world. It was not simply an "agrarian" society. The next issue is chronology. The emphasis in this study is on the Roman Principate. However, occasionally discussion of examples and evidence from both the late Republic and late antiquity has been included in order to throw light on the problems under examination. Though clearly seeing changes, the broader timespan was also marked by one fundamental continuity: the presence of a vast tributary empire in the Mediterranean world.

Finally, a word about citation of Greek and Latin texts. These are normally reproduced in English translation as a help to the reader. The argument, however, is based on the language of the original. Sometimes, therefore, I have not indicated the source of the English text, so as to be free to make the changes, modifications and adjustments I deemed necessary, whenever the translation did not originate with the present author. In most such cases the text has been taken from the standard translations of the Loeb series.

The first part of this study seeks to identify and develop the most suitable comparative framework for the analysis of trade in the Roman Empire. Chapter I treats the debate on the Roman economy as an expression of a set of problems common to pre-industrial studies in general: to what extent should the evolution of European capitalism be treated as a general template for analysing trade in other complex agrarian societies? The evolution of a system of emergent nation states in early modern Europe is now seen as instrumental in the development of modern capitalism. Fierce competition and rivalry forced governments to promote economic development and often trade in particular. The Roman imperial government was under no similar constraint. The ancient process of state formation had united the greater Mediterranean under the rule of the Romans. Interstate competition was a much weaker

---

[23] Tilly 1992; Watson 1992.

force. The Roman state was already the most powerful and had much less need to privilege commercial groups; it could concentrate on taxing its vast population, particularly the peasant masses. In that respect, the Roman Empire resembles the early modern empires of Asia, the Ottomans, the Mughals and China of the Ming and Ch'ing dynasties. These empires were all tributary and the chapter concludes by suggesting them as constituting a more proper category within which to analyse the character of Roman trade.

Chapter 2 explores the character of economic integration in the Roman world. Through a comparison with surplus extraction in Mughal India, it is shown how the formation of a tributary empire affects the main driving forces behind long-distance or intercity trade. The imposition of an imperial tax saw a concentration of wealth in the hands of the imperial government and aristocratic elites. Political consumption of the agricultural surplus, however, depended on the availability of markets and long-distance trade. Intensified surplus extraction therefore went hand in hand with increased commercialisation. Market formation was driven by politically determined consumption rather than economic competition. This argument is supported by a hypothetical quantitative model of the Roman economy.

The second part of the study, "Imperial Bazaar", moves on to examine the institutional conditions of trade and the shape of markets produced by the tributary empire. Its basic aim has been to redress the balance in our image of trade under Roman hegemony. While Roman historians have frequently been impressed by the image of tranquil order projected by the Empire, Mughal historians have, in comparison, paid much more attention to the predatory dimensions of imperial rule. Both aspects, however, need to be accommodated within our understanding. Increased surplus extraction, the creation of imperial coinages and the imposition of imperial law, all facilitated trade and markets. But there were clear limits to this process. Many irregularities still continued to characterise the world of trade under the imperial peace. State personnel did not only offer protection, they were also a source of predation and insecurity for merchants. The administrative and judiciary machinery was of very limited extent. Much was still left to the initiative of merchant communities and their capacity for self-organisation. Chapter 3 analyses market integration and argues that Roman merchants would generally have been less able to integrate markets than their later early modern European colleagues. Instead, it suggests the bazaars of the Mughal Empire as a useful parallel, presenting an image of more fragmented integration, many local monopolies and relatively greater uncertainty. Chapter 4 examines the question of uncertainty in greater detail by looking at protection and customs duties in the Roman and Mughal Empires. Though customs claimed by the state were predominantly fiscally motivated and frequently predatory, the ability of merchants to smuggle and to circumvent the harshest collection points checked abuse by officials and kept the burden of indirect taxes within bounds. In the absence of elaborate state guarantees, the merchants of the bazaar developed their own private, social institutions to tackle the uncertainties of commercial life. Chapter 5 examines these in terms of communal, religious organisations and the role of the household in supplying trading capital. The epilegomena conclude the study; they sum up the argument and identify some themes and avenues for further research with respect to the development of imperial styles of consumption.

PART I

THE ROMAN EMPIRE AND THE COMPARATIVE STUDY OF PRE-INDUSTRIAL SOCIETY

Ideally we should create a third discipline, the comparative study of literate post-primitive (if I may), pre-industrial societies.

M. I. Finley, *Anthropology and the Classics*

After all, something *has* changed in the course of human history. We need terms which can size the *differences*.

E. Gellner, *Plough, Sword and Book*

I

BEYOND *THE ANCIENT ECONOMY?*
TRADE IN THE ROMAN EMPIRE AND THE PROBLEM OF COMPARATIVE HISTORY

Aber diese Analogien mit mittelalterlichen und modernen Erscheinungen, schein-
bar auf Schrift und Tritt vorhanden, sind zum nicht geringen Teile höchst
unverlässlich und oft direkt schädlich für die unbefangene Erkenntnis. Denn
jene Aehnlichkeiten können leicht trügerische sein und sind es tatsächlich nicht
selten.

Max Weber, *Agrarverhältnisse im Altertum*, p. 4

En Asie, on a toujours vu de grands empires; en Europe, ils n'ont jamais pu
subsister.

Montesquieu, *L'Esprit des lois*, 3.17.6

Rome – the battlefield of Orient and Occident

Some years ago the world of classical scholarship saw one of
those rare genuine sensations. A manuscript was found and published containing a set of very full notes, taken by father and
son Hensel, of Mommsen's lectures on the history of the Roman
emperors. Here at last was the almost mythical, long hoped for and
never published fourth volume of Mommsen's legendary *Römische
Geschichte*. After having dealt, in three volumes, with Rome from
the earliest times up to the battle of Thapsus in 46 BC, the history
had been planned to proceed with a treatment of the political history of the Roman emperors. It never happened. The subject held
little appeal for Mommsen. In his view the system of monarchical
government had worked best "when second-rate men were at the
head".[1] Instead, a gap was left in the series and Mommsen continued his history of Rome with volume 5, published in 1885,
which contained a ground-breaking survey of the conditions prevailing in the provinces. Rather than the decadent and mediocre
emperors, long familiar from the narratives of Tacitus and

[1] Mommsen 1992: 231 (my translation). Skydsgaard 1997.

17

Suetonius, the matter of real importance and interest, as Mommsen saw it, in the history of this period was the gradual spread
of Greco-Roman civilisation throughout the provinces of the
Empire.[2] Among the chapters on the eastern provinces he included
a treatment of the border zone between Rome and its formidable
neighbour and adversary, the Parthian Empire. What clashed here
were not just two ancient, competing empires but two fundamentally opposed principles of society and culture – the city-
based, Western-style bourgeois, Greco-Roman civilisation versus
the Eastern civilisation of the Parthians, almost without towns and
based on the despotic control of large masses of toiling peasants
living in villages. The border thus took on an almost mythologi-
cal dimension in Mommsen's analysis, constituting a demarcation
line between East and West, Orient and Occident.

A few years earlier that great English historian of comparative jurisprudence, Sir Henry Sumner Maine (1822–1888), had
defined the difference between East and West as a question of
societies based on status rather than on contract – hierarchy versus
liberal egalitarianism. As the *ancien régime* gradually gave way
in Europe during the eighteenth and nineteenth centuries and the
continent established world dominance, the civilisations of Asia
came to be seen as specimens of an unchanging traditional and
hierarchic social order, which history somehow had left behind.
Hegel, and later Marx, placed the Orient outside the dialectical
progression of world history. China and India were seen as static
social systems betraying no signs of development, always remaining the same. They were without history.[3] Thus, to Maine as to
many others, Indian society with its age-old Vedic cultural tradition, composed in an Indo-European language, offered the student
of history a glimpse into the long bygone past of Europe. What
he saw was a society consisting of quasi-autarkic villages made
up of patriarchal households with the division of labour organised
along caste lines and only limited influence exerted by the market.
He believed that it was possible to detect the same traits in the

---

[2] Mommsen 1904, Introduction.
[3] Hegel 1996: 122–123; Marx's views on India are best expressed in his dispatches to the
New York Daily Tribune, e.g. 10 June 1853 and 22 July 1853, easily downloaded from
the Web or available in e.g. Marx and Engels 1960.

earliest remnants of Roman law. But Roman law had not remained caught in the fetters of status society. It had continued to progress until it achieved a fully developed system of rational law based on contractual obligations and rights. Thus Roman law represented a bridge, figuratively speaking, between the old status-based developmental stage and modern Western rational, commercial society. By studying the evolution of Roman law and its culmination in the classical Roman jurists, it was possible to follow the birth process of the founding principles of Western civilisation.[4]

So Greco-Roman civilisation, or rather its greatest achievements, were in many ways perceived as presenting a developmental history similar to that of Europe since the Middle Ages. This is, of course, a way of thinking which ultimately traces its roots back to Renaissance ideology, proclaiming the new times as a rebirth of Greco-Roman antiquity, and which later received a new boost from the art historian and archaeologist Johann Joachim Winckelmann (1717–1768), who inspired the neo-classicist adoration of the Greeks and to a lesser extent the Romans. Even in such an inclusive, overtly anti-classicist, history of antiquity as that of Eduard Meyer (1855–1930), which also insisted on the importance of the various Oriental or Levantine cultures as background and predecessors of the Greek and Roman world, only this last civilisation is depicted as progressing through all or most stages of historical development. In contrast, Pharaonic Egypt is seen as history gone wrong after a promising start, a case of Oriental stagnation caused by religious superstition and an oppressive clergy.[5] Thus the economic historian, Karl Bücher (1848–1930), could hardly avoid appearing strongly provocative when he dared in his *Die Entstehung der Volkswirtschaft* of 1893 to view Greco-Roman antiquity in its entirety under the same heading, that of household economy (*Oikenwirtschaft*), in order to distinguish it from the Middle Ages characterised by a city economy (*Stadtwirtschaft*) and the modern period with its national economies (*Volkswirtschaft*).[6] Meyer immediately felt the need to rebut what he saw as a dangerous, simplistic unilinear view of history, and chose an official meeting

---

[4] Maine 1871, chapter 1 and 1861.   [5] Meyer 1910: 192–193, 247–252 and 1924: 89.
[6] Bücher 1911: 85–150.

THE ROMAN EMPIRE AND COMPARATIVE STUDY

of German historians in 1895 to dismiss rudely Bücher's views as those of an amateur, unfamiliar with the sources. Bücher's description might, albeit with difficulties, fit the earliest, most primitive, periods of Greco-Roman culture; but for later times with the progress of civilisation, the extent of trade had become much too large. Here one had to employ his later economic types of *Stadt-* and *Volkswirtschaft*. This analysis Meyer concluded with the now legendary dictum that the ancient economy "in every respect, cannot be considered modern enough. Only one should avoid drawing on the nineteenth century for comparison, but use rather the seventeenth and eighteenth centuries."[7]

One of the classic debates of historiography had been born, the struggle between "primitivists" and "modernists", which still, a century later, continues to haunt scholarly discussions, often under the revealing name of minimalists versus maximalists, signifying that the problem has often wrongly been reduced to one of quantities, mainly of trade. Yet, Max Weber (1864–1920) in his 1909 article *Agrarverhältnisse im Altertum*, had already objected that the main point of Bücher's models was not to assign antiquity to a first, primitive stage of economy or to deny it the existence of historical development.[8] On the contrary, Bücher's message was strongly historicist and had developed from a critique of the English classical economists' attempt to explain all economic phenomena within one comprehensive or universal theory. Hence he tried to identify the organising principles, the economic structure, particular to each historical society and epoch, rather than subsuming them all under one unifying logic. The ideal-type of the oikos economy, in fact, far from being a first primitive stage of economic development, was rather an attempt to grasp what set antiquity apart as a historical epoch among the group of advanced civilised societies.[9]

---

[7] Meyer 1924: 141: "in jeder Hinsicht nicht modern genug gedacht werden kann. Nur darf man nicht das neunzehnte Jahrhundert zum Vergleich heranziehen, sondern das siebzehnte und achtzehnte" (my English translation). See further pp. 81–82 and 88–89; Schneider 1990.

[8] Weber 1924a: 7–13.

[9] Bücher 1911, pp. 85–92 are instructive for his historicist critique of classical economics. Meyer missed both this dimension of Bücher's thought and its separation of oikos economies from the "primitive" economies of anthropology. In Bücher's scheme the latter preceded the former category (pp. 92–116). Finley 1977: 315–317 saw this clearly.

20

Here it occurred to Weber that in certain respects the fundamental principles governing the economy of the Greco-Roman world had more in common with the Levantine or Oriental societies of antiquity than with the kind of economic formation one found in early modern Europe. Therefore he treated the various ancient civilisations known to him within a broad, common analytical framework, trying not to sacrifice historical development or particulars by developing a range of more specific models to describe the characteristics peculiar to each society and period.[10]

Meyer, however, was blind to this historical aspect of Bücher's and Weber's economic types and the accompanying comparative perspectives, even though he himself insisted that history was a discipline of the singular and the particular. In his interpretation, Greco-Roman civilisation remained a quintessentially Western bulwark against the Orient. In fact, the decline of the Roman Empire was portrayed as a reversal, beginning in the East, to more Oriental forms of society dominated by religion and stiffening tradition.[11] This idea received its fullest exposition in M. I. Rostovtzeff (1870–1952) and his monumental *The Social and Economic History of the Roman Empire* of 1926. Here he set out to supply the empirical underpinning of Meyer's basic interpretative framework for Roman economic history during the Empire, not least through an innovative attempt to bring the growing archaeological record to bear on the historical problems. To all intents and purposes the history of the Roman Empire came to an end with the beginning of the fourth century, from Rostovtzeff's point of view. To him the rest was, indeed, silence, and the remaining centuries, today known as late antiquity, were cursorily dealt with and hurried to their tragic end under the heading "The Oriental Despotism and the Decay of Ancient Civilization". Greco-Roman civilisation in all its constituent forms had now ceased to exist. It had become a foreign world – an Oriental world.[12]

[10] Weber 1924a, Einleitung. See Bruhns 1985; Capagrossi Colognesi 1990; Love 1991; Capagrossi Colognesi 1995; Bruhns and Nippel 2000; Nafissi 2005 on the Weberian approach to ancient economic and comparative history.

[11] Meyer 1924: 142–160. 1910: 123–153 and 192–193 makes the connection of the Orient, stagnation, tradition and religion clearer.

[12] Rostovtzeff 1957, chapter 12. Most of his overall interpretative schema can be found in Meyer 1924: 142–160. This ought to temper the current ritual praise of Rostovtzeff's

Today such an evaluation seems somewhat dated, given the flourishing state of late antique studies. One might even think in terms of a paradigm shift in classics and history having taken place in the last half century or so. A seminal work in this process of change was A. H. M. Jones' study of *The Later Roman Empire* of 1964, which demonstrated that late antiquity could be studied as an epoch in its own right and not just as an era of decay and disintegration or a prologue to the final liquidation of the classical world. Moreover, by reflecting upon the relative weight of agriculture and trade in the economy of the Empire, Jones came to hold a notion of the ancient economy fundamentally different from that of Eduard Meyer or Rostovtzeff. He characterised the Roman world, in late antiquity as in other periods, as overwhelmingly agrarian. Trade, so much emphasised by the modernists, he relegated to a minor position in the overall structure of the economy. Thus changes in the patterns and volume of trade might not, after all, be indicators of fundamental economic change.[13]

In many ways the task of teasing out the implications of Jones' decisive shift of emphasis for our understanding of the economy of the Roman Empire remains at the very centre of scholarly activity and controversy. One result has been that people are now less inclined to take a view of late antiquity as fundamentally different from and completely alien to the preceding periods, and tend instead to emphasise many continuities, without denying changes.[14] A good example, and one of the most persistent attempts to come to terms with the agrarian "nature" of the Greco-Roman world is, of course, the ground-breaking *The Ancient Economy* of 1973, composed by Moses Finley, Jones' successor as professor in Cambridge. Here developments in late antiquity, such as increased state control, contraction in the market sector, tying of peasants to the land and a crisis in the economy of the towns, are seen as the result of limitations, imposed by the

utilisation of the archaeological material as against Finley's alleged neglect (Harris 1993: 14–15 and n. 26; Horden and Purcell 2000: 612). It is doubtful whether his basic interpretation was in any determining way formed by archaeology. See Salmeri 1998 for a sobering reading of Rostovtzeff.

[13] See Jones 1964, chapter 21, and more broadly 1974; Christiansen 1995: 51.

[14] Pleket 1990: 29–30; De Ligt 1993: 4; Garnsey and Whittaker 1998; Garnsey and Humfress 2001.

core institutions of Roman civilisation, in the Empire's ability to respond to increased military pressure along the frontiers. This is Finley, doing the sums: "The Ancient World was hastened to its end by its social and political structure, its deeply embedded and institutionalized value system, and, underpinning the whole, the organization and exploitation of its productive forces."[15] The Empire of late antiquity had now been firmly located within the defining cultural characteristics of the classical world; during the same exercise Finley had radically shifted the focus of our understanding of the Greeks and Romans, stressing the "otherness" of the ancient world and rejecting the alleged close affinity between the social and economic forms of antiquity and early modern Europe.

Instead, Finley sought his inspiration from the, formerly unacceptable, analyses of Bücher, Weber and their pupils, and in addition from the writings of various anthropologists. The economist and anthropologist Karl Polanyi (1886–1964), whose seminar at Columbia during the late 1940s and early 1950s Finley attended, was cited for the fundamental inapplicability of "market-centred", modern economic theory to the study of antiquity; further, Polanyi's notion of economics as the study of "the satisfaction of material wants" echoes through Finley's discussion of the issue of the presence or absence of an economic policy, modern style, in Greek and Roman states.[16] But there were limits to the usefulness of Polanyi's conceptualisation for Finley's project. Reciprocal gift-giving and authoritarian redistribution, the two modes of economic organisation seen as characteristic of pre-modern economies by Polanyi, were inadequate to explain the ancient reality. Even if the Greco-Roman world did not operate on capitalist lines, markets still played too much of a role in the economy to describe it in terms of Polanyi's alternatives.[17] For the concrete analyses, Finley

---

[15] Finley 1985a: 176.   [16] Finley 1985a: 26 and 160–161.

[17] Cf. the important role ascribed to Athens' function as a commercial centre for the Aegean world in generating income to the city after the loss of the empire (Finley 1985a: 131–134). It is commonly forgotten that Finley rejected Polanyi's concrete models for not allowing enough influence to markets and trade (Finley 1970). It is, therefore, not a little ironic when Nafissi 2005, chapter 10 describes *The Ancient Economy* as a decline into Polanyian orthodoxy and at the same time takes it to task for excluding the ancient Middle East from the analysis. Yet, the latter was not included on the express grounds

turned to inspiration taken from more complex pre-industrial societies. The growing body of peasant studies, with its emphasis on locating markets in "traditional" settings, was a key influence.[18] In another place, the work of the anthropologist Louis Dumont on the Indian caste system, *Homo Hierarchicus*, is utilised to embark on a long discussion emphasising the role of hierarchy and social status in Greco-Roman society.[19] Thus, new and exciting comparative perspectives were opened up; and aspects or themes, often associated with the exotic societies of anthropological discourse or pre-modern Asian civilisations, were now allowed to appear and come to the forefront in the picture painted of the classical world.

Of course, Finley was far from alone in this. It is easy to forget this today, but the 1960s and 1970s were also the era of decolonisation and the *tiersmondiste* movement, fired by the writings of Jean-Paul Sartre and Franz Fanon. New prominence was given to notions of cultural relativism, and the limitations and historicity of Western concepts were explored and highlighted by thinkers such as Foucault and, in the field of economics, by the sundry critics of development theory. It would be difficult to maintain that all that was said and done during these years was for the good. After all, this was also the period that produced the various kinds of very dogmatic Marxism and the horrifying crimes of a Pol Pot, trying to realise *the third way* in a version profoundly different from current

that markets seemed to play less of a role and that it resembled more a Polanyian scenario (28–29). This view of the ancient Near East may be mistaken (cf. n. 19), but hardly makes the picture rendered of Greco-Roman antiquity any more Polanyian. Above all *The Ancient Economy* was a Weberian study.

[18] See Finley 1985a, chapter 4, n. 2 (referring to a now classic collection of peasant studies edited by T. Shanin), further nn. 29, 33, 34, 70. In his essay "Anthropology and the Classics" (1975), Finley insisted on a comparative category of complex pre-industrial societies as the most relevant for classical studies rather than the primitive tribes often the object of anthropological research.

[19] Finley 1985a: 43–44, though there are remnants of the old Orient–Occident divide on pp. 27–29; but there the question is of delineating the boundaries of the subject, not of seeking out comparanda. Manning and Morris 2005 convincingly argue that the various Near Eastern societies could usefully be included in our concept of the ancient economy; they were not as different as was previously thought. But for Finley (1985a: 30–31 with n. 31), following Braudel, not ignoring him as Manning and Morris 2005: 15–17 claim, the Greco-Roman world was a Mediterranean world, not a river valley world.

political usage.[20] Still, one should not lose sight of the liberating perspectives – for which the close relationship between history and anthropology to this day can work as a suitable symbol – that have allowed new questions to come to the fore and not least sought to provide more historical and often also more theoretically refined answers by exploring the limits of the experience and concepts of the modern world.[21]

Even if we stay within the field of Roman history, a long series of studies, influenced by anthropology and comparative history, springs to mind. I shall restrict myself to mentioning just a few. Paul Veyne asserted the primary importance of gift-giving, traditionally the preserve of anthropologists, to the Greek and Roman world in his *Le Pain et le cirque* of 1976. A few years previously, Ramsay McMullen in *Roman Social Relations* (1974) had called attention to the high levels of extra-legal violence and the limited extension of official authority. Before that, Peter Garnsey had documented the profound importance of status, social and legal, in the heyday of classical Roman law, where Maine had interpreted the elaboration of the juristic literature as a transition to a modern, egalitarian contract-based form of society. Even more systematic comparisons between the Roman and some of the more famous Asian pre-modern empires and civilisations have been attempted. Keith Hopkins drew continuously in his work on comparisons with, especially, Chinese imperial history.[22] In his study of *Patronage under the Early Empire* (1982) Richard Saller included comparisons with the administration of the Ottoman and Chinese Empires; and Dick Whittaker (1994) has recently attempted to understand the Roman imperial frontier through a model developed by Owen Lattimore to explain Chinese history. Inspired by these studies, a number of collaborative efforts in the field of Roman imperial comparisons have also seen the light of day during the last few years.[23]

---

[20] Finkielkraut 1988.   [21] Contra Engels 1990: 131–142.

[22] Hopkins 1978a; 1980; 1983a; and 1995–6.

[23] Bang *et al.* 1999; Alcock, D'Altroy, Morrison and Sinopoli 2001; Bang and Bayly 2003 and a project conducted by Walter Scheidel (2008) comparing Rome and Han China.

Returning to Rostovtzeff?

All the same, these tendencies have hardly gone uncontested. For instance, in a recent collection of essays, *Inventing Ancient Culture*, the editors set out to restore the prominence of Greco-Roman antiquity in our understanding of the birth of modernity, which they find has come to be too strongly associated with the Enlightenment era.[24] Certainly, in the field of social and economic history debate has been heated, to say the least, from the very beginning, and one cannot help but feel that it was somewhat premature when Keith Hopkins, introducing a collection of articles presented to Finley in 1983, termed Finley's and A. H. M. Jones' jointly developed interpretation "the new orthodoxy". After all, that very collection did not display such a consensus. The impression was rather that of a multiplicity of viewpoints and strong disagreements.[25] Even if we allow that *The Ancient Economy* has occupied a dominating position at the very centre of scholarly debate, the direction of research has to a large extent been decided by Martin Frederiksen's dismissive review in the *Journal of Roman Studies*. Coloured by a general distrust of the theoretical reflections in which Finley so excelled and by a strong positivist inclination, he set out to show that the ancient evidence revealed a more complex and varied reality than allowed for by Finley's simplifying models.[26]

That sort of objection, however, is banal. No treatment of a bygone world, however detailed, can ever claim to be more than a simplification. The important question to ask is whether in the chosen perspective a specific analysis seems to be a fair approximation of the ancient reality for which it seeks to account. Seen in this light much of the criticism has been less than successful.[27] Nonetheless, Frederiksen's positivist objections have struck a strong chord in academe, and have, of late, received somewhat

---

[24] Golden and Toohey 1997. Schiavone 2000 elegantly demonstrates the futility of such an enterprise.   [25] Garnsey, Hopkins and Whittaker 1983.

[26] Frederiksen 1975. See Drexhage, Konen and Ruffing 2002: 11 and 21 for some very recent echoes of Frederiksen's objections. Bang, Ikeguchi and Ziche 2006 for a collection of papers which, on the contrary, advocate the need for the conscious use of theory in the study of the ancient economy.

[27] Erdkamp 2001; see Saller 2002 for some cautionary observations.

unexpected assistance from the present postmodernist dislike of generalised explanations. One view asserts "that whatever classificatory or analytical system we use has to accommodate, in a way that the *monocolore* and essentially synchronic constructs of Bücher and Finley cannot, a possible extreme diversity of types of activity within the same society".[28] Another book, edited by Helen Parkins, confidently declares that we are now *Beyond the Consumer City* – the model Finley used to describe the economic foundation of Greco-Roman urbanism – and emphasises the need for a diversity of approaches.[29] One can readily applaud Parkins' desire to have ancient urbanism examined from a variety of viewpoints. After all, no model can ever hope to be exhaustive; its application is of necessity restricted to a limited number of problems. But it is less than clear why an openness towards a plurality of approaches would require the theory of the consumer city alone to be banned or left behind. Certainly, Parkins presents no very convincing case to back up her claim. On the contrary, in her own contribution to the book she is hard pressed to find her way. "None of this contradicts Weber's consumer city model", she has to admit; indeed her analysis sets out from a perspective "that incidentally underlines the validity of Weber's model while adding some significant refinements".[30] One could reasonably have left it at that. Even so, Parkins still insists that the level of involvement in the urban economy of the land-based elite was somehow too large to be accommodated by Finley and Weber's model. The logic is far from compelling.[31]

There is something a little doctrinaire about this kind of reaction, yet the style of argumentation is widespread. In their book *The Corrupting Sea*, Peregrine Horden and Nicholas Purcell manage within the space of two pages on the one hand to concede that the understanding of the city as a centre for aristocratic consumption of an agricultural surplus is what best sums up the phenomenon of ancient urbanism and on the other to reject the model as "dated": for there was allegedly more growth in the economy than allowed for by Finley.[32] The issues raised by Parkins, Horden

---

[28] Davies 1998: 241.   [29] Parkins 1997b, preface. See further Parkins 1998: 11–13.
[30] Parkins 1997a, citations from pp. 107 and 84.   [31] *Pace* Mattingly 1997a: 215.
[32] Horden and Purcell 2000: 106–107.

and Purcell are not unimportant. In the final analysis, however, the model survives and this is, more or less, openly admitted. Thus Horden and Purcell depend to a large extent on Morley's thought-provoking study of classical Rome – the quintessential consumer city – which argues that the immense buying power created by the politically directed concentration of economic resources from an extensive empire in the capital also acted as a stimulus on its Italian hinterland, promoting more intensive forms of agricultural production.[33] In Parkins' case, an acceptance of even extensive aristocratic investment in the urban economy does not alter the fact that the wealth of that class was grounded in agriculture or that the cities depended for the satisfaction of their consumption needs on the surplus from its landed estates. A strong presence in the urban economy would rather serve to put even further emphasis on aristocratic dominance in the city and thus underline the cities' general dependence on the large households of the elite.[34] Far from having made the consumer-city model obsolete, the critics seem to be exploring aspects or areas of activity where the model can accommodate several variations. Not polarised confrontation, but constructive engagement is what is needed here. This would allow a more fruitful debate about the model to emerge where attention could be clearly concentrated on charting variations, identifying sub-types and adding new dimensions to our understanding of ancient urbanism, for instance by exploring the formation of urban networks and hierarchies.[35]

Further examples of misdirected critique at Finley and the "primitivist" postion need not detain us here. Enough has already been said to make it clear that the unconstructive, sometimes almost extreme reaction against "the Cambridge orthodoxy" has been accompanied by a tendency to blur discussions and more importantly to allow a much less precise use of analytical concepts to reassert itself. The unfortunate outcome has been that the debate on the ancient economy has become stuck on a well-worn

[33] Morley 1996.
[34] Parkins 1997a: 88–89 is not far from that conclusion. Wallace-Hadrill 1991 and Whittaker 1993, chapter 12 and 1994b are very clear about this.
[35] Whittaker 1995 is an interesting exploration of the limits of the explanatory power of the model.

track as attempts are made to pinpoint its precise location on a linear spectrum between the two opposites of primitive and modern, as indeed recommended by Frederiksen in his review.[36] In that analytical game, less is never more.[37] A tendency has emerged in current scholarship almost automatically to support taking a *more* optimistic view of the ancient phenomena, be it rationality, growth, trade, market integration or the economy in general.[38] No wonder then, that Rostovtzeff is again celebrated as *the greatest* economic historian of Mediterranean antiquity and attempts have been made at resurrecting his general interpretation of economic development in the first centuries AD. Once more the story has been told of how a flourishing empire-wide market developed under the favourable influence of the *Pax Romana*, in which the provinces competed for market shares and gradually ousted Italian products.[39] More broadly, this return of "modernism" can be seen in what one of the veterans of the struggle has called "a drift back to the bad old ways when huge trade, industry and capital formation

[36] Frederiksen 1975: 171. Whittaker 1995; Bang 1997a; and Drinkwater 2001 warn against this tendency.
[37] Attempts at quantification, for instance, often incline towards the highest possible estimate, e.g. van Minnen 1986 (extrapolation from very thin and fragmentary material to postulate a very large global estimate of the Oxyrhynchite cloth trade, though we would expect seasonal fluctuation rather than permanent high activity); Wilson 2001 (twenty-two household establishments, with small fulling installations in Timgad dated broadly within a band of three centuries, are taken as a sign of large-scale activity. Yet, the twenty-two individually small establishments are unlikely all to have existed at the same time, much change happens over three centuries, and even if they did, at five members per household, the entire "industry" could be accounted for by some 100–120 persons); Adams 2007: 227–228 (focusing on a Ptolemaic village customs register indicating brisk activity in one month. But, as he also notes, this may be due to a post-harvest peak in grain transports. The more numerous Roman customs registers indicate less intense activity to be the norm, cf. Alston 1998 for a more cautious analysis).
[38] Harris 1993; Greene 1994: 25–26; Harris 2000 and Temin 2001 for systematic surveys of the economy and trade of the Roman Empire seeing *more* growth, trade, markets and development than Finley allowed. Horden and Purcell 2000 simply define exchange (market, gift, redistribution) as *the* central characteristic of pre-modern Mediterranean civilisation.
[39] Tchernia 2006 for a critique of this trend. A new example of the continuing cache of Rostovtzeff's general interpretive framework is provided by Rizzo's discussion of the changing patterns of imports to Rome (2003: 230) as reflected in ceramic assemblages, seeing Italian production decline in the face of provincial competition. Carandini 1983b; 1988; 1989 are the most outspoken examples. But elements can also be found in e.g. Paterson 1998; von Freyberg 1989, chapters 2 and 3.5 and in the very interesting and balanced attempt by Lo Cascio 1991 to "unite" Rostovtzeff and Weber. For Rostovtzeff as *the* great historian, see note 12 above.

were discovered in every petty street-corner workshop of Roman towns".[40]

Two examples will suffice. One deals with the production of Italian *terra sigillata*, the mould-cast, red-slip ceramic tableware found by archaeologists in widespread locations during the late Republic and early Empire. The other is a broader discussion of the market in the Roman world. Let us take *terra sigillata* first. Surveying recent archaeological developments in our picture of Italian production centres, Philip Kenrick concluded: "The level of organization and the closeness of relationship which this implies seems to me to justify us in regarding this as an industry *in an entirely modern sense*."[41] Yet, one looks in vain for any attempt at a close definition of modern industry that would justify the label in this particular context, especially in view of a whole series of studies that have emphasised the large differences to the modern world in the production of ancient fine ware.[42] Apparently the mere existence of branch workshops, maintaining connections with a mother unit, is taken as sufficient "proof". But we find Assyrian merchants establishing branches in other cities in the early second millennium BC. In fact, the very same archaeological excavations have shown, and mapped with increasing detail, that production remained decentralised and not just confined to a few centres or large workshops. Ironically, Rostovtzeff himself, the leading proponent of the old-style modernism, saw precisely this as what marked the limits to the modern nature of the Roman economy. The technological and economic advantages to be gained from a concentration of capital and production in large units were insufficient to produce and sustain an industrial development, modern style.[43]

Second, the nature of the market in the Roman world. Finley took the seemingly unproblematical view that the ancient economy

---

[40] Whittaker 1995: 22.   [41] Kenrick 1993: 36. See also Wilson 2001.

[42] Cf. Fülle 1997 and Prachner 1980 on the organisation of Italic *terra sigillata* production, stressing the limited scale of most potteries and the importance of travelling potters. Further on the interpretation of Gallic *terra sigillata* production, see the discussions by Woolf 1998, chapter 7 and Whittaker 2002. Seminal are Goudineau 1974 and Marsh 1981.

[43] Rostovtzeff 1957: 172–179. See Larsen 1976 for the organisation of early Assyrian merchants.

was not organised as "an enormous conglomeration of interdependent markets". Recently, however, the economist Peter Temin argued that Finley was quite simply wrong, the economy of the Roman Empire represented just such a conglomeration.[44] This is an extraordinary claim. One might conceivably imagine that some markets had begun to be linked by middle- and long-distance trade. But to see the entire economy, spanning several continents, as organised by a set of interlinked markets is quite another matter. It is doubtful whether the mature eighteenth-century European economy, outside some restricted pockets, could be described in such terms.[45] Given our almost complete lack of price data which could substantiate this conclusion, caution might be advisable.[46] But to Temin the mere occurrence of markets is enough to justify the claim. "If about seventy-five per cent of the population of the Roman Empire was engaged in farming, then it is not unreasonable to suppose that over half of production was carried on by householding rather than by market exchanges", he observes undeterred. For, according to Temin, the prevalence of households in organising economic activity does not mean that peasant production was not determined by the market, only "that most of each farm's activities were devoted to maintaining its workforce".[47] This will not do; it is an attempt to explain away the fact that for most peasants, the market will only have constituted a subsidiary outlet and did not provide them with their primary means of subsistence.

---

[44] Temin 2001: 181.

[45] Cf. the cautious analyses of Persson 1999 and Erdkamp 2005. See Osborne 1996 for an interesting study of some link-up between market and production in the archaic age. But that does not make the economy as a whole a conglomeration of interdependent markets, cf. Morley 2007: 96.

[46] A later MIT working paper by Kessler and Temin (2005) reasserts this claim of such Empire-wide integration based on a good handful of price observations scattered across several centuries. The scarcity of observations, however, only serves to reinforce the pattern detected, the authors declare optimistically. That is methodologically unwarranted; there is simply far too little data even to begin that form of analysis. An Empire-wide study of market integration on the basis of price data is beyond our reach. At best, and even that is debatable, the price data recovered from Egypt may allow us a broad impression of conditions in one province. See Chapter 3 of this book for what can hesitantly be achieved and with the opposite conclusion.

[47] Temin 2001: 180. The observation that even in today's rich societies a large part of economic activity is still kept within the family misses one crucial distinction. Most middle-class households depend on wage income for their subsistence, whereas peasants have historically produced their own subsistence outside the market.

A peasant household, therefore, cannot easily be abstracted to the model of a profit-orientated firm, as Temin seems to be doing; its primary objective was different, the reproduction of the family unit. In other words, even on Temin's own premises more than half of the Roman economy was not organised as "a conglomeration of interdependent markets". The question of a market economy in the Roman Empire is clearly less straightforward than Temin allows.

On closer inspection the various modernising uses of concepts, which have been explored here, seem to a large extent to have been guided less by analytical than by value judgements. A clear indicator is the recurrent use of terms such as "complex" and "sophisticated", qualifying or supporting the descriptions. By themselves these are almost empty words, meaning as little as "not primitive" or "something not inferior". Struggling to free themselves from the confident shadow of nineteenth-century evolutionism, twentieth-century social anthropologists have taught us that there is no such thing as a primitive culture, only imperceptive investigators. Hence words such as complex and sophisticated often appear in texts mainly as apologetic or defensive value markers. A remark made in connection with a discussion of ancient accounting by historian William Harris illustrates my point neatly. Against the claim that the ancient agricultural writers did not show any signs of modern economic rationality and capitalist accounting practices, the objection is voiced: "But Columella has in turn been *defended*."[48] Observations that the Greeks and Romans structured their thinking about estate management on other principles than those at the core of modern accounting and management theory, are taken as making an implicit statement about their cultural shortcomings and lack of rationality. But that is not the case; it only means that they organised their thought in a fashion different from some patterns which have been gaining ground since the birth of modern capitalism.[49] Essentially the problem is one of empathy. To Weber and Finley, as to most anthropologists, the culturalist

[48] Harris 1993: 25 (my emphasis). For a further example, see Rathbone 1991, chapters 8–9.
[49] Cf. Kehoe 1997; see Mickwitz 1937 for a classic analysis. See Tchernia 2005 for a recent collection of papers dedicated to this issue.

solution, Herder-style, was the most appealing. This meant under-
lining the differences between "us" and "them" and subsequently
seeking to understand the logic governing "the other" rather than
applying our own habitual notions of normalcy.

To the critics, however, it is exactly that approach which is
the central problem. Here are Peregrine Horden and Nicholas
Purcell: "The consequence has inevitably been to devalue practices
which cannot be usefully seen as embryonic modernity . . . For
the telescopic perspective encourages the itemizing of absences
and shortfalls . . . Ultimately, however, the project was sabotaged
by the use of the 'minimalizing' comparative technique. Its trust
remained essentially negative: a generation was taught . . . what
was not important in the pre-medieval Mediterranean."[50] The con-
trasting comparisons between the ancient and the early modern
world, inherent in the Weberian approach, are (mis)perceived as a
derogatory portfolio of defects and flaws – in the Italian archaeologist Carandini's words "an annihilation of the past" and "self-
deification of the modern world".[51] But it is difficult to see how
one could argue against a strongly modernist position, preferring
instead to emphasise the unique or historical characteristics of the
Greco-Roman world, without showing the contrasts and differences. That does not imply an essentially negative argument. On
the contrary, it is the central point in Weber's and Finley's analyses
that we find a world governed by other principles: the dominance
of agriculture, the dependence of urbanisation on aristocratic consumption, the importance of slavery and the all-pervasive influence of an ideology of social status which privileged political over
entrepreneurial activities.

In any case, the current dissatisfaction with comparisons focusing on the contrasts and differences between the Greco-Roman
world and later European developments has brought about a very
interesting change in the use of comparative history for the study of
the ancient economy. Pioneered by works such as D'Arms' *Commerce and Social Standing*, a number of scholars have taken up
the theoretical challenge of the "primitivist" position and begun in
a more systematic fashion to re-examine the relationship between

---

[50] Horden and Purcell 2000: 146.   [51] Carandini 1983a: 178–179.

the economy of the Roman Empire and that of medieval and early modern, capitalist Europe. Rather than differences and contrasts, it is now similarities and analogies which are sought out and emphasised.[52] Observing that the Empire contained a number of very large cities, with the one million inhabitants of Rome at the apex, they justly note that only at a very late stage was the European economy able to equal that achievement. London, the largest city in the eighteenth century, did not reach a million inhabitants before 1800. Hence, for instance, they warn against postulating any significant difference in the size of the market. Instead, they take their lead from the many developments in the study of the pre-industrial, still agrarian-based, European economy, emphasising the slowness and limited extent of change. In the larger perspective, this was a world, in the catchphrases coined by the French *Annales* historians, of *la longue durée* or *histoire immobile,* where economic change tended to be cyclical, caught as it was in the Malthusian trap where productivity gains in agriculture were undermined by growing population. The crucial development first came about with the Industrial Revolution around 1800. Until then the productive and technological base of society was organic and set clear limits to growth. Faced with this more "primitive" or static version of early modern Europe, the Dutch historian and epigraphist Harry Pleket concludes that it is now time "finally to call into question the view of the primitivists that the world of the Roman Empire was so very different from later pre-industrial Europe as they claim. In this . . . I would like to suggest that the economy of the Roman Empire was more closely related to the economy of pre-industrial Europe until the eighteenth century than our own time."[53]

---

[52] The approach was pioneered in studies of e.g. D'Arms 1981 and Schleich 1983. By far the best and most important specimen is Pleket 1990 which is a systematic attempt to produce a synthesis of the Roman economy by analogy to early modern Europe (1400–1800). Other examples include Harris 1993; van Nijf 1997; Laurence 1998 and 1999; Harris 2000; Horden and Purcell 2000; and Temin 2001.

[53] "endlich die Auffassung der 'Primitivisten' in frage stellen, dass sich die Welt des Römischen Reiches so wesentlich von der späteren vorindustriellen Europa underscheide wie behauptet. Indem . . . möchte ich die Vermutung aüssern, dass die Wirtschaft des Römischen Reiches mit der Ökonomie des vorindustriellen Europa bis zum 18. Jh. vielleicht enger verbunden war als mit unserer Gegenwart" (my translation). Pleket 1990: 28.

It is difficult to disagree strongly with Pleket's position, stated in such very general terms. It is certainly salutary to be reminded in our comparisons that the scale and dimensions of pre-industrial economies were of another, much smaller order than in the modern world, that they, so to speak, belong on the same baseline.[54] However, this is not where the main argument is. Even Finley, for instance, emphasised that urbanisation in Greco-Roman antiquity reached a historical high point, only equalled very late in history. He also expressed strong doubts about relying too much on analogies furnished by anthropological studies of, say, gift-giving in much simpler societies. The market as a form of exchange was far too important in antiquity; and no one who has walked around the Monte Testaccio – the man-made, almost eighth hill of Rome consisting (for the most part) of oil-bearing amphorae discarded in the days of the Empire – can seriously doubt the existence of quite large volumes of exchange within the Roman Empire.[55] But Pleket takes the analysis much further, constructing the Roman Empire closely on the model of early modern Europe. Thus a picture emerges where regions of relative low-level agriculture and only sparse urbanisation intermingle with dynamic, more modern centres dominated by highly specialised agriculture in the Dutch style, and towns relying more on trade and export manufacture for their survival than on aristocratic consumption. Other contributions to the debate point in the same direction when they suggest that the Roman Empire should be seen as a market economy working essentially at a level comparable to that of the Atlantic world in the eighteenth century.[56]

The problem with such analyses is that they depend on a very loose use of the notion of functional equivalents. Being strongly disinclined even to consider the possible importance of differences, they tend to prefer either to declare them marginal or automatically

[54] Nicolet 1988: 37–38 and e.g. Andreau 1994b: 191 and 1995: 948 point in the same direction.
[55] Finley 1970, 1975, chapter 6 and 1977, for instance. On Monte Testaccio, see Rodríguez-Almeida 1984; Blázquez Martínez and Remesal Rodriguez 1999–2001.
[56] Temin 2001. Also Harris 1993: 19.

assert that "the methods may have been different, but the economic consequences are the same".[57] A discussion of the rank-size distribution of Roman towns is symptomatic. Referring to De Vries' influential study of urbanisation and urban networks in early modern Europe, Pleket concludes that the rank-size distributions of Roman cities can be seen as roughly similar, even if admittedly there are some differences, especially among the very large cities of the Roman and early modern world. In De Vries' study, however, it is a central point that the shape of urban systems is closely linked to the specific socio-economic structure of any given particular society. Differences at the top of urban hierarchies, therefore, ought not to be quickly brushed aside as of only trivial importance; they may reflect significant differences in economic organisation between the two societies.[58] Braudel, after all, argued that capitalism was a higher-order phenomenon, connected precisely with the top of societal hierarchies in early modern Europe rather than the virtually immovable mass of peasant producers and small towns.[59] In Pleket's analysis, however, this type of issue is simply bypassed in favour of a broader, more inclusive understanding of "modern" economic phenomena.[60] But there is a price to be paid for such a manoeuvre: a potential loss of explanatory power. Ultimately, the economies of early modern Europe and the Roman Empire followed very different paths of development. The more we downplay the differences, the less able are we to understand why. That is unsatisfactory. The aim should be to find better historical models to help us elucidate the particular nature of the Roman economy.[61]

---

[57] Pleket 1990: 39: "die Methoden mögen verschieden sein, aber die Wirtschaftlichen Folgen sind dieselben" (my English translation). The method was pioneered by D'Arms 1981: 165–169.

[58] See Woolf 1997 for a discussion linking these differences to the presence of a single unifying empire in the Roman world.

[59] Braudel 1982: 455–457.

[60] Pleket 1990: 146. Similar in style is Harris 1993: 24, advising Love 1991 to adopt a more inclusive definition of capitalism so as to make room for antiquity. De Vries 1990 explains his approach to urban networks.

[61] For a similar wish to transcend this problem cf. the introductions to Mattingly and Salmon 2001 and Manning and Morris 2005.

From traditional Asia to early modern Eurasia

At first sight the persistent attraction of early modern Europe as yardstick for the ancient world appears curious. The last half century has seen a strong challenge building up to the notion of European developments as the quintessential expression of history. Europe's paradigmatic status in world history has suffered considerable erosion and is no longer self-evident.[62] Nonetheless, the current modernising trends in ancient history are not an isolated phenomenon. Similar doubts about the legitimacy of analysing differences between "the West and the rest" have occurred in a whole range of disciplines. During the 1990s a rather curious debate took place between Marshall Sahlins and Gananath Obeysekere, both distinguished American anthropologists, about the proper interpretation of Captain James Cook's death on Hawaii on his second return, 14 February 1779. To Sahlins the explanation has to be found in the particular cognitive and cultural universe of the Hawaiians. Unfortunately for Cook, his arrival was linked to their calendar of religious ritual by the Hawaiians, who saw him as their returning god Lono. Cook willingly played along, not knowing that the festival part of the year would end in the king re-establishing his primacy by appropriating the powers of Lono. Even then nothing would have happened if Cook had not been forced by a broken mast to return after first having left the island. This action was perceived as a threat to the cosmic order where the king was now in command. That order had to be re-created and Cook/Lono was killed so that his powers could properly be passed to the king. To Obeysekere such a culturalist interpretation is the result of blatant racism, making a mockery of the cognitive abilities of the indigenous population and denying them their rightful place within common humanity; of course, the Hawaiians could tell the difference between a white explorer and their god. Instead he wants to *render fuzzy* the clear distinctions between the visiting Westerner and the indigenous culture. One cannot avoid

---

[62] Hodgson in 1974 and 1993, presents one of the most thoughtful attempts to re-evaluate the position of Europe in world history.

recalling the defensive dismissals of Finley. Still the incidents are quite mystifying and Obeysekere has to introduce a post-mortem deification of Cook by the Hawaiians to tie the loose ends together. To the innocent bystander it is not altogether clear why the very thought of Cook as a god to the Hawaiians while alive should be seen as a monstrosity when it is apparently acceptable that they should have worshipped him after his death. In both cases the explanation depends on the particular cultural universe of the Hawaiians, even if one of the commentators tries to disguise it.[63]

The clash over the interpretation of Cook's death testifies to a certain ambiguity in the status of "the other" in our political and scholarly discourses. On closer inspection, the tension between cultural differences and universal similarities lies at the very heart of social anthropology. Malinowski, for instance, made his name as one of the founders of the discipline by developing Bücher's theories to portray the economic world of Melanesia as functioning according to principles very different from those imagined by modern economic theory. Yet, he also attempted to show in a discussion of Lévy-Bruhl's work on "primitive" mentality that so-called primitive peoples were guided by the same kind of utilitarian rationality as modern English people.[64] Recently the Indologist Sheldon Pollock aptly described this situation as the general epistemological trap of non-Western studies where the universal value of Western categories and analyses stressing the "otherness" of those societies are equally rejected as unacceptable. The student of non-Western societies seems to be confronted with the impossible challenge of having his cake and eating it too.[65]

Sometimes pictures say more than many words (Fig. 1.1). The problem is clearly brought out by the symbolism in a picture showing the moment when Olusegun Obasanjo was sworn in as president of Nigeria on 29 May 1999. Here he appeared in an ethnic national costume whereas the officials surrounding him and the president of the high court, who was in charge of the ceremony, were all dressed in uniforms unmistakably European in style. The concept of power has never convincingly been separated from the

---

[63] Obeysekere 1992 (quotation from p. 16), answered by Sahlins 1995.
[64] Malinowski 1948 vs Levy-Bruhl 1985. Littleton 1985.   [65] Pollock 1998: 43.

Fig. 1.1 Olusegun Obasanjo is sworn in as president of Nigeria (PolFot, Denmark)

West. Indeed, how could it possibly be in the present world? The legacy of European imperialism is a heavy one and the romanticist emphasis on the native cultural tradition has more often than not, quite understandably, been combined with a wish to gain access to the technological and economic resources of modernity. The scenes which one could see some years ago of Hindu nationalists celebrating in the streets of Delhi because India had now joined the atomic powers are only an extreme illustration of a more general condition.[66] In his essays on Istanbul, Orhan Pamuk, the great novelist, has managed to capture well the tortured and complex relationship between Westernising and "othering" in the cultural identity of third world countries:

The vicious cycle is fed by Westernising intellectuals who long to hear the prominent writers and publishers of the West praise them for being like Westerners. Writers like Pierre Loti, by contrast, make no secret of loving Istanbul and the Turkish people for the opposite reason: for the preservation of their Eastern particularity and their resistance to things Western. In the days when Pierre Loti was criticising Istanbullus for losing touch with their traditions, he had only a small following in Turkey, most of this ironically, among the Westernising minority. But whenever the nation is embroiled in an international dispute, the Westernised literary élite makes an indignant peace with the "Turkophilism" of Pierre Loti's highly sentimental and exotic writings.[67]

The position of being "other" both holds out a promise of autonomy and a danger of falling into the trap of the merely quaint and exotic, an object of domination.

This problem of "empowerment" was accentuated by the process of de-colonisation in the decades following the Second World War. No longer was it possible for historians to regard the Western world as the sole agent of social development, the *faber historiae,* when it now became clear that history did not end with the European colonial empires. Hence there has been a growing dissatisfaction with the traditional view of world history as the unfolding drama of Western development from the birth of civilisation in Mesopotamia through antiquity, the Middle Ages and Renaissance to modernity, leaving the rest of the world in the sidings until it

[66] Even Huntington 1996, chapters 4–5 sees how "indigenisation" and modernisation may go together.
[67] Pamuk 2005: 213.

came under the influence of Europe. Instead the main concern has been to establish a more global point of view and, in the words of Eric Wolf's influential book, include *The People Without History*. One of the most remarkable results of these endeavours is the American Islamist Marshall Hodgson's great work of comparative history *The Venture of Islam*. Hodgson asked how world history should be conceived before the establishment of European world hegemony. His answer was to relegate Western feudalism to the margins of the historical narrative. The dominant force in the world from the seventh to the seventeenth century was, he observed, the civilisation of Islam. Europe need not, in other words, be taken as paradigmatic of history as such.[68]

In the study of India and the Indian Ocean economy Hodgson's analysis was foreshadowed by the Dutch historian J. C. van Leur. In the 1930s he began to reject the notion of European superiority right from the arrival of Vasco da Gama in the early sixteenth century. European hegemony was a much later development, van Leur maintained; during the first centuries of their presence the influence and importance of the Europeans were only marginal and certainly amounted to far less than commercial, let alone political control. This is how he drew the larger picture:

Such an East, retiring into isolation, standing to one side along the path of the West, the path of hurried activity, world trade, world economy, modern life, seems to have been foreign to the eighteenth century. That century did not know any superior Occident, nor any self-isolating Orient no longer progressing with it. It knew a mighty East, a rich fabric of a strong, broad weave with a more fragile Western warp thread inserted in it at broad intervals.[69]

For a long period after the Portuguese first established their sea empire in the Indian Ocean, Asia remained largely unaffected and followed its own course of history. The application of European periodisations was therefore meaningless.

At a general level, van Leur's ideas have formed the basis of a new paradigm which has been developing since the Second World War. One important implication of his view, which has emerged with ever greater clarity since the 1950s, is the existence of a strong,

[68] Hodgson 1974. See further Hodgson 1993: 44–71 and 91–94.
[69] Van Leur 1955: 289.

independent, South and South-East Asian trading world and merchant community before the beginning of European colonialism from the middle of the eighteenth century.[70] The Asian merchants proved to be highly competitive. Only in a certain restricted number of trades where the European chartered companies were able to impose their own terms of commerce did they lose out. But for a long period they held their own in most other fields, restricting the influence of the Europeans to that of yet another participant in the already existing trading system.[71] In that respect, van Leur's analysis was only the beginning. Stressing, like Finley, the clear limits of commercial development in the pre-modern world, he emphasised the ephemeral position of trade within "the highly traditional agrarian world still based completely on self-sufficiency, with little independent city life" and "closed village communities as social and economic basis".[72] However, as the resilience of Indian and other Asian merchants has been documented, the emphasis has changed markedly and is now placed rather on the large amounts of trade and the vigorous commercial developments in that part of the world. As the controversial historian of early modern trade, Niels Steensgaard, has remarked, it is as if the myth of the immense riches of Asia has been substituted for that of the static, traditional Orient.[73] Even so, the foundation of van Leur's judgement has suffered some erosion. The study of the allegedly autarkic Indian village communities, the archetype of traditional society, has all but gone through a revolution. It is now clear that these villages were not entirely closed economies but also entered into wider marketing networks. For the Mughal Empire, its leading historian Irfan Habib has identified a long period of commercialisation of the agricultural surplus provoked by the tax demands of the state. This has been followed by seminal works of scholars such as B. R. Grover, K. N. Chaudhuri and C. A. Bayly, linking the rural world

---

[70] Braudel 1984; Arasaratnam 1990; Marshall 1993; Wills 1993; and Disney 1995: 484–535 are convenient and short overviews. For more detailed treatments, see Chaudhuri 1985; 1990 and Das Gupta and Pearson 1987.

[71] Steensgaard 1973a: 405–411, though often misunderstood, is the best analysis of the resilience of Asian merchants, together with Das Gupta 1979; Prakash 1985; and Banerjee 1990.

[72] Van Leur 1955, quotations from 283 and 282.   [73] Steensgaard 1987.

of northern India in the seventeenth and eighteenth centuries to a hierarchy of markets.[74]

Similar developments have taken place in other branches of Asian or Oriental studies. In 1966 Maxime Rodinson countered the widespread assumptions about the cultural blockage of Islam towards capitalism. In his analysis, he objected that even Mohammed had been a trader and that the religion was, in many ways, quite favourable towards mercantile activities; Islam and capitalism were not mutually incompatible. The following year, Goitein published the first volume of his extraordinary account of a community of Jewish traders centred in medieval Cairo, showing a strong and highly developed commercial world. In Ottoman studies, the picture of a stagnant and inefficient empire in the plundering hands of an Oriental despot has been discarded. Before it became "the sick man of Europe" the Ottoman Empire had been a strong and equal adversary with a flourishing economy, a highly developed market sector and capital formation.[75] Then there is China, where research seems to defy everything we take for granted about pre-industrial societies. Joseph Needham and his team of assistants, for instance, have identified a strong scientific tradition under the various Chinese imperial dynasties, in many ways the equal of Greek and, for a long time, European science. This is to say nothing of the spectacular rise in steel production under the medieval Song dynasty, not significantly surpassed again before the Industrial Revolution, or the large internal rural commercial developments under Ming and Ch'ing, all brought to our attention by scholars such as Elvin, Hartwell and Skinner.[76]

The result of all this has been a strong challenge to our very notion of modernity. As it has become increasingly clear that the concept of traditional society is difficult actually to locate empirically in the pre-industrial world, even in the archetypal case of India, the very notion of differences between early modern Europe and the other complex civilisations of Eurasia has come

---

[74] Habib 1963; Grover 1966; Chaudhuri 1978; Bayly 1983. See Inden 1990: chapter 4 on Indian village economies.

[75] Inalcik 1969; Faroqhi 1991; Inalcik and Quataert 1994; Adanir 1997. Bjørkelo 1999 is a convenient survey.

[76] Some of their more optimistic conclusions may be in need of moderation. For some cautionary critiques, see Finlay 2000 and Wagner 2001.

under strong attack. In the now classic, if controversial, *Orientalism* (1978) and the sequel *Culture and Imperialism* (1993) it was argued by Edward Said that the differences were but a romantic fiction of the European mind, longing for the exotic. This was in the best case. In the worst, they were an imperialist construction designed to dominate the colonised societies. Thus static traditional society with all its connotations of communal heart-warming *Gemeinschaft* and lack of commercial activity had not been there before. Rather, it was imposed on the dynamic Asian societies by the colonialist regimes – a case of the development of underdevelopment.[77] Understandably, we are now called upon to undo the wrong and re-admit these societies into modernity. Here is Sanjay Subrahmanyam, a prominent historian of South Asian economies: "Having taken away so much from the societies of South Asia, it seems to be high time that social science at least gave them back what they had by the sixteenth and seventeenth centuries – their admittedly very ambiguous 'early modernity'."[78]

If the developments in the study of the economy of the Roman Empire are added, an image gradually emerges of a very old pre-industrial Eurasian world of comparable high cultures. Lately, there have been a number of attempts to synthesise this condition. Most radically, some have posited the existence of an all-embracing world system of long-distance trade across Eurasia since the Bronze Age, determining the fate of its constituent societies. However, that is an extreme position, considering the limited amounts of trade passing across the Eurasian land mass.[79] Rather more challenging are the recent attempts to reinvigorate a diffusionist approach to the study of historical societies. So far, the Cambridge anthropologist Jack Goody has provided the most systematically worked-through version of this line of thought. To him the great divide does not run between Europe and Asia but between Eurasia and black Africa. The latter never shared in the Bronze Age urban revolution and this explains the problems of the

---

[77] Wolf 1982 is the most systematic attempt to develop this idea. More nuanced discussions of India can be found in Bayly 1988: chapter 5; Breckenridge and van der Veer 1993; and Bayly 1999.

[78] Subrahmanyam 1998: 100 and 1990b. See also Pomeranz 2000.

[79] Frank and Gills 1993 and Frank 1998, inspired by Schneider 1977 and Abu-Lughod 1989. See Subrahmanyam 1996: xv–xvi for a sceptical note.

continent in modernising today. The many, presently, much more successful Asian economies can, on the other hand, be seen as the result of a much greater infrastructural compatibility between East and West which ultimately dates back to common roots in the Bronze Age and the rise of civilisation. This shared legacy consists in the development of similar socio-economic institutions which Goody summarises as social stratification, literacy, specialisation, division of labour and a mercantile capitalism.[80] The result was a series of complex and broadly similar pre-industrial agrarian economies shaped by Smithian market dynamics and Malthusian constraints, to borrow a set of concepts developed within late imperial Chinese history by R. Bin Wong and more extensively by Kenneth Pomeranz.[81]

From "primitive" capitalism to agrarian empire

However, it is difficult not to feel a little uneasy about this attempt to inscribe capitalism into the DNA string of civilisation as such. There is a very real danger of doing away with most of human history, lumping it together under the same heading as a mirror image of early modern Europe: a kind of Eurocentrism by the backdoor. Of course, on a very broad, minimal, definition such as the existence of market trade, generating Marx's famous sequence of M(oney)-C(ommodity)-M(oney), capitalism probably has to be seen as ubiquitous in civilised societies. However, market trade already provides conceptual coverage for that phenomenon. Capitalism, on the other hand, will always remain linked to the developments culminating in the Industrial Revolution. True, the link was a complex one rather than a linear progression, as E. A. Wrigley insisted two decades ago. The Netherlands, which had spearheaded economic developments in the seventeenth century, fell behind during the eighteenth century and failed to make the transition to coal and steam till relatively late. The Dutch, though,

---

[80] Goody 1990; 1996; 1998: 1-26. Perlin 1983; 1993.
[81] Pomeranz 2000 developing an idea of Wong 1997: Part 1. Further Goldstone 1998; 2002. See Parthasarathi 2002 for a critique of Pomeranz, pointing out that he underestimates the importance of European market developments and state policies.

THE ROMAN EMPIRE AND COMPARATIVE STUDY

had begun to use peat on an extensive scale for production purposes, but their industries lost out to protectionist competition
from French and British manufacturers.[82] Capitalism was gradually coming together to drive economic development in a system
which transcended individual countries and produced a dynamic
succession of leading economies, as Braudel described it in the
final volume of his great work on capitalism. Why these developments took place in early modern Europe rather than somewhere
else is a question that cannot be avoided, indeed should not, considering their world-shattering effects. Of course, there is a risk
of seeming Eurocentric in providing answers. But that should be
treated as a challenge, not as an excuse to brush aside the issue.
The task confronting us is to provide explanations of early modern
European developments without denying the existence of historical dynamics in other cultures and times.[83] Here neither Goody and
Pomeranz, nor Pleket, with their strong determination to identify
analogies and parallel patterns, have much to say. Yet, if the basic
tenor of their argument is correct, suggesting answers seems more
necessary than ever, unless we have given up trying to understand
the different trajectories of world history. To cite a recent collection of papers, we need a kind of historiography "committed
neither to justifying European domination, nor to explaining it
away".[84]

---

[82] Wrigley 1988. Jongman 2006 takes Wrigley to show that the economic developments
preceding industrialisation were unimportant, and that there is therefore little to distinguish early modern capitalism. While I agree with Jongman that we need not shape our
analyses of the ancient economy on the early modern model, his reading of Wrigley
is an overinterpretation. Wrigley describes the period of vigorous pre-industrial economic development as a necessary precondition, but not an automatic guarantee for
an industrial breakthrough (1988: 11–12, 113–118). Even so, Wrigley's vision of the
process remains heavily Anglocentric and pays little attention to the overall dynamic of
the emerging capitalist system. That would have come out more clearly if he had also
included processes of state formation and military competition, cf. McNeill 1982 (military competition); Wong 1997: chapter 6 (comparative differences in state formation
between Europe and China); De Vries and Woude 1997 (on the modern character of the
Dutch economy).

[83] On this latter aspect I agree with Morley 2007: 6–9, but that does not require the student
of ancient trade to play down the differences to early modern capitalism. Landes 1998:
415–418 is a pointed, if perhaps too strong, critique of this basically Saidian tendency
to ignore or tone down the question of differences. Pearson 1991: 45; Wong 1997: 1–8;
and Bayly 2000 insist on the continued need to differentiate our image of pre-industrial
Eurasia.

[84] Manning and Morris 2005: 9.

I do not advocate introducing a ban on comparisons between the Roman Empire and early modern Europe. Recently, for instance, attention has been called to a possible similarity in the effects that eighteenth-century London and early imperial Rome had on their respective hinterlands. The two capital cities were of comparable size and both represented an enormous concentration of spending power; the effects of Rome on her hinterland might have been parallel to those of London on hers, where the rising demand of the city generated economic development in the countryside, marked by rising productivity and an increased commercialisation of agriculture.[85] But we also need to explore the limits to this comparison. The enormous spending power of the Roman market was the result of the concentration in that city of a large part of the resources generated by a territorial empire spanning the Mediterranean world with a population of perhaps 60 million. In 1750, on the other hand, when London's population reached 700,000, she still had to rely mainly on the British Isles and a few commercial colonies and outposts around the world, in all comprising a population in the order of magnitude of say 10 million. In comparison with the ancient imperial metropolis, London's resource base was much smaller. The English capital had to compensate by making much larger earnings from foreign trade than did Rome to finance its consumption.[86]

The relationship between empire, concentration of spending power and commercialisation-cum-growth was first brought to the forefront of the debate on the economy of the Roman Empire by Keith Hopkins, three decades ago.[87] Taking his point of departure, like Weber and Finley, from the politically defined consumption patterns of the agricultural surplus, he drew attention to the way these were modified by the creation of large empires.[88] A part of the resources which had formerly been available to the multitude of local cities around the Greco-Roman world was now confiscated and redirected to serve the purposes of the Roman imperial

---

[85] Hopkins 1995–6: 59; Morley 1996.
[86] *Pace* Morley 1996: 29, who tends to underestimate the significance of this difference. See Wrigley 1987: chapter 6 and Reed 1996 for the economy of London.
[87] Hopkins 1978a; 1980; 1983c; 1983b; and 1995–6.
[88] See now also Erdkamp 2001 on the similarities of the "consumer city" and Hopkins' model.

authorities. Basically, that meant that they were channelled to Rome, the capital of the Empire, and the army, stationed along the frontiers. Since many of these taxes were, presumably, paid in coin or at some stage after delivery in kind, sold on the market and converted into money, most areas of the Empire where there was no government spending would have had to earn their tax money back if they were going to continue to be able to pay their annual taxes and not run out of coin. The result was a limited growth and commercialisation process where taxpayers around the Empire entered the market to earn their tax money, and export flows of manufactured products arose between the areas in tax deficit and those in surplus.

Hopkins' model has justly attracted much attention. Not surprisingly, given the current climate of discussion, many have emphasised the elements dealing with growth and commercialisation, whereas the limits to these processes and the close affinity of the model with that of "the consumer city" tend to be ignored or dismissed.[89] Hopkins has even been criticised for underestimating the amount of trade and the penetration of market forces in the Roman Mediterranean.[90] Here, Harry Pleket's endorsement and the special twist he gives to the taxes-and-trade model are of particular interest. Rejecting its Weberian foundations, he sets out to compare the tax system of the Roman Empire with that of the early modern European nation states. He stops at the need of the latter to borrow from private financiers and the gradual creation of a permanent, funded government debt. This institution is wholly lacking in the Roman Empire. In Pleket's view, this is a reflection of the greater strength of the imperial state; it did not need to resort to such measures to finance its activities. It could simply rely on taxing its subjects directly. From an economic perspective, however, the two fiscal regimes would have produced similar results. In both cases the state absorbed the wealth of its citizens and created a similar amount or kind of economic activity through its consumption.[91]

---

[89] See Erdkamp 2001 for a similar view of the "consumer city".
[90] See Paterson 1998: 153 and Pleket 1990 for critique along these lines. Greene 1986 is a typical example emphasising commercialisation and growth. The model has also been criticised from more "primitivist" perspectives, e.g. Jongman 1988; Whittaker 1989; Duncan-Jones 1990; and Whittaker 1995.
[91] Pleket 1990: 39 and 46–47.

I do not share the confidence of this conjecture in its reliance on functional equivalents. A basic, if rarely noted, premise of Hopkins' argument is that there is no such thing as the market, in the abstract general sense. It is not just out there, happening on its own. Rather, it needs to be created and often even pressed or forced into existence under pre-industrial conditions. Hence it becomes crucial to understand how the particular markets are articulated, how they are moulded and shaped by the social and political institutions of society and the context in which they appear. This, of course, was Polanyi's point and the one that has survived the many empirical criticisms of his economic models. It has even entered the mainstream of economics through the institutional analysis of Douglass North.[92] In this particular instance, the relative weakness of the rising nation state and its consequent reliance on private loans cannot just be reduced to a matter of consumption in relation to the economy. A main result of that situation was the formation of an efficient international market in capital. The development began when the large medieval fairs of Europe were turned into meeting places for the rich banking firms, connected with the European monarchs, where they could settle accounts and deal in bills of exchange. Gradually, as the scale of transactions increased, more permanent structures became necessary and in the seventeenth century this function was taken over by the stock exchanges of Amsterdam and London. During the same period the government debts of the Netherlands and England were put on a more stable basis in the form of negotiable, interest-bearing, bonds. Thus this line of investment was now effectively opened up to groups other than the closed cliques of leading financiers. The result was an important extension of investment opportunities for commercial capital.[93] The point is that such an institutional development seems to be largely absent from the Roman Empire. We do find a hierarchy of periodic fairs and markets. However, they remained, to a very large extent, gathering places where the rural population could sell its surplus production and have its limited

---

[92] Steensgaard 1981; 1984 and Lane 1966: 383–428 are some of the most perceptive analyses of the close bonds between markets and the socio-political formation. See further Polanyi, Arensberg and Pearson 1957; North 1990; and Morris 2002.

[93] De Vries 1976: chapter 7 and Braudel 1982: 81–114.

needs for market services supplied. The larger fairs also seem to
have played a role in regional and interregional trade. A few even
developed into important foci of long-distance trade, such as the
one on Delos. But they do not appear to have fulfilled the role of
"international" credit markets. We should, perhaps, rather turn our
attention to the cities. Here we do, of course, find market buildings and squares, but there is nothing to suggest that they would
have operated on lines resembling those of the formalised stock
exchanges of seventeenth-century Amsterdam and London. What
is more, on Pleket's interpretation of the taxes-and-trade model,
stressing the absence of government debt, we would not expect
this either.[94]

Nor should we, as Pleket concedes, expect any kind of bourgeois
development giving rise to a class of large merchants and financiers
able to challenge the economic preponderance of the political elite
based in landed wealth. However, that cannot just be written off as
a difference in social structure. It had economic consequences as
well. It would, for instance, be difficult to imagine a situation like
that described by Braudel for the West Indies, where the plantation
owners often had large problems making ends meet while the merchants who bought their produce and sold it back in Europe made
huge profits.[95] Indeed, in the Roman Empire things took place in
the opposite fashion. Wealthy landowners remained firmly in the
driving seat. In parting with their produce, they seem generally
to have been able to shift most of the risk onto the commercial
middlemen, to judge from the business procedures envisaged in
legal regulations and prevailing forms of contract.[96] This impression is confirmed by what we know about elite mobility in the
Empire. The crucial component seems to have been access to large
agricultural resources; it was the cities with the largest and richest countrysides available that proved most successful in getting
members of provincial elites promoted into the imperial aristocracy. The spectacular rise of members of the elite of North African
Lepcis Magna, culminating in the Severan emperors, should not

---

[94] Finley 1985a: 195–196, confirmed by de Ligt 1993 and Frayn 1993. On Delos, see Rauh
1993. See Andreau 1999: chapter 11, pace Harris 2006, for the relative weakness of the
financial "sector" in the Roman economy.

[95] Braudel 1982: 272–280. [96] Morley 1996: 159–166.

be seen as the result of profits generated from the *administration* of Mediterranean trade. Rather, their success came about because they controlled an unusually large hinterland which provided them with a vast agricultural surplus, especially in olive oil, that could be exported.[97] In other words, Pleket tends to ignore the fact that differences in social organisation produce the articulation or dominance of very different economic interests. The Roman Empire may, on very rare occasions, have allowed considerations about the safety of its traders against encroachments in foreign countries to enter into decisions about war and peace. But that is a very far cry from the active strategies of Dutch merchants in the seventeenth century, successfully waging war around the globe to secure and conquer markets. Here commerce was the dominant motive. Could we imagine the Roman Empire in a situation like that of the Spanish Habsburgs fighting on and off against the Dutch rebels for eighty years and in the end depending on the very same Dutchmen to provide credit to finance their armies? It all came to an end in 1648 when the Dutch merchants finally decided that peace was more profitable than war, and shut their coffers.[98]

In a historical perspective this early modern European development, often described in the convenient shorthand of mercantilism, appears to be very much the exception, a unique occurrence.[99] Adam Smith sensed this clearly when he chose in *The Wealth of Nations* to portray the preceding centuries of European economic history as a perversion of the natural hierarchy between agriculture, manufacture and commerce. The so-called mercantile system had allowed the merchants too much power and far too many privileges, and had made it possible for them to appropriate and control a disproportionately large part of the total wealth of society to the detriment of the overall well-being of the economy. This should, according to Adam Smith, now be brought to an end; the leading position of agricultural production should be recognised and mercantilist policies abandoned. The principle of laissez-faire

[97] See Mattingly 1988b on Lepcis Magna's aristocracy; Syme 1977 and Corbier 1991: 223 for the situation in general.
[98] Burke 1988: 229–230. On Dutch trade, see Israel 1989. See Lo Cascio 1991 and Andreau 1994a and 2003 for the relationship between market and government in the Roman Empire. Harris 2003 effectively confirms their description.
[99] Gellner 1988b; Pearson 1991.

would then operate to restore the proper and economically most beneficial relationship between the different sectors of the economy.[100] We are a far cry from the horizons of modern-day free trade enthusiasts. Indeed, it is striking when one reads through the pages of *The Wealth of Nations* how Smith's vision of the Chinese Empire, resting on the backs of a multitude of hard-working peasants and a large internal market, in some respects came quite close to his ideal of the natural relationship between agriculture and trade.[101]

China may even be much closer to the historical norm than the liberal Smith, who also saw oppression and consequent distortion of the economy caused by the political elite, would have liked to admit. In post-war scholarship the Chinese Empire has, in analytical contrast to Europe, come to represent the more normal pattern of development, where a political elite, depending on agricultural rent-taking, is able to dominate the commercial groups of society. The *locus classicus* of this literature is a counterfactual explanation of why China, clearly the leading economic power in the world around 1400, eventually lost its lead to Europe.[102] In the thirteenth century a brisk trade had developed in South East Asia, dominated by Chinese merchants. But when the Ming dynasty took over from the Mongols in 1368 this foreign trade was prohibited. Instead the authorities tried to control contacts with the world outside and attempted to organise foreign exchange relations within a large imperial tribute system. As a consequence a number of very large naval expeditions, headed by the legendary eunuch admiral Zheng He, were sent out from China between 1405 and 1433, navigating the South China Sea and the Indian Ocean, even reaching the coast

---

[100] Smith 1976: 276–85, 360–427 and Book 4. Smith's analysis lives on in the new economic history which downplays the significance of foreign trade to eighteenth-century Britain, e.g. Wrigley 1987 and 1988. The argument ignores the contribution of a much strengthened commercial infrastructure (institutions), that is simply taken for granted, cf. O'Brien 1998.

[101] It is no coincidence that Elvin's classic analysis of late imperial China (1973), describing the country as caught in a high-level equilibrium trap, is right out of the pages of Smith (as is Pomeranz 2000). Smith expected something similar to happen for England, Wrigley 1988.

[102] McNeill 1982: chapter 2. See further Wallerstein 1974a; Jones 1981; 1988; and Landes 1998.

of East Africa.[103] The scale of operations was truly magnificent. The first expedition is believed to have been made up of some 28,000 men and perhaps up to 255 ships of varying sizes, including 62 enormous treasure ships. This was far beyond anything the small European states at that time could even dream of achieving. The handful of Portuguese ships that began to arrive in the Indian Ocean at the end of the fifteenth century would have been no match for these gigantic fleets. This has led a number of scholars to ask why it was not the Chinese who sailed around Africa and began to establish colonies in Europe.

As it happened, the Chinese had already aborted their expeditions when the Portuguese arrived. A mounting Mongol threat on the inner Asian frontier, a war in Vietnam and the building of Beijing as the new capital strained imperial finances. In 1421 the undertaking of new expeditions was called off temporarily. A final voyage was completed between 1431 and 1433 before the project was finally abandoned. In 1436 the building of new sea-going vessels was prohibited, and the crews and resources were channelled into traffic on the Grand Canal and public building activities. After a few years the know-how necessary to resume the expeditions had been lost. The scene was set for the Portuguese and other Europeans to embark on the slow and very gradual road towards dominance. This is as far as the counterfactual will take us. Normally, the ills of despotism or Confucian dislike of eunuchs and trade are called upon to explain this historical "mistake". A closer look, however, reveals that the very size of the Chinese expeditions marks a very significant difference from the much more commercially motivated European fleets. There was no way that the stupendously costly activities of Zheng He could ever have been profitable in a commercial sense. They have to be understood within the more "traditional" framework of the imperial tribute system. The motives were never commercial and it would be a mistake to see them as an abortive attempt to establish a commercial world-system, in what would become the European style. They were intended to announce the might of the Ming emperor

---

[103] See Dreyer 2007 for the history of the these fleets.

and bring foreign princes to recognise his suzerainty by rendering tribute.[104]

Such an interpretation would also help to make sense of the situation prevailing in the following centuries, where the ban on foreign trade was upheld for long periods. China is a large area to control, and it turned out to be impossible to prevent even large numbers of Chinese merchants setting out to sea. However, the ban meant that the merchants were, so to speak, outside the sphere recognised by the state. One consequence was, that they often had to depend on the protection of local Chinese gentry, who knew the "value" of their service; another, that they were left in a vulnerable position vis-à-vis the emerging aggressive European merchant empires. Thus we have examples of massacres in the Chinese overseas trading communities carried out by various European nations without the Chinese imperial state paying much notice. It did not recognise the existence of these traders. In other words, the interests of the commercial groups in Chinese society were never articulated to the same extent as those behind European mercantilist policies.[105] Therefore we do not find attempts by the state to support the formation of commercial institutions as powerful as those developed in cooperation by European merchants and states to strengthen and stabilise the market system – state bonds, joint stock companies and the like. It follows that we should imagine the Chinese Empire as going along quite another historical trajectory. It was not a failed or trapped move towards what we have come to understand as modernisation.[106]

Montesquieu more than 250 years ago provided an important clue to the understanding of the reasons of this development, when he seized on the difference in state formation processes.[107] Focusing his attention, as did many Enlightenment intellectuals, on the large Asian empires facing Europe and its traders, such as the Ottoman Empire, Safavid Persia, Mughal India and Ch'ing China, he was struck by the contrasts and noted that large agrarian empires

---

[104] Pearson 1991: 104–105; Landes 1998: 93–98. Elvin 1973: 220 describes the voyages as "prestige ventures". In general, see the analysis of Dreyer 2007: chapters 1 and 3.

[105] Elvin 1973: 215–225; Gungwu 1990.

[106] Wong 1997: chapters 4–6 is a pertinent demonstration of this. Pomeranz 2000 underestimates issues of state formation and institutions, cf. Bayly 2000 and Pamuk 2000.

[107] See Roberto 2003 for an interesting analysis of Montesquieu.

had always failed in Europe whereas they seemed to prosper in Asia. The reasons for this "failure" are now sought in the feudal society that arose in Europe after the disintegration of the western parts of the Roman Empire.[108] An important characteristic of this social system was the fragile position of centralised forms of power, which produced a very fragmented kind of social formation split up into many small units. There were several attempts to re-establish a strong imperial system in the European theatre. The dramatis personae include such prominent figures as Charlemagne, the Catholic Church and the Holy Roman Empire. Yet, these ambitions always faltered, if sometimes only just, and suffered their final defeat with the compromise in Augsburg in 1555. This settlement left in tatters whatever was left of the dreams of the Habsburg emperor Charles V to unite most of Europe under his authority. Disillusioned, the emperor left it to his brother Ferdinand to negotiate the peace and instead began to organise his abdication in the following year. This saw the division of the Habsburg heritage into an Austrian and a Spanish branch.

Instead of an empire, a system of smaller competing states gradually evolved out of the feudal world. Yet, central royal power remained relatively weak against the multitude of feudal baronies. For our purposes, the most important result of this state of affairs was that the king often had to ally with mercantile groups to consolidate his authority. This brought these groups into much closer proximity to state power than had been the case historically. To begin with, this gave rise to the numerous strong medieval cities where the merchants were allowed freedom of rule to a very large degree. Sometimes they even became *the* government, such as in the rich communes of northern Italy, with Venice, Florence, Pisa and Genoa leading the way, and in the northern parts of Europe with the Hanseatic league. Trade and the interests of commerce were fast becoming of great importance to the state. As arms technology developed and became much more expensive, especially with the

---

[108] Landes 1998: chapter 3, though too simplistic. For the general processes at work see North and Thomas 1973; Anderson 1974; Wallerstein 1974: chapters 3–4; Braudel 1981; Jones 1981; Braudel 1982: McNeill 1982; chapters 3–4; Braudel 1984; Wickham 1985; Mann 1986: chapters 12–15; Burke 1988; Jones 1988; Kennedy 1988: chapter 2; Crone 1989; Mauro 1990; Brady 1991; Østergaard 1996; Bayly 2004.

introduction of artillery and new forms of fortification designed to withstand bombardment from cannons, royal power was strengthened in relation to the feudal barons, who could not afford the new technology on their own. Centralisation followed and the nation states of Europe came into being. However, increased interstate competition and the enormous, continuously rising costs of warfare caused by the ensuing arms race made it crucial for state power to cooperate with all propertied groups of society in order to secure ever larger revenues. Thus the alliance with the commercial sections of society was continued; numerous measures, known in the convenient shorthand as mercantilism, were introduced, even aggressive warfare, in order to favour and promote the interests of the traders of each nation, with the motive of generating as much income as possible. The military balance of power now went hand in hand with an unprecedented kind of economic interstate rivalry. The result was a much strengthened and stabilised institutional base for the mercantile sector of society.[109]

Characteristically, the states which formed the closest alliance with the commercial parts of society proved strongest during the seventeenth and eighteenth centuries. Hence the spectacular rise of the Dutch Netherlands and the repeated British victories over much larger France. On the face of it, one would have expected it to be otherwise, given the fact of French absolutism and the need for the weaker British state/king to come to terms with parliament. Voltaire captured the situation vividly when he noted that

What has made England powerful is the fact that from the time of Elizabeth, all parties have agreed on the necessity of favoring commerce. The same parliament that had the king beheaded was busy with overseas trading posts as though nothing was happening. The blood of Charles I was still steaming when this parliament, composed almost entirely of fanatics, passed the Navigation Act of 1650.[110]

Interestingly, among the states contending for a dominant position in Europe, it was Habsburg Spain – the state formation most resembling an old-style territorial empire – in spite of all her gold and silver flowing in from the New World, that proved least able to accommodate the demands of the new situation of intensified

---

[109] Hont 2005. De Vries 1976 is excellent on the resulting institutional arrangements.
[110] Cited from Landes 1998: 234. See also Gellner 1988b: 114–115.

commercial rivalry. It was, quite simply, difficult to run a vast territorial empire along the same lines of policy.[111]

An early and almost too perfect illustration of the difference between agrarian empires and the emerging new organisational forms in Europe is provided by the relationship between a number of Italian merchant republics, with Venice in the forefront, and the surviving, Byzantine, part of the Roman Empire in the first centuries of the second millennium. During a period of political and military weakness the Byzantine emperor found himself forced to concede various trading privileges to the Italian merchants in return for military support. In effect, a situation arose where the Empire's own merchants were put at a disadvantage in Constantinople in comparison to the Italian merchants – this was mercantilist protectionism stood on its head. The point about this is not its "perversity" from a European point of view, as Donald Treadgold, the author of a recent synthetic history of the Byzantine Empire, would have us believe. It is rather that the economic weight of the commercial groups was normally simply not sufficiently important in a large agrarian empire, which could draw on income from huge masses of peasants, ever to give rise by itself to a similar strong position for the mercantile sections of society.[112] This does not mean that merchants in such imperial formations were entirely powerless. We can turn to the richest trading city of the Mughal Empire, Surat, in the eighteenth century for indications of the limits within which they could act. Rising up against an unusually extortionate governor, the rich merchants of the city actually managed to drive him out of the town. But that was the end of it. There was no attempt at systemic change, and they had to settle for a new governor, belonging to the nobility. Thus the old order was restored.[113]

All this makes early modern Europe a very bad guide indeed for understanding the economies of the large agrarian empires of Eurasian history. Quite simply, they do not appear to provide any

[111] Wallerstein 1974a: chapter 4; De Vries 1976: 249–250; North 1990: 112–115.
[112] Treadgold 1997: chapters 18–21, especially pp. 699–706. On p. 704 the situation is described as "the perverse policy of reverse protectionism". Pearson 1991 and Wong 1997: chapter 6 make the point in general for these empires.
[113] Das Gupta 1979: Chapter 4.

strong parallel to the pattern of institutional developments we find in the competitive state system of the early modern period. The, at times, very large observable amounts (hence the modernising critiques of "othering" analyses) of trade in these empires were located in a different structural and institutional setting. In some respects, the empires even seem incompatible with the expanding capitalism of the eighteenth and nineteenth centuries. There is a strong argument that they may have fallen victim to its development. A large and growing literature focuses on how the Ottoman Empire found it very difficult to keep up with European developments and was gradually undermined and incorporated into the European economic system.[114] The Mughal Empire had disintegrated before the beginning of the British conquest of India, though there were perhaps signs that a reestablishment of imperial authority was imminent under the leadership of one or other of the Mughal successor states. In the event, it all came to nothing with the rise of British supremacy. More important from our point of view is the possibility that the initial weakening of imperial authority came about through the increased involvement of India in the growing European world-system. The resulting large imports of bullion into the Indian economy as payment for spices and cotton calicoes may have contributed to undermining the established power structure.[115] The humiliating defeat of the Chinese Empire in the Opium War (1839–42) spelled out to the authorities the need for modernisation and industrialisation. But this proved a goal difficult to achieve within the already existing system. Eventually "industrialization did take place in twentieth-century China, but this China was no longer an agrarian empire."[116]

Thus it appears futile to insist on envisaging these empires in analogy to the competitive system of more or less mercantilist nation states arising in early modern Europe. Such comparisons, when scrutinised closely, seem destined to end up in a catalogue of failures and near misses. The large traditional or classic agrarian

---

[114] See Keyder 1997; Landes 1998; chapter 24; and Pamuk 2000 for brief surveys. Inalcik and Quataert 1994: vol. 2, parts 3 and 4 for greater detail. Islamoglu-Inan 1987 and Masters 1988 for world-system-inspired approaches.

[115] Steensgaard 1990a. Wink 1989 for re-establishment of central control.

[116] Wong 1997: 151. McNeill 1982: 257 about the Opium War.

empires were, for all we know, not on the same path of historical development. The strategy of reverting to explanations of the functional equivalent type is ultimately unsatisfying, as I tried to argue from the example of Pleket. Being mainly defensive in character, it only succeeds in taking a very narrow view of the phenomena and ignoring their markedly different contexts. For the study of the Roman imperial economy this carries, at least, two implications. First, it is time, finally, to abandon *the tyranny of Europe over Rome*. The unusual pattern of European history cannot do service as a yardstick to measure the very different imperial experience. Second, in terms of comparative history it seems reasonable to suggest that analogous or parallel comparisons to help understand the institutional and structural characteristics of the Empire should rather be sought among the Asian empires that so impressed the Enlightenment intellectuals.

Certainly, in terms of sheer scale, the Asian empires constitute a much more fitting parallel to the Roman world. From a historical perspective, all of them, like Rome, are characterised by quite substantial amounts of trade and urbanisation. They also seem to show significant similarities in the structural location of commercial groups and the market sector in society. In respect to state formation, they represent an alternative path of development during the early modern period to that experienced by Europe. While the feudal fragmentation of Europe eventually crystallised into a system characterised by medium-sized states, these empires emerged as hegemonic powers dominating their regions. The establishment of the Ming dynasty in 1368, later succeded by the Ch'ing in 1648, saw the restoration of a Chinese Empire dominating East Asia. During the fifteenth and sixteenth centuries, the Ottoman sultans conquered vast stretches of the Mediterranean and Middle East. Finally, the Mughals rose to dominate India during the sixteenth and seventeenth centuries. None of these empires was initially locked into interstate competition to the same extent as the emerging nation states of Europe. Therefore they were not under the same pressure to generate new revenues from their existing tax bases to survive, for instance by granting commercial privileges. Instead they enjoyed the benefits derived from expansion. Having conquered many of their neighbours, each of the empires controlled a much bigger agrarian economy than the European monarchies. The imperial governments were able to field vast armies by relying on collecting (land) taxes from their extensive provincial territories; they were, in that sense, "tributary empires" rather than mercantilist states.[117] Enjoying the benefit of at least another millennium of slowly accumulating social developments, these empires hold the further attraction as comparanda that they are unlikely to be more "archaic" than Rome in any meaningful sense. Making a shift in our comparisons of the Roman world to this group of Asian tributary states, therefore, would allow us to explore in greater detail the relationship between market system and agrarian empire, in other words to understand it as a particular type of political economy or system. The next chapter will begin to explore how this can be done.

[117] Woolf 1990 points in the same direction. Pleket 1990: 151 remains sceptical on the distinction between empire and mercantilist state system, but does not see the consequences of the very different articulations of commercial interests.

2

AN AGRARIAN EMPIRE BETWEEN MARKET AND TRIBUTE: SITUATING INTERREGIONAL TRADE IN THE ROMAN WORLD

[T]he decline of Rome was the natural and inevitable effect of immoderate greatness . . . as soon as time or accident had removed the artificial supports, the stupendous fabric yielded to the pressure of its own weight. The story of its ruin is simple and obvious; and instead of inquiring why the Roman empire was destroyed, we should rather be surprised that it had subsisted so long.

Gibbon, *The Decline and Fall of the Roman Empire*, vol. IV, p. 119

Those are the immortal words of Gibbon, uttered with his characteristic acrimony while contemplating *the decline and fall of the Roman Empire*. At first, they may come as a surprise. After all, this was the very same man who proclaimed the age of the Antonine emperors "the period in the history of the world during which the condition of the human race was most happy and prosperous".[1] But to Gibbon, the golden second century was an aberration. Only a fortuitous succession of unusually capable, conscientious and moderate emperors had made it possible. In the long run, the corrupting influence of absolute power was bound to prevail and turn the enlightened monarchy into an oppressive tyranny. Ironically it was left to Commodus, son of the philosopher king Marcus Aurelius, to bring out the true face of imperial rule. With his accession to the throne the history of the Empire became one of despotism, corruption, military anarchy, brutal oppression and the withering away of its powers. And yet, in spite of its alleged pernicious influence on society, the Roman Empire lasted for centuries. Indeed, it came as a shock to Gibbon in writing his history to realise the almost, from this point of view, perverse ability of the imperial system to renew itself and regain its strength;[2] he needed six long volumes finally to lay the leviathan to rest.

[1] Gibbon 1993, vol. 1: 90 and further 90–99. Garnsey and Humfress 2001, chapter 10 on Gibbon.
[2] Robertson 1997.

The relationship between the predatory and benign aspects of imperial rule remains a key issue in our understanding of the effect of Rome and other agrarian empires on their economies. This chapter argues that these two aspects of the imperial experience cannot be separated, but have to be seen as two sides of the same coin. Economic development was the result of political exploitation, not its victim. This requires us to shift our attention from markets as the organising force in the economy to the process of tribute extraction and mobilisation of peasant surplus production. A comparison of the interlinked processes of surplus extraction and elite building in the Mughal and Roman Empires demonstrates the importance of imperial tribute in determining economic flows in the empires. Markets, from that perspective, do not determine the structure of the economy; instead they play a crucial role in mobilising the agricultural surplus and turning it into a disposable resource. The chapter concludes by discussing to what extent the processes of tribute extraction spawned economic growth in the Roman Empire.

Agrarian empires between market and tribute

Ultimately, the universal empire had presented itself as a paradox to Gibbon, a perception he shared with many of his contemporaries. In *The Wealth of Nations*, Adam Smith described China of the Ch'ing dynasty as one of the richest societies in the world with a highly productive irrigation agriculture, substantive division of labour and an extensive inland trade. But at the same time he saw the rule of the "Son of Heaven" as inimical to the economy; the imperial tributary elite depressed the economic performance of the country through political privileges, taxation, arbitrary administration and outright predatory encroachment on the wealth of the producing and mercantile layers of society.[3] Market and tribute existed in contradiction to each other; they seemed incompatible and yet they were co-existing. The Enlightenment philosophers never really managed to dissolve this tension and incorporate both

---

[3] Smith 1976: 111–112.

elements in their understanding of the great empires. Some, like Voltaire, chose to ignore the "darker" side and instead eulogised the imperial claims to absolute power. In his *Essai sur les moeurs et l'esprit des nations* he presented imperial China as the paragon of rational order, an idealised counter-image to *ancien régime* France. This solution failed to win the majority opinion. Most intellectuals were more impressed by the oppressive effects of imperial rule. In *L'Esprit des lois* Montesquieu fiercely denounced the rosy image of China; tributary empires were based on the principle of fear.[4] Later, Adam Ferguson followed suit in his tract on civil society. The absence in the empires of a close alliance with commercial groups and the concomitant predominance of political consumption (cf. Chapter 1), was fundamentally at odds with the world view of the increasingly powerful and confident bourgeois societies of Europe. Empires seemed the embodiment of everything adverse to the kind of social order they promoted, with clearly defined civil liberties and parliaments to contain the ruling power. In the bourgeois view, the empires appeared to be antagonistically opposed to their very economic and societal bases. Here is one of Adam Ferguson's damning observations:

Were despotic empire ... to continue for ever unmolested from abroad ... it appears to have in itself no principle of new life, and presents no hope of restoration to freedom and political vigour. That which the despotical master has sown, cannot quicken unless it die; it must languish and expire by the effect of its own abuse ... National poverty, however, and the suppression of commerce, are the means by which despotism comes to accomplish its own destruction.[5]

Stagnation and misery were all that agrarian empires had in store for their poverty-stricken subjects. Commerce and the market were left very little room in the imperial order.

It took Max Weber to realise that the picture was much overdrawn and strongly stereotyped; empires would not have been able to exist under such purely traditional conditions. Here he made the fundamental observation that once a traditional, or in his terminology, patrimonial state began to grow, the household of the ruler would no longer be able to control the entire area of his realm. The ruler had to form alliances with local communities, mainly

---

[4] Montesquieu 1955, part 1: 3, 9–10; 7, 7 and 8, 21.   [5] Ferguson 1995: 262–263.

aristocracies, in order to establish longer-lasting control and have representatives carrying out his commands. The much dreaded despotism of the sociological tradition was not really possible. The power of emperors and the imperial state was only apparently absolute and arbitrary. In practice, the ruler over extensive areas had to negotiate and accept limitations on his exercise of power. Consequently the empires were characterised by a tension or uneasy co-existence between the tax-extracting central power of the emperor (tribute) and locally entrenched power wielders (feudal elites), living off agricultural rents. The resulting institutionalisation of government into relatively stable patterns of activity was, as Weber saw it, the beginnings of more complex types of society with a more pronounced specialisation of functions. This led him to include his treatment of tributary empires in a general discussion of the development of modern forms of state and bureaucracy.[6]

For our present purposes, however, this choice has had some unfortunate consequences. An opportunity was partly missed to break free from the contradictions in the Enlightenment tradition. In Weber's analysis of the origins of modern states, the crucial factor became the ability of the feudal level of society to curb what seemed the arbitrary aspirations of the tributary state. However, the more successfully this was done, the less chance the empire stood of survival. Only where feudalism had been triumphant and the imperial superstructure had disintegrated, did society set off on a developmental path eventually leading to modernisation. In the last analysis, the antithetical relationship between empire and its economy and civil society therefore remained central for Weber. The tributary systems may have shown some signs of institutionalising social and economic diversification. But ultimately the two phenomena were incompatible. Conceptually, this resulted in a hybrid characterisation of these systems as patrimonial–bureaucratic.[7]

That was problematic. It was the tensions in Weber's conceptualisation which came to define the path ahead for later work in historical sociology. Several influential studies in the Weberian tradition have tended to disregard the cautiously balanced

---

[6] Weber 1972: 580–652. See also Wickham 1985.
[7] See Weber 1972: 619. See pp. 593, 604 and 625–653 for his continued adherence to the Enlightenment interpretation.

observations of Weber and instead accentuated and aggravated the internal contradictions in the concept of tributary empire. In *The Political System of Empires* (1963) Shmuel Eisenstadt attempted to develop Weber's basic analysis of complex agrarian societies. Eisenstadt's analysis is not without merits. Its focus on the ability of the empires to generate "free floating resources", that is their capacity for mobilising the agricultural surplus outside its immediate context, has much in common with the view which will be presented here. But the study has one crucial drawback. It treats the empires entirely within a framework of very abstract 1950s modernisation theory. This prevents the empires from appearing in their own right. Analysing Roman imperial administration in terms of a modern-style bureaucracy is, for instance, not very revealing when we remember that it had no institutions which served to guarantee that promotion happened on the basis of merit or professional qualification rather than through personal favour.[8] Eisenstadt's approach tends, in other words, to miss some of the important organisational characteristics of the empires. They are perceived as incipient cases of modernisation still needing to shed much of the dead weight of traditional society before coming to fruition. Essentially this confronts agrarian empires with two options: either they transform successfully into mercantilist nation states and modernise or they remain traditional empires and eventually kill off whatever modern elements they possess.[9]

John Kautsky has taken this further in *The Politics of Aristocratic Empires* (1982) by sharpening the contrasts appearing in Eisenstadt's image. Here the empires are simply defined as essentially traditional. Trade and other such phenomena are, on the other hand, seen as signs of modernisation per se and hence as fundamentally outside the aristocratic order. This is a very unfortunate solution. Most agrarian empires and certainly the best known had considerable amounts of trade taking place within them. But Kautsky's system cannot really account for this. Commercial phenomena are left in a kind of analytical no-man's land between the aristocratic and the present world until the agrarian or tributary empires finally had modernisation forced upon them from without

[8] Saller 1982: 111–116.   [9] Eisenstadt 1963: 351–360.

by a conquering European modernity and in that process were transformed into a new type of society.[10]

A conceptualisation of trade and economic activity that situates these phenomena firmly within the tributary empires constantly eludes us. The relationship between traditional empire and trade seems to defy our accustomed categories. According to established notions they ought to be like oil and water: mutually exclusive. The essence of the orthodox view is neatly summarised in John Hall's notion of *capstone government*. Apparently, an imperial centre could only maintain control by weakening its underlying society and economy. For its own survival, it was forced to prey on any dynamic development and finally to block and destroy it. In that way, the empire prevented local groups from becoming wealthy and strong enough successfully to challenge its authority and refuse to pay taxes. Thus imperial rule was secured by creating a power stand-off which lowered the level of social activity and put a lid on creative energies. Empires had "strong blocking but weak enabling powers", as Hall has phrased it.[11]

Redistribution or integrated market systems?

To be sure, it is not difficult to find examples of imperial authorities abusing their power to plunder and depress the subject populations. A recent book on Roman Syria stresses how the imperial army damaged the local economies to a large extent. The soldiers often proved a dangerous presence, being only too prone to terrorise provincial inhabitants in order to extort money or other desirable resources for their own benefit.[12] Yet, there are some very important aspects of the imperial experience for which the whole label of capstone government seems inappropriate. For instance, the empires were able to create some of the largest urban concentrations in the pre-industrial world. Metropoleis such as Mughal Delhi, Peking and Rome represent, by pre-modern standards, not

---

[10] Kautsky 1982, chapters 1, 2 and 15.
[11] Hall 1985: 35. See further chapter 2 and pp. 99–109. Mann 1986, chapter 5 for a critique of this whole tradition.
[12] Pollard 2000, chapters 3 and 7.

only an enormous concentration of spending capacity, but also with populations reaching up towards the million mark (or above), a gigantic logistical accomplishment.[13] "Low enabling powers" does not appear an adequate expression with which to capture such phenomena. Thinkers less suspicious of state power have therefore been more inclined to note a paternalistic, beneficial side to imperial government. This point of view can be traced back to the Jesuit missionaries reporting about the enlightened, orderly rule of the Chinese emperor to the reading public of Europe in the seventeenth and eighteenth centuries.[14] In more recent times, Weber tentatively suggested that the imperial inclination to give priority to consumer over producer interests was a first premonition of the welfare state.[15] More than anyone else, however, it is Karl Polanyi who has given expression to this view with his notions of *redistribution* and *administered trade*. Disgusted by capitalism he set about exploring historical alternatives to a modern market economy. One such alternative he found in a group of ancient Middle Eastern empires. Apparently the economies were organised without price-fixing markets. Instead resources were allocated within a framework of state-controlled redistribution of production and legally fixed prices. To Polanyi's mind, this was a planned economy of a sort and he did not hesitate to draw parallels between his ancient redistributive empires and the economy of the Soviet Union; essentially they were of the same kind.[16]

Polanyi's ideas have proved fertile in Roman soil. They have stimulated a substantial number of studies which have been able to show the large influence that state-administered redistribution exercised on the movement of material resources around the Roman Empire. The archaeological record showing the distribution of exported oil and wine amphorae has, for instance,

[13] See Braudel 1981: 489–491, 498–504 and 525–559 about pre-industrial metropoleis; Blake 1991 on Delhi; Morley 1996 on Rome.
[14] See Bitterli 1991: 60–65 and 270–272 about the place of China in early modern European discourse. The reports of the Jesuits had a strong influence on philosophers such as Leibniz and Voltaire. One of the central works in the genre is father Du Halde's *Description géographique, historique, chronologique, politique et physique de la Chine et de la Tartarie*, Paris 1735. Whereas Voltaire was delighted with it, Montesquieu, with his doctrine of the division of power, attacked it vehemently in *L'Esprit de lois* (1955, part 1: 8, 21).
[15] Weber 1972: 651–653.   [16] Polanyi, Arensberg and Pearson 1957, chapters 2 and 13.

to some extent been persuasively linked to the so-called *annona* system, or rather systems which the state used to organise food supplies for Rome and the armies.[17] Yet, in its pure form the notion of redistribution cannot be elevated to *the* organising principle of the imperial economy. It is in a way, modernising in spite of itself. Polanyi's redistribution simply exaggerates the organisational strength of imperial systems such as that of the Romans. From *a modern perspective* the striking thing is rather the very limited capacity for bureaucratic control of pre-modern states and often their outright impotence.[18]

Some administrative documents from the Egyptian nome (district) Panopolis, dating to around AD 300, offer ample illustration and deserve to be presented in some detail. Two papyrus scrolls contain copies of letters sent to and from the office of the *strategos*, the local representative of the imperial authorities.[19] From this correspondence we learn that the *strategos* was expected to submit monthly accounts of the collection of taxes and the expenses incurred in government service. However, the predecessor had neglected his duties for some time and had now left the area without leaving a proper record behind. In practice, therefore, the accounts, which according to imperial command and expectation ought to have been kept in scrupulous order, were in a mess and could not easily be corrected.[20] Of course, we know of this affair because an attempt was made to remedy past neglect, though precisely with what effect is uncertain. The letter scrolls do not uniformly document governmental failure; they also reveal an administration, at least periodically, attempting to tackle attempts at evasion.[21] But, they do indicate that the gap between imperial prescription and reality would often have been a wide one. The scrolls are also full of letters from higher-level officials giving and repeating orders,

---

[17] Peacock and Williams 1986, chapter 5. Some single studies emphasising state redistribution: Middleton 1983; Wickham 1988; Whittaker 1994a; Foraboschi 1994; Remesal Rodríguez 1997.

[18] Saller 1982, chapters 3 and 5; Garnsey and Saller 1987, chapter 2.

[19] *P. Beatty Panop.* 1 and 2.

[20] *P. Beatty Panop.* 1, lines 64–71 and 90–107. The problem of disorderly or imperfectly submitted accounts occurs repeatedly in the correspondence, e.g., *P. Beatty Panop.* 1, lines 72–76; 2: lines 10–14 and 61–67.

[21] Cf. *P. Beatty Panop.* 2, lines 68–71 and 128–152 (seeking a pragmatic settlement rather than effectuating punishments for tax evasion).

often several times over, that had so far been disregarded locally in spite of dire threats of heavy and frightening punishments. Even officials in charge of the cultivation of government land could not, as a rule, be expected to obey orders promptly, if at all.[22]

Thus, on closer inspection the idea that the imperial economy was controlled by a large redistributive system that organised all or most of the transfer of resources in the Roman world has shown itself to be inadequate and also somewhat unrealistic.[23] The Empire simply lacked the bureaucratic capacity for such a thing. The redistributive measures were very restricted in number and scope and only comprised a small part of the economy. In the first two centuries AD they were mainly limited to supplying much, though not all, of the grain needed to feed the population of the capital, and most, though even that is contested by some, of the requirements of the army.[24] There are indications in the sources that the system grew larger, mainly from the Severan dynasty onwards. But the extent is quite unclear and it has recently been concluded that the evidence does not lend support to any notion of radical change. The system remained limited in scope.[25] Correspondingly, the pendulum is now swinging back towards (re-)assigning the central state apparatus a traditionally more marginal position in the economic life of the Roman world.

As was to be expected, while the dimensions of the state have been shrinking in the eyes of modern commentators, so the importance of private market trade has received new and increased emphasis, as already noted in Chapter 1. One theme which in particular has been able to command scholarly attention in the last decade or more is the possible formation of large markets and their integration on an empire-wide scale.[26] Much of this reads like a catalogue of "free trade" promotion. The role of the Roman

---

[22] For repetition followed by threats, see for instance *P. Beatty Panop.* 1: lines 110–119 and 166–179 (lines 184–187 show one of the repeated orders having gone through). For officials on state land ignoring orders *P. Beatty Panop.* 1, lines 205–212. Another example of "juicy" threats *P. Panop.* 2, lines 100–108.

[23] Harris 1993: 14–18.

[24] Garnsey and Saller 1987, chapter 5. Harris 1993: 17 is too sceptical about state control of military supplies.

[25] Garnsey and Whittaker 1998.

[26] Fulford 1987; Carandini 1988; von Freyberg 1989; Harris 1993; Parker 1996; Harris 2000.

state is mainly perceived as indirect, assisting the trading world more or less consciously by providing a better infrastructure. In this context many old ideas have been recycled and brought to new prominence. Here we find the notion that the *Pax Romana*, the imposition of a common currency, standardised measures, the highly developed system of Roman law and more orderly administration, all worked to improve economic efficiency, lower the costs of trading and promote market integration. Characteristically Hopkins' model, linking imperial monetary taxation with interregional trade flows, which was discussed in the previous chapter, has been adopted within this picture, not as providing the dominant mechanism, but at most as just one factor within the whole range of economic catalysts.[27]

Some go even further and relegate the state to a position of pure exploitation on the fringes of the economy. In *The Corrupting Sea* Peregrine Horden and Nicholas Purcell argue that the pre-modern states in the Mediterranean mainly worked to intensify exploitation, sometimes with locally disruptive effects.[28] The basic pattern in the economy, however, was defined rather by the regional ecology. According to their argument, extreme geographical fragmentation, splintering even micro-regions into many sub-types, combined with an unstable and erratic pattern of annual rainfall to make subsistence agriculture an impossibility; there was no such thing as an average harvest which the peasants could depend upon, only extreme variability. The much praised and idolised autarky of the peasants is a modern myth. In the Mediterranean reality, aiming for self-sufficiency was a suicidal strategy. To survive, peasants had to rely on surplus production and exchange. "Every crop is a cash-crop", the authors assert. The crucial role of exchange was much helped by the sea which served to bind the fragmented localities together. It made the transfer and exchange of agricultural products between individual localities a fundamental feature of the Mediterranean world. Interdependence and economic integration, though varying with levels of exploitation, were, so to speak,

[27] Lo Cascio 2000c is the best-argued example. Paterson 1998 is extreme, rejecting the relevance of Hopkins' model.
[28] Horden and Purcell 2000, chapter 7.

written into the DNA of Mediterranean civilisation. Here is one of their observations: "We may even regard the state of affairs today, in which the Mediterranean lands produce a fifth of the planet's vegetables and a third of its fruit but depend on imports for two-thirds of their own grain, as a logical extension of the intensification that we have been discussing."[29] Of course, there is an element of rhetorical hyperbole here which perhaps ought not to be given too much weight. Yet, William Harris has made a comment to much the same effect, namely that the economic integration of the Empire was probably equal to that of the European market system including the colonies around 1750.[30]

These are extravagant claims, as can be briefly shown with the aid of a few examples. Let us leave the position of the Mediterranean in the modern world economy aside and take a closer look at the formation of the early modern European colonial market system. During the Middle Ages the sugar consumed by Europe was produced in the Mediterranean area. But that was almost brought to a complete end when sugar cultivation was moved, first to the plantations of the Atlantic islands and then to Brazil and the West Indies, whose production systems became completely organised around this activity. Later the same thing happened to coffee, which was moved from Yemen to Java and the plantations of the New World; meanwhile tea was brought from China to India and Ceylon. The driving force behind these relocations of the production of export crops was the search for greater profits; in the new locations production was either cheaper, more easily controlled and organised or had greater room for expansion.[31] Sugar, coffee

---

[29] Horden and Purcell 2000: 279 and 273 for the first quotation. Pp. 270–274 summarise their views. Chapters 5, 6 and 9 develop their view of Mediterranean interdependence, *connectivity* in their terminology. *The Corrupting Sea* is a bold work of synthesis and should be admired for that. However, it is also a very difficult book and does not always appear consistent in its views. For instance, while elite exploitation is seen as an extension of the basic productive pattern, it is still mostly viewed as disruptive and a threat to the well-being of the "victim" population (278–287, in contrast with p. 223), in other words, as representing a break from the ecological standard pattern. If that is so, it becomes crucial to explore how different regimes of elite exploitation mould economic activity. However, that is precisely what they rule out by blurring distinctions between the Bronze Age, classical antiquity and the Middle Ages. For a critique, see Bang 2004.
[30] Harris 1993: 19; Temin 2001.   [31] Steensgaard 1990a and 1990b.

and tea, however, are only examples of a general process in which the economic geography of Europe and large tracts of the world were gradually reorganised to fit the needs of a commercial system based on a steadily deepening regional specialisation.[32] The underlying principle received its classic expression in David Ricardo, the father of modern international trade theory, when he observed that foreign commerce and the resulting international division of labour ensured that:

each country naturally devotes its capital and labour to such employments as are most beneficial to each . . . while by increasing the general mass of productions, it diffuses general benefit, and binds together by one common tie of interest and intercourse the universal society of nations throughout the civilized world. It is this principle which determines that wine shall be made in France and Portugal, that corn shall be grown in America and Poland, and that hardware and other goods shall be manufactured in England.[33]

Subscribing to a *Ricardian* vision of the Empire, in other words, involves positing a radical, artificial, commercial remoulding of production patterns in the Roman world. The result would have to be a system where provincial economies were transformed to serve the needs of a steadily deepening interregional division of labour based on regional specialisation, economic competition and comparative advantages in a conglomeration of interdependent markets. Spelled out in such detail, few, perhaps, would be prepared to accept the implications of some of the optimistic assertions made on behalf of the Roman and ancient Mediterranean economy. It is doubtful, for instance, whether this image is in fact what Horden and Purcell intended to create in their analysis. After all, the ambition to integrate history and ecology can be read as an attempt to create a completely new framework for our understanding of exchange activities in the ancient world. Even the old Polanyian notion of redistribution is developed and expanded, in *The Corrupting Sea*, to cover a broader range of types of exchange. Clearly, an alternative to the *Ricardian* notion of long-distance trade is needed.

[32] See Wallerstein 1974 and Wolf 1982 for a world-system description of this development.
[33] Ricardo 1996: 93.

Interregional trade and agricultural surplus areas

Now, obviously all interregional trade which achieves a degree of regularity implies some kind of interdependence; a great city like Rome would not have existed without grain imported from the provinces. But we are still far from the kind of economic integration demanded by the modernising model. Take two of our archaeologically best-recorded products: wine and oil. The beginning of wine imports to Rome in the late Republic/early Empire from Gaul and Spain, carried in the so-called Dressel 2–4 amphorae, did not bring an end to the delivery of Italian supplies to the capital.[34] Similarly, the enormous growth in the early Empire in production and export of Spanish and, later, African olive oil did not extinguish oleo-culture in other areas of the Roman world.[35] The extent of regional specialisation, in other words, remained quite limited. A recent archaeological survey of the city of Leptiminus in modern Tunisia offers a strong additional confirmation.[36] The town seems to have had a very substantial export of olive oil and fish sauce from the second to fourth centuries AD, to judge by the amounts of waste from amphorae production found on the site. On the other hand, the city had no local supplies of iron and had to cover its needs through imports. Yet, the archaeological survey documents the existence of a local iron "industry"; substantial amounts of debris from the smelting of iron ore was found on the site. The most likely explanation is that ore was brought in as ballast in the ships carrying off the oil. Significantly, it was apparently not more expedient to import the metal after it had been processed into bars, let alone manufactured into finished products. Undeniably, this is

---

[34] Tchernia 1986. Panella and Tchernia 1994. Whittaker 1985: 50–51 summarises the amphorae material.

[35] Keay 1984; Mattingly 1988a; and Remesal Rodríguez 1998 are good treatments of African and Spanish olive oil. In late antiquity but beginning at an earlier date, olive oil, produced in the numerous villages dotting the limestone massif of northern Syria, has also been interpreted as an instance of regional specialisation in the pioneering survey work of Tchalenko. However, re-examination of this material in the last decades has undermined his interpretation. The agriculture in the area was "a mixed regime dominated by arable cultivation" and did not depend on the export of oil for its existence, so Pollard 2000: 201–203 and 232–236, building on Tate 1992.

[36] Mattingly et al. 2001.

an example of regional interdependence, but also of very fragile and limited specialisation. This conclusion ought not to be controversial. It has been repeatedly observed that Greek and Roman states failed to take commercial advantage of their colonies in the way that early modern European states attempted to in the organisation of the Atlantic economy. Montesquieu must have been among the first to make this observation, when he noted that ancient states did not treat their colonies as opportunities for increasing economic specialisation and the division of labour. In contrast to the mercantilist strategies pursued by his contemporaries, the ancients did not attempt to secure the continued commercial dependence of the colonies on the metropolis through the granting of export and production monopolies.[37] In spite of countless claims to the contrary, archaeology has, by and large, confirmed this picture. Interestingly, it was Rostovtzeff, the founder of the *concorrenza* paradigm, who first supplied the evidence. With the coming of the "Roman peace" he found it increasingly difficult to make the patterns produced by the archaeological data fit the *Ricardian* model. Rather than going their own way, specialising in particular goods, the provinces began to emulate the products of Italy.[38]

This is the problem known in the historiography as the (very questionable) "crisis of Italy".[39] In the second century BC considerable quantities of Italian exports start to appear in the Mediterranean, especially in the Aegean and Gaul. To judge from archaeological finds, these exports seem primarily to have consisted of wine (carried in Dressel 1 and Lamboglia 2 amphorae) and fine pottery (the black-glazed Campanian, followed by the red-glossed Arretine *terra sigillata*) riding "piggy back" on the shipments of wine. In the final phase of the Republic with the conquest of Gaul, the consolidation of empire in the eastern Mediterranean and the coming of Augustus, the level of activity dropped significantly. In the West, for instance, the wine exports from Italy to Gaul experienced a steep fall and then petered off during the first century AD. In the same period, Gaul gradually established a domestic

---

[37] Montesquieu 1955, part 4, 21, 21.   [38] Rostovtzeff 1957, chapters 3–5.
[39] Carandini 1988 is the most outspoken proponent of the decline of Italy theory.

production of the former imports of wine and pottery and eventually even began to send substantial consignments of wine to Rome.[40]

Thus through the lenses of modern trade theory, the inclusion of Gaul in the Empire paradoxically appears to undermine the existing regional specialisation; economic integration seems to suffer and the Empire enters upon a process of *Entspezialisierung* (declining specialisation), to quote the recent work of a German economist.[41] Rather than the expected increased regional division of labour where Gaul would have specialised in a different product (say, ham or iron tools) it could use in exchange for Italian wine, Roman exports collapsed and the province became self-sufficient in goods it had formerly imported.[42] According to modern economic perceptions this apparent decreasing division of labour ought to be a sign of economic crisis and decline. And this, too, is what Rostovtzeff and his modern Italian followers have suggested. The fall in Italian exports has been seen as an indication of a growing economic crisis, as first Italy and then the Empire as a whole entered a downward spiral of declining division of labour and diminishing economic integration.[43] This is unconvincing for several reasons. First, however one estimates the condition of Italy from the second century AD onwards, a hotly debated issue, the peninsula seems to have been in good economic health at least throughout the first century AD and probably for much longer. The changes that do occur are better described as transformations than decline.[44]

Second, to describe the incorporation of Gaul in the Empire as a process of decreasing economic integration is to take too narrow a view of the relationship between province and imperial

---

[40] Panella 1981; 1993. Panella and Tchernia 1994 survey the evidence.

[41] Von Freyberg 1989: 151–152. Woolf 1992: 283–293 also sees integration culminating in the first century BC.

[42] Gren 1941 also noted how imports from Asia Minor to the Balkans were never balanced by a counterflow of specialised goods produced in the Balkans.

[43] For this school of thought Giardina and Schiavone 1981 and Carandini 1988.

[44] Tchernia 1986 is a devastating critique. See further Patterson 1987; Whittaker 1994b; Vera 1994; and Giardina 1997, chapter 5. The development of Italy is better explained in terms of developments in patterns of landholding and political office among the political elites. See Patterson 2006 for an attempt to synthesise such a view of Italy. Sallares 2002 raises the question of epidemic diseases for our understanding of imperial Italy.

centre. It significantly overestimates the economic effects of the Italian wine exports. These exports were not the result of a deep economic interdependence between the two regions. On the contrary, they seem to have been the outcome of a very restricted set of circumstances, mostly depending on a very low degree of integration between the two areas. During the age of expansion the demand for "barbarian" slaves and metal increased in Italy. With contacts increasing between Roman and Celtic civilisations, the Gaulic nobility acquired a taste for wine, a product of the Mediterranean. In return for this exotic and luxurious product, Gaulic nobles seem to have provided Roman merchants with an abundant supply of metals and slaves of Celtic origin. After Gaul was made a province this traffic became unacceptable and came to a swift end. With the loss of these very particular conditions, the wine trade was doomed.[45] At the same time, however, social and economic integration became more extensive and involved greater resources. Gaul may have stopped sending many slaves to Rome, but it now had to pay a far more substantial imperial tribute and supply troops for the Roman army.[46] The imperial system made greater demands on the economic resources of post- rather than pre-conquest Gaul. On top of this, the province entered a phase of partial adoption of Roman institutions, material culture and productive strategies. Urbanisation increased and production both grew and became more diversified.[47] It simply does not make much sense to describe this process of inclusion and intensified contact spanning a much broader spectrum of activities as one of decreasing economic integration and specialisation. Social complexity did not decline, it increased. It is, in other words, difficult to explain the experience of Roman imperialism within a *Ricardian* framework. Economic integration developed according to different principles.

In fact, a better comparison than the strongly articulated commercial specialisation that we find in the European capitalist world-system, is the situation in the Indian Ocean world before the arrival

---

[45] Tchernia 1983; 1986: 74–100, 140–146 and 158–172; and 2006.
[46] Tacitus *Hist.* IV, 26 and 71 portrays tribute and army levies as important factors behind the Gallic rebellion in 69–70.
[47] Woolf 2001 and 1998.

of the British Raj.[48] Chaudhuri summarises the basic conditions of interregional trade in that part of the world: "But the composition of trade... was not mainly determined by the nature of that specialisation [i.e. interregional division of labour]... The most important consideration was the ability of a local economy to create a surplus over and above subsistence demand and to maintain this level."[49] The generation of an agricultural surplus was a key factor in enabling the development of other commercial and productive activities within a region. Most of what happens in the Roman Mediterranean fits nicely into such a pattern. In the western part the link between commercial prosperity and sustained agricultural surplus production is pretty straightforward, with agricultural products dominating the scene. It is the regions showing considerable agricultural expansion such as the Guadalquivir valley in Spain or much of Roman North Africa which turn up in the evidence as commercially dominant. The study of the eastern Mediterranean is, at least in terms of archaeology, less developed. Still, what we know seems consonant with this model. Alexandria, for instance, praised by Dio Chrysostomus as the leading entrepôt in the East, was also the "capital" of Egypt, the most fertile agricultural province in the Empire.[50] Ephesos, another emporium often mentioned for its prosperous trade, was one of the most important cities in the agriculturally rich province of Asia.[51]

For what it is worth, the close connection between the creation of an agricultural surplus and commercial prosperity also appears as a dominating feature of a late antique work of commercial geography of the Roman world known as the *Expositio Totius Mundi*. The author notes, for example, that the cities of Phoenicia, famed for their trade, all had an abundant production of grain, oil and wine.[52] Inevitably, in the short-term, such a trading system

---

[48] Habib 1999: 39–62 and Moosvi 2000: 345–346 underline that a closely integrated market system did not develop in India before the construction of railways in the late nineteenth century.

[49] Chaudhuri 1985: 182.

[50] Strabo 798.13 and Dio Chrysostomus XXXII, 35–36. Dio's description of Alexandria's grandeur characteristically starts by noting its basis in the rich Egyptian hinterland.

[51] Strabo 641.24. Pleket 1994 and Kobes 1999 emphasise the importance of trade to Ephesos, though they underestimate agriculture, in my view.

[52] *Expositio Totius Mundi* 23–33 (confirmed by Millar 1993: 274–295). The close link between trade and fertile cultivation is ubiquitous throughout the work.

would be susceptible to fluctuations caused by harvest failures or other shocks to the agricultural economy that eroded the surplus and thus "dried up supplies of commercial goods and destroyed the livelihoods of both artisans and farmers". To return to our Indian comparison, during a disastrous famine in the province of Gujarat in 1630 the substantial export production of cloth dwindled away as scores of spinners, weavers and peasants alike either fled the province in search of food or succumbed to hunger.[53] A similar image of the vulnerability of the commercial sector in the face of agricultural failure in surplus areas is painted by a late Roman chronicle describing a famine in Edessa: "Everything that was not edible was cheap, such as clothes and household utensils and furniture, for these things were sold for a half or a third of their value, and did not suffice for the maintenance of their owners, because of the great dearth of bread."[54]

Catastrophic famines, however, were rare. Normally the fluctuations in output would be less severe, though far from insignificant.[55] In the longer term, other factors take on greater prominence in shaping the size and distribution of the surplus. Chaudhuri lists conditions such as the general fertility of the area, population density and the level of technology. One factor, though, is conspicuous by its absence: surplus extraction. One of the great accomplishments of the vast body of peasant studies has been to make clear that peasant households are not normally orientated towards producing a large surplus for circulation outside the farm. They aim rather to fulfil the basic needs of the household with as little effort as possible. Usually they have not been the main beneficiaries of the production of substantial surpluses above their own subsistence needs. The bulk of their surplus produce was normally claimed by various political lords and would not have been produced without pressure from above.[56] Changes in the patterns of surplus

[53] See Chaudhuri 1985: 32–33 and 182–183 about the effect of short-term shocks on trade. Quotation from p. 182.
[54] *The Chronicle of Ps.-Joshua the Stylite*, chapter 39, trans. W. Wright, cited in Garnsey 1988: 4.
[55] Garnsey 1988, chapters 2 and 3.
[56] Chayanov 1986 remains fundamental on the productive logic of the peasant household. Peasants will normally aim to produce a little above their subsistence needs. This strategy ensures protection in years of less than average harvest results and enables

extraction are thus likely to constitute a key factor in explaining developments in economic circulation. Compared to the ecology, it represents a much more dynamic variable. So, the discussion has come full circle. We are back with tribute extraction and the Roman state.

The place of tribute extraction in the economy: Rome and Mughal India compared

Consonant with the prevailing "minimalist" view of the Empire, it has become customary to stress the markedly small share of the total economy which the Roman state was able to command. By the most probable estimates, it was in the region of 5–8% of gross production. Some are inclined to go even lower and opt for 3–5% or less. But this does not seem realistic; it hardly allows any room whatsoever for the state in the economy.[57] Historians of Mughal India struggle with the opposite problem: the state seems to take up too much of the economy. For centuries the Mughals have served as the quintessential example of an oppressive despotism ruthlessly plundering its miserable subject population down to the very last penny. It might therefore be useful to confront the experience of the two empires in order to sharpen our idea of the impact of the Roman state on the Mediterranean economy.

The Mughal Empire was a large and powerful state based on the floodplains of northern India.[58] It was founded in the 1520s by Babur, a central Asian aristocratic warrior adventurer, claiming descent from the great conqueror Timur Lenk. Sometime ruler of Samarkand, and later Kabul, his luck changed dramatically for the

---

storage of supplies for bad years (Garnsey 1988: 54). However, this "normal" surplus is part of subsistence production and should not be confused with the surplus produced for the political elite. Horden and Purcell 2000, chapter 7, in spite of perceptive comments on the effects of political pressure on surplus production, fail to make that crucial distinction. Wolf 1966, chapter 1, treats the different "surpluses" produced by peasants.

[57] Hopkins 1995–6: 46–48 for 5–7%; Lo Cascio 2000c, following Goldsmith 1987: 47–48, for an estimate of 3–5%, but suspecting that even this may be too high. This is unlikely. Duncan-Jones (1994: 52–55) estimates the revenue of the Roman state in Egypt in the second century at 20–25% of the province's GDP. This revenue alone would suffice to bring state income close to the threshold suggested by Lo Cascio, with Egypt producing a disproportionately large share of the Empire's GDP (see further note 176 below).

[58] See Richards 1993a for a survey of Mughal history.

better when, in a series of invasions, he succeeded in conquering the remains of the Delhi Sultanate. During the next two centuries the Empire continued to expand and develop. Akbar who ruled from 1556 to 1605 is generally recognised as the consolidator of the mature Mughal state. Under his grandson, Shahjahan (r. 1628–57), the Empire seems to have reached its "Antonine" moment, embodied in spectacular architectural feats such as the Taj Mahal and the Red Fort of Delhi. Aurangzeb (r. 1658–1707), his successor, seemingly continued the triumphal march of Mughal arms with large conquests in the southern parts of India. At the end of his reign, however, strains had built up in the system. It had proven impossible to consolidate some of the new acquisitions. In the decades after the death of Aurangzeb, the Mughal Empire entered its "third-century crisis", from which it was never to recover. Frequent challenges to the reigning monarch and regional fragmentation gradually divested the Mughal emperor of his power and territories many years before the British delivered the *coup de grâce* and deposed the last incumbent in the aftermath of the Great Indian Mutiny of 1857.

In terms of size and dimensions, the Mughal Empire may arguably be seen as the most attractive of the potential early modern comparisons sketched out in the previous chapter. The Ottoman Empire admittedly shared much of its territory with the Romans, but the total extent, both in terms of geography and population, was significantly smaller. The reach of Mughal territories was smaller, too, though with an action radius of some 1,200 km protruding from the capital Delhi, it was distinctly sizeable.[59] The population, however, was bigger than the Roman, but still within a comparable order of magnitude. By the turn of the sixteenth century, the Mughal Empire is generally estimated to have comprised some 100–110 million inhabitants.[60] By then, the Chinese population had already grown to an even bigger size. The Mughals, therefore, provide the closest bigger early modern parallel to the Roman economy (see Fig. 2.1 for a map of the Mughal Empire).

---

[59] Gommans 2002: 108.

[60] Moosvi 1987, chapter 17 estimates 100 million in 1600. Habib & Raychaudhuri 1982, chapter 6 estimate 110 million for the Mughal Empire and 150 million for all of India in 1600, growing moderately to 200 million in 1800.

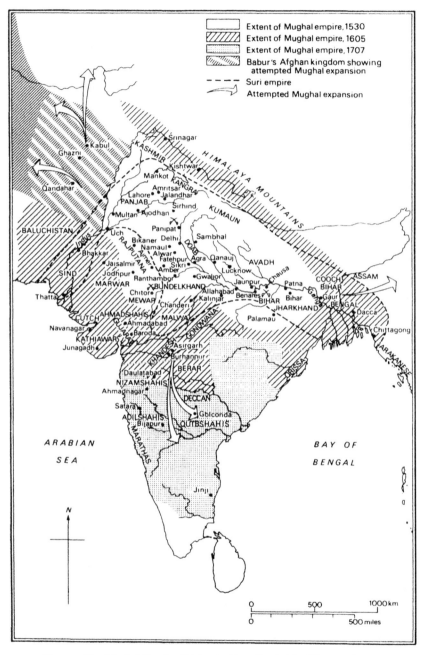

Fig. 2.1 The Mughal Empire (Richards, New Cambridge History of India, 1993, p. iv)

Despite its reputation as an insatiable Leviathan, the Mughal Empire also resembled the organisation of the Roman Empire in several ways. To begin with, it was a conquest state. A unitary system was therefore out of the question. In spite of the imperial façade of homogeneous administration, the system can best be described as a patchwork, accommodating a large variety of local and regional arrangements of submission.[61] Next, both polities belong to the category of patrimonial–bureaucratic empires.[62] This means that the state was based on a large imperial household, the army and an imperial aristocracy filling important positions within the system. In the Mughal Empire the title used to describe the imperial elite was *mansabdar*, which would be roughly the equivalent of Roman senators and knights in the imperial service and officers in the army. Bureaucratic features, on the other hand, were not strongly developed. The mechanisms governing the administrative and military system, for example, depended more on patronage connections to the emperor than bureaucratic principles such as promotion on merit, clearly defined lines of command and spheres of authority.[63] Similarly, both empires divided provincial rule into two branches. The governor would be in military command and responsible for keeping the province loyal and peaceful. The collection of taxes, on the other hand, took place under the authority of a separate official, answering directly to the imperial centre.[64]

An exhaustive listing of all similar features is unnecessary. Clearly, the two tributary systems resemble each other sufficiently

---

[61] On the Mughal Empire and its heterogeneous composition, see Richards 1993. See further Alam 1986; Blake 1991; Hintze 1997; Alam and Subrahmanyam 1998; Habib 1999, chapter 5. See Richards 1975 for a monograph studying the provincial settlement in Golconda. For the Roman Empire Garnsey and Saller 1987; Jacques and Scheid 1990; and Lepelley 1998 emphasise organisational heterogeneity and the importance of patrimonialism rather than bureaucracy.

[62] Weber 1972: 580–624 developed by Blake 1979 on the Mughals. Lo Cascio 2000b: 8 dismisses the notion of a patrimonial–bureaucratic empire. But his own analysis, pp. 13–79, 97–149 and 163–176, of the complexities of the Roman imperial *patrimonium* does not convincingly bring it beyond the model.

[63] Blake 1979, Alam and Subrahmanyam 2000: 112–130. See Saller 1982, chapter 3 on Roman imperial administration.

[64] The third book of the *Ain-i Akbari*, a grand description of the Mughal Empire *c.* 1600, explains the principles of imperial provincial administration. See further Blake 1979: 86–90; Richards 1986, introduction and 1993: 58–59. See Eck 2000 on Roman provincial administration.

to warrant closer comparison. Of course, there are also important differences, the most obvious being that the Mughal Empire was landlocked whereas the Roman surrounded the Mediterranean Sea. From the present perspective, however, this rather works to our advantage. Traditionally the realm of the Mughals has been seen as the quintessentially land-based, destructive, predatory empire that kept the economy in a stranglehold. In recent years, this image has gradually begun to disintegrate and new interpretations, exploring a more positive connection between economy, trade and empire, have evolved.[65] At the heart of this historiographical turnabout is a model which links the collection of imperial taxes with an increasing monetisation of the economy, much as Keith Hopkins has suggested for Rome. This makes the Mughal Empire an attractive comparative tool for identifying alternative approaches to the Roman trading system.

A central concern for historians of the Mughal Empire has been what one might call "the taming of the revenue intake". Our sources for Mughal taxation are dominated by official, administrative records, often of an ideological nature such as the courtier Abu al-Fazl's survey of the Empire and its institutions, contained in the late sixteenth-century *Ain-i Akbari*. Working from these it seems that the Empire aimed at taking half of the gross agricultural production in taxes.[66] This is incredibly high. It implies that the Empire came close to confiscating the total agricultural surplus and sometimes even more. In practice, that must have been impossible. An anecdote about one of the nawabs of Awadh, Burhan-ul-Mulk, is revealing about what must have happened. When trying to increase tax collection, he was asked which set of tax rolls he wanted employed, those of the coward or those of the man. Only the coward's lists were normally in use and they operated at a more moderate level of extraction.[67] The Mughal Empire also seems to have recognised the precarious connection between official claims and actual revenue. Discounting systems were

---

[65] Habib 1999 (1963) is a first step. Later research has taken this further and parted with the notion of destructive despotisms: Bayly 1983, Alam 1986, Richards 1993a, Hintze 1997 and Alam and Subrahmanyam 1998.

[66] Habib 1999: 230–236.

[67] Alam 1986: 212–213; n. 28 relates the anecdote about the tax lists.

introduced that allowed the imperial administration to allocate parts of the revenue, not at the exaggerated (imaginary) official level but at something which at least for a while resembled the actual figure more closely.[68] In the *Ain-i Akbari* one also reads the advice that the level of taxation should be adjusted so as to take account of the strongly varying agricultural potential and hence tax-carrying capacity of different areas.[69] A recent estimate, therefore, more moderate, but still high, sets imperial tax as one-third of staples such as rice, millet and wheat. More valuable crops were probably taxed closer to one-fifth.[70]

Several aspects of this can be brought to bear on the Roman case. The following sections will deal with the imperial state and the economic surplus and with the process of taxation and elite formation. State and surplus, first. Our Mughal comparison teaches us, that 5–7% of gross production is a misleadingly low measure of the Roman state's impact on society. To be sure, in modern terms the figure clearly is absolutely low; a welfare state such as Denmark claims approximately one half of GDP in tax and still leaves people more for private consumption than ever before. Yet, the Mughal case reminds us that the limits set on the scale of activities in a pre-industrial economy dominated by agriculture are much narrower than we are accustomed to thinking of today. If the dimensions of the Roman state were small, so was the size of the economy.[71] Agriculture may in general have been a little more productive on the floodplains of northern India than in the Mediterranean. Still, pre-colonial Indian conditions provide us with a rough idea of the space we are operating within. Not much more than half of total production, and often less, would have been available for extraction in the first place (see Fig. 2.2).[72] Therefore a more realistic appreciation of the scale of state expenditure can only be gained from seeing it in relation to the total disposable surplus; it is the size of the disposable surplus which effectively defines the amount of resources that can be diverted for purposes

---

[68] Alam 1986: 24–25. Habib 1999, chapter 7 treats the discounting methods in greater detail.

[69] *Ain-i Akbari*, book 3, chapter 7.   [70] Richards 1993: 85.

[71] Braudel 1981 is fundamental.

[72] Moosvi 2000: 330 posits a fifty-fifty scenario for the Indian agricultural economy around 1600.

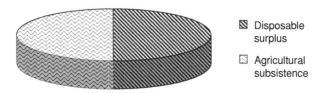

Fig. 2.2 Rough model of agrarian economy

other than the immediate reproduction of the agricultural sector. This was the negotiable part of the economy. The rest was spoken for in advance to cover the subsistence requirements of the food producers themselves.[73]

The implications of this can be brought out with greater clarity by attempting a simple quantitative model of the Roman economy. The very attempt at quantification may seem of dubious worth, given the many uncertainties in our knowledge of macro-economic parameters in the Empire. The results, however, must not be mistaken for exact figures. Quantitative speculation cannot generate the statistics which we do not possess. Nonetheless, as a heuristic device it can provide us with a rough idea of orders of magnitude. Even imprecise figures can be an advantage here. Economies are finite, quantifiable entities. By giving the Roman economy a hypothetical, quantitative expression we can control our qualitative analyses with much greater precision than would otherwise be possible. Quantification, however imperfect, helps us to choose between competing hypotheses by making their implications clearer.[74] It is also important to recognise that the construction of this sort of model is not completely arbitrary, in spite of the uncertainties. We do have bits and pieces of the information we need from the Roman world. This can be combined with what we know of agricultural economies from other periods and regions to provide us with a reasonably realistic impression of the Roman situation. Only industrialisation has created enormous differences in the productive capacities of complex societies. Agrarianate societies do show local and regional variations in wealth, but these

---

[73] Haswell 1967: 88; Kula 1976: 62–75; and Garnsey 1998b: 22–28 about the centrality of the surplus.
[74] Hopkins 1995–6: 41–46 is a strong defence of the approach. Bang 2002b attempts to develop the distinction between heuristic device and statistical model.

fall within a relatively narrow range. And what is more important, the differences tend to be ironed out when very large areas such as the Mediterranean, India or China are compared.[75] It follows that estimates on a global scale, such as are relevant to the Roman Empire, operate within a fairly manageable margin of uncertainty, say 30 or 40%.

I take my lead from Hopkins' recent attempt to quantify the size of the Roman economy.[76] The calculation has been summarised in Table 2.1. The all important component in an estimate of the Roman, as of any agrarian, economy is the size of the population. Due to the relatively modest differences in productivity the number of producers is going to be the single most important determinant of the size of the economy. The population of the Mediterranean world around 1600 was set by Braudel at 60–70 million.[77] The number in Roman times is unlikely to have gone far beyond that; neither Gaul nor northern Italy were as densely populated as later. Moreover, historical demographers operate with a slowly rising secular trend beneath the cyclical pattern of pre-industrial population growth and decline.[78] Taking that into account, Frier's recent more detailed estimate of the Empire, province by province, cannot be wide off the mark. Allowing for a slow rise during the first two centuries AD, he sees the population as reaching a peak of approximately 60 million in the middle of the second century just before the arrival of the Antonine plague.[79]

From there it is possible to derive an estimate of the minimum agricultural production needed to keep this population alive. Modern studies, based on observation in developing countries and colonies, provide a fairly good idea of the minimal material requirements of populations living in agricultural societies. On average a person needs to consume 250 kg wheat equivalents per year to subsist at an absolute bare minimum level. Within this

[75] Bairoch 1993: 101–110 and Pomeranz 2000, chapters 1 and 3.
[76] Hopkins 1995–6: 44–48.   [77] Braudel 1972: 394–398.
[78] Scheidel 2000: 63–76 suggests the possibility of a maximum population of 80 million. But that does not take account of a rising secular trend through Eurasian pre-industrial population history. On this see Braudel 1981: 31–34 and 88–92 and Livi-Bacchi 1992: 29–34.
[79] Frier 2000a: 812, building on Beloch 1886, now followed by Scheidel 2007a. See also Frier 2000b.

Table 2.1 *Estimate of disposable surplus, state impact and interregional trade in the second century AD*

1. The population of the Empire in the mid second century AD is set at 60 million.
2. Minimum subsistence is set at 250 kg wheat equivalent per person per year.
3. Agriculture was relatively low-yielding. A reasonable estimate puts average yield at 4 × seed. This means that 25% of total minimum produce would have to be put aside for next year's crop.
4. Minimum GDP will then be:

   60 million × (250 kg subsistence + 83.33 kg seed)
   = 20 million tonnes wheat equivalent

5. A large part of the population will have had to live close to this level. But cities were normally privileged, some people were also very rich and not all peasants were equally poor. Production of manufactured goods and services by the 10–20% not employed in primary agricultural production also needs to be added. It seems reasonable with Hopkins to increase total production by half in order to get to actual GDP: 20 million tonnes × 1.5 = 30 million tonnes wheat equivalent.
6. The average price of wheat is set at HS 3 per modius (6. 55 kg). To judge from prices in Egypt this may be a bit on the high side. But since this operates against the point I am trying to make it only serves to strengthen the model.
7. This makes GDP: 30 million tonnes × HS 3/modius = HS 13,700 million
8. From comparative evidence of other pre-industrial societies we can operate with a proportion of 10–20% living in cities and 80% working the land to feed the remaining 20%. The total disposable surplus can then be defined as GDP minus minimum subsistence for 80% and seed required to produce subsistence for 60 million. That is unrealistically generous, but by increasing the surplus which actually entered circulation outside the peasant household and its village network, I work against the point I am attempting to make.
9. In numbers this makes our estimate of the total disposable surplus: 13,700 ÷ (48 million × 250 kg + 60 million × 83.33 kg) × HS 3/modius = HS 6,000 million (in round figures) or 40–45 % of GDP.
10. Following Duncan-Jones, set state expenditure in the middle of the second century AD at approximately HS 900 million. Direct state expenditure then constitutes 15 % of the disposable surplus.

(*cont.*)

87

Table 2.1 (*cont.*)

11. To this should be added the imperial elite: 600 senators with an annual income (not to be mistaken for the census requirement) of around HS 1 million each, and a similar number of knights, whose income is estimated at half that of senators. The income of the imperial elite then can reasonably be assumed to be in the same range as that of the state: HS 900 million. In other words, the central aristocracy can account for another 15% of the disposable surplus.

12. 10% of GDP, entering interregional (intertown) trade, works out at 23% of disposable surplus.

    20% of GDP, entering interregional (intertown) trade, works out at 46% of disposable surplus (add another 10% and we would reach 69% of surplus which would be totally unrealistic).

13. Increasing GDP by one-third would accommodate, in the model, either raising the price of grain from HS 3 to 4/modius, or setting population at 80 rather than 60 million, or seeing actual production taking place at 2 times rather than 1.5 times subsistence. That would bring GDP up to approx. HS 18,000 million, and reduce the combined weight of imperial state and aristocracy to 17–23% of the surplus. Follow any two of these three options and the corresponding figures would be 13–17% of the surplus. That would still denote a significant influence on the economy, but with GDP at some HS 24,000 million, the costs of the central government institutions (HS 900 million) would now only take up a miserly 3–4% of the total economy.

To conclude, any understanding of economic integration in the Empire must needs take the imperial tribute extraction as its point of departure. It is able to account for a very substantial part of all interregional flows of resources, be they in the form of trade or of redistribution.

figure food accounts for around four-fifths, the rest is provision for a little clothing, firewood, housing etc. It should, perhaps, be stressed, that these are real minimums, presupposing a low level of activity, rather than the somewhat generous prescriptive standards of calorific intake recommended by United Nations agencies.[80]

The notion of wheat equivalents may require a little further explanation. Ideally, of course, we would like to have statistics for all the different products that people consumed apart from wheat, in order to determine their relative significance in the economy.

---

[80] Clark and Haswell 1970, chapter 1 and pp. 57–62.

In the absence of that, wheat equivalents are a useful fallback. Before industrialisation food grains play a dominant role in the economy of the vast majority. As a consequence, the value of the rest of production tends to stand in a rough relationship to the price of grain. In times of famine, for instance, the value of non-essentials drops sharply because people need to draw heavily on their resources to procure highly priced cereals or their substitutes. Therefore it makes good sense initially to express an agrarian economy in terms of wheat equivalents.[81]

Thus, by combining population size with subsistence requirements minimum production in the Empire can be set to 60 million × 250 kg = 15 million tonnes wheat equivalent. The imperial economy, however, could not have functioned at this level. Two more factors should be added to the calculation. First, it takes seed to grow grain. Now the seed : yield ratio is far from an uncomplicated expression of productivity. High yields may for instance be obtained by a low sowing rate, making the return per hectare more modest. For our present purposes we need not go into the finer details of these problems. What we need is a rough measure and 4 times seed has been adopted, acknowledging that behind this figure there were enormous local differences. We do not possess much good information on yields in the Greco-Roman world, but the scraps we do find in the various agricultural treatises do not strongly contradict this choice. Moreover, scientific analysis of ancient grains found by archaeologists confirms that they will have been fairly low-yielding.[82] Finally, on comparative grounds, we can also argue that yield must have been higher than three-fold because otherwise the peasants would have found it difficult to support the elaborate urban-centred social system. On the other hand, they would probably also have been below five-fold or we would have to accept a much higher level of urbanisation than most are willing to concede.[83] So 4 times seed can be used with reasonable confidence as a broad measure. This adds an extra 5 million

---

[81] Garnsey 1988: 3–7 citing the chronicle of Joshua the Stylite on a famine in late Roman Edessa. For comparative confirmation of the rough relationship between prices in food and non-essentials, see Chatterjee 1996: 54.

[82] In addition to Hopkins, see Garnsey 2000: 706–709 on grain productivity.

[83] De Vries 1984: 242–243 works with a standard peasant household of 5 members and 8 hectares of land. With yields of 3 : 1 the household would produce less than its own

tonnes wheat equivalent, and subsistence production in the Empire comes out at 20 million tonnes wheat equivalent (Table 2.1, steps 3–4).

While many peasants, village artisans and poor townsfolk probably existed at or close to subsistence level, considerable numbers had a standard of living above this.[84] Cities, for instance, were privileged places where large resources were concentrated. It is not uncommon to hypothesise city populations as consuming agricultural products at twice the minimum level.[85] Some of this will have been used as raw materials by urban manufacturers. This reminds us that we also need to include the production of higher-value goods and services performed by the 10–20% of population living in the cities as well as manufacturing in the countryside. All in all, our minimum estimate of the economy probably needs to be increased by half in order to arrive at the *real GDP*. This brings our estimate of the Roman GDP to 30 million tonnes wheat equivalent. Finally, this number must be converted into monetary terms to enable comparison with state expenditure. Our information on wheat prices in the Empire is fragmented, but suffices to give a broad impression.[86] In most parts of Egypt the price of wheat seems to have been around HS 2 per modius, at least until the late

subsistence. At 4 : 1 the household would be able to support 1.4 persons employed outside agriculture. With yields rising to 5 : 1 the number of persons would go up to 3.4 or about 40% outside agriculture. Erdkamp 2005: 34–54 argues, perhaps a little one-sidedly, for the possibility of higher yields in the Mediterranean, especially Italy, with a potentially even higher surplus to sustain non-agricultural activities. But, as he also emphasises, his model farm is a utopia, designed to draw attention to the significance of peasant agriculture for creating a low-yield regime. The model "high-yield" farm would only be possible on the best of lands, and could not reproduce its own labour force. In other words, it depended on the availability of a peasant population in the surrounding countryside. Average productivity would thus be much lower than the hypothetical maximum.

[84] See Garnsey 1998, chapter 4 on the near subsistence existence of many groups in the Greco-Roman world.

[85] Habib 1999: 84–85. See further De Vries 1984: 242–243, who observes that it is relatively more demanding on resources to maintain people in cities than in the countryside.

[86] For Hellenistic Babylon an impressive continuous series of prices have been preserved in the astronomical records. Aperghis 2001 makes use of this material to model the macro conditions of the Seleucid economy in Mesopotamia. Unfortunately, he has forgotten to include production above subsistence, which weakens his results considerably. For example, the state is seen as confiscating 60% of GDP, even though that means that the peasants are left with less than their subsistence requirements. He also opts for a level of urbanisation at 50% of population. That seems extremely optimistic. See Aperghis 2004 for a broad study of the Seleucid economy.

second century. Similar prices are attested for Pisidian Antioch (HS 2.25), a small town in Asia Minor, and Roman Africa. On the other hand prices in Rome were probably more like HS 8–10 per modius.[87] Hopkins has chosen HS 3 as his average. If anything, that is probably on the high side, since most grain was consumed outside the large urban concentrations where food was more expensive. Using a price of HS 3 per modius brings our estimate of GDP in the Roman Empire in the mid second century roughly to HS 13, 700 million (Table 2.1, steps 5–7).

Admittedly there are great uncertainties involved in the calculation. But as a rough measure I think it will do. Stated in per capita income it works out at HS 229.[88] Some years ago, an economist estimated per capita income in the Empire in the first century AD as HS 380.[89] That is problematic. This figure was reached without using any significant analytical checks to assure that the estimate would be realistic. As an average HS 380, in fact, seems unrealistically high when we compare it to what we know of Roman wages. Adjusting for differences in wage levels between city and countryside and between men and women, it implies that the average male working income was higher than the pay of a legionary in the first century and only a little less in the second century. This is implausible. The legionaries were a powerful and privileged group in Roman society. We would expect them to do considerably better than the average adult male labourer. Consequently, per capita income should be comfortably below HS 380. Indeed, if the information preserved about the wages of Roman labourers is used as an alternative basis from which to calculate a possible GDP, we arrive at a per capita income a little below our estimate.[90] It looks as if the dimensions of the model are roughly correct.

---

[87] Duncan-Jones 1982: 144–147 and Rickman 1980a, chapter 6 collect much of the evidence. The normal price range was HS 2–4. Egyptian wheat prices are collected in Duncan-Jones 1990: 151; Drexhage 1991; and Rathbone 1997.

[88] In wheat equivalents the figure is 500 kg per person or net production of seed 417 kg. In 1960, India, still heavily dominated by a very basic agricultural regime, had a net per capita agricultural production of 382 kg wheat equivalent (Clark and Haswell 1970: 78). This lends credence to our estimate.

[89] Goldsmith 1987: 35.

[90] I am much obliged to Richard Saller for presenting this argument to me in correspondence. Using Duncan-Jones 1982: 54 Saller sets urban male labour at HS 3 a day and rural at HS 1.5. He sets population at 60 million with half actually working (250 days per year), 20% living in cities and female income at half the rate of male, a practice that

We can now use our GDP as the basis for an attempt to quantify the disposable surplus, the really crucial element in the Roman economy. In this exercise, it is important to reach a generous estimate, more likely to be an overestimate than the opposite, since this will work against the point I am trying to make. Therefore I have tried to include some analytical "buffers" which will be able to absorb most of the effects on our conclusion of an increase in GDP of, say, 10 or 20%. Again, taking the better-known situation around 1600 as our starting point, urbanisation seems to have reached a new high of 16–17% of the Mediterranean population.[91] Figures for the Roman Empire are unlikely to have been significantly higher, but we allow a generous 20%. This leaves 80% of the population to produce the agricultural surplus. To do that, it needed its minimum subsistence requirements and seed for producing the minimum GDP. All production in Roman society above those two elements, I take as the disposable surplus. This is, in fact, very generous. Peasants also had to feed their draught animals and would probably in many areas have been able to reserve a little more than the bare minimum for the consumption of the household.[92] Leaving this aside, the disposable surplus comes out at roughly HS 6,000 million. Basically this means that only about 40–45% of the Roman economy would have been available for taxation, market circulation and so on (Table 2.1, steps 8–9).

Roman government expenditure in the second century AD can be estimated at approximately HS 900 million.[93] Combining this estimate with our GDP enables us to see that the net expenditure of the imperial system (mainly the emperor's household, "bread

is attested from antiquity. Finally he assumes that the sex distribution of the population was fifty-fifty. This works out at HS 10,000 million. To this he adds 20% for elite income and 7–8% for state income. The final result is approximately HS 13,000 million or HS 217 per capita. If we insert Goldsmith's estimate of HS 380 into the equation we see, since only half of the population worked, that average working income would be twice the base figure, that is 760. If male income is double that of female, average male working income would then be HS 1,013. For comparison the annual pay of a legionary was HS 900 in the first century and HS 1,200 in the second century (Duncan-Jones 1982: 10). Temin 2006 goes even lower in his estimate, also based on prices, but with less analytical sophistication.

[91] De Vries 1984: 69–77.
[92] Clark and Haswell 1970, chapter 4 argues that of production up to 350 kg wheat equivalent per person, most will usually remain within the peasant household.
[93] Duncan-Jones 1994: 45; Hopkins 1995–6; Wolters 1999: 202–234.

and circuses", and the army) probably took up at least 15% of the disposable surplus, as opposed to only 6% of gross production. This is quite substantial, especially when we remember, as pointed out by Hopkins, that the state often spent its tax income at some remove from where it had been collected (Table 2.1, step 10).[94] If, for example, we hypothesise that interregional transfer of resources amounted to something like 10% of GDP, *c.* 65% could arguably be accounted for by the flows of money, goods and redistribution in kind caused by net tribute extraction. If the figure for intermediate and long-distance exchange of resources is increased to 20% of GDP, the proportion comes down to 33%. But at 20% of GDP intercity transfers will amount to more than two-fifths of the disposable surplus (Table 2.1, step 12). Since a large part of the surplus was undoubtedly consumed in its region of origin, interregional exchange cannot easily have been much higher. I will return with some more detailed reflections to support this view later in the chapter. For now it will suffice to observe that even in what seems a "worst case scenario", net government expenditure is still far from a marginal economic force. Thus as a preliminary conclusion it seems clear that the imposition of imperial tribute cannot easily be bypassed in our understanding of the development in the intermediate and long-distance transfer of resources. At the very least, it must have significantly modified the pre-existing pattern in the Mediterranean world. The Roman state may after all not have been quite so marginal an economic presence as our GDP figure initially indicated. In that way it is moving closer to our Mughal example.

Tribute extraction, elite building and economic integration

Our comparison with the Mughal Empire, though, still confronts us with a glaring discrepancy between the size of the two states: the Roman state probably took up less than 10% of GDP whereas the Mughal state controlled perhaps up to one-third. That is curious and should make us wonder. In terms of organisation, we

---

[94] Hopkins 1978b; 1980; and 1995–1996.

remember, the Empires looked much alike. Could they really have experienced such differing success rates? If we compare the imperial armies, by far the largest items of state expenditure in both realms, we would not expect such a stark contrast. The army of the Great Mughal seems to have comprised around 200,000 cavalry and 40,000 infantry, whereas the Roman, consisting mainly of infantry, counted approximately 400,000 soldiers at the end of the second century AD.[95] Even allowing for the greater expenses connected with the equipment of armed horsemen, the Mughal army is still surprisingly small, especially when we add that the size of the Mughal population was around double that of the Roman.[96] Apparently, the greater share of the surplus in a much larger economy did not easily translate into military striking power of vastly different dimensions. Something is missing from the equation. We forget that we are comparing net expenditure of the Romans with gross income of the Mughals. Taxes never come in cheaply. Being without a large, disciplined, but costly modern-style bureaucracy to effectuate their commands, the Mughals instead had to create loyal and powerful aristocratic groups at various levels of imperial society to perform the functions of government. In return, these groups were supported by the assignment of very substantial shares of the tax revenue.

Thus the Empire came to reshape the structure of north Indian elite society. At the base of the imperial formation alliances were formed with village headmen and local bigwigs, the so-called *zamindars*.[97] Their position in the countryside was strengthened as they were left in charge of collection and payment of the imperial taxes. This enhanced their control and authority over the peasantry and enabled them to increase their incomes, often substantially, from their share in the imperial revenues and from tax rebates or exemptions of substantial areas of land under their direct control, not to mention from the increased opportunities to impose illicit or unofficial extra "taxes"; a Mughal letter formula for the appointment of the headman for a district of villages includes an

---

[95] Hassall 2000: 320–321 and Duncan-Jones 1994: 34.

[96] Moosvi 1987, chapter 17; Habib and Raychaudhuri 1982, chapter 6.

[97] Bayly 1983; Alam 1986, chapter 3; Richards 1993a: 86–91; Ali 1997: 84–87; Hintze 1997, chapter 6; and Habib 1999, chapters 4–5.

admonition to the appointee not to make any charges unsanctioned by local custom.[98] Clearly, even officially, to say nothing of actual practice, the state had to recognise considerable room for "creative" interpretation by its various representatives. The price the local elite groups had to pay for their increased powers was greater dependency on the state for their position. Though still in a position of substantial autonomy in the day-to-day running of things, openly disloyal, rebellious or overly recalcitrant *zamindars* risked facing the Mughal army and replacement by a more manageable substitute, for instance a local rival.[99]

The increased flow of surplus production out of the Indian countryside, brought about by this alliance of local and state power, went into financing the central imperial institutions: the large household of the great Mughal himself and the imperial, military nobility, the so-called *mansabdars*, who controlled and recruited the largest part of the cavalry army. Of those two the lion's share was taken by the *mansabdars*. It has been estimated that they were allocated about 80% of the enormous revenues of the Empire, whose collection they had to organise through their agents and in collaboration with the local elite groups. Most of this, probably around 60% or so, was intended as salary for the soldiers they were obliged to maintain. The rest mainly consisted of a personal payment for their services rendered towards the great Mughal and was intended to finance their aristocratic and luxurious lifestyle. Thus the Mughal Empire can be likened to a giant revenue pump at the end of which was created an incredibly rich imperial elite with large followings organised around their grand households dominating the main cities of the Empire.[100]

---

[98] Richards 1986: 41. Imposition of taxes is never neutral in relation to the existing social structure. They are bound to invest their administrators with increased powers which *will* be used to their private benefit. Hinton 1966, chapters 2–4, an anthropological micro-study of the Chinese village of Fanshen, provides one of the most revealing descriptions of the repertoire of coercive tools available to a gentry in control of state taxation for bringing the peasantry into economic dependence and for the eventual confiscation of its lands.

[99] Alam 1986, chapter 3, especially 92–93; Richards 1993a: 86–91; Ali 1997: 84–87; Habib 1999, chapter 5, especially 208–222.

[100] Richards 1993a, chapter 3, especially 75–78. See further Qaisar 1967 and Moosvi 1987. See Blake 1991 for grand households.

As sketched here, much in this process of intertwined state and elite formation seems rather familiar from what we know about the development of the Roman Empire. Perhaps, it is time for a more inclusive understanding of the Roman imperial state or rather a less unitary one? One peculiarity of the Mughal arrangement, though, would normally be taken to contradict this. The majority of the *mansabdars* were not allowed to form more enduring links with the countryside which could be transformed into permanent landholdings. Every so often their revenue assignments would be reshuffled and they were allocated new areas from which to collect their taxes.[101] This contrasts with the Roman world, where the resources of the imperial elite, consisting of senators and knights, were invested in enormous conglomerations of private landholdings. Ever since the famous French traveller and dealer in diamonds, Jean-Baptiste Tavernier (1605–89), reported back to a horrified European public on how the so-called despotic practices of the Mughals denied the nobility the right to private property, this has been taken as the defining difference between the powerful, independent more feudal forms of aristocracy found in the West and the weaker, state-dependent Oriental nobilities.[102] Therefore the tribute extraction of the Roman state is generally described as being structurally opposed to the independent rent-seeking activities of the landed elites. They are perceived as two separate forms of power competing for the limited surplus production of the peasantry.[103]

There is no denying that the Empire knew a structural conflict between, for example, senators and emperor, about the distribution of the surplus, but so did Mughal India. An important concern of the imperial establishment was to prevent the *mansabdars* from maintaining fewer soldiers than they were required to while pocketing the saved expenses for their own benefit.[104] The ultimate

---

[101] Richards 1993: 66–68. See further Alam 1986, chapter 1; Ali 1997, chapter 3; Hintze 1997, chapters 4 and 8; and Habib 1999, chapter 7.

[102] Tavernier 1889: 260 (book II, chapter 1).

[103] Thus Hopkins 2000: 254–257 and Rathbone 2000.

[104] Ali 1997: 53–59 and Habib 1999 discuss this question, but tend to underestimate the extent of the phenomenon; even if the *mansabdar* maintained the full number of soldiers he might still pocket a profit if he could hire the soldiers for less than the awarded amount, e.g. Richards 1993: 64–65.

control claimed by the Mughal emperor over the landholdings of the imperial elite was a tool which enabled him to punish and reward individual members of the imperial aristocracy. It could not, however, be used to reserve all revenue for the emperor himself; he had to allow the aristocracy effective control of much of the imperial revenue. The regime of the great Mughal depended on his ability to attract the service of great and powerful men. Such men expected to be granted areas from which to collect revenue in return for their loyalty. The Mughal emperor had to assign to his aristocracy most of his notional rights to agricultural revenue in a form of prebends called *jagirs*, a term which is perhaps best described as denoting a kind of fief with the restriction that the monarch retains a greater degree of ultimate control than was normally the case in feudal Europe. A failure by the monarch to secure access for his aristocracy to collect the wealth of extensive agricultural areas would plunge Mughal rule into crisis.[105]

The contrast between the two systems, one based on private, the other on prebendal, aristocratic land tenure, can, in other words, easily be made too stark and risks concealing a more fundamental similarity. In many ways, observing the Mughal system, where tribute dominated rent-taking, provides a truer picture of the workings of the Roman system.[106] Certainly, the accumulation of vast property portfolios in the hands of the Roman imperial elite was intimately connected with its access to the resources generated by the acquisition of empire in the Mediterranean. It is in no way clear that the Roman imperial elite was more independent and powerful than its Mughal equivalent. The *mansabdars* may not generally have been allowed the luxury of vast private landholdings, but then they constituted the army and administered most of the imperial revenues. Had they in that position been conceded even more, one may seriously doubt that there would have been an empire rather than a string of petty principalities. On the other hand, the Roman senate, in spite of its landed wealth, usually found itself

---

[105] Richards 1975; Pearson 1976; Ali 1997 (1966): 92–94.

[106] Cf. Haldon 1993: 63–87 who argues against Wickham 1985 that aristocratic rents should not be seen as structurally distinct from tribute extraction. Wickham 2005: 57–60 now accepts this, but with an important modification: only as long as a centralised state maintains an ability to tax the peasantry.

the weaker party when it confronted the emperor and/or the army. It was that experience which gave the historical work of Tacitus both its impassioned verve and disillusioned detachment. In times of dynastic turmoil, it was not in the senate that the new emperor was made; strong support in the army was overwhelmingly the decisive factor. When the courtier and senator Nerva was put on the throne in Rome after the murder of Domitian in AD 96, his feeble hold on power was only secured through the adoption of one of the foremost generals of the Empire, Trajan, as heir to the throne.[107]

Nothing illustrates better the relative weakness of the senatorial order as opposed to the imperial system than its manifest failure effectively to make membership of the senate hereditary. As shown by Hopkins and Burton, even in the case of the more successful senators, who rose to the highest offices and obtained the consulship, only a third managed to have male descendants within the next three generations reaching a similar standing. Some families would have died out in the male line. But a significant number would just have withdrawn from politics in the capital altogether.[108] Participating in politics at the imperial court was a high-risk activity. The expenditure alone required to maintain a senatorial household and lifestyle could be crippling to any fortune, however big.[109] Most senators would have found it necessary to add to their income the substantial profits that could be made from holding high offices in the imperial administration, such as army commands or governorships of provinces.[110] Indeed, senators expected to be allowed a substantial share of the resources generated by the imperial system. The senatorial historian Dio Cassius, for instance, makes Maecenas advise Augustus to take the leading magnates across the Roman world as "partners in empire". There is a distinct businesslike flavour to the choice of vocabulary. Later in the *Roman History*, Dio criticises his own emperor, Caracalla, for giving his freedmen too great a share of the imperial proceeds while the

---

[107] Syme 1958, chapters 1 and 2 for Nerva and Trajan. See Roda 1998: 213–221 in general about the impotence of the senate. Cf. Tac. *Hist.* I, 4.
[108] Hopkins 1983a: 134–146.   [109] Hopkins 1983a: 149–175.
[110] Suet. *Vesp.* 4.3 is quite telling about this. Here it is a cause for comment that Vespasian refrained from enriching himself during his governorship of Africa, so endangering his credit. Most aristocrats knew better, cf. Brunt 1990, chapter 4.

senators received nothing.[111] It is the same pattern of thought we find behind Pliny's description of Trajan, donating and selling off parts of the imperial estates to members of the Roman elite; the *princeps* is complimented for allowing his friends (*amici*) to benefit, instead of treating the Empire as identical with his own household.[112]

Of course, that was precisely what tended to happen. Being so closely woven into the fabric of the imperial system, the fortunes of the elite were highly vulnerable or permeable. The great narrative histories of the early empire of Tacitus and Dio Cassius provide ample illustration of greedy emperors killing senators and other aristocrats in order to confiscate their property. Yet, it would be a mistake to see this only as a question of periods of terror under a few mad and cruel rulers. The phenomenon had much deeper roots than this, and found its truest expression in a set of practices common to "good" and "bad" emperors alike. During the early Empire the custom developed among members of the elite and various sections of the imperial apparatus to include the *princeps* as co-heir in their wills. Furthermore, the emperor appropriated the right to properties left without an heir, without a valid will, and those belonging to people condemned on serious charges such as murder or offences against the state.[113] Here is how Pliny, in his *Panegyric to Trajan*, elegantly labours to turn black into white, pressure into heartfelt gratitude:

You are not named as heir because someone else has given offence, but on your own merits, set down by your personal friends and passed over by strangers. The only difference in fact between your former private life and your present supreme position lies in the greater number of those who love you, as your own affections are more widely spread. Only continue on this course, Caesar, and experience will show whether the reputation and purse alike of a prince are not better enriched when his subjects make him their heir at their death from choice rather than from compulsion.[114]

---

[111] Dio Cassius 52, 19, 1–3 uses the expression "κοινωνοί σοι τῆς ἀρχῆς". The term is also used about proper business partnerships, e.g. Liddell and Scott, *Greek–English Lexicon s.v.* I, 2. For Caracalla, Dio Cassius 78, 18, 4. See further Cassius Dio 52, 5, 1–2; 52, 12; 52, 28 about the expectations of senators of sharing in the proceeds of the empire. Millar 1964: 102–118 and chapter 5 is still valuable.

[112] Plin. *Pan.* 50.   [113] Millar 1977: 153–174.

[114] Plin. *Pan.* 43, citation from paragraphs 1–4, with Millar 1977: 156–157 and Saller 1982: 71–73.

One gets a very clear sense of the harsher reality behind this glossy rhetorical image when Pliny goes on to describe it as a favour if the emperor accepts being passed over in a will by someone whom he had benefited in some material way or other.

Any absolute distinction between the *private* fortunes of the elite and the imperial state therefore seems mistaken. The estates of senators and knights equally belonged to the world of high politics. The connection comes out in full clarity during times of dynastic collapse. The ensuing struggles for the throne and changes in power relationships were normally accompanied by a redistribution of the wealth of the elite on a considerable scale. Aristocrats linked with the losing factions risked facing destruction, confiscation of their property and its subsequent redistribution among the members of the victorious coalition, many of whom would have been "stimulated by the desire for spoils or by the unsettled state of their private affairs".[115] It is telling that the rate of hereditary succession among the highest-standing and hence best-established consulars seems to have fallen from around 50% to only 30% in times of political instability.[116] Basically then, the enormous fortunes of the imperial elite depended upon having access to the power resources generated by the empire and ultimately controlled by the emperor.[117] This reflected the fact that they were also very much the creation of the empire. The period of republican expansion had witnessed the build-up of property and wealth in the hands of the Roman elite on a steadily increasing scale, financed by profits drawn from the exploitation and conquest of the constantly expanding Empire.[118]

The growth of aristocratic property portfolios continued under the Principate. It was fuelled by a stronger integration of provincial landholdings into the tributary system of the Roman state. The

---

[115] Tac. *Hist.* II, 7. The close link between violent dynastic struggles and redistribution of aristocratic wealth is a main theme of Tacitus' *Histories*, e.g. I, 2; I, 20; I, 88; and II, 84. Of course one should be cautious of taking Tacitus' laments too seriously. The suggestion, however, that aristocrats with financial problems had everything to gain from the turmoil surely is quite revealing, not because we should accept Tacitus' sneer that all the "troublemakers" were bankrupts, but because of the underlying expectation that such people would be able to profit substantially from joining a rebellion.

[116] Hopkins 1983a: 138–139, including table 3.6.

[117] Saller 1982, chapter 2 and Millar 1977: 275–355 show the integration of the elite in a network of imperial patronage.

[118] Hopkins 1978a: 39–56. See further Shatzman 1975: 11–176.

process went in two directions, from the centre to the provinces and from the provinces to the centre. Already established members of the imperial elite would to a larger extent than hitherto acquire estates scattered around the provinces. As provincial administrators, they profited from the dispensing of justice and the collection of taxes by various more or less sinister methods such as acceptance of gifts, "bribery", pocketing of parts of the imperial revenues and collection of extra dues.[119] Some of this would have been transformed into provincial real estate. Through prosopographical studies it is possible to follow how some senatorial families, based in Italy, gradually built up large estates in parts of the provinces where they had governed.[120] An important aspect of this process was the lending of money at high rates of interest by wealthy Roman aristocrats to provincial communities, lacking money to pay their taxes.[121] Seneca is said to have lent something like HS 40 million, at a very high rate of interest, to needy communities in the newly conquered province of Britain, only to have the debt called in shortly after. The harshness with which he proceeded to collect the debts was supposed to have been an important contributing factor to Queen Boudica's rebellion.[122] Undoubtedly, an exacerbating factor was that many had seen their lands confiscated in the process of settling the debt. In the late fourth century the Syrian orator Libanius complained that aristocrats in state offices exploited their positions to lend money to town councillors and then took over their estates when payment failed.[123]

A central element in all of this was the easier access enjoyed by people of high standing to the coercive machinery of the Empire.

---

[119] Plutarch's description (*Moralia* 814D) of the leading imperial offices in the provinces as "πολυταλάντους" (generating much money) is revealing. On provincial administration: Saller 1982, chapter 5; Woolf 1998, chapter 2; Eck 2000: 281–288. Specifically on taxation: Neesen 1980; Garnsey 1988, chapter 15; Merola 2001.

[120] Roda 1998: 214–215 with bibliography.

[121] Howgego 1994. *Dig.*18.5.9 discusses the selling-up of land burdened with tax arrears.

[122] Dio Cassius 62, 2, 1.

[123] Lib. 48, 3 and 14. Though late, Libanius is no less relevant for the earlier period. The practice was ingrained in Roman provincial administration. Apart from Seneca, it is vividly attested in the correspondence of Cicero. The letters, *Att.* 5.21; 6.1; 6.2 and 6.3 (with Rauh 1986), discuss Brutus' usurious loans to provincial communities. See further Plutarch's essay, "That we Ought Not to Borrow", in the *Moralia*, paragraphs 828E–829E on the general importance of money lending for the redistribution of land in provincial communities.

Senators, knights and other persons of substance would often, for instance, have been able to use their connections within the imperial system to secure the support of government troops to settle conflicts to their own advantage, not least in connection with the collection of debts.[124] The importance of this should not be underestimated. Roman society was not strongly regulated and peaceful. Violence was endemic. People who suddenly found themselves in weaker positions, such as orphans and widows, frequently experienced difficulties in holding on to their material possessions.[125] Claims needed to be defended and asserted in order to count.[126] This was also true of the legal system. Hearing a case, as Aulus Gellius informs us, was not just a matter of weighing the evidence. The general standing and social clout of the litigants were equally important matters to take into consideration.[127] A trial was to a very large extent a question of measuring out the relative power and influence of the contestants.[128] Hence the established practice of using one's powerful connections to influence the outcome. Again it does not require much imagination to see how a Roman senator or knight with a stake in the financial exploitation of the provinces would benefit from this. To judge from the collections of letters preserved from antiquity, it was an aspect of the mutual exchange of favours inside the personal networks of the imperial elite to write to provincial governors with whom one had links, asking them to look kindly on the cases of one's friends, protégés and connections. Of course, it is difficult to know how much influence such recommendations exercised on the governor/judge, and it will in any case have varied from case to case, according to the circumstances. But the very fact that these letters were written, shows that people expected them to have an effect.[129] Thus, it seems reasonable to suggest that the various kinds of support that the imperial elite could mobilise from the state system must have

---

[124] Brutus attempted to obtain military support for the collection of provincial debts from Cicero as governor of Cilicia, Cic. *Att.* 6. 1.5–6. See further the anecdotal evidence in Apuleius' *Metamorphoses* (VII, 6–7) and MacMullen 1990: 191–193.

[125] Krause 1994, chapter 10 and pp. 232–235 and Krause 1995, chapter 13, especially pp. 195–200.

[126] Millar 1981: 66–71 and MacMullen 1990, chapter 18.

[127] Gellius 14.2 with Garnsey 1970: 210–211.   [128] Saller 1982: 56–60.

[129] Saller 1982: 152–154.

played a crucial role in enabling it to acquire and maintain estates in different regions of the Empire.[130]

Another way forward was to team up with a local aristocrat and town councillor who enjoyed sufficient influence locally to promote and guard the economic interests of rich outsiders. Libanius, for example, complains about how the leading members of the town councils as middlemen for people in government positions handled ruinous loans that deprived their less prosperous colleagues of their landholdings.[131] Undoubtedly these local bigwigs profited substantially from their involvement in those transactions with people in higher positions. As such, this only represents a particular instance of a more general phenomenon. Plutarch urged the leading town councillors to cultivate the patronage of members of the imperial provincial administration because "the Romans themselves are most eager to promote the political interests of their friends" and would serve them "as a firm bulwark".[132] The reason for this was, of course, that the Empire depended on the payment of taxes. But being without a large bureaucratic corps, it needed to create a group of local allies who were strong enough to control the area, ensure its continuous peaceful subjugation and handle the actual collection of the imperial tribute. In his autobiography Josephus, a local Jewish grandee, provides us with a close-up of how this was done in practice. When the Jewish rebellion had been almost quelled, Titus, the Roman commander, offered to spare Josephus' friends and relations from punishment and captivity, thus preserving his network of social contacts. Afterwards Josephus was presented with lands in Judaea, first by Titus and then later by his father, the ruling emperor, Vespasian. Later still, the emperor Domitian added to the gift by granting tax immunity to his properties in Judaea. Throughout this period of imperial favouritism Josephus also enjoyed the support and protection of the emperors against political rivals who tried to bring him down by accusing him of treason against the Roman cause.[133]

[130] Saller 1982, chapter 4 for the importance of access to the resources generated by the Empire to the imperial elite.
[131] Libanius 48, 37–41.   [132] Plutarch *Moralia* 814c.
[133] Josephus *Vit.* 422–430. The autobiography is itself a defence written to counter the accusations of a rival, Justus of Tiberias (*Vit.* 336–367, 410). Brunt 1990, chapter 13 on Josephus and Empire.

Josephus, however, was also exceptional. The vast majority of local aristocrats would never have experienced anything resembling the close direct patronage of the ruling dynasty that he enjoyed. Yet on a scale less grand, the privileged cocktail of protection, land and tax benefits was offered to those in powerful positions, who where willing to co-operate, around the provinces of the Empire.[134] In organisational terms, the Empire was only loosely integrated. As has been said so many times before, the world of the Romans was, rather, a patchwork of conquered city states. These were retained at the time of conquest as the basic and internally largely self-governing administrative units. In areas where city state organisation had been lacking, the Roman conquerors introduced it in order to satisfy the needs of the imperial administration. Among the functions of city government was the responsibility for the payment of the imperial taxes. Each city territory was assessed at a set amount of tribute, and the leading and richest citizens were effectively left in charge of distributing the burden internally within the landowning segment of the citizen body.[135] Obviously, this gave them considerable power and room for manoeuvre. To begin with, they were normally able to ensure that their own property would be underestimated, one way or another.[136] Moreover, this did not just enable them to avoid paying their full share of the taxes. Usually, it also meant increasing the burden on those less well off and hence less able to shoulder it.[137] Thus an avenue of access was opened up for the extension of rural credit. We have already seen how this was used as an investment opportunity by rich outsiders, but it was also open

---

[134] Some general references must suffice: Jones 1940; Garnsey 1988, chapter 15; Brunt 1990, chapter 12; Jacques and Scheid 1990, chapters 5–7.

[135] *IG* V(1), 1432–1433 (with Hopkins 1995–6: 68, n. 28) show how the city of Messene allocated its tax of 100,000 denarii among its citizens. See further Bay 1972: 32–47; Jones 1974, chapter 8; Neesen 1980; Brunt 1990, chapter 15.

[136] *P. Beatty Panop.* 2, lines 68–71 and 145–152 is a good example. The leading magnates in Panopolis had colluded with a village official to leave some cultivated land undeclared, thereby effectively carving out tax-free lands for their own benefit.

[137] Cic. II *Verr.* 2, 138 is clear about this mechanism. See Veyne 1990: 200 (and note 292) who also adds the testimony of *Codex Justinianus*, XI, 58 (57), 1: a law of AD 313 which observes that "the *tabularii* of the cities, in collusion with the powerful, shift the burden of taxes onto the lesser people".

to the prosperous insiders themselves. Plutarch admonished the leading citizens not to (ab)use the support of the Roman authorities to satisfy their own greed and drive away the less powerful.[138] Libanius adds greater detail to the picture. Much to his dismay, the local landed magnates did not just act as middlemen for people in higher positions. They also took advantage of their power actively to increase their own wealth by imposing too heavy burdens on their lesser colleagues in the city councils and afterwards forcing expensive loans upon them that made them lose their lands.[139]

True, both Plutarch and Libanius criticise the system. In that respect, they are also witnesses to ideological attempts to limit the most brutal effects of its workings. The Roman jurists, too, gave rulings that prohibited the uneven distribution of tax burdens and government requisitions.[140] Such ideological misgivings and legal admonitions, however, should not be interpreted as fundamental attempts to combat and change the basic principles of the exploitative machinery. Plutarch, after all, recommended municipal rule by the leading and richest members of each community, supported by Roman government representatives. Rather, these phenomena should be seen as (feeble) mechanisms to contain those activities within bounds in order to ensure the longevity of the system. The sheep had to be sheared, perhaps even fleeced, but not gutted. Too harsh a regime might undermine the tax-paying capacity of the cities by causing social unrest, banditry or just impoverishment and abandonment of cultivated land. It was a question of maintaining a balance. But that balance remained heavily tilted towards the members of the most prominent families around the cities of the Empire because they were the most important guarantors of social stability.[141]

---

[138] Plut. *Moralia* 815a.

[139] Libanius 48, 37–41. The practice of overburdening weaker members of the councils is confirmed by rulings in the *Digesta*, e.g. *Dig.* L.4.3.15 (Plutarch *Moralia* 827–832 warns more generally against the corrosive effect of credit on the economic fortunes of councillors). Control of taxation and loan-giving was a powerful tool of wealth-acquisition in the hands of pre-industrial elites. Hinton 1966: 50 is illuminating.

[140] *Dig.* L.4.3.15 (Ulpian).

[141] Cic. *Q. fr.* I, 1, 25 is clear about the need to avoid internal struggles in the cities, banditry etc. to maintain the tax capacity of the province.

One gets a very clear idea of this from the institution of courts to hear complaints of provincials about the activities of Roman governors. In Cicero's speeches against the most notorious culprit in provincial maladministration, Gaius Verres, a recurrent strategy of discrediting the accused is to emphasise how he alienated and encroached on the wealth of the leading members of the Sicilian provincial communities. Verres' crime as governor was not just his deeds of self-enrichment, but more the damage done to those upon whom Roman rule was based. In seeking to profit from his office Verres had not respected the established social hierarchy. Therefore, according to Cicero, he could only muster the support of small fry and persons of dubious reputation and power who had gained from his attacks on the *homines nobilissimi primique*.[142] Whether a governor would be prosecuted and punished for his (mal)administration seems, in other words, to have been decided less by what he did than whom he did it to. It was essential that he secured support from a section of the provincial upper classes with sufficient strength to be able to block attempts to have him indicted after his time of office had expired.[143]

As in the Mughal Empire then, the imposition of Roman hegemony considerably modified the pre-existing pattern of power around the numerous cities of the empire. The administration of imperial tribute extraction enhanced the strength of the leading local landowners. As a result, these elite groups were able gradually to accumulate wealth and property on a larger scale than before.[144] A clear sign of this is that "big men" with very large financial capacities indeed begin to surface in our sources. The province of Lycia, on the south coast of Asia Minor has revealed some of the best evidence for this process through its very strongly developed epigraphic habit. A whole dossier of inscriptions, recovered from a funerary monument, describe the brilliant career of

---

[142] Cic. II *Verr.* 2, 11. Further II, 2, 14, 22, 35–49 dismissing provincial supporters of Verres as small fry and desperate people hoping to benefit by turning the social order upside down.

[143] *CIL* XIII, 3162, with Saller 1982: 132.

[144] See Brunt 1990, chapter 12 and Garnsey 1988: 246–251 for this development. For studies of individual provinces, see e.g. Garnsey 1978 (Africa), Millet 1990 (Britain), Jones 1940; Quass 1993; Merola 2001; Dmitriev 2005 (Greek East), Woolf 1998 (Gaul) and Ørsted 1986 (Noricum and Illyricum).

a certain Opramoas of Rhodiapolis.[145] Normally attention has focused on the enormous gifts that he bestowed on the Lycian communities during a period of a quarter century (AD 125–52). They seem to add up to something like 1,000,000 denarii or about four times the minimum legal requirement of a senatorial fortune.[146] This is munificence on a truly staggering scale. In Paul Veyne's interpretation, Opramoas is the ideal embodiment of the spirit of euergetism, a virtuoso taking to an extreme the habit of the aristocracy of making public benefactions by performing financial suicide in a kind of ancient potlatch.[147]

I remain sceptical about that interpretation. Opramoas was not alone in the province and neighbouring regions in demonstrating such spending capacity.[148] Ultimately, of course, in the absence of his private accounts we will never know whether he did indeed ruin his patrimony. But what we do know is that gift-giving on this level, sustained for many years, requires a substantial build-up of wealth and the generation of very large incomes. Altruism is not nearly enough to maintain such activity. Here we find Opramoas and his family, exactly as we might expect, playing a central role in the political life of the province and cultivating the patronage of Roman magistrates and emperors. According to the inscriptions the family had a prominent record of office holding within the Lycian *koinon*, or league, perhaps stretching back before Roman rule.[149] But the first member for whom we have more detailed information is Opramoas' father Apollonios. He played a dominant role in his hometown Rhodiapolis, holding all its major offices, and attained a position of some prominence in the provincial council, though he does not seem to have reached the highest office of *lykiarch*.[150] However, he had certainly managed to concentrate enough wealth and influence during his career to see two sons, including Opramoas, off to even greater glory and influence. We meet Opramoas first in AD 125, when his father performed the office of *archiphylax* both in his own name and in the name of

---

[145] *TAM* 905. Kokkinia 2000 presents a new improved edition of the text, with detailed "real kommentar". Heberdey 1897 reconstructed the chronology of the information contained in the inscriptions.

[146] See Coulton 1987: 172 for a recent discussion. [147] Veyne 1990: 149–150.

[148] Coulton 1987. [149] *TAM* 905, IVC, lines 13–14.

[150] *TAM* 905, IIB, IIIE–F and VIIIC.

his two sons. This was an office which required great financial resources. In the honorary decrees Opramoas is described as having paid "the taxes owed to the imperial coffers by the province with his own money and only afterwards began the collection with great philanthropy".[151] One would like to know the economic reality behind this phrase. But in the light of the foregoing discussion it seems far from unlikely that Opramoas or, to be more precise, his father, would have been able to profit from handling the provincial taxes. If nothing else, we find the family securing the patronage of the governor Iulius Frugi, who praised them in official letters.[152]

At any rate, the patrimony of the family was certainly not ruined or endangered by this. On the contrary, during the following twenty-five years Opramoas (and his brother) expanded the power of the family and rose to the highest positions in the province, including secretary and *lykiarch*, the leader of the provincial council and high priest of the imperial cult. All of this brought him into close contact with successive Roman governors. Their many letters of praise addressed to the provincial council allow us a glimpse of how Opramoas continued the work of his father and expanded his network of imperial supporters.[153] Several of the governors even assisted in bringing Opramoas to the attention of the emperor Antoninus Pius, who honoured him in letters on more than a dozen occasions.[154] This does not look like a man eroding his economic

---

[151] *TAM* 905, IIE, lines 10–14. From the proceeding information and text 14 and XIIIC, line 4, it is clear that his first positions were held through his father.

[152] *TAM* 905, IF. Contra Quass 1993: 177–178, who only sees the euergetistic side of the handling of taxes.

[153] Opramoas enjoyed the patronage of effectively every governor in Lycia during the period. We know the name of the governor in twenty-two years of the twenty-eight years covered by the inscriptions, and all of those more than ten governors found it worth their while to support Opramoas – one or two of them, though, only after some initial resistance. On completion of the *lykiarchy* Opramoas was voted *extraordinary* honours. Asked to support this, the governor cryptically replies that the *koinon* ought to follow established practice. This is probably not support, as Kokkinia takes it to be, but rather an attempt to curb the ambitions of Opramoas. The following governor continues the resistance to these extraordinary honours but is outmanoeuvred by Opramoas who secures the backing of the emperor (*TAM* 905, VIIA–VIIIA, Kokkinia 2000: 225–228). Rather than a "potlatch" aristocrat, Opramoas better fits Tacitus' category (*Ann.* xv, xx) of leading provincial magnates whose great wealth allowed them to dominate the province and were of crucial importance to the governor.

[154] *TAM* 905, texts 37–51 are letters from the emperor honouring Opramoas. Several had been supported by the patronage of governors. Heberdey 1897: 70–71 has a convenient list.

base by excessive expenditures. Instead, the inscriptions convey the impression of a family steadily increasing its resources and sphere of influence. A further indication of this is that as his career progressed he seems to have acquired considerable interests in the province outside his hometown Rhodiapolis. Some of the later inscriptions show him as having acquired citizenship in several other Lycian communities. He is also described as pursuing politics actively in all the cities of Lycia – a fact which is documented by the very wide distribution of his benefactions across a broad selection of the cities in the province.[155] They could, of course, be interpreted as an instance of pure generosity, but it seems more reasonable to take them as a sign of Opramoas' need to cultivate his interests on a province-wide scale. He had now grown beyond his hometown.

In this connection, it is certainly not without interest that the family continued its expansive move in the next generation. One of the last inscriptions proudly records that a niece of Opramoas had entered the imperial elite by marrying the senator, Claudius Agrippinus.[156] The couple is also known from a fascinating inscription found in the Lycian city Oenoanda, listing a genealogy of another leading Lycian family.[157] From that we can see that Agrippinus eventually reached the office of consul. In the generations following this union we find senators, consuls and even a governor for the province of Lycia and Pamphylia from this family. Agrippinus himself was from an old family of *lykiarch*s. One of his forefathers was *lykiarch* as early as around the middle of the first century. Two generations later we find Agrippinus' grandmother marrying a Roman aristocrat, who held the governorship of Spain and also commanded a legion. The daughter of this marriage married a *lykiarch* and in the next generation we then find the son, Claudius, and the daughter, Claudia Helena, re-entering the imperial aristocracy.

As a group the inscriptions show in detail how the interaction of local elites with the tributary empire gradually led to the

[155] *TAM* 905, VIIIB–E mentions six cities without being exhaustive. Texts 53 and 59 show the wide dispersal of Opramoas' benefactions.
[156] *TAM* 905, XVIIID, lines 12–13.
[157] *IGR* III, 500. See Heberdey and Kalinka 1896 for a graphic representation.

formation of stronger and richer elite groups. At the pinnacle of this elite, are to be found some families which had risen to a level of wealth that made them big even in a provincial context and whose interests would often have exceeded the bounds of their local community. This made them attractive partners for already established members of the imperial elite, both in terms of marriage and as resourceful allies who could be promoted into the highest orders of imperial society as they invariably needed replenishment.[158] Detailed and painstaking prosopographical research into the composition of the Roman senate has revealed how during the first two centuries AD under the auspices of the emperors, it changed from a body of Italian aristocrats to a gathering of the "best men" from across the Empire.[159] This is, of course, a sign of the relative weakness of the senatorial aristocracy. But it also reveals the strength of the imperial system. It managed, as it were, to (re)fashion and (re)produce its own elite.[160] What is more, this was done on a steadily increasing scale as larger and larger accumulations of provincial land were merged into the existing stock of wealth in the hands of the imperial elite. Thus, to talk about the weakness of the imperial aristocracy is paradoxical, for it grew richer and came to command larger social resources through its dependence on the imperial system. Like the Mughal Empire, the Roman Empire appears to have worked like a powerful revenue pump.

Tributary integration: the market as surplus transformer

Thus the comparison with Mughal India adds a new perspective to our understanding of patrimonial bureaucratic empires. The

---

[158] Saller 1982, chapter 5 on the patterns of the provincial patronage of the imperial elite.

[159] The expression is commonplace in the contemporary literature: Aristeides *Or.* 25, 40–71 and Dio Cassius 52, 15 with Oliver 1953; Millar 1964: 102–118 and chapter 5. Chastagnol 1992 and Roda 1998: 172–213, chapter 11 survey the research on the changing composition of the senate. Stein 1927, chapters 3–4 and Sherwin-White 1973a, e.g. 402–417 are still valuable. Hammond 1957 is fundamental. See further Alföldy 1977; Halfmann 1979; *Epigrafia e ordine senatorio* 1982. Particularly on knights, see Pflaum 1950; Demougin 1988; Demougin and Devijver 1999.

[160] A clear expression of this was the creation of a second leg of the imperial elite, as knights were admitted to powerful positions in the Empire next to the senate; see Saller 1982, especially chapter 3; Hopkins 1983a: 176–184.

customary emphasis on a conflict of interest between tributary empire and various rent-taking aristocratic strata is only one part of the imperial experience. The empire is not just engaging in a socially destructive war against its aristocracy where it will either, as a capstone in John Hall's phrase, curtail and break the landed elites or disintegrate into numerous small cells. Rather, the central power depended for its existence on partly dissolving the opposition and successfully integrating the more local forms of power into the imperial fabric. Some years ago the late Burton Stein, a historian of pre-colonial India, put forward the concept of segmentary state to denote this kind of political system. By this he meant that the imperial state could not be reduced to the central institutions of the emperor's household and the army, it also encompassed "a large sub-stratum of local lordships, magnates or . . . honoratiores".[161] The great advantage of Stein's formulation is that it recognises that state (tribute) and local forms of power (feudal rent) are not absolutely separate. As aristocracies come to participate in the functions of the state system, through office holding and the collection of taxes, the two forms of authority begin to blend. Invariably they become intertwined and, depending on the success and durability of the imperial formation, mutually supportive.

Tribute extraction, in other words, was never just a question of depleting the resources of local communities. In return for handling taxation, aristocrats were, as we have seen, allowed to profit substantially at various strategic points in the process. This needs to be added to the bill if we are to reach a proper assessment of the economic impact of the Roman state. At least for the central aristocratic groups, senate and knights in the imperial administration, it is possible to get an idea of how this works out in our quantitative model of the imperial economy (Table 2.1, step 11). Based on Pliny's letters, Duncan-Jones has estimated the annual income (not to be mistaken for the census requirement) of a middling senator at approximately HS 1 million in the early

---

[161] Stein 1985a, especially 387–388 and 410–411, citation from 411. See further Stein 1998: 18–30, stressing the duality of conflict and dependence.

second century AD.[162] Some senatorial households would have experienced much greater incomes. On the other hand, some also had problems even in meeting the economic requirements of a political career.[163] Hence it seems reasonable to adopt the figure based on Pliny's experience as an average annual income for the 600 or so senators, even though we might actually be underestimating the wealth of the senate then.[164] The contours of the equestrian tranche of the central imperial elite are more hazy. But to judge from the growing number of equestrian procuratorships (127 are attested in the reign of Marcus Aurelius) it would have required a group more or less equal in size to the senate to fill the spaces.[165] The wealthiest and most powerful knights clearly were richer than many members of the senate. But this would not generally have been the rule, rather the opposite would have been the case if the lower property qualification of this group is anything to go by. A fair guestimate would put the income of the equestrian members of the central imperial aristocracy at half that of the senate. In numbers this gives 600 × HS 1 million + 50% = HS 900 million or an extra 15% of the disposable surplus to be added to the 15% which was estimated above for central government expenditure (Table 2.1, step 11).

This makes the Roman Empire look a lot more like the Mughal Empire, especially if we take into consideration that the Mughals' notional intake of one-third of production in reality would probably have been closer to one-fourth or one-fifth.[166] Then when we subtract the substantial part that went into the pockets of the local aristocracies, the *zamindars*, the two empires come to look very much alike. The revenue of the central imperial system seems to

---

[162] Duncan-Jones 1982, chapter 1. See also Hopkins 2000, n. 5 for some comments on the material informing us of the scale of aristocratic wealth.

[163] Millar 1977: 297–300.   [164] Chastagnol 1992, chapter 10.

[165] Whittaker 1993, chapter 12: 61–62 adopts a similar figure for the size of the equestrian section of the imperial elite. Pflaum 1950 and 1960–1 are the classic studies of the equestrian imperial procurators.

[166] The Mughal revenue intake is a thorny issue. But independently of how we assess this problem two things operate in favour of lowering towards one-fourth or one-fifth of GDP. The figure of one-third is of agricultural production. To be strictly comparable to our Roman figure, it should be adjusted to take account of urban production and services which only contributed modestly to Mughal taxes. On top of this, many cash crops were only taxed at a rate of one-fifth. Taken together these two factors go a long way to bring the Mughal tax figure within "our" range.

have been within a range of 10–20% of GDP in both cases. This does not look impressive. But when we realise that this would have constituted close to one-third of the disposable surplus in the Roman case (and it cannot have been wildly different in the Mughal case) it is clear that it could not easily have been much larger (Fig. 2.3 is a graphic representation of the model).[167]

As already mentioned, the revenues of the imperial system (emperor, army and central aristocracy) were spent unevenly across the empires and often at a considerable distance from their collection point. In the Roman case it was to a very large extent consumed by emperor and elite in the capital and in the border regions where the army was stationed.[168] This means that much of the revenue intake had to enter regional and interregional circulation in order to reach its point of expenditure. In Table 2.1, step 12, I have tried to indicate the consequences of different proportions of GDP going outside its nearest marketing network, that is, entering intercity resource flows. At 10% of GDP, about 20–25% of the disposable surplus would be spoken for in this way. At 20% of GDP it would be 45–50%. Clearly this must be pushing against the maximum limit of what could have happened. Even though the consumer-city model has been hotly debated, few people would doubt that a very large section of the surplus was spent locally by the municipal aristocracies around the numerous ordinary cities of the empire. Data from both eighteenth- and nineteenth-century India and late imperial China, too, suggests that we should envisage a level of intercity exchange of between 10 and 20% of GDP in the Roman Empire.[169]

---

[167] Huang 1974: 159–161 on Ming China shows the narrow limits for imperial taxation.

[168] Whittaker 1993, chapter 12: 61–62 for a balanced account of imperial aristocratic consumption.

[169] Yang 1998: 223–224 lists a number of estimates from eighteenth- and nineteenth-century India. They indicate a rise in the marketable surplus from 20 to 30% of production. Of this a significant portion is bound to have been sold within the region of production. One estimate saw about 10% of agricultural production enter wider networks of circulation. Expressed as a proportion of GDP, when manufactured products and other luxuries are added into the calculation, this suggests a level of interregional trade of about 10–20% of GDP. Perkins 1969: 115–120 estimates total value of interregional trade in late imperial China at 15–20% of gross farm output. Expressed as a proportion of GDP (farm output plus production and services in the cities) the figure will be a little lower, perhaps 10–15%.

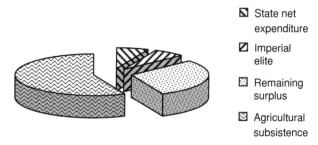

- ◩ State net expenditure
- ◪ Imperial elite
- ▨ Remaining surplus
- ▧ Agricultural subsistence

Fig. 2.3 Roman GDP, surplus and tributary empire

For our understanding of the economy of the Empire this scenario has important implications. To begin with, it is difficult to identify market exchange as the dominant organising force of economic integration in the empire. At our imagined maximum level of interregional resource transfers, expenditure related to the central imperial system would be able to account for up to two-thirds. In practice, some of this would have gone into property transfers from tribute payers to the tribute-receiving groups in society. This is the implication of the processes of increased concentration of agricultural land in aristocratic hands described above. But even in that case, a large part of the politically extracted surplus would still have had to be exchanged between the different regions of the empire.[170] No wonder that archaeologists again and again emphasise the different scale of activity between Greek and Roman history.[171] Imperial tribute extraction must have dramatically changed and expanded or at least considerably modified the pre-existing pattern of economic circulation in the Mediterranean world. If we want to speak of economic unity in the Roman Empire we would do well to start by looking for tribute extraction and the shared processes of elite formation and concentration of landed property rather than a conglomeration of interconnected capitalist markets. Consumption related to the profits of empire comes out as such a powerful stimulus that there cannot be much room for a development in interregional trade driven by regions

---

[170] See Jongman 2006: 248–50 for an attempt to model the scale of property transfers spawned by the imposition of an imperial tribute.
[171] Mattingly and Salmon 2001: 3–14.

specialising in single products and exchanging them with one another.[172]

This may be stated with confidence. Even if we should have underestimated the value of the economic surplus and interregional trade in our model by, say, a third, the conclusion is not much affected; imperial expenditure would still be able to account for up to 50% of our maximum level of intercity transfers. This would, for instance, be the case if the average price of grain rather than the HS 3 adopted in our calculations was closer to HS 4 per modius. But that would have to be considered a high price in many regions of the empire, acceptable perhaps in times of threatening famine, but not characteristic of the prevailing conditions.[173] A similar effect would be produced by increasing the estimate of the Roman population from 60 to 80 million. However, that population figure represents the plausible maximum. It is as high as the more optimistic of modern considered estimates go. Of course, the compounded effect of adopting both modifications to the model would be more serious, though far from damaging. Such a procedure would reduce the combined weight of imperial state and aristocracy in the surplus to approximately 15%. That would still be a very noticeable, but admittedly weaker, force in the imperial economy (see Table 2.1, step 13 for a summary).

But why would we choose to compound our most optimistic estimates? It is certainly not necessary in order to accommodate "a more optimistic" view of exchange in the empire. A model of an agrarian economy which provides for some 10–20% of GDP to be transferred between localities does not present a "minimalist" scenario of Roman exchange activities, quite the reverse. It bears emphasis that the different parameters adopted in the model cannot simply be increased at will. One of the advantages of quantitative speculation is that it enables us to observe how the different parameters are interrelated. Increasing the value of GDP, without changing our estimate of state expenditure, has the questionable

---

[172] Cf. Perkins 1969: 120–123 on the pattern of interregional trade in the Chinese Empire; the politically determined consumption of emperor and his elite dominated over interregional specialisation.

[173] Cf. the edict of the governor Antistius Rusticus proclaiming 1 denarius per modius of grain (twice the normal level) as the maximum permitted price during a famine in Pisidian Antioch (*AE* 1925, 126 = Sherk 1988, no. 107).

implication of reducing the weight of government institutions to almost nothing in the economy. In the present case of a compound increase in grain price and population size, the costs of imperial court and army are reduced to 3–4% of GDP. That would be difficult to justify.[174] The model already operates with a "small-scale" Roman state. There is little reason to make it even smaller. Only a generation ago, leading historians such as Jones and Brunt thought of Roman taxation as oppressive.[175] The Roman emperor was the single biggest landowner in the empire; and the fiscus drew substantial rents from these extensive properties. A recent estimate of taxation in the province of Egypt sees the Roman authorities claiming perhaps some 20% of provincial economic output. Taken together, these two observations alone would suffice to bring Roman government income within the range of 3–4% of GDP, thus precluding the need for any further taxation around the rest of the empire. To this list must also be added income from precious metal mines and stone quarries. It is difficult to fit the Roman state within the narrow limits of 3–4% of GDP.[176]

[174] For some general reflections, Hopkins 1995–6 (more accessible in Scheidel and von Reden 2002: 201–203).

[175] Brunt 1990, chapter 15; Jones 1974, chapter 8.

[176] Exact figures cannot be hoped for, of course. But 'crown' lands, as in most other pre-industrial monarchies, are unlikely not to have constituted several per cent of agricultural property. Egypt, however, allows at least some hypothetical reflection; it is the province which provides us with the most abundant evidence of levels of taxation and production. Working from this Duncan-Jones (1994: 52–55) has estimated the revenue claim of the Roman state in Egypt in the second century to be in the area of HS 250 million. Very roughly this can be estimated as 20–25% of the province's GDP. Egypt was an extremely productive province with grain yields beyond comparison in the Roman world. It also had a rich luxury trade passing through it. If we estimate Egypt's GDP as at least 10% of the imperial total we cannot possibly be going too high, rather the opposite. This means that the tax claim on Egypt alone will have equalled at least 2% of imperial GDP (one-fifth of 10% of imperial GDP). As already noted, Duncan-Jones (1994: 45–46) estimates government expenditure in the second century to be around HS 900 million. This is about 3.6 times the value of the Egyptian tax figure which equalled a minimum of 2% of GDP. HS 900 million, and hence state expenditure, will then have been around 7% of GDP. This is, at least, suggestive. The figures are very uncertain and the method of calculation is too simplistic. Thus Hopkins 1995–6: 44 finds Duncan-Jones' estimate of Egyptian revenue implausibly high, partly because Hopkins overestimates the proportion of this revenue in the state budget, partly because he forgets that a substantial part of the revenue was likely to "disappear" between collection point and state consumption. However, there is no doubt that the Egyptian revenues were of extreme importance for the Roman state.

In other words, though we do not and never will know the exact size of the Roman economy, our speculative modelling has to operate within certain constraints. Increasing one parameter may well require us to reduce another in order to keep the dimensions realistic. Perhaps the most problematic parameter in the quantification of the Roman economy is the choice of multiplier from minimum subsistence to GDP, set by Hopkins to 1.5. One cannot claim that it could not possibly be any bigger. But it could not be much bigger. The limits can be explored by setting up a simple equation describing the living standards which are possible for different population segments under different productivity/income regimes (how many times subsistence). Table 2.2 explains the mathematics and summarises the results of using different values for the agricultural population, for economies in the range of 2–3 times minimum subsistence. Let us examine the implications of the most prosperous scenario sketched in the table, 3 times minimum subsistence. If 80% of the population was engaged in agriculture then it would be able to have a living standard at 2.5 times minimum subsistence while the 20% non-agricultural/urban could live at 5 times subsistence. Make the agricultural population 60% and the corresponding figures would fall to 2 and 4 times subsistence. With the agricultural population constituting only 40%, it could still live at 1.88 times minimum subsistence and the non-agricultural population at 3.76 times. This does not seem a realistic possibility for the Empire taken as a whole, which mixed rich and poor regions. Three times subsistence would imply that the entire Roman world was approaching the level of productivity which was achieved (exceptionally) in England by the middle of the eighteenth century, one of the most prosperous pre-industrial economies on record, where only four out of ten had to be employed in agriculture. Stated differently, it would require the Roman economy as a whole to sustain a level of production which was probably not even achieved in its agriculturally most prosperous region, the fertile, Nile-inundated province of Egypt.[177] Both conditions are implausible.

---

[177] The study by D. Thompson of the Ptolemaic village Kerkeosiris revealed an agricultural regime with 7 aroura available per family. With yields at 10 times seed, and 1 artaba of wheat sown per aroura, then if all land for convenience's sake is imagined to have been planted with wheat, total net production would be 63 artabai. A family of five would

Table 2.2 *Living standards for different groups of population under different productivity regimes*

Let a be the proportion of the population engaged in agriculture, then the non-agriculturally employed population is (1–a); and let x represent the basic standard of living for the agricultural population and allow the non-agricultural population to live at twice this level. S equals subsistence and y is the number of times subsistence at which per capita production takes place.

$2x(1-a) + xa = y * S$
$x(2-a) = y * S$
$x = y/(2-a) * S$

Living standards (x) expressed as times subsistence for the agricultural/ (urban) population at different production levels

(a) Population in Agriculture	(y) Production at:		
	3 times subsistence	2.5 times subsistence	2 times subsistence
80%	2.50 (5)	2.08 (4.16)	1.67 (3.34)
60%	2.14 (4.28)	1.79 (3.58)	1.43 (2.86)
40%	1.88 (3.76)	1.56 (3.12)	1.25 (2.5)

At 3 times subsistence a scenario of only 40% of the population employed in agriculture begins to look plausible. Standards of living for the agricultural population can be maintained at a reasonably generous level while the non-agricultural population does very well. Both groups would in fact be marginally better off than a population with 80% in agriculture with per capita income at 2 times minimum subsistence. The latter scenario, however, would still be a reflection of fairly wealthy conditions far away from an agricultural minimum state, and most likely represents a hypothetical maximum for the Roman economy.

When we look at the Roman Empire in its entirety, comparisons of averages are more appropriate on a continental scale, rather than with smaller, particularly prosperous regions. Estimates of average per capita incomes for pre-industrial Europe as a whole

require some 32 artabai for a very minimal own consumption, a family of four some 24 artabai. Total production would therefore be between 2 and 2.5 times minimum subsistence. The Roman world could not possibly have exceeded that.

would suggest that the plausible range for the Roman economy would have to be placed somewhere between 1 and 2 times minimum subsistence.[178] This locates the hypothetical maximum at the low rather than the high end of our table of alternative, more optimistic scenarios for Roman living standards. Pressing the Roman economy to a maximum of 2 times subsistence would as much as double my estimated surplus (though in practice probably less since it was calculated generously). The imperial state and aristocracy would then account for a minimum of 15% of the surplus. As already stated, that would be far from a negligible influence on economic circulation; it would still represent a very significant change from conditions before the imposition of Empire. But this low result would have to be considered an absolute minimum and, as explained, an unlikely estimate of the share of the imperial system in the overall economy. Within the plausible limits for the Roman economy, therefore, it would be difficult not to ascribe to imperial surplus extraction, the role of a key stimulus of interregional economic flows.

This stimulus, however, did not play itself out only or primarily within a state-redistributive system of goods in kind, such as might be envisaged along the line of thought of Polanyi. The imperial state, for one thing, as already argued, did not have the organisational capacity. Markets were a necessary intermediary. Taking a last glance at our Mughal comparison, we can say that in the kind of tributary system described here, the role of market exchange and interregional trade is not first and foremost that of co-ordinating and organising the economy in an interregional division of labour. Rather its task is the subordinate one of acting as transformer and

---

[178] Maddison 2001, 46 (figures for the "developed" world). In general chapter 1 and appendix B. I suspect that Maddison underestimates production both in the ancient world and in early modern China. The European figures, however, are more reliable. Here he presents a development rising from a real minimum per capita of $400 around AD 1000 to approximately twice that level in 1700. In general, as North 2005: 91 observes from these data, the difference between rich and poor countries fluctuates between 1 and 2 times. Jongman 2006: 241 is right in guessing 2–3 times subsistence as the upper limit for productivity. But the larger the geographical area under consideration, the closer the maximum average will approach 2 times. The richest agricultural regions were generally fairly circumscribed and appear against a more extensive background of considerably less productive regions. Saller 2002: 259–261 places the Roman economy in a band between 1.2 and 1.5 times subsistence.

conveyer of the extracted surplus.[179] The majority of tax payers were grain-producing peasants, but the requirements of the imperial state were much more diverse. Neither the Roman nor the Mughal government and different layers of imperial elites, would have been able to put to good use all the food grains which they potentially commanded.[180] "The good husbandman", as even that arch-proponent of traditional agricultural virtues, Cato, admonished, "should be a seller, not a buyer". Therefore government and aristocratic elites required the services of markets and traders to mobilise parts of the surplus by converting agricultural produce into money which could be stored and used later in other contexts to buy different products. In the Mughal Empire, a significant part of the taxes came to be remitted in coin rather than kind. Something similar was suggested by Hopkins for the Roman Empire. But in both Empires, this process of commercialising the agricultural surplus is likely to have been uneven. Some, even many, taxes would still have been paid in kind; not all peasants would have been heavily involved in market transactions. Often, the peasant would have handed over part of his production to bigger landowners or tax collectors, who would then have undertaken to cart the produce to market, near or distant according to circumstances. Alternatively, the landowner might pass on the produce to merchants at the farm gate or even unharvested on the field.[181] The imperial government would also frequently have availed itself of markets to convert excess produce into monetary wealth. Instalments of the Egyptian grain tax found their way onto the private market in Puteoli, the harbour where the imperial grain fleet arrived from Alexandria before the construction of better port facilities at the mouth of the Tiber. Even surplus medicinal herbs from the Cretan estates of the emperors were sold on the market through commercial agents.[182]

---

[179] Bayly 1983: 63–68. This is the frequently overlooked implication of Hopkins' taxes-and-trade model.
[180] Hopkins 1995–6 (cited in Scheidel and von Reden 2002: 216–17).
[181] Cato *Agr.*, quotation from II.7 ("patrem familias vendacem, non emacem esse oportet"); advance sales: CXLVI–II; sale of wine in jars: CXLVIII.
[182] Galen XIV, 9 (on the medicinal herbs), *TPSulp.* 45, 46, 51, 52, 79 (on Alexandrian wheat used for commercial speculation in Puteoli). Lo Cascio 2006 for the imperial state as a large seller in the market.

Merchants and traders, to borrow an expression commonly used by Mughal historians, served to oil the wheels of the agricultural economy and the process of tribute extraction. Sometimes, this saw the creation of links between commercial investment, money-lending and collection of taxes. In Roman history, such activities have traditionally been connected with the great companies of *publicani*, the tax-farmers who played a prominent role in middle and late republican history. But the phenomenon should by no means be seen as confined to that period or as restricted to that scale of activity only.[183] In early imperial Pompeii we find the more humble auctioneer Jucundus also engaging in farming urban revenues.[184] Documents from second-century Egypt add a few more tesserae to our fragmentary mosaic. One contract reveals a member of the local political elite, who was active in the collection of taxes, financing the trading trip of a group of merchants. Another, recent, and by now famous, papyrus, the so-called Muziris Papyrus, provides evidence of a loan to finance a cargo of Oriental luxury goods, presumably intended for the market in Rome, to the value of almost HS 7 million. As Rathbone, among others, has suggested, it is difficult not to see the involvement of the imperial aristocracy here. Investing in a cargo worth several times the minimum fortune of a Roman senator was an efficient way of transferring wealth from the provinces to the imperial capital.[185] In that perspective, the dichotomy between market and state redistribution, which has attracted so much attention over the years, reveals itself to be a modernist construct. In the Empire both activities, often in direct collaboration, aimed at turning the extracted tribute into flexible resources which could be disposed of in other contexts.[186]

---

[183] Bang 2007: 31–54 for a general discussion, but with a focus on late antique material.

[184] Cf. the tablets from his archive containing receipts confirming payment by Jucundus to the city of what is due on these account: *CIL* IV, suppl. 1, pp. 382–404 (tablets nos. 138–151) with Andreau 1974: 53–71.

[185] Rathbone 2003: 215–225. For analysis of the documents, see Casson 1986; 1990; and Rathbone 2001.

[186] De Salvo 1992: 69–78 is a good example of how meaningless the distinction between free trade and state redistribution can be. The boats carrying the grain arriving in Rome may have been free but their cargoes were dominated by state shipments.

Growth and/or tributary concentration

Such a system of markets developing around political exploitation is what Weber referred to as political capitalism or even "Raub Kapitalismus" (robber capitalism).[187] According to the standard view, this is an arbitrary and disruptive sort of economic activity. But there is an "error" in perspective here. Clearly the type of economic exploitation which I have described in such detail above does not fit the doctrines of liberal, legally ordered economics well.[188] However, while it did not offer the stability and security of economic assets which we have come to expect today, the close alliance between empire and aristocratic groups did nonethelcss constitute a solid and enduring kind of order. In a closely argued critique of the sociological tradition on tributary empires, Michael Mann has suggested that the alliance between state and aristocracy was socially productive; their mutual collaboration produced a synergistic effect which increased extraction and the agricultural surplus and therefore allowed greater scope for the development of manufacture and trade.[189]

This brings us to the question of growth. But first some clarification of the meaning of the term is called for. Growth is far from being an unambiguous concept. Clearly, from a modern perspective the most interesting question to pursue is whether the economy of the Roman Empire experienced significant growth in per capita incomes.[190] Some have argued along these lines, albeit with considerable differences in degree.[191] Central to this argument has been the identification of some gradual developments in technology, such as growth in the tonnage of ships, reduction of the weight of amphorae in relation to the volume of their contents, investment

---

[187] Lo Cascio 1991; Whittaker 1994; Schiavone 2000, chapter 3 have a clear understanding of the submission of the market to tributary forces. Love 1991: 223–245 on Weber's political capitalism.

[188] Jones 1988: 135 notes that it is difficult from a modern perspective to understand how markets could work under those circumstances.

[189] Mann 1986: 167–174 and chapter 9.

[190] Millett 2001 discusses modern notions of growth and the ancient economy.

[191] Compare the cautious account of Hopkins 1995–6 with Mattingly 1996 and Hitchner 2005.

in bigger olive presses and the like.[192] There may also have been some pockets of rising agricultural prosperity where producers were able to take advantage of expanding markets to increase specialisation and improve productivity. Such processes have been suggested for Rome's Italian hinterland (Etruria–Campania) during the late Republic and early Empire.[193] Yet it is difficult to reach an assessment of the impact of those and similar developments in terms of increasing overall productivity in the Roman economy at large. Most such developments, I suspect, will have improved economic performance only marginally.[194] Elsewhere I have argued that the greater efficiency of African as compared to Spanish oil amphorae would have lowered the sales price of oil by less than 5%.[195]

Ultimately, in the absence of statistics, the measurement of per capita growth will remain beyond our grasp. This should be no cause for sleepless nights. Per capita growth is in any case a very problematical concept to apply to an economy which was heavily dominated by pre-modern agricultural production. The classic illustration of this is economic developments in Europe following the Black Death. In the aftermath of the pandemic, aggregate production plummeted while the decimated population experienced a strong growth in per capita income as more and better land became available to the individual peasant.[196] In traditional agriculture, increased production is often only achieved at the price of falling marginal returns. Essentially the peasant is faced with the choice of working existing land harder or expanding the cultivated area by bringing more marginal lands under the plough. Either way the increase in production tends to require a proportionately bigger increase in the amount of labour. Production expands, but

---

[192] Hopkins 1983b; Peacock and Williams 1986: 51–53; Greene 2000; Wilson 2002.

[193] On this, see Scheidel 2007a (building on Morley 1996) and 2007b.

[194] Saller 2002 for some cautionary observations; moderate growth can easily explain developments.

[195] Bang 2002a, n. 69. Cf. Lelener 2006.

[196] Livi-Bacci 1992: 47–54; more generally Braudel 1981: 32–34, *pace* Persson 1988 (in the long run no pre-industrial agrarian economy can really escape this constraint, cf. Wrigley 1988. Stagnation should not primarily be put down to a result of exogenous shocks, as Persson 1988: 131–135 also has to concede). See Scheidel 2002 for an attempt to understand the economic effects of the Antonine Plague affecting the Roman world in the 160s AD in terms parallel to the Black Death.

productivity declines. The income of the peasant grows but it is by no means clear that his living conditions improve correspondingly.[197] Obviously this puts very severe limits on how much the production of the individual peasant households can be increased. That being so, the total command over or availability of human labour is probably a much better key to unlocking the secrets of the economic performance of the Empire than the notion of substantial and sustained increases in productivity in the economy at large.

To begin with, the increased power of the tribute-cum-rent nexus may have succeeded in forcing peasants to work harder. This can be seen as a process in which the tributary system mobilised the resources of rural underemployment. The scope for such intensification varied considerably according to local conditions. It was greatest and most visible in the western provinces where surplus extraction was brought closer to the greater level of intensity required to sustain Mediterranean civilisation.[198] But both the growth of slavery in the wake of the Roman conquests and the development which can be followed in the legal sources, where a distinction between *honestiores* and *humiliores* from the early second century AD gradually overtakes the distinction between Roman citizens and aliens, may indicate a general intensification in the exploitation of *il populo minuto*.[199]

It is questionable, however, whether this trend towards intensified cultivation ever materialised as a sustained increase in per capita production. There were countervailing forces. Completely stationary populations are rare. It now seems generally agreed that there was a modest rise in the population figure during the first two centuries AD. The most plausible recent estimate sees the population growing from around 45 million in the age of Augustus to just over 60 million in the middle of the second century AD before the onset of the Antonine plague.[200] As a consequence, existing fields

[197] Boserup 1965; Sahlins 1972; Chayanov 1986, chapter 2.
[198] Woolf 2001. See Hopkins 2000: 257–259 for some model calculations showing how rents and taxes increase the area of cultivable land needed by the peasant household to sustain itself. Instead of more land, peasants may have to work existing fields more intensively.
[199] Nørlund 1920; Garnsey 1970; Finley 1980, chapter 4 on this. Garnsey and Humfress 2001, chapter 5 for a nuanced discussion.
[200] Frier 2000a: 812–813.

would have had to be shared by more producers and the area of cultivation to be extended into new zones, bringing less fertile, more marginal lands under cultivation.[201] This would have pulled in the opposite direction, producing a tendency towards falling per capita production, as individual peasant families would have had to work harder simply to achieve the same outcome. Even so, in aggregate terms the economy would still have continued to expand as long as the new producers were able to grow a surplus.[202] Obviously, it will never be possible to work out the combined economic effect of these two countervailing forces of agricultural intensification in exact terms. But we may gain a clearer understanding of the problem through a hypothetical experiment. If we assume that the politically induced increase in household production would have been nullified by a fall in productivity caused by the need to cultivate more marginal lands, thus preserving per capita production at an unchanged level, we are still looking at an aggregate expansion of the economic surplus by around one-third between the time of Augustus and the early years of Marcus Aurelius. In other words, actual per capita growth is not necessary to explain much, if not most, of the increased level of activity that archaeologists have documented for the early Empire.[203]

This points to by far the most important aspect of the developments presented by the Roman economy: sheer mass. The formation of a Mediterranean empire need not necessarily have led to a substantial growth in per capita production, at most only a moderate increase.[204] But the Empire brought together the productive capacity of many more people under the same tributary

---

[201] Developments in Africa are a good example, Barker and Mattingly 1996, Dietz, Sebai and Ben Hassen 1995, Ørsted et al. 2000. So is the Syrian limestone massif, Pollard 2000: 201–236. Both expanded the agricultural frontier into marginal zones.

[202] *Pace* Hitchner 2005: 222, n. 30 who holds that the Roman Empire stayed clear of the constraint of falling marginal returns. But he has misunderstood the concept. It does not imply that production falls off, as he thinks, only that increased production happens at lower productivity.

[203] Mattingly and Salmon 2001: 3–14 in general emphasise the difference in scale of individual economic phenomena as a central distinction between Greek and Roman economic history. Greene 1986; 2000, Wilson 2002 assembles much of the archaeological evidence for the increased scale of Roman economic activity.

[204] See Saller 2002 for a moderate growth scenario.

umbrella.[205] That was the decisive feature of the imperial economy. It enabled it to mobilise, amass and concentrate resources from a much wider area than its predecessors. As a result, the dimensions of the political economy changed dramatically onto a vastly different scale of activity.[206] The clearest illustration of this is the formation of very large, individual market concentrations. The imperial capital Rome is, of course, the leading example. With a population generally believed to have reached the million mark, it constituted a concentration of demand not to be equalled in Europe again until the Industrial Revolution. However impressive, Rome should not monopolise our attention. Compared with the urban network of early modern Europe, the system of cities which made up the Empire stands out by the more dominant position occupied by large urban concentrations (over 100,000). Alexandria, Antioch and Carthage taken together are generally believed to have comprised perhaps another million inhabitants.[207] In addition, there are almost a dozen other putative candidates for the over 100,000 category. As late as 1700 Europe still did not decisively exceed that number, even though it had a larger population base. Instead it had many more medium-sized cities (over 10,000). In 1800, between 300 and 400 had reached that level. The numerous, but quite modest, cities in the Roman world notwithstanding, a similarly dense layer of medium-sized cities is hard to identify. In other words, the tributary system maintained a much steeper urban hierarchy, concentrating resources from a very broad base into a relatively restricted number of very large cities.[208]

[205] Livi-Bacci 1992: 109 following Boserup 1981 sees the aggregate effect of large populations as more important for the formation of large urban concentrations than marginal variations in per capita income under pre-industrial conditions.

[206] Cf. Wickham 2005 arguing that the key difference between the economies of the Roman and post-Roman West is the gradual collapse of taxation; this significantly reduced the scale of economic activity.

[207] Hurst 1993 reminds us not to inflate ancient urban populations. Carthage, though still large, may have been smaller than is often thought.

[208] Woolf 1997 points in the same direction but warns against seeing the empire as primarily responsible for the strongly pronounced hierarchy in the East. The urban system had already existed before imperial rule. Therefore he points to trade and cultural exchanges as equally important in shaping the system. But, as he also recognises (p. 12), the growth of large cities in the eastern Mediterranean was closely linked with the formation of larger states. Moreover, Roman rule maintained this hierarchy by underwriting the strength of the aristocracies residing in the most prominent urban centres. Antioch

If the Mughal comparison is anything to go by, the stronger concentration of surplus consumption would have increased the scale of individual resource flows, creating some large "centralised trades" and "arterial routes".[209] Such a scenario seems equally relevant for the Roman Empire. The supplies reaching Rome are an obvious case in point. But the pattern is also found in the provinces. Gaul, for instance, presents an image of strongly concentrated trades closely linked with the imperial system. Here the Rhone–Saône–Rhine axis stands out as the dominant artery, serving as the supply route for the imperial legions stationed on the Germanic border. This gave rise to a system where the need for servicing the state transports favoured the development of a private commercial infrastructure and trade. But outside this interregional arterial channel, the exchange economy seems to have been operating in rather more local or regional cells.[210]

in Syria was given a very large hinterland to dominate and administer. Alexandria, too, benefited enormously from its dominant political position in Egypt. The same goes for Carthage, which received an extensive *chora* (territory) to draw its resources from. Again, the effects of empire were manifest, not only in direct expenditure of the imperial patrimonium, but also in the fashioning and maintenance of provincial elites.

[209] Bayly 1983: 65 and 159 and chapter 3.
[210] Middleton 1983; Whittaker 1994a; Jacobsen 1995.

PART II

IMPERIAL BAZAAR

The bazaar is more than a place set aside where people are permitted to come each day to deceive one another, and more, too, than one more demonstration of the truth that, under whatever skies, men prefer to buy cheap and sell dear... It is a distinctive system of social relationships centering around the production and consumption of goods and services (i.e. a particular kind of economy), and it deserves analysis as such... Bazaar, that Persian word of uncertain origins which has come to stand in English for the oriental market, thus becomes, like the word market itself, as much an analytic idea as the name of an institution.

Clifford Geertz, *Meaning and Order in Moroccan Society*

That that trade was not of a "bourgeois commercial" sort has already been indicated... The financiers of trade were often princes, religious dignitaries, and nobles. The merchant gentlemen, as *popolo grosso*, led a seigneurial way of life when compared to the *popolo minuto*, the masses of craftsmen and "actual traders". Furthermore, the princes and lords were themselves often merchants... Their trade could be occasional or regular. The former could result in sudden obstruction of markets, forced purchases, temporary monopolisation.

J. C. van Leur, *Indonesian Trade and Society*

3

A ROUGH TRADING WORLD: OPAQUE, VOLATILE AND DISCONTINUOUSLY CONNECTED MARKETS

> We know how varied the prices of things are between individual cities and regions.
>
> Gaius, *Digesta* 13.4.3

> In short, whatever is obstructing the development of a modern economy out of the general background of the bazaar economy, it is not lack of a "business-like" orientation on the part of the *pasaar* traders . . . What the bazaar economy lacks is not elbow room but organisation, not freedom but form.
>
> Geertz, *Peddlers and Princes*, p. 47

Some thirty years ago a sanctuary for a hitherto almost unknown ancient goddess, Nehalenia, was found on the Dutch coast, in the former Roman province of Germania Inferior. The most remarkable part of the find was the discovery of a fairly large body of votive inscriptions put up mainly, it seems, by sailors and merchants thanking Nehalenia for their safe return: "To the goddess Nehalenia for the good preservation of his merchandise Marcus Secundinius Silvanus, trader in pottery to the province of Britain, kept his promise freely and dutifully."[1] Even in their concise, matter of fact appearance the inscriptions provide us with a chilling glimpse into the world of merchants and other travellers in ancient times. At best, travel was a slow and arduous trial; complaints over long delays, bumpy roads and never-ending nausea are legion. At worst it was a dangerous undertaking for which you might have to pay with your life; wreckage, illness or assault by pirates and highwaymen were always lurking just around the corner.[2] In such

---

[1] *AE*, 1973, 370: "Deae N[e]haleniae | ob merces recte conservatas M(arcus) Secund(inius?) Silvanus | negotiator cretariu[s] | Britannicianu[s] | v(otum) s(olvit) l(ibens) m(erito)." The inscriptions can be found in *AE* 1973, 362–380 and 1975, 641–656 with further examples in 1980 and 1983. See also Stuart and Bogaers 1971 and 2001, two catalogues from exhibitions presenting the find.

[2] Successfully completed travels were accomplishments to take notice of. Hence the funeral inscription (*SIG*³ 1229), mentioning the seventy-two safe journeys made by a trader from

circumstances one could never be too sure. The protection of the gods was enlisted as a matter of routine. Indeed, the superstitions of mariners have at all times been legendary and have provided a rich material for novelists across the centuries. Think, for instance, of Melville's immortal description of an American whaling community in *Moby Dick*, not to mention the more comical chord struck by Petronius exploiting the prohibition against cutting one's hair at sea to put his hard-tested (anti)heroes in yet another ridiculous pickle.[3]

This second part of the book will explore the conditions of trade in the Roman Empire. The first part identified the broad characteristics of the political economy and the main driving forces behind interregional trade. The inquiry now proceeds to examine how the formation of a tributary empire affected the institutional set-up for trade. Further comparisons drawn from Mughal India will be employed to suggest new ways of thinking about Roman traders. A central concern will be to integrate the risks and uncertainties of ancient commerce into our general understanding of market institutions. This third chapter will deal with the basic character of markets and conditions of trade in the Roman Empire. Emphasis will be placed on the limits to market integration and the volatility of commercial links. A middle section attempts to deepen the image of market fragmentation through a very tentative analysis of the few and scattered price records surviving from Roman Egypt. The chapter then moves on to consider evidence of enduring cultural and institutional fragmentation within the Roman trading world, in spite of the greater legal and monetary coherence brought about by the imperial government. At the end, the bazaar, with its many irregularities and uncertainties, is suggested as a model for the functioning of Roman markets.

Hierapolis, Flavius Zeuxis, around Cape Malea to Italy. André and Baslez 1993: 437–447 and 483–526 is a convenient selection of the material pertaining to the *insécurité chronique* of travel in the Greco-Roman world. See also Millar 1981 using Apuleius' *Metamorphoses* to give a vivid impression of the hassles and uncertainties of ancient travel.

[3] Petr. *Sat.* 104–105.

Transport

By modern standards, the means of transport were both slow and very much at the mercy of the elements.[4] The latter was more true of travel by water than by land. However, even on land the weather could affect travelling conditions significantly. During the rainy seasons, rivers and lakes might rise above their usual boundaries and cause roads to flood, flush away bridges and seriously impede crossing. Roads, either not built to the best of Roman standards or not properly maintained, might turn into bottomless mud holes. In the colder regions of the empire winter could see roads transformed into slippery ice patches whereas burning sun in some of the hotter areas would often have forced travellers to go by the cool but also more frightening night rather than during daytime. Employed as pack animals or used as traction power for carts, donkeys, mules, oxen and camels (horses only to a lesser extent) constituted the basis of Roman land transport. That made it, on average, considerably slower than waterborne transport, but above all a lot more expensive, both relatively and absolutely. The animals needed considerable amounts of fodder to keep going.[5] Working from Diocletian's price edict, A. H. M. Jones suggested that, roughly speaking, transport on land by wagon increased the price of wheat by 50% for every 100 miles whereas the corresponding figure for sea transport was only 1.3%. One should not pay too much attention to the exact figures. The relative proportions of the price of land and water transport would have varied considerably according to local circumstances. As a rule of thumb, however, the relationship, which seems to receive comparative confirmation, between the price of sea, riverine and land transport can be estimated as 1 : 5 : 50.[6]

---

[4] Braudel 1972: 246–311 remains one of the best descriptions of pre-modern transport in the Mediterranean. What follows draws heavily on his analysis. For ancient travel, see Casson 1974; Chevalier 1988; and André and Baslez 1993: 373–412 collect much interesting material. See Bekker-Nielsen 2004 for a study of a regional road network.

[5] See Finley 1985a: 126–128 in general. See further Jones 1964: 841–842, working from the price edict of Diocletian, with the adjustments of Duncan-Jones 1982: 366–369.

[6] See further Hopkins 2000: 263, n. 18 and 1983b, 102–105. Clark and Haswell 1970, chapter 12 lists some comparative figures of transport costs.

As Braudel was one of the first to observe, and as many ancient historians now agree, that did not reduce land transport to total insignificance.[7] The high price on land transport was more of an impediment to low-value bulky goods, such as grain, than low-bulk, highly priced luxuries where transport costs constituted a much smaller percentage of the total price. In special circumstances land transport might even compete successfully with water. During the first century AD the caravan route bringing frankincense, of the best and purest crop, from southern Arabia to Gaza on the Mediterranean seaboard, continued in spite of increasing navigation in the region. The caravans could leave in the beginning of the autumn while ships had to await the arrival of the north-east monsoon. This gave the caravans a time advantage. They could normally expect to arrive in Gaza as the ships left South Arabia. The caravan merchants were thus able to bring their goods first to the market. This would quite possibly have been sufficient compensation for their higher transport costs.[8] Even more bulky goods such as pottery can at times be found to have travelled considerable distances overland in large quantities. The famed production of red-glossed fine ware in La Graufesenque (floruit first century AD) in southern France had no nearby waterway. Pots, cups and bowls would have travelled in the thousands on the roads leading away from the production centre each year.[9] Even so, in general there is no way of escaping the fact of the primacy of water for transport over longer distances. The economic logic dictated this and this logic was not lost on the ancients either. It is noticeable how the elder Pliny in his geographical description of the Empire, when assessing the potential resources of an area, repeatedly takes time to observe whether a river is navigable or not; that would determine how easily the surplus produce could be mobilised.[10] In terms of the value of transported goods, Braudel estimated that in the sixteenth century the relation of water to land transport was

---

[7] See Braudel 1972: 284–295. See Laurence 1998 and Horden and Purcell 2000, chapter 9 for two recent discussions stressing the vitality of land transport.

[8] Young 2001: 104–106.

[9] See Whittaker 2002; see Goody and Whittaker 2001; for proto-industry in southern France. See further, Vernhet 1991.

[10] E.g. Plin. *Nat.* III, 12: "Singilis fluvius...ab ea navigabilis" and 21: "Hiberus amnis navigabili commercio dives".

something like three to one in the Mediterranean. We cannot know whether it would have been exactly the same in Roman times. But it does provide us with a useful pointer.

So it is almost true of the pre-industrial world that land divides whereas water unites – but only almost. Sea transport was far less expensive and often a necessary requirement for large bulk transfers. However, it was also much more sensitive towards changing weather conditions. On the micro level, we see it when a ship en route had to go into the nearest harbour and wait, in unfavourable seasons perhaps even for weeks, until the storm blew itself out and the sea calmed down again. If the ship found no ready shelter and still survived the adverse conditions it might find itself blown off course, occasionally to such an extent that the only practical response was to change its destination. On the other hand, sometimes there would be too little wind and the ship would just have been drifting with the currents until the wind rose again, or the crew would have had to row.[11] On the macro level, we encounter the great dependency on the weather as an organisation of navigation around the rhythm of the changing seasons. During wintertime the risk of sailing increased substantially in the Mediterranean and navigation came almost to a standstill or at least the intensity of shipping was much reduced. The Romans talked of a *mare clausum* at least between November and March/April, with most navigation probably taking place safely within the margins of the summer period.[12]

All this worked to make travel times on the sea very uncertain and highly fluctuating. In his *Natural History*, Pliny informs us of some record crossings, such as from Puteoli to Alexandria in nine

---

[11] Heliodorus *Aethiopica* V offers many illustrations of the changing fortunes of life at sea, especially in the more unfavourable seasons (chapter 23 for roving). See Synesius *Litt.* 129 for an example of a ship being blown so much off course that it changes its destination to Alexandria.

[12] See Rougé 1966: 32–33 for *mare clausum*. It is clear, however, that some sailing did take place during the winter season. In the eastern Mediterranean, for instance, sailing during the winter between Rhodes and Egypt is attested for an earlier period, cf. Demosthenes *Against Dionysodorus* 30. Heliodorus *Aethiopica* V, chapter 18 points in the same direction. But here it is also observed that it took special skills and, in the end, even navigators possessing those might choose to winter in a harbour, at least for part of the bad season.

days.[13] But that was unusual. If we are to judge from the speed of imperial communication something like three or four times that number of days would have been more common, but with considerable individual variations and with some trips taking substantially longer.[14] The general situation does not seem to have been very different from the Mediterranean in the sixteenth century. For that period, Fernand Braudel estimated the length of a sea voyage from east to west to have been in the order of two to three months and often even more, with substantial additions to be made for penetration beyond the coastal regions. There had of course been some technological modifications since antiquity, but they were marginal improvements. The pattern of relatively slow, irregular and for periods even discontinuous transport and communication lines, had still to be broken. The same goes for tonnage. Most ships in both periods would have been relatively small, below 100 tonnes and more often than not closer to 50 tonnes. Bigger ships were certainly built and used, especially on routes between the largest cities, but they were far from the norm.[15]

Volatile and opaque markets

Mysteriously this basic continuity over many centuries has been taken by some classicists as confirmation that communication and transport did not impose strong limits on the economic performance and workings of markets in (Roman) antiquity. To be sure, a lot of movement of commodities on sea and on land did occur.

---

[13] Plin. *Nat.* XIX, 3.   [14] Duncan-Jones 1990, chapter 1.

[15] In general Braudel 1972: 295–311 and 354–375 remains fundamental on these problems and *la longue durée* in Mediterranean transport, in spite of the ambitions of Horden and Purcell 2000 to overtake him. Parker 1992: 26, based on a catalogue of some 1,200 ancient shipwrecks, concludes that most ships were a good bit below 100 tonnes capacity. *P. Bingen* 77, treated by the editor Heilporn and by Rathbone 2003: 226, contains information about some eleven ships arriving in an Egyptian port, probably Alexandria during the second half of the second century AD. Two of these, one a Roman grain freighter, the other used to carry pine trunks, were well above 100 tonnes. The majority, however, had a tonnage between 30 and 75 tonnes. Rougé 1966: 47–80 argued, before the rise of underwater archaeology, for the comparable dimensions of shipping in the Roman Empire and the early modern Mediterranean. His general conclusion is convincing, but he tends to overestimate the size of the ships. He would have done well to consult his great compatriot, Braudel, who had already written on this.

But the optimism of Horden and Purcell, reflected in the deceptive catchphrase *connectivity*, is misplaced. The proper point to make is rather the opposite: transport remained a serious challenge or even obstacle to economic integration for most of pre-industrial history.[16] Individual markets were not easily tied together so as to behave in unison. With slow, irregular and periodically discontinuous transport and communication it was simply very difficult, on a regional basis, on the continental scale of the Roman Empire quite impossible, to match demand and supply across individual marketplaces in an even, steady and predictable way.[17] Rather, resources would normally have come in uneven, not easily predictable, clusters. The problem is conveniently illustrated from Apuleius' *Golden Ass* by the story told by one of its characters, a small trader. Having had news of the availability of some good-quality cheese at a very attractive price in a neighbouring area, he rushed to the place only to find that everything had already been sold. His efforts had been in vain; the market had already been cleared.[18]

Acting on wrong or out-of-date information, which did not correspond to the actual situation in the marketplace on the time of arrival, was an ever-looming risk for the pre-industrial merchant. It was not just that the goods might have cleared by the time of his arrival. Too many competitors might have picked up the same news, flocked to the market and caused the low price to increase violently so as to endanger the profitability of making the trip in the first place. On the other hand, high prices might attract too many sellers trying to out-compete each other; or, alternatively, buyers might fail to show, causing a shortage in demand and the market to plummet well below normal levels.[19] The latter seems to describe the situation in the example above from the point of view of the cheeseseller. He had to part with his goods at a very low price to a single well-positioned merchant who just happened

---

[16] Braudel 1972: 375–379 conveys a good sense of the problems and frequent breakdowns in economic integration. See also Shaw 2001: 423–425 for a related critique.

[17] See Erdkamp 2005, chapter 4 for an analysis of the Roman grain market stressing low carry-over of stocks in the operation of markets through time and across distances.

[18] Apul. *Met.* I, 5.

[19] See for example *P. Oslo* II, 63 (third century). This is an estate letter in which an agent reports that he cannot sell his goods at the price at which he has been instructed to sell them. The market is much lower.

to be in the area. Another illustration can be found in one of the letters of Cassiodorus. The state needed to make some requisitions from an area with plentiful stocks. But it was out of season and there were few merchants in the area. Therefore demand was low and people were forced to accept a very unattractive price for their goods.[20]

Closely connected to the information problems were logistical difficulties. A merchant might act on correct information and still see his plans fall through. His shipment of goods might be seriously delayed en route. Or, alternatively, he might have to leave a market before the goods he wanted to buy had arrived, either due to delayed cargoes or because fair weather made it expedient or the close of the trading season made it imperative for him to set sail.[21] It would also, occasionally, be difficult to find a ship which could bring orders to an agent in another harbour at the required time. Equally it could be a problem to find cargo space for hire when needed. Surplus of shipping in an area with nothing to export and shortage in a neighbouring region with stocks ready for export were not unheard of.[22] In other words, the pre-modern merchant had to act in a highly uncertain market situation, governed by the rhythm of the seasons, where it was difficult to predict or estimate the amounts of goods brought to the individual marketplace and the number and buying capacity of his competitors. Such markets would normally be quite prone to violent fluctuations in the short term. Price changes of say 10, 20 or 30% within a few months, weeks or sometimes even between days were the order of the day, making it a very risky business environment. Under the ruling regime of communication and transport it is difficult to imagine

---

[20] Cassiodorus *Variae* XII, 22.2. Rougé 1966 diligently gathered much late material showing the irregularities of Roman trading, especially pp. 416–417 for more examples.

[21] Seasonality of trading: Philo *Leg. Gai.* 15; Sirks 2002 (on *Dig.* 45.1.122.1). *TPSulp.* 46, 53 and 79 (as explained by the editor Camodeca) show a loan being advanced in March to a Puteolan grain trader on the security of a consignment of grain. Had the loan not been repaid by the Ides of May, the lender was entitled to auction off the grain just in time to beat the arrival of the Alexandrian grain fleet whose fresh supplies would cause prices to fall in the market. See also Cic. *Fam.* XIV, 4, 5 (ship departing Brundisium before arrival of letters in order not to lose fair weather).

[22] Cassiodorus *Variae* XII, 24. The letters of Synesius offer some striking illustrations. No. 129 mentions letters which have gone astray and have been delayed many months. Nos. 134 and 148 describe problems about finding cargo space and ships heading to the required destination.

how *the hidden hand* could ensure that such fluctuations would find a strong and ready response in other markets that would be able to iron out the differences and create a more stable situation – except in a very imperfect, almost haphazard, way.

Ceteris paribus, the volume of transactions alone was not enough to establish stable markets with closely correlated movements of prices. In the short run there would normally be only a very weak link between price developments in particular demand markets on the one hand and the quantities of a given commodity sent from the various individual supply markets on the other hand.[23] The result was a trading world characterised by chronic bottlenecks, imbalances and asymmetries in the supply of available information and goods. A humorous letter of Pliny sums up the situation of dearth in one region and glut with collapsing prices not too far away:

My Tuscan fields, I hear, have been wiped out by hail, and in the Transpadane there's a bumper crop but prices have collapsed in consequence. Only my Laurentine yields me a return. Of course I have nothing there beyond house, garden and sandy beach hard by; still for me it is the sole source of profit. For that's where I do most of my writing. I don't cultivate the land – for I have none – but myself in my studies.[24]

In recent years economists have become increasingly interested in the consequences of such market imperfections and asymmetries. So far their efforts have been rewarded with several Nobel prizes since the 1990s.[25] The recipients argue that traditional economics have overestimated the tendency of markets to become integrated and move in unison. A classic illustration of this is the huge gap between the comparatively moderate interest rates in Indian cities and the usurious rates that Indian peasants have often had to pay to the village money lender. For he, unlike the

---

[23] Steensgaard 1973a: 58; in general pp. 22–59 for an incisive analysis of markets characterised by weak integration and short-term fluctuations.

[24] Plin. *Ep.* IV, 6, 1–2: "Tusci grandine excussi, in regione Transpadana summa abundantia, sed par vilitas nuntiatur. Solum mihi Laurentinum meum in reditu. Nihil quidem ibi possideo praetor tectum et hortum statimque harenas, solum tamen mihi in reditu. Ibi plurimum scribo, nec agrum quem non habeo sed ipsum me studiis excolo." The passage is analysed by Tchernia 1986: 178. Erdkamp 2005: 167–169 is speculative and overcomplicates the issue.

[25] For example Douglass North, George Akerlof, Michael Spence and Joseph Stiglitz.

banks, knows the individual borrowers. He can therefore better assess the risk involved in advancing a loan to a particular peasant, the argument goes. Should a middleman attempt to bring the city and village credit markets together, he risks attracting all the bad payers, due to his lack of local knowledge, and soon goes out of business. Consequently the village money lender rests secure in his local monopoly and the markets remain separate. The lesson can be put in more general terms: market environments, with huge irregularities, low transparency, great uncertainties and slow and at times erratic transport, make it expensive and difficult for economic agents to transact and move goods from market to market. When transaction costs are high, it cannot be taken for granted that markets will tend towards the same equilibrium.[26] Such considerations are of obvious interest to students of pre-modern trade. One crucial implication for our understanding of the Roman (as of most of the pre-industrial) trading world, is that any notion of the empire as constituting one generalised market, where prices converge around a common equilibrium price across the many individual markets, cannot easily be maintained.[27]

In contrast to market in the abstract, generalised, modern sense, it is customary to speak of concrete, individual marketplaces existing in isolation. But here it is important to keep in mind that we are dealing with two ideal-types at each end of a broad spectrum of varying degrees of integration.[28] The purely concrete market-type might reasonably catch the situation in some Roman inland towns far from waterways or the most frequented roads. Gregory of Nazianzus, explains the plight of food shortage in the inland city of Caesarea in Cappadocia: "Coastal cities support such shortages without much difficulty, as they can dispose of

---

[26] For some pionering studies of the new perspective, see the now classic paper by Akerlof (1970), also Rotschild 1973 and North 1990, especially pages 60–80.

[27] Temin 2001: 179 is an example of the tendency of traditional economics to play down the effects of market imperfections: they might in the short run create imbalances but they could not prevent an equilibrium from materialising across the Roman Empire in the middle- or long-term perspective. It is precisely this expectation that the new institutional economics has undermined.

[28] Marshall 1890: 323–330, the founder of neo-classical economics, already made this observation. But neo-classical economics has never been very interested in exploring the space in between the two extremes. Hence the success of institutional and transaction cost economics today.

their own products and receive supplies by sea; for us inland our surpluses are unprofitable and our scarcities irremediable, as we have no means of disposing of what we have or of importing what we lack."[29] But even inland areas were not completely isolated. Grain, for instance, was certainly transported out of the inner parts of Anatolia to be sold in Mediterranean markets.[30] Nonetheless, it was a costly and burdensome undertaking from which cities sometimes sought to relieve themselves at a price. As Cicero explains, inland cities might accept to pay, in lieu of their grain taxes, a lump monetary sum calculated on the basis of the higher prices prevailing in more busy coastal markets, rather than having to deliver their taxes in kind on the coast.[31] With cities enjoying close access to waterways, however, the concrete market-type begins to require considerable modification. Perhaps the situation can be more usefully described in terms of concrete connections. It is the density and stability of those that we need to look at.

Most cities in the Mediterranean world were small (less than 10,000 inhabitants). Markets, therefore, were generally small too and could not easily sustain close permanent connections, especially because the needs of many cities will have fluctuated from year to year. This is most marked in agricultural products where the strong interannual fluctuations in harvests would have made cities constantly change between the roles of exporter and importer of small amounts of grain etc., as illustrated by the above quotation from Gregory. Those markets were normally served by a system often referred to as *cabotage*: small merchant ships would more or less casually tramp along the coast from harbour to harbour in search of a good bargain.[32] This, combined with the constant shifts in the needs of markets, did not work in favour of bringing areas closely together. On the contrary, the loosely linked small *cabotage* markets, characterised by impermanent connections, accentuated the uncertainties and risks of pre-modern trade. The arrival or non-arrival of as little as one or two extra ships during the sailing

[29] Gregory of Nazianzus *In Laudem Basilii* 34–35 (Migne, *Patr. Gr.* 36, 541–544, quoted from Jones 1964: 844). See further the discussion of Garnsey 1988: 22–24 for a perceptive analysis, pointing out that Gregory probably overstates his case.

[30] Mitchell 1993, vol. I (last chapter, analysing the economy).

[31] Cic. II *Verr.* 3, 191 with Erdkamp 2005: 197–198.

[32] Horden and Purcell 2000, chapters 4 and 5 make a great deal out of this.

season might have had a decisive influence on the price in the market. Consequently prices would often be highly volatile and the markets would be dominated by interlocal asymmetries and imbalances.[33]

The situation begins to change somewhat when attention is turned to the small group of very large cities/markets in the Empire: Rome, Alexandria, Antioch, Carthage, Ephesos and a few others. In some commodities, such as the most highly priced luxuries, markets will still have been very narrow. This is what Cicero alleged had been the experience of the Roman knight Rabirius Postumus, who had imported a valuable Egyptian cargo of "paper, linen and glass" to the imperial capital. But the promise of a rich profit had turned out to be "treacherous and deceptive", because many other ships had arrived in Rome carrying the same goods and caused prices to fall.[34] But such luxury markets were nonetheless very much larger and represented a far more stable concentration of demand than could be mustered in the smaller towns. This is even more true in the case of staple foods. The requirements of the large cities were of a size that could not be supplied in the small scale, ad hoc manner of *cabotage*. To take the most extreme example, Rome would probably have required something like 1,500 shipments of 100 tonnes to supply its needs for grain.[35] Clearly, more permanent connections and larger concentrations of merchants, transport facilities, infrastructure and routes to maintain these had to come into existence in order to serve the needs of such giant markets. The big cities thus represent several steps up the ladder of integration.[36] From the merchants' perspective, they offered a higher,

---

[33] *Pace* Horden and Purcell 2000, chapters 5 and 9. Gibson and Smout 1995: 270 provide a clear exposition of the low degree of economic integration created by phenomena such as *cabotage*, characterised by impermanent connections, and of the structural difference from larger markets. See also Tchernia 1986, 172–193. Goitein 1967, chapters 3 and 4 provides a very useful description of the uncertainties of a world of small Mediterranean markets in the early Middle Ages. The general conditions would not have been very different in antiquity.

[34] Cic. *Pro Rabirio* 40 ("fallaces quidem et fucosae") with Erdkamp 2005: 177. It does little that the passage has been emended, best by Mommsen; the general meaning is quite unequivocal.

[35] Garnsey 1983b: 118 estimates Roman grain imports at between 150,000 and 200,000 tonnes wheat.

[36] See Tchernia 1986, 189–193 for a related point. Morley 1996 explores the creation of more stable connections of economic integration created by the demand of the Roman

more steady and predictable demand than other markets. In that respect, the large consumptive nodal points reduced commercial risks. But they were far from unproblematic markets to negotiate. Coming to a large city, without a prior established social network, carried risks of its own. That theme, however, will be developed more fully in Chapter 5. For the moment, I am interested in a different aspect; the giant markets were logistical feats that strained capacities to the full, and supplies were in constant danger of breakdown or temporary interruption.[37] In that way they remained nervous and volatile. In a tense situation, even the arrival of as few as five ships with grain might suffice to ease for the moment the worries of a riotous urban mob, as one of the letters written by Sidonius during his tenure of the urban prefecture in fifth-century Rome demonstrates.[38]

Finley's classic illustration of the vulnerable and unstable character of the larger urban markets was the food crisis in fourth-century Antioch during the stay of the emperor Julian. Only with Julian's intervention was the emerging crisis averted, but not even then without problems, through the importation of grain from nearby imperial estates and later from Egypt as well. Market networks had been unable to solve the problem by responding to the growing demand and bringing in supplies from surplus areas.[39] The various accounts of the crisis add an extra dimension to our understanding of the problem. It was not only a question of high transportation costs. Local power wielders exploited their control of the agricultural surplus in the region to take advantage of the shortage and increase the local market asymmetries by very considerable hoarding in order to drive up prices further and make

market. The interpretation offered above clashes directly with Horden and Purcell 2000, e.g. p. 121, who reduce the larger markets to an outgrowth of *cabotage* and therefore tone down their importance. These markets, in fact, represent a qualitative change. They could not possibly be sustained by the casual small-scale movements of coastal tramping. They needed a far more permanent infrastructure. It is in this perspective that the major shipping (and land) routes take on a very important role as the main conveyers of economic integration.

[37] The phenomenon should not be seen as restricted to grain supplies. Thus Suetonius' biography of Augustus (42.1) and Ammianus Marcellinus book 14, chapter 6, 1, report of wine shortages in the Roman market.

[38] Sidonius *Epistulae* I, 10 with Garnsey and Humfress 2001, 114.

[39] Finley 1985a: 127. See further Garnsey and Humfress 2001: 120–121 and Hopkins 1978a: 46–47 for discussion of the emperor Julian's relief of the food crisis in 362–3.

a killing. The intervention of the emperor provoked resistance in these groups. They continued to keep their grain from the market in the city and even had the "audacity" to buy up some of the imperial "relief" supplies brought to Antioch. One can easily understand why more modest merchants hesitated to step in and alleviate this particular crisis. It would have amounted to commercial suicide for such people, outsiders at that, to challenge the deeply entrenched local monopoly position enjoyed by a very powerful group of local landowners.[40] The example carries a significant lesson which is rarely drawn: in the pre-industrial world closer integration of economic resources and tighter coordination of markets, in particular, depended on a hand anything but hidden. It was impossible without the intervention of very tangible and overt forms of organisational power, to tie supply and demand across locations into a more stable relationship where markets would be more closely integrated and behave more uniformly.[41]

A further clear demonstration of this is provided by India in the aftermath of Mughal rule and the early beginnings of British hegemony. After a disastrous famine in Bengal in the 1770s the British East India Company attempted to organise a more stable and integrated company/state-controlled grain market in the province. The scheme was a fiasco and quickly abandoned; the Company had failed to gain control over the numerous rural supply networks. Short of that, it was unable to establish a more stable and transparent situation in the grain markets in Bengal. The internal grain market in Bengal, however, was only a secondary concern of the Company. In areas of crucial importance for its operations, such as opium production and trade, it did not tolerate defeat. Here control was pursued ruthlessly, with whatever means necessary, until it was achieved and the market situation stabilised.[42] The Indian example is particularly instructive because it so clearly shows the clash of two different market regimes. There is a growing awareness among economists that markets are never "just" markets; they have

[40] Julian *Misopogon* 368c–370b confirmed by Libanius *Oratio* 18, 195.
[41] Contra Harris 1999, who supposes that the mere existence of a substantial trade in slaves would have worked to create uniform movements of prices across a large group of individual, separate markets.
[42] Chatterjee 1996, chapter 5 offers a very clear analysis of the British East India Company's first decades in Bengal.

significant individual characteristics shaped by the institutional fabric which supports them.[43] This is what historians should be studying.

In dealing with markets in Bengal the East India Company drew on a set of trading strategies which in the two preceding centuries had transformed and gradually created a number of more coherent and integrated markets in Europe.[44] The various chartered joint stock companies were themselves a prime expression of this development. The crucial characteristic was the ability to create greater and more long-lived concentrations of trading capital than hitherto. This enabled the merchants to adopt a longer-term perspective of the market and create buffers which could absorb some of the endemic irregularities of pre-industrial trade. The larger capital base enabled them to extend control over trading in many individual markets. Control is here to be taken literally. It was far from uncommon that military force was employed to achieve the objective.[45] A report submitted to the Dutch East India Company (VOC) in the late 1620s by Francisco Pelsaert, the Dutch factor in the Mughal capital, Agra, conveys a very clear idea of this process.[46] VOC's commercial presence in the Agra area was primarily motivated by the local production of indigo, a highly desired dye. It bought considerable quantities, to a large extent financed by selling its primary commodity, spices imported from various South-East Asian islands. These spices, however, were also marketed in large quantities by the company on the Coromandel Coast (the south-east Indian litoral). In too large quantities, as a matter of fact, according to Pelsaert. The problem was that

---

[43] North 1990. North, in a way, has brought the challenge of Polanyi into the mainstream of economic theory.

[44] Braudel and Spooner 1967 offer a useful overview of the gradual creation of more stable, less fluctuating and more uniform price movements in European markets during the seventeenth and eighteenth centuries. See Granger and Elliott 1967 and Gibson and Smout 1995 for two case studies of this process. For the extremely close correlation of the price of grain in Amsterdam and in Danzig, see De Vries and Woude 1997: 414–419.

[45] See Steensgaard 1973a, chapter 3 and Chaudhuri 1985, chapter 4 for analyses of the chartered companies. Glamann 1958 demonstrated how the Dutch East India Company did not possess a simple monopoly, but together with the other chartered companies created and developed a competitive European market in spices. Cf. Pearson 1993, who provides another example of the importance of the development of organisations for the integration of markets.

[46] Pelsaert 1925, chapter 5.

many Indian merchants, willing to accept a lower profit, imported the Dutch spices from the Coromandel Coast to the Agra area and destabilised the market with falling prices as the result. This did considerable damage to the Dutch capacity to procure indigo in the area. Lower prices on spices meant less money to buy indigo. On top of that, it became more difficult to reach an advantageous price with the indigo sellers. Seeing that the factor was financially vulnerable they could press him harder and claim a higher price. Therefore Pelsaert suggested that the company should make better use of its control over the spice trade to cut the supplies from the Coromandel Coast of his Indian competitors in Agra. This would, of course, mean smaller profits in the trade on the Coromandel Coast. But they would be more than compensated by the greater income generated by the operations in Agra. What is remarkable here is the conscious formulation of a strategy to coordinate and integrate operations in widely separated markets into a coherent system.

Other aspects of this process included the financial ability to fund the build-up of extensive stocks, sometimes equal to the turnover of several years, in order to make trading less dependent on the erratic fluctuations in supplies. In addition, attempts were made by merchants to push beyond wholesale markets and extend control right to the door of the producer through the advancement of large credits or, if more forceful methods were required, through military action. Thus the greater organisational power of merchants enabled them to get a much firmer grip on the erratically working supply networks and re-shape the basic conditions of trade. The result was the gradual growth of more stable and integrated markets where it made good sense to coordinate activities in individual locations closely in order to achieve long-term goals rather than to obtain short-term profits. For instance, in spite of achieving a very high degree of control with European pepper imports, the East India companies did not take advantage of the situation to drive up prices excessively and make a quick monopolistic profit. Instead, they preferred to keep the price at a level where the temptation to challenge their dominance would never be too great. In fact, they were able to operate a gradually narrowing profit margin. While prices rose in the production areas in Indonesia they still managed to lower the price of pepper in Europe throughout the seventeenth century.[47]

Perhaps some will argue that the joint stock companies were exceptions, not even representative of European trade in the period. On formalistic grounds that is correct. But in real terms it would be more precise to say that they were the most articulated examples of a general trend in institutional developments. When Dutch supremacy in European trade during the seventeenth century receives explanation, it is the same general features that are evoked. Exemplified by such institutions as the *Beurs, Korenbeurs, Wisselbank*, enormous warehouses and publication of printed biweekly price notations, it is the unprecedented strength and capacity of Dutch commerce to control, organise and integrate markets which repeatedly receive emphasis.[48] Perhaps its biggest achievement was the level of integration it achieved in the Baltic grain trade. It is truly astonishing to observe how closely the price in Danzig followed developments in Amsterdam in the eighteenth century (Fig. 3.1).[49]

Strong political support, greater and more permanent concentrations of capital and much improved information, the achievements of Dutch international capitalism were an expression of a general process in parts of Europe which saw the position of the middleman strengthened considerably. The wave of mercantilist privileges, employed particularly by the rivals of the Dutch, were aimed precisely at this goal. Later the process was given a fresh impetus by absolutist governments seeking to push through a programme of free trade, in emulation of eighteenth-century Britain. This strategy was pursued by governments to open up their territories for trade and loosen the control of local societies over their own markets. For, as Adam Smith remarked about the grain trade,

---

[47] Steensgaard 1973a: 146 and 152–153. In general Chaudhuri 1985, chapter 4.

[48] Apart from Steensgaard 1973a and Chaudhuri 1985, see Klein 1965; Barbour 1966; Wallerstein 1974a; Israel 1989; De Vries and Woude 1997; Lesger 2006 for expositions of the principles and institutional strength of Dutch trade. See also Braudel 1982 for numerous perceptive comments about the growth of the modern world economy.

[49] See de Vries and Woude 1997: 414–419 for the integration of the grain markets in Amsterdam and Danzig. Christensen 1941 is the classic analysis of the Dutch Baltic grain trade and its institutional strengths.

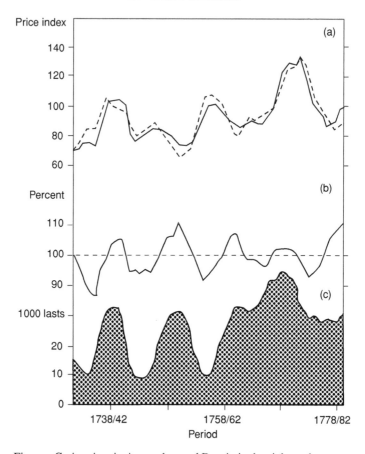

Fig. 3.1 Grain prices in Amsterdam and Danzig in the eighteenth century
(De Vries and Woude 1997: 418)

"no trade deserves more the full protection of the law, and no trade requires it so much; because no trade is so exposed to popular odium".[50] Imperfections and fragmentation did not disappear from European trade. Nevertheless, the result was a gradual stabilisation and tighter integration of markets, both nationally and internationally, created across large stretches of Europe and the Atlantic world from the seventeenth till the nineteenth centuries

---

[50] Smith 1976, vol. I: 527.

"literally with recourse to the forces of order" in the face of local opposition.[51]

The question at hand now is whether we should expect the tributary-fuelled process of market formation, described in chapter 2, to have caused a similar set of closely integrated markets to emerge in the Roman Empire. Finley was adamant in his denial.[52] Not surprisingly, his critics have seized the opportunity to argue the opposite.[53] If we turn once more to our Mughal parallel, it does not warrant such a reaction. As the experience of the chartered companies shows, markets did not easily adapt to the more stable forms gradually developing in Europe. Rather they seem in general to have remained less strongly integrated. Volatile prices, erratic fluctuations and significant local differences and asymmetries continued to dominate the bazaars of north India.[54] It would be wrong, though, to mistake this for a sign of a primitive trading world; in certain limited ways the Indian bazaar had at its disposal tools for transacting business which were, in evolutionary terms, more advanced than those at the command of the Roman merchant. Most important among those was the *hundi*, an Indian form of the bill of exchange.[55] It is now clear to Roman historians that merchants may to a limited extent have been able to organise cashless transfers of money, for instance with bankers acting as intermediaries. But it is equally clear that a fully fledged and solidly institutionalised system of bills of exchange did not materialise in the Roman world. Otherwise, we would expect it to have left far stronger traces in the historical record than is in fact the case (see Chapter 5). The performance of the Mughal trading

---

[51] Persson 1999: 146, in general chapters 4 and 6. See further Braudel and Spooner 1967. On local opposition to the process, see Thompson 1993, chapters 4 and 5. The lack of interest of large empires in pursuing such policies of favouritism, would thus carry significant consequences for the development of trade, *pace* Morley 2007: 58.

[52] Finley 1985a, "Further Thoughts", first section.

[53] Harris 1993, 1999 and 2000 (the latest piece was written before the two first mentioned and is more cautious as befits a chapter in *The Cambridge Ancient History*), Rathbone 1997 (on Egypt), and Temin 2001.

[54] Blake 1987: 451–455; Prakash 1991: 64–65; Habib 1999: 39–62, 68–82 and 90–102; and Moosvi 2000 on the "imperfections" of markets in the Mughal Empire. Marshall 1976 and Chatterjee 1996 complement with material from the late Mughal and post-Mughal period.

[55] Habib 1972 for an exposition of the *hundi* system in the Mughal Empire.

world can therefore be seen to offer an upper benchmark for the Roman experience. At the same time, it provides us with a useful guide for our understanding of Roman trade. In spite of the few limited technological advantages that it held over Rome, it was unable to transform the basic irregularities and volatile conditions of pre-modern trade. Even after the introduction of the railway and the telegraph under British colonial rule at the turn of the nineteenth century – two features which significantly reduced many of the obstacles to economic integration – the Indian "bazaar" remained a very risky and fragile business environment. Many European companies, therefore, preferred to do business in India outside the sphere of the indigenous market; they needed far greater stability and predictability to satisfy their profit requirements.[56] This goes to show that the chronic economic imbalances of the bazaar world cannot be reduced to a simple question of technological deficiencies. Social institutions played a crucial role.[57] The tributary process of commercialisation rested on a very different social balance of power. It did not invest the merchants of the Mughal "bazaar" with the kind of strong organisational powers and corporate influence that were necessary to control and conquer the endemic irregularities of pre-industrial trade and production. A telling index of this is that Indian traders were not normally in a powerful position vis-à-vis the aristocratic and political elite.[58] A small poetic autobiography written in the seventeenth century by a Jain merchant, Banarasidas, provides interesting evidence of this condition from a merchant's horizon. Aristocrats and imperial authorities in his story often prey on the readily consumable riches of merchants. Time and time again traders are taken hostage in order to fill the empty or just insatiable coffers of Mughal nobles.[59]

[56] Ray 1988. Steensgaard 1973a made the same point for an earlier period.
[57] Marshall 1976 offers a pertinent argument in support of this.
[58] Marshall 1976; Pearson 1976; Das Gupta 1979; Habib and Raychaudhuri 1982: 183–202 and 339–41; Das Gupta and Pearson 1987, chapters 4 and 6; Chatterjee 1996; Subrahmaniam 1999. *Pace* Subrahmanyam 1995, who remains unconvincing. The few examples he can point to are marginal and tend rather to reinforce the validity of the established historiography.
[59] Banarasidas' poem, the *Ardha-Kathának*, written in a dialect of Hindi, has received two recent translations: a drier, but literally more direct by Sharma 1970 and a more

The experience of Banarasidas can easily be matched by material from the Roman Empire. In times of military upheaval we hear of trading wealth being a convenient target for cash-hungry generals and soldiers. In Appian's history of the civil wars, the merchants of Palmyra barely avoid the onslaught of Antonius by escaping to the other side of the Euphrates.[60] During the so-called year of the four emperors, Tacitus tells of a town in northern Italy which, swelled by merchants coming to a large fair, became a tempting target for the approaching armies.[61] Even more revealing about the general conditions is the comic anecdote in Apuleius' *Golden Ass* about the zealous market official whom the hero encounters during a visit to the marketplace.[62] When the *agoranomos* (market overseer) discovers that the hero has been overcharged for a fish, he rushes down to the poor market seller to set him right. Now, the comic point hinges on the fact that the unfortunate *agoranomos* makes a fool of himself by *failing* to give the petty huckster his just deserts and put him in his proper place, while destroying the fish. Our hero is left with neither fish nor revenge. Leaving the world of literary fantasy behind, we have a letter among the Vindolanda tablets that conveys a similar impression.[63] There we encounter an overseas trader, a *homo transmarinus*, filing a complaint about a beating he has received from a centurion. Likewise, aristocrats could occasionally be found to intervene in the operation of markets and exploit their greater musclepower to corner a line of trade in order to make a quick profit, as Vespasian reputedly did.[64] In general, the position of the commercial middleman remained vulnerable. Roman authorities often looked with suspicion upon his activities. Inscribed on a stele in the Piraeus, a set of regulations of Hadrian attempted to secure a plentiful and cheap supply of fish for Eleusis, presumably during the Mysteries, by, among other things, seeking to limit the role of middlemen in the trade; their activities were denounced as harmful speculation which only served to drive up prices.[65]

poetically evocative in the early 1980s. See Snell 2005 for a study of the literary aspects of this text.

[60] App. *BC* 5, 9.   [61] Tac. *Hist*. III, 30–34.   [62] Apul. *Met*. I, 24–25.
[63] *Tab. Vindol*. 344.   [64] Suet. *Vesp*. 16.1.   [65] Oliver 1989, no. 77.

It would be wrong to mistake this greater social vulnerability
of merchants in tributary empires with an absolute powerlessness
or complete lack of political influence. Merchants were far from
always passive victims, as the letter from Vindolanda also informs
us. They, too, could stand up for themselves or seek the patronage
of powerful people.[66] However, compared to the world of their
early modern European counterparts theirs was a *rougher* place,
a less secure business environment.[67] But it was not an impossible one. We even find some examples of officially empowered
merchant organisations in the Roman Empire. One example is the
small association of salt traders in Tebtunis in Egypt, known from
a papyrus dated AD 47.[68] It shows that the merchants possessed a
monopoly in salt in the area and regulated their mutual relationships. This has been taken as evidence of something approaching strong medieval guilds.[69] That would be wrong, though. The
Egyptian salt merchants had not really acquired a similarly strong,
independent corporate power. The monopoly exists entirely within
a context of state regulation and, most importantly, state taxation.
It is clear from the papyrus that that the monopoly rights are wholly
dependent on the merchants administering and paying the salt tax
due to the state. It was, in other words, totally subordinate to the
fiscal requirements of the tributary system.[70]

Political leaders, thus, might both recognise and make use of
the services of traders. But this generally happened in a context
which valued urban consumers over the interests of exporters and
the middleman. Illustration is provided by Hadrian's restrictions
on the export of olive oil from Athenian territory. Measures were
taken to ensure that local needs were met before export could
take place.[71] In many respects, as Adam Smith pointed out, such

[66] E.g. the letter from Cicero (*Fam.* 13.75) asking for the prolongation of some privileges
the grain merchant C. Avianius Flaccus had enjoyed regarding his deliveries of grain
to Rome. For the Mughal Empire, the studies by Das Gupta 1979; Chatterjee 1996;
chapters 3 and 4; and Hasan 2004 offer telling illustrations of the more fragile power
and influence enjoyed by Indian merchants.
[67] Bayly 2000 is, to date, one of the best attempts to balance the greater institutional
security of the rising European capitalism with a recognition of the non-passivity of
merchants in the agrarian, aristocratic world.
[68] *P. Mich.* V, 245.   [69] Van Nijf 1997: 13–14 suggests such an interpretation.
[70] See Weber 1972: 592, 644–645 and 652 for this distinction.
[71] *SEG* XV, 108. See in general Finley 1985a: 160–164. The famous passage from Cicero
Off. 1.150–151, in fact, illustrates the ideological ambivalence in relation to trade:

procedures were just the opposite of the policies that were gradually introduced during the early modern period in Europe.[72] What
mattered to the Greco-Roman elites, however, was the availability
of well-supplied markets in the many cities which made up the
political framework of the Empire and of which they continued
to be the local leaders. Placed under the supervision of the local
aedile or *agoranomos*, whose task it was to regulate business and
ensure that traders acted fairly without, as they saw it, undue speculation, the markets of the Roman world remained subject to the
"moral economy" of the *polis/civitas*.[73]

Sojourn on the Nile: the Egyptian price series

So far the discussion has been conducted mainly on impressionistic evidence. Historians and economists examining market integration, however, are normally used to basing their analysis on
long, continuous series of recorded prices in different locations.
But such statistical analysis is beyond the means of the historian
for vast swathes of pre-industrial history. Records were either not
collected or have not survived. Only in exceptional cases is it

---

basically in the eyes of the aristocrat a sordid activity, particularly as practised by those
that buy up goods only to sell them on. Yet if conducted in a grand manner, which
brought goods not otherwise available to market, then it might be deemed worthy of
respect. See Giardina 1986 for the complex ideological web surrounding merchants in
antiquity, though he makes too much of a contrast between the despised small trader
and the honourable big merchant. The wholesaler was also subject to social prejudice
and suspected of immoderate greed, speculation and lying, as is clear from Cicero's
own discussion of the secretive merchant in *Off.* 3.50 and the contempt administered
by Petronius to his literary character Trimalchio, the stereotypical freedman, vulgar and
greedy beyond measure (cf. *Sat.* 75, 8–76, 9).

[72] The theme of the third book of the *Wealth of Nations*, e.g. Smith 1976, vol. 3: 380,
422. See Bang 2006 for an attempt to relate the problem of Roman markets to the
questions raised by Smith's understanding of history. The formation of empire should
not automatically be assumed to have created a similar strengthening of commercial
networks; *pace* Erdkamp 2005: 196, it gave rise to a very different process of market
formation.

[73] See Alston 2002: 274–277 and 337–339; Garnsey 1988: 257–268; Jones 1940: 215–
219. See Jakab 1997, chapters 2 and 3 for a legal analysis of the functions of the
aedile and *agoranomos*. Thompson 1993, chapter 4 contrasted the moral economy of
local communities, privileging the interests of consumers, with the new economy in
eighteenth-century England, which strove to break down barriers between markets and
ensure greater economic integration by siding with the middleman. See Erdkamp 2002
for an attempt to employ this concept in an analysis of food riots in the Roman Empire.

possible to break through the mist of pre-statistical time. The fortuitous preservation on clay tablets of astronomical records from Hellenistic Babylon, for instance, does make it possible to catch a glimpse of the vicissitudes of commodity prices and pre-industrial trade for long stretches of time.[74] The Roman historian can explore the extent to which markets were integrated with reference to price material from Egypt, owing its survival to the protection offered to papyri by the dry conditions of the desert.

No papyri records, however, can match the continuity of the Babylonian material. In that respect, the Roman is more fragmentary and episodic. But what it lacks in continuity, the Romano-Egyptian evidence does to some extent make up for in geographical variation. The Hellenistic clay tablets, it seems rather ungracious to observe, are restricted to one city. A significant feature of pre-industrial trade was the relative unpredictability of prices. Yet, prices fluctuate in all markets, sometimes violently, even in quite well-integrated systems. Price instability may be a symptom of limited market integration, but is no absolute test. Two other, complementary, criteria are normally employed to determine the degree of commercial integration: unity of prices and parallel developments. Generally, integration of individual markets works as a stabilising influence on prices. The effect of small changes in local supply and demand is evened out through exchange with other localities. This, in turn, will cause prices in individual locations to converge towards the same equilibrium. Near unity of prices in different markets is a useful indicator of market integration. But there are always costs involved in moving goods from one location to another. Even in well-integrated markets, prices are never completely identical; they may vary between two locations within a span defined by the costs of bringing the two markets together. If this span is wide, the single markets will remain largely autonomous of each other.[75] On the other hand, price similarity need not necessarily be the result of commercial integration.

---

[74] See Aperghis 2004: 78–86 for an analysis, noting the volatility of the Babylonian market.

[75] This is an important modification which Erdkamp 2005: 199–200 fails to accommodate fully in his exposition of the theoretical issues involved in measuring market integration. Gibson and Smout 1995; Stiegler and Sherwin 1985 set out the different criteria for examining market integration.

Coincidence, regulation or some other extra-economic cause may be equally responsible. A useful additional test of market integration is whether developments in individual markets follow the same course. If prices develop in parallel fashion there is a good chance that it is the outcome of commercial integration. Providing information on prices in different markets, the Egyptian evidence makes it possible to explore tentatively all three dimensions of commercial integration.

The material mainly originates from urban and rural, half-commercialised, contexts in Middle Egypt.[76] No major market is represented. This is both a strength and a weakness. It is a strength because the testimony offered by this material can be taken as broadly representative of conditions in the vast majority of markets around the Empire, which would have been no more, in fact in most cases even less, centrally placed in Roman commercial life. It is a weakness because it tells little about the situation in leading markets that might be expected to have pioneered a movement towards greater integration, had such a process occurred. Yet, we are in no position to choose. The inhabited part of the region consisted only of a narrow strip of land following the course of the Nile and the Bahr Yusuf canal running parallel to it, and widening for a distance to include the Fayum with Lake Moeris. This was, in fact, a physical environment which ought to have favoured integration. With easy access to water and only short distances to cover by land, transport would have been far less of a problem than in most other places. The relevant evidence spans a period from the early first to the early fifth century AD. Unfortunately, most prices in the first- to third-century papyri are only mentioned in isolation. This makes the density of information which can be gained from these, a few exceptions apart, insufficient to study short-term market developments in any detail. The early prices mostly only allow us to form an impression of the level of prices in the region.[77]

---

[76] Rathbone 1991 clearly shows how market trade co-existed with forms of natural economy on the Appianus estate in this area. Farm labourers were not just employed on a free contractual basis. Various ways to tie at least some of them to the estate were pursued. Wages would, for instance, often have been paid in kind.

[77] Rathbone 1997 offers an interesting analysis of this material, but overestimates its potential for studying market integration. The evidence only allows a very broad impression of some long-term trends, cf. Erdkamp 2005: 204.

In late antiquity, however, the Roman state began gathering information on prices. Relevant urban professional associations, the *collegia*, were asked or required to submit monthly reports to the authorities about the prices, especially of raw materials, current in the marketplace. A considerable number of these individual declarations survive.[78] These were then compiled and drawn up in surveys at various levels in the administrative hierarchy, listing recorded prices over a time period for the different nomes (districts). Two such price series have been published among the *Oxyrhynchus Papyri*, one from the second quarter of the fourth century and one from the early fifth.[79] Official registration of commodity prices was intimately linked with the changes introduced to late antique taxation. The government needed information on which to calculate the value of tax claims and consumption demands. Forced purchases of goods were a regular feature of this system and were supposed to be remunerated at the rates current in the local market. Similarly, dues in kind were often converted into a lump cash payment according to the going market price.[80]

While the broad picture is reasonably clear, some uncertainty still remains as to the details. It is not known how the *collegia* arrived at the prices they submitted to the administration. We can see that most prices did vary over time and according to location, which is an indication that they do bear some relationship to the situation in the marketplace. But records were "only" submitted on a monthly basis. If prices changed it is unlikely that they did so only once a month. Presumably the *collegia* registered the daily

---

[78] E.g. *P. Oxy.* 3624–3626. For basic discussion of these and the other late antique price records, see the editor's introductions to *P. Oxy.* 3628–3636, 3773 and 3624–3626. See further Lo Cascio 1998 and Bagnall 2000: 89–91 decisively contra Fikhman 1991–2 (the prices are market prices, not administratively fixed prices).

[79] *P. Oxy.* 3773 (dating to *c.* 340) and *P. Oxy.* 3628–3636 (dating probably to the early fifth century) are by far the best specimens. The first of these was probably produced by the local authorities in Oxyrhynchus, the other compiled in a provincial office based on material submitted by "the tabularii of each city", as stated in *P. Oxy.* 3628, lines, 1–3.

[80] E.g. Justinian, *Appendix Constitutionum Dispersarum* vii, § 26 (in *Corpus Iuris Civilis* III, Novellae, ed. Schoell and Kroll), *C. Theod.* VII 4, 10 and 46; XI 15, 2. Lo Cascio 1998 removes any remaining doubts as to the character of these documents. They must be understood in the context of late antique taxation practices. Cerati 1975 remains fundamental on the importance of so-called *coemptio* and *adaeratio* in the fourth and fifth centuries. Bang 2007: 31–39 attempts to place the phenomenon in its economic context.

prices and then presented the authorities with an average or the predominant price. We must also allow for significant differences in standards here. Not all *collegia* are likely to have been equally rigorous, nor will information about all products have been equally important. By far the most elaborate of the preserved surveys, for instance, documents developments in grain and wine prices quite closely, whereas the prices for less important products such as meat or radish oil are consistently registered as unchanged throughout the year.[81] The quality of single records is bound to have varied, though it is impossible in individual cases to ascertain with certainty whether a record is false or not. Even so, none of this is likely to distort the information so as to render the overall impression of the market situation unreliable. Generally the image emerging from the dossiers seems to fit quite well with our knowledge of markets in Roman Egypt. Thus the documents do not fail to register the existence of the government monopoly in the salt trade familiar from the Principate; they also, as will appear below, reveal that of the agricultural products wine probably had the most "developed" market in the province. This is just what we would expect of the primary cash crop of the estates of the landowning elite.[82] Taken as a whole then and bearing in mind the poor state of the evidence for prices in most pre-industrial societies, the Romano-Egyptian government price series do provide an extremely detailed image of the situation in the markets of Middle Egypt at two cross-sections in time. Some distortion in the details is probable, but not enough to invalidate a tentative analysis.

The fifth-century series consists of a centrally drawn-up set of lists of the price of gold, silver and eight commodities in each of the nine nomes of the province of Arcadia in Middle Egypt. The records span one year and the prices are given in four-monthly

[81] This is most conveniently seen from the table on pp. 73–74 of the editor's introduction to *P. Oxy.* 3628–3636, summarising the information of the reports. The permanence of prices of some goods such as meat could very well be a reflection of the existence of only a very limited market in those goods rather than failure to report developments. On top of this is the question of tax-inspired monopolies in Egypt. The salt trade was a monopoly contracted to private individuals (*P. Mich.* V, 245), which explains the uniform rate of salt in the survey.

[82] See Rathbone 1991, chapter 6 on the agricultural production of large Egyptian estates; see further Sarris 2006 on the great Egyptian estates.

intervals.[83] This makes the data inadequate for investigating short-term fluctuations, other than in a very broad way. Limiting the number of recorded prices to three each year for a particular commodity inevitably serves to underplay change. This is particularly so since the prices recorded are likely to represent four-monthly averages. The calculation of averages automatically irons out differences between months and thus artificially minimises the level of fluctuation occurring in the market. From our present perspective, however, the set of lists is of particular interest because, uniquely, they allow us to test for the two other criteria for measuring the degree of market integration: variation in price levels between markets and the degree of uniformity in developments in commodity prices across locations. In theory, it should have been possible to achieve a cross-section of prices at three points in time for all nine nomes making up the province. But the document, as we have it, was never finished. Gaps for three nomes have been left by the scribe to be filled in later. Wear and tear of the papyrus has further reduced the available information. The names of two of the nomes are lost, as is a considerable number of prices. Of the eighteen originally recorded wheat prices, only eleven are still legible, of wine only twelve. Yet, enough survives to enable a tentative analysis.

First, let us deal with the variation in price levels. Comparing the quotations of commodity prices reveals the existence of remarkably large differences between the prices current in the individual cities, even within the relatively small area covered by Arcadia, not more than 100 miles in length (see Fig. 3.2). For instance, the difference between the lowest and highest prices simultaneously listed for meat is 25%, for radish oil, 31%, and 32% for lentils. Even the value of the gold coin, the solidus, expressed in myriads of denarii, shows some rather surprising differences. Thus in the period from September to December there was a 5% gap between the price in Cynopolis and neighbouring Oxyrhynchus,

[83] *P. Oxy.* 3628–3633. In working on the papyri I have checked the *Berichtigungsliste* and used the images made available in electronic form by the homepage of the Centre for the Study of Ancient Documents, University of Oxford (www.csad.ox.ac.uk) to confirm some uncertain readings of prices in the material. In that connection, I should like to express my warm gratitude to Dorothy Thompson for spending a most enjoyable Thursday morning with me, trying to decipher the script used by the scribe.

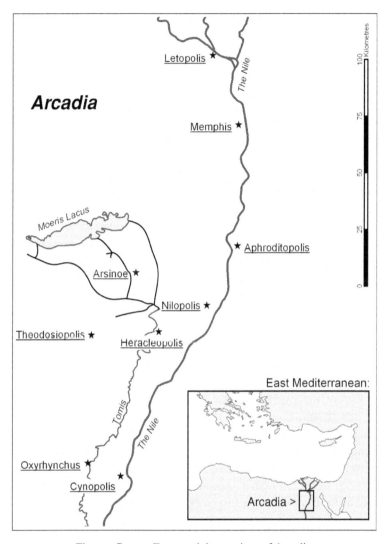

Fig. 3.2 Roman Egypt and the province of Arcadia

less than 20 miles apart. This is the sort of behaviour we would expect from a system of imperfectly integrated markets.

This impression is confirmed if we model the market conditions in greater detail for some of the most important products, wheat, barley and wine. They all reveal the existence of considerable price spans between individual markets (see Table 3.1). For wheat, the difference between highest and lowest simultaneously recorded price is between two-thirds and, if we can trust the very low Arsinoite values, a little more than 100% in the year under examination, though the figure is of course less for some cities. For instance, the level in the Aphroditopolite nome, less than 100 miles downstream, is 46% higher than the corresponding price recorded for the Cynopolite nome in the September–December interval. In order better to assess this difference we must adjust for transport costs. To take advantage of higher prices the grain would have needed to be taken down the Nile by boat from Cynopolis to reach the Aphroditopolite market. Information pertaining to the cost of transport is scanty. But the papyrus evidence we do have shows with consistency that the rent of a boat, including some basic handling charges, is unlikely to have been very substantial. Most grain transport on the Nile seems to have cost less than 3% of the value of wheat. Cynopolite wheat could easily have absorbed this extra cost.[84]

Part of the explanation for the very high discrepancy may lie in that pronounced enemy of market integration, the levying of local customs (see further Chapter 4). We know, though the evidence is heavily weighted towards the high empire, that it was normal for customs dues to be paid on exports from and imports to each nome. Whether this also included paying for goods in transit on the Nile each time a boat crossed a nome boundary is

---

[84] See Adams 2007 for a recent analysis of Egyptian transport. The price evidence is collected by Johnston 1936 and Drexhage 1991. *P. Oxy.* 522 (second century AD) gives a pure freight rate of 21 drachmae (dr.) per 100 artabai for Oxyrhynchus to Alexandria. Setting wheat at a reasonable 8 dr. per artaba this comes out at 2.5%. The boat, dealt with in the papyrus, carried 3,400 artabai making the freight rate 712 dr. To this were added various handling and loading charges, bringing the total bill to 762 dr. 3 obols (ob.) or 2.8% for wheat at 8 dr./artaba. Other papyri state freight rates in kind, e.g. *BGU* III, 802, col. 22 giving prices for boat transport from the Arsinoite nome to Alexandria of three different agricultural products. All come out at less than 1% of the cargo.

Table 3.1 *Variation in price levels in Arcadia*

1: Variation span of prices, the difference between highest and lowest price

	Sept.–Dec.	Jan.–Apr.	May–Aug.
Wheat	88%	67%	108%
Barley	30%	78%	33%
Wine	7% (43%)	15%	27%

2: Commodity prices, real figures (indexed numbers) in the nomes of Arcadia

Wheat (den. myr./art.–index)	Sept.–Dec.	Jan.–Apr.	May–Aug.
Cynopolite	307.7 (100)	300 (97)	325 (106)
Oxyrhynchite	316.7 (103)	–	–
Uncertain	450 (146)	500 (162)	500 (162)
Uncertain	–	–	450 (146)
Arsinoite*	240 (78)	–	240 (78)
Aphroditopolite	450 (146)	450 (146)	–

Barley (den. myr./art.–index)	Sept.–Dec.	Jan.–Apr.	May–Aug.
Cynopolite	285.7 (100)	278.6 (98)	300 (105)
Oxyrhynchite	292.3 (102)	–	–
Uncertain	270 (94)	400 (140)	270 (94)
Uncertain	–	–	–
Arsinoite	225 (79)	225 (79)	225 (79)
Aphroditopolite	225 (79)	–	–

Wine (den. myr./sex.–index)	Sept.–Dec.	Jan.–Apr.	May–Aug.
Cynopolite	20.6 (100)	20.6 (100)	22.5 (109)
Oxyrhynchite	–	22.5 (109)	–
Uncertain	21.4 (104)	23.6 (115)	28.6 (139)
Uncertain	–	–	–
Arsinoite	20 (97)	23.8 (116)	27.5 (133)
Aphroditopolite	? 28.6 ?	–	28.6 (139)

* The grain prices in the Arsinoite nome may be suspiciously low since they also fail to register any developments during the year. But this is a matter for speculation. Therefore these data have not been excluded from the calculations. Exclusion would, in any case, not alter the basic picture. The variation span in grain prices would be lessened, especially for wheat, but it would still be high.

unclear. The craftiness of custom officials is legendary and, to judge from comparative examples, it would not be at all surprising if transit boats were charged too, possibly at a lower rate. The Cynopolite nome is separated from the Aphroditopolite by the Hermopolite. Customs would then at a minimum be exacted on departure and on entering Aphroditopolis. The going rate seems to have been around 3% each time.[85] To the approximately 3% needed for transport, this might have added an artificial barrier of at least 6%, or more if dues also had to be defrayed for transit through the Hermopolite nome. Neither cost would in this case have been prohibitive. But the need, willy-nilly, to pay perhaps up to 10% of the value of the grain in the process of bringing it to market may have discouraged the establishment of a routine commercial infrastructure, able to take advantage even of smaller price differentials.

The impression of relatively low and fragile integration between the individual markets in the province of Arcadia receives further confirmation when we proceed to compare the development in grain prices over the recorded year. Unfortunately, the damage to the papyri means that not all price information has been preserved. We can only follow the price during all three four-monthly intervals for Cynopolis and a city whose name does not survive (Fig. 3.3). This and the fact that there are only three prices recorded during the year, mean that the result must remain very tentative. From the graph it appears that price developments do not conform to the same pattern. While prices stay essentially the same in Cynopolis in the second interval, the price increases 11% (index price from 146 to 162) in the unidentified city. In the third interval, the pattern is turned around. Now Cynopolis experiences an increase of some 8%, whereas the price remains unchanged at its high level in the anonymous city. The situation for barley puts this pattern into sharper relief (Fig. 3.4). The uncertain city experiences a sharp rise from the first to the second interval and Cynopolis remains stable. By the third interval Cynopolis shows a slight increase in

---

[85] See Sijpesteijn 1987: 19–25 and de Laet 1949, 324–329 for customs rates in Egypt. Sijpesteijn 1987: 6–7 is not justified in taking the virtual disappearance of evidence pertaining to customs from the third century onwards as a sign that the exaction of tolls had been discontinued.

Price of wheat in fifth-century province of Arcadia

In myriads of denarii per artaba   In indexed numbers

nome	Sept.–Dec.	Jan.–Apr.	May–Aug.	Interval	1	2	3
Cynopolite	308	300	325	Cynopolite	100	97	106
Uncertain	450	500	500	Uncertain	146	162	162
Arsinoite	240		240	Arsinoite	78		78
Aphroditopolite	450	450		Aphroditopolite	146	146	

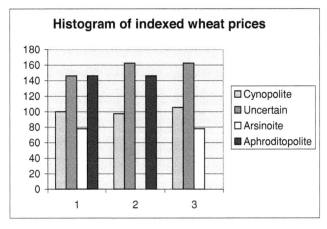

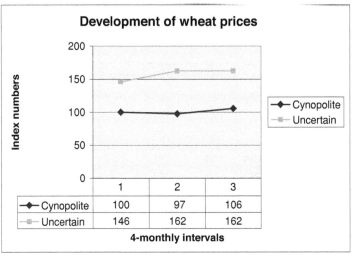

Fig. 3.3 Price of wheat in fifth-century province of Arcadia

163

Price of barley in fifth-century province of Arcadia

In myriads of denarii per artaba   In indexed numbers

nome	Sept.–Dec.	Jan.–Apr.	May–Aug.	Interval	1	2	3
Cynopolite	286	279	300	Cynopolite	100	98	105
Uncertain	270	400	270	Uncertain	94	140	94
Arsinoite	225	225	225	Arsinoite	79	79	79

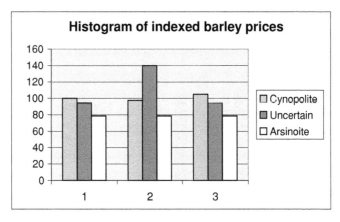

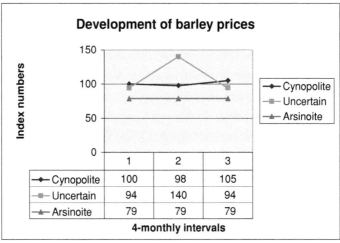

Fig. 3.4 Price of barley in fifth-century province of Arcadia

the price of barley, whereas the city of uncertain identity now has a steep fall in the price of barley. The prices are very far from moving in unison and market developments appear to vary considerably between the cities.

Perhaps, a little surprisingly the harvest cycle fails to manifest itself clearly. The main grain harvest in Egypt seems normally to have taken place in May. Prices could therefore be expected to rise in the second interval of the year as stocks began to wear thinner, and drop again in the third interval after the new crop. Only the unidentified city conforms more or less to this pattern. But its wheat price remains high for the May–August interval. A possible explanation would be that the harvest came late in this particular year. The delayed rise in the Cynopolite grain prices could then be a reflection of this and perhaps also indication of a bad or disappointing crop.[86] Another likely explanation might be distortion caused by the method of registration. However, if market integration was fragile, we should expect local deviations from the "standard" pattern. If it had been possible to test for a much greater number of cities and perhaps over a longer timeframe, and the average pattern still failed to conform to the rhythm of the agricultural year, it would be a greater cause for concern. In this case, however, the number of examples is so small that individual irregularities are only to be expected and may, in fact, be a result of market imbalances.

Finally, let us consider wine. In contrast to the grain prices, a very clear harvest cycle pattern comes through in the evidence; prices are low in the post-harvest interval (September–December) and rise steadily towards harvest time in August, reaching culmination in the the third interval. This requires introducing extra subtlety into the analysis. Shared patterns of price development cannot, in and of themselves, be taken automatically as evidence of close integration. They may not be due to a close coordination of supply and demand across marketplaces. Equally important may be exogenous influences common to all the markets, such as the arrival of a plague, political collapse or shared weather

---

[86] Rathbone 1991: 228–231 documents the prevalence of a harvest pattern later than the norm for the Fayum.

conditions. This last factor, by producing similar harvest results across the region, is undoubtedly part of the explanation for the shared pattern in the wine markets. However, wine was the primary cash crop of Egyptian agriculture, and we should probably be prepared to accept some integration of markets.

Thus, even though their courses are not absolutely identical, with the price leader changing twice during the year, the curves for the unidentified city and Arsinoe do appear to show some resemblance.[87] On the other hand, the fragile and limited nature of the integration in the wine trade is clearly brought out by the overall development in the market. At the beginning of our period the prices of the unidentified city, Arsinoe and Cynopolis are very close together within a range of 7% from bottom to top, while at the end of the year that gap has increased to 28%, and Cynopolis has seen a significantly different development than the other two markets (Fig. 3.5). Incidentally it is worth observing that local customs duties might have been an important barrier to integration in the wine markets. All in all, this leaves an image of a set of markets where integration was limited, links were fragile and vulnerable, and coordination between the individual markets fairly weak. As a result conditions varied considerably from city to city, even within this very limited territory.

Moving on, a fourth-century papyrus lists information on the monthly, presumably average, prices for gold, silver, wheat, barley, lentils, vegetable seed and wine over a fifteen-month period (see Table 3.2).[88] As was to be expected we find a pattern for the agricultural goods heavily influenced by the seasons with a pronounced tendency for prices to peak just before harvest and to slump with a little delay after. But the agricultural seasonal cycle cannot account for all developments. Again some irregularities, now less surprising to us, emerge. Other factors clearly also had a strong influence in the short term as the monthly averages show.

---

[87] One reason for their close resemblance could be that the unidentified city was located close to Arsinoe, e.g. if it was identical with Herakleopolis at 26 km's distance, which might well be the case.

[88] *P. Oxy.* 3773. The editor assumes that the prices are real market prices. However, if government officials could calculate four-monthly averages, I have no doubt that *collegia* would be able to produce average monthly prices too. In view of the violent fluctuations of some of the prices, it would be highly unlikely that prices within each month were absolutely fixed.

Price of wine in fifth-century province of Arcadia

In myriads of denarii per sextarius   In indexed numbers

nome	Sept.–Dec.	Jan.–Apr.	May–Aug.	Interval	1	2	3
Cynopolite	20.6	20.6	22.5	Cynopolite	100	100	109
Uncertain	21.4	23.6	28.6	Uncertain	104	115	139
Arsinoite	20	23.8	27.5	Arsinoite	97	116	133

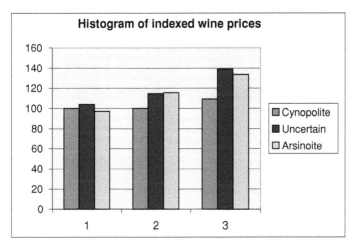

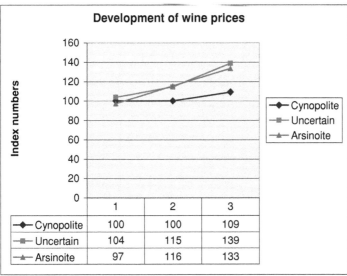

Fig. 3.5 Price of wine in fifth-century province of Arcadia

167

Table 3.2 *Commodity prices, probably in Oxyrhynchus, during fifteen months of the fourth century AD*

	Toth	Phaopi	Hathyr	Choiak	Tybi	Mecheir	Phamenoth	Pharmouthi	Pachon	Payni	Epeiph.	Mesore	Toth	Phaopi	Hathyr
1 solidus (talents)	190?	206.67?	233.33	233.33?	233.33	233.33	233.33	233.33	243.33	243.33	243.33	243.33	243.33	240	240
Silver (talents/lb)		950?	1,033.33	1,033.33?	1,033.33?	1,166.67	1,166.67		1,186.67	1,186.67	1,186.67	1,186.67	1,213.33	1,213.33	1,123.33
Wheat (talents/art)	45		45		45	46.67	50		50	45	45	45	40	40	40?
Barley (talents/art)	20		20? or 25		25	20	25		15	15	20	20?	20	22	
Lentils (talents/art)	20		22		25	22	25		20+	30	30?	30	35	30	
Vegetable seed (talents/art)			50		50	45	50			75	75		80	75	
Wine (talents/sext)	1		1		1	1	1.33	1.33	1.33	1.33	1.67		1	1	

Note: the table is based on R. Coles' summary table of *P. Oxy.* 3773, published on p. 208 in the *Oxyrhynchus Papyri*, vol. LIV, 1987. A ? indicates uncertain reading, a blank slot equals a gap in the papyrus record. Egyptian months correspond approximately to modern as: Thoth/September; Phaopi/October; Hathyr/November; Choiak/December; Tybi/January; Mecheir/February; Phamenoth/March; Pharmouthi/April; Pachon/May; Pauni/June; Epeiph/July; Mesore/August.

The price of barley is revealing. It sets off with the expected rise as stocks wear thinner during winter. Then in Mecheir it suddenly drops by 20%, only to rise to its former level in the following month. The harvest sees a slump but only for two months, followed a little surprisingly by a steep increase of 33%. The script for wheat is slightly different. It shows an 11% increase from Phaopi until Pachon, then drops in Pauni to the previous autumn level as the crop is harvested. But then in Thot a fall of another 11% follows rather unexpectedly. For lentils, a similar pattern of some erratically fluctuating prices appears. Here, as for barley, there is a surprising drop in Mecheir (12%) and the fall in prices after harvest is very quickly offset by a large increase in Pauni. Did the crop fail? Or was there some other shock, unknown to us? Be that as it may, the situation seems to have been unstable – as the further 17% increase in Thoth and its immediate nullification in Phaophi indicate. Something similar could be said about vegetable seed, where we observe an increase of some 60% during the time we can follow the price. From these observations it should be clear that seasonal and other changes combined to make the markets quite volatile during the year. Further, developments in individual goods show fairly divergent patterns, another sign of weakly integrated markets. That becomes even clearer when we include gold and silver in our observations. The document stems from the period of considerable inflation affecting the imperial coinage. The timeframe is not long enough for this to have a visible effect on the prices registered for the agricultural goods. But with gold and silver it is another matter. Both seem to rise in Athyr. Then silver sees an additional increase in Mecheir. In Pachon both silver and gold rise, though not by the same percentage. Very belatedly gold seems to follow suit (four months later, in fact), whereas silver climbs to its highest level hitherto in Thoth. In sum, the fourth- and fifth-century government price lists convey an impression of very opaque, weakly integrated markets with relatively frail stabilising mechanisms.

Consisting of monthly and even four-monthly price averages, the fourth- and early fifth-century lists must invariably have masked some short-term fluctuations. Some of this we can make up for by complementing our image of markets in Middle Egypt by drawing in some of the earlier, but more disparate information on prices we possess from the area.[89] Effectively we have only a handful of documents offering sufficiently detailed evidence on which to create short-term price series. Several of these relate to the price of wine. This carries problems of its own. Often it is not possible to ascertain whether a variation in price reflects different qualities of wine or changing prices.[90] A couple of other series come from internal estate accounts. While there is no doubt that they do reflect market prices, as argued by Rathbone, over the longer term, it is far from clear that they were adjusted according to short-term developments in the market. Thus one shows a surprising stability that does not even register the expectable seasonal changes. There is, for instance, no drop in the months after the harvest. To judge from the figures, the level of the accounting price seems to have been adjusted annually in June and more or less maintained for the next twelve months.[91]

This leaves us with the information that can be squeezed from the Tebtunis *grapheion*, or record office, for September and October AD 45.[92] Here we find a number of transactions for the

[89] H.-J. Drexhage 1988 and 1991 and Rathbone 1997 have gathered the material.

[90] The problem is a real one P. *Oxy*. 3513, 3515, 3516, 3518, 3519, 3520, 3521 (collected by Rathbone 1997: 231) inform of two sales of wine from an estate in the same month at very different prices. However, we are talking of two different vintages where the earlier one receives the highest price. I have therefore chosen to disregard the evidence of *BGU* III, 712 (listed in Rathbone 1997: 228). This problem, incidentally, is less serious for the late price series. In practice, these wine data project a fairly coherent image. Their price differential does not seem sufficiently significant to require explanation as a reflection of quality differences. Further, the prices were submitted to the authorities by collective commercial bodies and would most likely have been based on standard, bulk wine. The data therefore were the result of a much more homogeneous collection procedure.

[91] *P. Brux. inéd.* (listed by Rathbone 1997: 229–230). The information starts in November 247 with a price of 9 dr. 1 ob. per keramion monochoron. This level continues unchanged till May 248. We have no information for June but in August it has risen to 10 dr. 2 ob. Then there is some uncertainty. In October the price might have been raised slightly to 10 dr. 6 ob, and is presumably kept steady until June 249 where it is raised to 14 dr. 6 ob. When I say uncertainty, it is because in January 249 we get the price of 10 dr. 2 ob. again. Rathbone suggests it is a mistake for 6 ob. I have not seen the papyrus but have the suspicion that it could also be the 10 dr. 6 ob. which was a writing error, to judge from the continuity of the 9 dr. 1 ob. in the previous year. Jakab 2003 argues that prices in the Heroninos archive, the basis of Rathbone 1991 and a main source for prices in the third century, would often have been administratively fixed.

[92] *P. Mich.* II, 127 (i. 8–38 contain the grain prices) and *P. Mich.* II, 123 (mainly for wine). Grain prices are most conveniently listed in Duncan-Jones 1990, because he lists the grain prices according to date. See also Rathbone 1997: 217 and 224.

procurement of small quantities of wheat and wine. Taking wheat first, on 7 September in AD 45 the price is listed at 4.4 drachmae (dr.) per artaba. A fortnight later it has risen by 30% to 5.7 dr. Three days later it is 8 dr. or an extra 40% higher.[93] Two days later it drops to 7.3 dr., that is by 9%. In October it goes up in two instalments to 8 dr. again. It is clear that even in the very short term, prices fluctuated quite violently at times. This conclusion is further supported by the data on wine from the *grapheion*. In the same months, the prices for wine fluctuate within a band of 2.50 dr. and 4.58 dr. per keramion or by up to 80% in round figures.[94] This image of fragile market integration would appear to clash with Rathbone's analysis, partly based on the same data. By a comprehensive statistical analysis of the fairly few attested prices for wheat, wine and donkeys from Middle Egypt in the first three centuries AD he concluded that markets seemed to be well integrated in the region. His conclusion was based on the identification of a common long-term pattern with two periods of relative price stability within *relatively broad* price bands from *c.* AD 40 to 170 and again from 190 to 270.[95]

First, the price bands are very broad. That for wheat in the first period lies in an interval between 5 or 6 and 12 dr. per artaba. This leaves plenty of room for local intra-annual variations. If we look at the very small amount of data that constitutes this band we find that it is essentially based on ten prices from the Arsinoite

---

[93] One possible explanation for this extraordinarily high leap could be a very poor Nile inundation. Prices will therefore have soared in response to the expectation of a bad harvest in the coming year, Rathbone 1997: 193. However, that remains only one possible hypothesis. If we are to judge from slightly later material, the start-out price of 4.4 dr. per artaba was very low. We could therefore also just be seeing a return to more normal prices.

[94] *Pace* Rathbone 1997: 196–197, who concludes that changes over the very short term were minimal. To support this conclusion he calculates the variation from the median (the middle point between the two extreme points in the price range). Over the short term that is going to produce a false sense of continuity. For instance, a price rise of 100% is only going to appear as a variation of 33% around the median (example: price goes from 5 to 10. Variation around the median will be only 2.5 around 7.5 or 33%) and a rise of 50% will come out as a fluctuation of 20%. The merchant, however, is not going to pay the median price. His profit is going to depend on the variation in real prices. Cf. Steensgaard 1973a: 42–59 for a similar approach to the calculation of short-term fluctuations in pre-modern markets. Working on early modern trade he even considers as violent much smaller variations than our evidence shows.

[95] See Rathbone 1997: 210–216 for a summary of his results. H.-J. Drexhage 1988 is much closer to the present author's analysis.

nome and seven from the Hermopolite. Taken separately, the data produce an average of 7.36 dr. for the Arsinoite and 9.55 dr. or 30% higher for the Hermopolite. This difference may be coincidental. Ten and seven figures respectively from a period of over 100 years can hardly be considered adequate evidence to allow conclusions regarding differences in the price levels between the two nomes. But they do remind us that we cannot exclude local differences within the very broad trends located by Rathbone. In fact, for our fifth-century dossier basically all the wheat prices fall within a similarly wide span, and yet considerable fragmentation characterised the market. The broad comparability of early and late prices, incidentally, corresponds quite well with recent trends in late antique scholarship stressing the continued economic health and vitality of market trade in the fourth and fifth centuries.[96] The evidence of short-term fluctuation and the late antique records, therefore, both suggest that the parameters, never made explicit, of Rathbone's analysis are faulty. The Egyptian prices from the Principate are fully compatible with a scenario where market integration remained fragile.

Second, it is important to recognise that this is not a question of either total disintegration with completely isolated communities or fully correlated markets moving in absolute unison; we are trying to look at differences between a group of highly complex pre-industrial societies with forces working on several levels to tie localities into wider networks. The activities of the state would have been one significant factor in creating some broad overarching patterns, as was argued in the last chapter. On a micro-level, state-defined rates for compulsory purchase or the conversion of grain taxes into cash payments may have helped stabilise prices in the long term within the broad bands identified by Rathbone.[97] Compulsory purchases, of course, would often have served to

[96] Bagnall 1993, Banaji 2001, Sarris 2006 and Ziche 2006. They all insist on the continued vitality of economic life in much of the Empire during late antiquity, and in particular, Egypt. Therefore it is not unreasonable to use this material, at least as an indicator of conditions in the preceding centuries.

[97] See Rathbone 1997: 196–197 for this suggestion. State purchases and conversion rates can only have been very broad stabilising factors. According to Rathbone's price bands, the span of variations becomes narrower in the third century when evidence of conversion stops for a period.

increase uncertainty in the short run, as the many surviving complaints clearly testify; often people would have suffered losses and been forced to sell below the current market rate. Individual communities did not exist in perfect economic isolation either. Trade clearly did take place. In the long run this must have worked to create some broadly coherent features. Even if prices in one Egyptian city would normally have differed from those of its neighbours, we would expect the variations to remain within limits. If they had consistently been of an entirely different order, landowners in the surrounding area would surely have moved in to benefit and thus gradually re-established a connection, however broad, between individual prices in the region.[98] The identification of some common long-term price trends, therefore, does not militate against the case for a relatively low level of market integration. They are only to be expected.[99] Rathbone, for instance, convincingly suggests that the caesura between the two identifiable price bands was caused by the disruption that followed the arrival of the Antonine Plague in Egypt.[100] A similar leap in prices can be observed across large sections of Europe after the shock caused by the Black Death. That was long before the arrival of more closely integrated markets. Rather than the result of a close integration of supply and demand, the jump in prices after the Antonine Plague was caused by an exogenous shock shared by the whole province.

The limited institutional coherence of the tributary empire

So, the question is whether the Roman world ever made the move beyond weakly integrated, volatile markets with some degree of long-term coherence to more closely correlated and stable markets. The Egyptian evidence surveyed, so far, suggests a negative answer. But this answer could admittedly be better supported. The evidence is disparate and spans approximately 400 years.

---

[98] Steensgaard 1973a: 58 argues that short-term weak integration of markets does not exclude the creation of broader conjunctures over the long-term.

[99] Grover 1966 provides an analysis of that sort of low-level integration in the Mughal Empire.

[100] See Scheidel 2002 for an analysis of the effects of the Antonine Plague in Egypt seen in the light of the Black Death.

Significant changes took place within that period. On top of this, the information does not originate from some of the more important markets in cross-regional trade, where the pulse beat quicker and closer integration was more likely to make its first appearance. However, we do have a few scraps of information issuing from people in touch with more central markets. One of those is provided by a letter sent from Coptos in the early second century. The city held a central position in the long-distance trade between Egypt and India, and developed into an important interregional market in the province.[101] The sender had been commissioned by a certain Apollonius to procure a number of goods there to the substantial value of a little less than 1,000 dr. The letter, therefore, offers an interesting glimpse of conditions in a fairly important commercial town and may help us to fill in the blanks. The writer tells of his careful efforts, mostly crowned with success, to secure a good bargain for his correspondent. At the end of the business report, he declares his willingness to undertake further commissions on behalf of Apollonius and then adds a bit of expert information: "the price of bullion is now 326 dr., for as you know, the prices at Coptos change from day to day".[102] Again, it is the impression of endemic and erratic local price fluctuations that seems to receive confirmation. This image also conforms to the general expectations of the Roman elite. According to the second-century jurist Gaius, prices of many important commodities such as wine, oil, grain and even credit, were likely to show strong local or regional variations.[103]

We can go further by contemplating whether it is possible to pinpoint any institutions with the capacity and sufficient power to be able to establish the long-term control of markets necessary to make them more closely interdependent. An obvious candidate

---

[101] Plin. *Nat.* V, 60 on Coptos. For a recent collection of papers, see *Autour de Coptos*.

[102] Translation, Johnston 277 of *P. Giss.* 47 (= *W. Chr.* 326). The text, however, must be read with the corrections to line 29 published in the first *Berichtigungsliste* by Preisigke from 1922.

[103] *Dig.* 13.4.3. Similar is Pliny *Nat.* XXXIII, 57. One might also adduce more literary forms of evidence. To satirists, novelists and philosophers alike trade remained an uncertain activity, a game of chance first and foremost. See Erdkamp 2005, chapter 4 for a broadly similar assessment of integration and fragmentation in the Roman grain trade.

would be aristocratic households. They often controlled enormous amounts of agricultural produce for sale, at least sufficient to make them important players on a local or regional scale. However, they did not depend on their ability to tie markets together. Their power rested on their position in the political hierarchy and in the control of the agricultural surplus. Indeed, often they seem rather to have exploited this position to benefit from enhancing the endemic market imperfections; I have already mentioned the resentment of the wealthy classes in Antioch to the various imperial attempts to alleviate a particular food crisis. Libanius gave words to the sentiment underlying the resistance. In a letter to a high-ranking official, the count of the Orient, Rufinus, he only grudgingly admitted that state interference in a food crisis had been necessary and that the interference with the "autonomy of the marketplace" had been the lesser evil.[104] Often landowners were unwilling to make even that concession. Some groups took their resistance to intervention all the way to the emperor's court: a ruling of Marcus Aurelius and Verus felt obliged to emphasise that "decurions should not be forced to provide grain to their citizens at less than the prevailing market price".[105] In general the elite did not look favourably on any attempt to reduce its capacity to exploit its economic resources. Hoarding and speculative manipulation of the market by the powerful, not least in the necessities of life during times of crisis and famine, is commonplace in the ancient sources.[106] It speaks volumes that among the relatively few directions about everyday life in the *Lex Irnitana* (a Spanish municipal law dating to the late

---

[104] Libanius *Ep.* 1379, 2 ("τὴν ἀγορὰν αὐτόνομον") with Garnsey and Whittaker 1998: 334.

[105] *Dig.* 50.1.8 (Marcianus). For this and a few similar passages, see most recently Lo Cascio 2006: 230–231 and Erdkamp 2005: 288–294 (the latter, however, makes too much of the fact that we are especially well informed about such resistance in fourth-century Antioch. That is a fortuitous coincidence, a reflection of the unusually dense preservation of the historical record in the writings of Julian, Libanius and Ammianus Marcellinus, rather than a symptom of significant social change. Dio Chrystostomus was not perceptibly less reluctant to give in to popular pressures to provide cheap grain in the early second century AD and risked being burned by an angry mob as we learn from his forty-sixth speech harping on about self-constraint to the hungry urban crowds).

[106] E.g. Philostratus *Vit. Apol.* I, 15 (treated by Garnsey 1988: 76). The Elder Cato (*Agr.* 3.2 with Nicolet 1988: 166) advised the aristocratic "farmer" to make sure he had sufficient storage capacity to be able to hoard his produce for sale in times of scarcity.

first century), we find a sombre prohibition against any kind of hoarding.[107] The political elite normally possessed sufficient social power to be able to benefit from the volatile market environment and the endemic, sometimes wilfully created, imbalances in supplies. It had no incentive to try to change things by investing in greater market predictability instead.[108] At times, exploitative, short-term speculation is even presented as a convenient solution for aristocrats in need of more cash.[109] This was an attitude the Roman elite shared with its later Mughal counterparts.[110]

Moving a step further up the ladder we find another possible candidate to exercise a stabilising and integrating influence on markets, the different segments of the imperial state. Faced with the danger of social upheaval, cities, provincial governors and the emperor occasionally all had a strong interest in checking the worst abuses.[111] But such intervention, as pointed out above, happened with a view to local conditions, not market integration. At any rate, most initiatives were discontinuous, implemented on an ad hoc basis and only during times of severe crisis to ensure social peace.[112] The big exception, of course, was the food supply of the imperial capital Rome, perhaps followed by some precautionary measures of more limited help in other large cities of the

---

[107] *Lex Irnitana*, section 75. (Though not the most recent Latin version, Gonzáles 1986 offers an easily accessible edition and with a parallel English translation.)

[108] Erdkamp 2005: 155–74 makes the important point that Roman landowners operated with a low carry-over of grain stocks from year to year. When prices were volatile, it made better economic sense to profit on high pre-harvest prices than on long-term storage. Big landowners therefore were part of a regime which reproduced market imperfections and fragmentation, *pace* Höbenreich 1997: 268–282.

[109] Suet. *Vesp.* 16.1. Whittaker 1985 suggests that there is a strong link between membership of the imperial elite and imports to Rome. Presumably senators exploited their power to gain advantages in the Roman market.

[110] Ali 1997, chapter 6, for examples. In that chapter he also treats an imperial *farman* (edict) denouncing the manipulation of the market by Mughal nobles.

[111] Apart from the *Lex Irnitana* (Gonzáles 1986) (the municipal level), one could point to evidence from papyri and inscriptions showing Roman governors ordering that stocks be made available for sale in the market, not exceeding a specified price, e.g. Lucius Antistius Rusticus' measures for a grain shortage in Pisidian Antioch (*AE* 1925, 126, trans. Sherk 1988, no. 107).

[112] The phenomenon has received full treatment in Garnsey 1988, with slightly different emphasis in Erdkamp 2005, chapter 6. See further Grenier 1997 for some perceptive comments on how ad hoc attempts to curb the market would have worked to increase commercial unpredictability rather than improve the functioning of markets.

Empire, such as Alexandria and Syrian Antioch.[113] From taxation the imperial state controlled enormous amounts of grain, sufficient to make it by far the biggest player in the field. This allowed it to organise the grain supply of the imperial metropolis into a much more settled and stable pattern than was achieved in republican times.[114] This did undoubtedly create a more predictable environment for the Roman consumer and secondary private suppliers. But the result was to a large extent brought about by crowding out the market. A very large part of the grain was simply handed out free to the citizen population as a privilege and what was left in the imperial granaries would have been sold, probably at a fairly low market rate.[115]

---

[113] Sharp 1998: 127–140 for some observations on a scheme meant to benefit the food supply of Alexandria.

[114] The grain supply of Rome has received extensive treatment. See Pavis d'Escurac 1976; Rickman 1980a; Garnsey 1988; Herz 1988; Sirks 1991; Höbenreich 1997; and Erdkamp 2005, chapter 5.

[115] The Roman state seems to have handed out grain free of charge to 150,000 to 200,000 people at an annual rate of 60 modii per person. At a generous annual consumption rate of 175 kg wheat per person this would have sufficed to feed with grain a population of 350, 000 to 450,000 in very round numbers. In other words, via the grain dole alone the Roman state probably satisfied the grain needs of not less than one-third of the population of the capital and probably closer to one-half. On top of this must be added state sales on the "free" market in the capital. Regrettably we are left very much in the dark by our sources. We should not imagine a static picture. The proportion of state sales in the market is likely to have increased as the state apparatus in the capital grew during the Principate. I suspect that during the Principate, the state would relatively quickly have become a very important supplier of the "free" market as well. From taxes, the state commanded far more grain than it needed for both the army and the free handouts. Rome would have been a convenient place to sell some of this. It is not necessary to imagine the creation of a strong centralised commercial administration in Rome. Documents in the banker's archive found outside Pompeii, the so-called Murecine tablets, show us that consignments of Alexandrian wheat were released on the market via small, individual private middlemen (*TPSulp.* 45–46 and 51–52, dating to the reign of Caligula, mention the giving of 13,000 modii of Alexandrian wheat, stored in a Puteolean granary, as security. *Dig.* 39.4.10.8 confirms that it was normal procedure for the state to avail itself of private merchants to sell the produce which it controlled). A letter of the emperor Hadrian (Oliver 1989, no. 187) refer to the state shipments of Alexandrian grain as intended for the market ("πρòς τὴν ἀγορὰν") of the capital. This may suggest that state sales were routine, which is why Nero hoped to gain on high grain prices in Rome (Suet. *Nero* 45.1). Finally, reports of an episode of speculative hoarding of state grain during Commodus' reign seem to imply that state grain played or had come to play an important role in the market (Herodian I, 12, 4 and Dio Cassius 73, 13, 1). Rickman 1980a seriously underestimated the role of the state in the grain supply because he assumed unrealistically high per capita grain consumption. See Garnsey 1988, 231–239 for a general, albeit on balance probably still too conservative, discussion of the role of the state in the Roman grain market;

The emperor did not run a commercial establishment. Movement of grain to the capital happened independently of market considerations. It was a question of state. The emperor could not, if he valued his own security, let increased demand in other areas of the empire have a decisive effect on the supplies brought to the Roman market. As Hadrian wrote in a letter to the council of Ephesos, only when the needs of the imperial capital had been served would other communities be allowed to buy state grain.[116] A bad harvest in a grain surplus-producing province such as Egypt, causing prices to rise in Alexandria, would not be allowed to have a strong effect on the market in the capital. If the emperor had grain to spare, he might open the state granaries in Alexandria or even ship back stocks from Rome and sell it at reduced rates. But this would only be done to avert disaster and the decision was taken without regard to commercial considerations.[117] Thus it is unlikely that there ever arose a very close link between the situation in the Alexandrian and Roman grain markets.

In years of abundance, on the other hand, the imperial state could dispose of far more Egyptian grain than it needed for the capital and the army. Some of this would have been exported from Alexandria to locations in the eastern Mediterranean experiencing a temporary or permanent grain deficit. This would, to some extent, have exercised a stabilising influence on the Levantine grain "market". However, as the above-mentioned letter of Hadrian to Ephesos goes on to show, being admitted to the market in Alexandria was a matter of acquiring a political privilege from the emperor or more often the prefects of either Egypt or of the grain supply. Much else other than commercial considerations was bound to enter into the decision whether access should be granted or not. Patronage connections and political influence

Erdkamp 2005, chapter 5 for a more generous estimate. As the biggest landowner in the empire, the imperial state was by implication a major seller in the market, as recently argued by Lo Cascio 2006.

[116] Oliver 1989, no. 187.

[117] See Plin. *Pan.* 30–32 on the re-shipment of grain to Alexandria to avert a famine. The fact that this occurrence received extensive treatment in a panegyric to the emperor goes to show how unusual it must have been. The same impression is conveyed by Tacitus' indignant report of Germanicus' opening of the granaries in Alexandria to alleviate high prices, *Ann.* II, 59.

would not have been the least important elements in this selection process. Josephus relates how Herod the Great, during a famine which affected large parts of the Levant, was able to secure a consignment of Egyptian wheat by exploiting his connections with the prefect of Egypt, C. Petronius. For he, "though many persons had come to him because of the same needs, was a friend of Herod and wished to rescue his subjects, and so he gave them priority in the export of grain".[118] Access to the market in surplus grain was, in other words, far from open or equal. It is not impossible to imagine that preferential treatment will often have increased market imbalances in the region, ensuring supplies where they were not urgently needed. Therefore it seems implausible to look to the Roman state, though it might quite possibly have created more stable conditions in some markets, for the creation of a set of tightly integrated markets between the core regions of the Mediterranean through the disposal of its surplus grain. It simply lacked the organisational apparatus necessary to make it respond quickly and effectively to market developments across the empire. It is telling that in the case of the food crisis in Syrian Antioch, treated above, there was no "marketing" agency which ensured that grain held on neighbouring imperial estates and in Alexandria was shipped to the city in need. That only happened at the emperor's personal intervention.[119]

Indirectly, of course, the state did promote some stabilisation of market conditions across the Empire. The development of a

---

[118] Josephus, *Ant. Jud.* 15.307. Garnsey 1988, 255–257 emphasises how commercial considerations would generally have been overruled by various political motives. Market response in the Alexandrian export market would therefore habitually have been heavily distorted.

[119] See Grenier 1997 for a related point. However, he goes further and sees state involvement in the grain supply of Rome as increasing uncertainty by making the market sector much smaller and hence more susceptible to shocks. Apart from sudden interventions, e.g. fixing a price level far below the market rate, I think this is going too far. The presence of enormous state supplies will simply have reduced the strategic bargaining power of private grain. Therefore it must have exercised a stabilising influence on the situation. However, this is not to deny that there were still occasional attempts to destabilise the market; sometimes they surface in the sources. But the contrast with the republican period is marked. Not least the risk involved in speculation must have increased in the imperial period. The executive powers of the emperor were much larger and above all faster-working than those of the republican state. He would have been able (and expected) to intervene more quickly if the situation threatened to get out of hand.

tributary empire extending over a number of diverse areas required some kind of administrative framework. Both the Mughal and Roman Empires gradually created increased monetary and legal cohesion between different regions. They also spread the use of coins and written forms of contract, in the Roman Empire, particularly in the west, which in many regions had only used such instruments rudimentarily before the conquest.[120] Though not to be belittled, I doubt that greater unity of law and coinage would have been anything more than facilitative in allowing more exchange to take place between localities. By themselves these were passive media. Roman commercial law, for instance, was mostly reactive. It did not so much drive institutional developments as develop in response to the practices emerging among traders. Law and coinage were part of the infrastructure. As such their creation did provide important support for and expand the sphere of commercial activities; but they did not constitute organisations which could actively coordinate and remould links between individual marketplaces.[121] Moreover, these institutions were not primarily meant to create unity between markets. They were designed to serve the needs of the imperial state: to ease the collection of taxes, allow it to make payments and regulate relations among its most important subjects. On special occasions that might be taken to imply a complete imposition of the institutions of the conquerors. "None of the cities should be allowed to have its own separate coinage or system of weights and measures; they should all be required to use ours", as the senator and historian Dio Cassius makes Maecenas proclaim in an advisory speech addressed to Augustus.[122] That was a statement of ideology. In both the Mughal and Roman Empires, though with variations in actual outcome and degree, the needs of the state fell far short of the creation of absolute and

---

[120] See Lo Cascio 2000c, chapter 1 for an interesting if perhaps too optimistic treatment of this. The same holds for Meyer 2004, chapter 7, treating the use of Roman tablets as a form of documentation in the provinces. The very few finds of tablets in the provinces do not warrant her wide-ranging conclusions. See Aubert 2004 on the use of writing among merchants.

[121] Morley 2007, chapter 4 is right to place the emphasis in his interpretation of Roman law and coinage on their providing some basic state services (see p. 66 for the mostly reactive nature of Roman commercial law).

[122] Dio Cassius 52, 30, 9.

immediate institutional homogeneity.[123] Pragmatism was crucial to the operation of empire.

The tendency towards homogenisation was greatest in the sphere of coinage. With the consolidation of Mughal rule under the emperor Akbar (r. 1556–1605), an imperial currency was introduced with gold, silver and copper coins.[124] Local coinages were discontinued; no new issues were struck. In some regions, for instance the commercially important province of Gujarat, the old currency remained in circulation for a considerable time next to the Mughal issues. But by and large, the imperial currency managed to establish an effective monopoly inside the realm within a surprisingly short span of time. The price the Great Mughal had to pay for this success was effectively to relinquish the ability to manipulate the coinage or pursue an active monetary policy. Instead the Mughal state made the coins attractive by striking them at almost 100% purity and by keeping the monetary system open; anyone with gold or silver could have it struck for a fee at the Mughal mint. The value of coins, therefore, was effectively identical with their precious metal contents.

The Roman state was unwilling or unable to go quite so far. The great consolidator of Roman rule, Augustus, also reformed the currency after the tumultuous civil wars of the late Republic.[125] He created a three-tiered system based on gold, silver and lower value brass/bronze coins and fixed the exchange rate between the different denominations by decree. In the western part of the Empire, the Roman experience resembles the Mughal achievement. The virtual purity of the golden aureus and the silver denarius secured their acceptance and dominance from the beginning. By the reign of Claudius, the cities of the western provinces even stopped striking their own base denominations. In the eastern part of the Empire, the situation was very different for silver and bronze. Here the

---

[123] Lo Cascio 2000c: 18, "L'evoluzione amministrativa accompagna e talora favorisce questo processo di integrazione, che è anche un processo di progressiva *uniformazione e omogeneizzazione*" (my emphasis). This is to go too far.

[124] Habib 1999, 432–435 for the basic facts. For a full treatment of the Mughal monetary system, see Haider 1997 and the various contributions in Richards 1987.

[125] My treatment of the Roman imperial coinage system is based on Crawford 1986b; Howgego 1992, 1994 and 1995, chapter 3 (with interesting comparisons to other ancient empires); Harl 1996, chapters 4 and 5; and Wolters 1999, chapter 6.

conquering power had encountered the well-established monetary practices of the Hellenistic states. To a large extent, the Roman administration was satisfied with continuing this system, partly leaving it to provincial communities, in groups or individually, to strike their coinage. Thus locally minted copper coinage of smaller denominations continued and proliferated throughout the eastern part of the Empire, reaching an unprecedented peak in the number of issuing communities during the reign of Septimius Severus (AD 193–211). A number of regional silver coinages, though now mostly issued by the imperial authorities, were maintained for a long time, in Asia into the second century, in Cappadocia and Syria into the third and Egypt only saw the abolition of her own closed-currency system under Diocletian (AD 284–305).[126] All this is not to deny that even considerable monetary transfers happened between the provinces. As is well known from later historical epochs, such transfers are possible without homogeneity and if the model presented in Chapter 2 is basically correct, those must have taken place. The aureus would probably have been the main medium for this; credit may also have played a role.[127] But the idea of the imperial monetary system as removing all obstacles to an unmediated transfer of economic resources between different areas needs serious qualification. Unity of currency only came about through a slow and gradual process. The fact that some of the most important and prosperous provinces retained valuable

---

[126] See Christiansen 1988 and 2004 for discussion of the Roman administration of the Egyptian closed-currency system. Nero seems to have exploited this to debase the Egyptian currency substantially, using the profits to fill his empty coffers in Rome and incidentally to create a fiduciary Egyptian coinage. On a smaller scale, the Roman state seems to have been able also to strike the other eastern silver coins with a slightly lower fineness than the mainstream imperial denarius (Harl 1996: 98–106). Tolerance in the east may, therefore, not just have been a sign of weakness. Compared to the Mughal state, the Roman administration was able to pursue a far more active monetary policy.

[127] Hopkins 1995–6 for the importance of the aureus in interregional transfers. Duncan-Jones 1994: 167–170 and 2003 suggests, on the basis of hypothetical extrapolation however, that the value of gold coins constituted a very significant part of the total imperial coinage. See further Hopkins 1980 contra Duncan-Jones 1990, chapter 2 for a debate about whether circulation of imperial silver coinage happened across the Empire or in regional cells. Howgego 1994 offers an interesting qualification of this debate. The two phenomena were not mutually exclusive. Significant monetary exchanges could take place between provinces without erasing all regional peculiarities in the composition of the coin population. See Harris 2006 and Rathbone 2003 for credit transfers; De Ligt 2002 for the prevalence of cash over paper transactions.

regional silver currencies for most of our period does say some-thing about the limits of institutional integration in the empire.[128]

Proceeding to the legal sphere, we find that ambiguous unity gives way to considerable institutional fragmentation. Again, the Mughal comparison offers a useful yardstick. The Mughals were Muslims conquering territories with a population predominantly subscribing to the variegated cults and practices we call Hinduism. As Muslim rulers the Timurids saw themselves as the upholders of Islamic law, the *shar'iya*. This was the law of the imperial administration and courts, supplemented with edicts issued by the emperor to tackle specific problems. Occasionally this gave rise to conflicts when imperial wishes clashed with established Islamic doctrine. However, the main institutional gap was in relation to the large non-Muslim population. The administration had, for obvious reasons, to respect the locally varying customs of Hindu law, and largely allowed the Hindu population to conduct its own admin-istration of justice. Thus within the Mughal realm several legal systems co-existed, and occasionally blended or clashed.[129]

The Roman emperors did not have to accommodate a canonical imperial law, at least not until well into late antiquity. They could therefore very gradually go further in legal integration. But essen-tially they were faced with the same problem as the Timurid rulers of north India. Roman law was primarily the law of Roman citi-zens. Originally this group denoted the conquerors. But gradually

[128] The services of money changers and assayers were, in other words, not made com-pletely redundant by Roman hegemony. This is, in any case, a problematic notion in a currency system based on the value of precious metals, as the Mughal case reminds us. Even without the need for exchanging currencies, the money changer still had an important role in assaying the genuineness, quality and weight of coins, for instance making a discount for older, worn coins. Apuleius *Met.* X, 9 shows us the need for a money changer in a transaction involving gold coins and Suet. *Nero* 44.2 distin-guishes between fresh and old coins. In general see Harl 1996, 113–122, 259–260 and Andreau 1999, 36–37 for the continued need for money changers and assayers under the Empire.

[129] Mughal historiography has not been heavily preoccupied with the legal system(s) of the Empire, but see Hintze 1997, 175–178 and Hasan 2004, chapter 6, documenting in detail the interaction in Gujarat of the imperial court with local legal customs and adjudicatory bodies. Not surprisingly in the light of the separation of India and Pakistan after independence from British rule, historians have been more interested in the religious dimension of the meeting of Islam and Hinduism and the degree to which individual Mughal rulers attempted to accommodate Hindu elements within the imperial umbrella, e.g. Hodgson 1974, 59–99.

under the emperors the right of Roman citizenship was extended to particularly privileged communities, groups and individuals in the provinces. In that way the right of citizenship spread, but it happened patchily and in an uneven pattern. The development was also far more a phenomenon of the west than the east in the empire.[130] Thus Roman citizens remained a minority until Caracalla (AD 211–17) issued the *constitutio antoniniana* and extended this right to most of the population.[131] Even after that date, however, the legal situation was far from homogeneous. At the time of conquest foreigners, *peregrini*, had to a large extent been allowed to maintain their old laws, just as they were left in charge of the local administration of justice. So beneath the umbrella of Roman imperial law a patchwork of local and regional practices and customs had continued to exist.[132] As Mitteis long ago was the first to observe, that could not have changed fundamentally after Caracalla's edict. It is a simple matter of logistics: the number of people thoroughly steeped in the complex rules of imperial law were far too few.[133] Neither was there any drastic attempt to discard suddenly provincial law en bloc. It was expected to live on, recognised as custom in a Roman law context. Thus we find Greek orators appealing to the particular customs of communities long after the dramatic extension of the citizenship, and occasionally it is possible to observe how local legal practices begin gradually to blend into and transform Roman law in the provinces.[134]

---

[130] See Sherwin-White 1973a for the spread of Roman citizenship.

[131] Though significant pockets of non-citizens continued to exist throughout late antiquity, see Garnsey 2004. As the Spanish *Lex Irnitana* (Gonzáles 1986) shows, some communities with Latin rights, a phenomenon restricted to the western part of the empire, might also have adopted Roman law. But this will have varied from community to community, see Galsterer 1997.

[132] Galsterer 1986 is a clear exposition of this. See Jacques and Scheid 1990, chapter 6. See also Lintott 1993, though he appears slightly too optimistic about the gradual uniformity of imperial law.

[133] Mitteis 1891, chapter 6. Modrzejewski 1970 provides an illuminating analysis of the relationship between Roman law and Egyptian customs both before and after Caracalla. See further Garnsey 2004, noting that the Greek orator Menander of Laodicea (trans. Russell and Wilson, Oxford, 1981) eulogised the continued existence of local customs even after the extension of Roman law to the majority of cities.

[134] The mixture of Roman law with local customs can for instance be gauged from the fifth-century Romano-Syrian law book. Mitteis 1891 remains the classic treatment. See also Taubenschlag 1955 and Modrzejewski 1970 and 1990.

In fact, the situation was even more complicated than this. Even before the *constitutio antoniniana* the divisions between the sphere of local and imperial law were never firmly settled. The boundaries were permeable. Provincial populations could and did sometimes avail themselves of Roman legal forms and brought their quarrels before the imperial provincial authorities.[135] A group of wooden tablets from the mid second century testifies to the spread of Roman forms of contract in Dacia.[136] These documents contain examples of provincial subjects availing themselves of legal forms which in strict law were only available to Roman citizens. Yet, as recently remarked by Eva Jakab, the legal niceties were not crucial to the contracting parties. They treated the Roman formula pragmatically; it provided documentation of their transactions.[137] A fairly recent find in a cave of some thirty-five documents dating from AD 93–132 in the newly established province of Roman Arabia reveal the same kind of pragmatic adaptation.[138] The dossier of papers concern the (family and property) affairs of a Jewish woman, Babatha, belonging to the village gentry in the province. We find her, among other things, engaging in a number of fairly prolonged conflicts over property which seem to have reached stalemate. In that situation, the parties try to involve the Roman authorities to tip the balance in their favour.[139] First the opponent is presented with a lawsuit at the governor's court. This was presumably intended as a threat because shortly afterwards the opponent is made a not very favourable offer to settle the dispute out of court.[140] What has especially caught the attention of scholars is the close adherence, in some of the documents, to the formulas and procedures of Roman law and litigation. All this has caused surprise since Jews were in general thought to have settled affairs in their own courts. In consequence, there has been a tendency to

---

[135] Augustus' Fourth Edict for Cyrene (in de Visscher 1940) rules that if the parties agreed to it they could have an all-Roman court. However, the Verrine orations of Cicero should teach us not to put too much emphasis on the aspect of consent to the use of Roman courts. In practice, the Roman governor must have had broad scope to exercise discretionary powers.

[136] *CIL* III, 2, pp. 921–960.   [137] Jakab 1997: 166–170. Cf. Meyer 2004: 182–183.

[138] Lewis 1989 (*P. Yadin*) has published and edited the twenty-six documents written in Greek.

[139] Cotton 1993: 102–107 for instance.

[140] The pattern can be seen in *P. Yadin* 14 and 15 and in *P. Yadin* 23 and 24.

make somewhat more optimistic assertions as to the unity of the legal system in the Empire.[141]

The evidence, however, does not so much support unity as patchy integration, fluidity and regional variation. Jews in Galilee are certainly known to have used both rabbinic and village/city courts controlled by the Jewish gentry in addition to Roman courts. In Egypt they, too, availed themselves both of Jewish and Hellenic courts.[142] If the Babatha texts demonstrate a use of Roman law to a surprising extent, they also contain testimony of major deviations, pointing to a continuation of local practice, such as polygamy and payment of taxes in pre-Roman coinage.[143] In one complaint to the governor over her son's guardians Babatha suggests she will be able to invest her son's trust fund at a rate of 1.5% per month. This probably implied lending the money out on interest. Thus there is a good possibility that Babatha in her complaint to the governor effectively suggested violating the normal Roman legal annual maximum limit on interest of 12%.[144] Roman law was appropriated by provincial subjects and adjusted to fit their own purposes and cultural contexts.

To estimate the level of penetration of Roman legal procedures it is also necessary to take the general conditions of the province concerned into account. Both Dacia and Arabia lacked *polis* institutions prior to the Roman conquest. This would make a more direct transfer of Roman institutions more likely. But other provinces complained against the use of Roman courts and defended their

---

[141] See Johnston 1999: 9–11 for a cautious, balanced attempt to formulate that position. Other examples are Nörr 1998 and Serrao 2000. Based especially on the *Lex Irnitana* (Gonzáles 1986), Hackl 1997 argues this specifically for court procedures, with Egypt alone as an exception. I find his conclusion unwarranted. It simply disregards the contrary evidence and fails to take account of differences in status between provinces.

[142] See Goodman 1983, chapter 10 for the co-existence of rabbinic, Jewish–Hellenic and Roman law courts in Galilee.

[143] *P. Yadin* 16 is a census declaration to the Roman authorities testifying continuity in money, measures and taxes. *P. Yadin* 26 documents polygamy. Wolff 1980: 797–804 rightly distinguishes between adherence to Roman procedure and continuation of local custom in substance.

[144] *P. Yadin* 15. In his commentary Lewis suggests that Babatha must have been thinking of lending the money out at interest. But he makes no connection to the maximum of 12%. *P. Yadin* 11 documents a loan advanced by a Roman centurion charging the legally prescribed maximum of 1% per month, so it was used by Romans in the area. But we should not be surprised if the suggestion made here is true. Mitteis 1891: 156–158 provides several similar examples.

legal "independence", as it were.[145] Egypt, where written records and notaries were widespread before the annexation, saw the continuation of much of her Hellenistic legal practices with relatively little Roman influence, particularly in the field of commercial law.[146] Newly enfranchised Romans in the provinces normally also seem to have retained the right to use the foreign laws of their home community.[147] This was not an empty gesture; a papyrus from Egypt shows two Roman citizens entering a contractual relationship with each other using a Greek formula.[148] Even in Italy we can find Roman citizens contracting with *peregrini* using elements of non-Roman legal forms. Among the wax tablets found outside Pompeii in the archive of the Sulpicii bank is a document pertaining to a contract for freight between the shipper Menelaos from Ceramos in Caria and the Roman merchant P. Attius Severus. In the document Menelaos, writing in Greek, declares that he has received a sum of money (the sum representing the cargo) from the slave of P. Attius Severus to be returned according to the contract for freight. On the next page follows a surety declaration by an M. Barbatus Celer, now written by a scribe in Latin. Formally, the document complies with the standards of Roman law. But it also reveals interesting deviations from the pattern otherwise attested in the Sulpicii archive. Both declarations conspicuously omit to present the obligation as arising out of a mutually expressed agreement about the contracting matter. Instead, they follow the Greek

---

[145] The Cyrene Edicts of Augustus provide evidence of this (especially nos. 1 and 4, in de Visscher 1940). They are a response to complaints from Greek provincials that they are, among other things, being submitted to Roman judges. Therefore the emperor rules that in complaints involving Greeks from different cities in Cyrene they shall, as a rule, have Greek judges and should never be judged, against their will, by a purely Roman jury panel. For the continued use of Greek law to regulate relations even at a provincial level among the different cities, see Marshall 1980. Another example of the continuing use of local law is Athens, cf. Lintott 1993: 158.

[146] Modrzejewski 1970; Taubenschlag 1955.

[147] The classic example is the *Tabula Banasitana*. Here a tribal chieftain is made a Roman citizen *salvo iure gentis* (cf. Sherwin-White 1973b). Interesting material for other aspects of this problem is provided by Augustus' Third Cyrene Edict (de Visscher 1940). It ruled that enfranchised provincials would not escape the duties of their home towns.

[148] *FIRA* III, 119: the contract was for *pignus* and the form was the un-Roman *synchōrēsis*. See also *FIRA* III, 120 with the editor's comment: "mutuum inter cives Romanos ad chirographi formam redactam". *Chirographum*, too, was not a standard form of contract in Roman law, cf. Gaius *Inst.* 3.133–134.

practice where contractual obligations are incurred by unilateral declaration: *un prodotto ellenistico-romano.*[149] Roman law did not create a homogeneous regime, it provided a flexible framework.[150]

This impression of mixture and fluidity is parallelled in courts presided over by Roman magistrates in the provinces. These will not always only have followed the prescriptions of Roman law. From Spain there is a very early illustration of this. The governor conducts the proceedings in a dispute over boundaries between two Spanish towns. He also defines the issue to the native jury according to Roman notions. But the jury is asked to reach a decision based on Spanish laws or customs![151] Several centuries later and from the opposite end of the empire a summary of some Egyptian court proceedings gives the same impression. A conflict has arisen between a certain Dionysia and her father. They take it to the Roman court. During the trial, the father suddenly attempts to close the question once and for all by claiming that according to Egyptian law the father was entitled, at any time he saw fit, to break up the marriage of his daughters and take them back into custody. The interesting thing here is the appeal to non-Roman laws in a Roman court. In this particular case, the magistrate decided not to condone the father's wish, probably on the basis of the precedent of a denial by another magistrate in a similar case. But we have several other instances where decisions are made expressly with reference to Egyptian custom.[152]

To sum up: there is no doubt that Roman law created a very gradual, piecemeal and patchy increase in legal unity across the empire during the Principate. But it never broke the pattern of strong local variations in customs and practices.[153] Indeed, implementing Roman law in the provinces required both pragmatism and flexibility. Even when Roman law was employed in some form

---

[149] *TPSulp.* 78 with the commentary by Camodeca.   [150] Jakab 2006.

[151] This is the so-called *Tabula Contrebiensis.* Cf. Galsterer 1986: 22.

[152] *P. Oxy.* 237: For an interesting discussion see Katzoff 1972. The interesting thing about the precedents cited (*P. Oxy.* 2, 237, col. vii, 19–43) is that the decision is left to the wife. So in a way Roman law does not really enter the picture. *P. Oxy.* 2, 237, col viii 21–43 cites precedents in other matters where the Roman authorities decided to uphold the local law traditions. For the co-existence of many layers of legal tradition in Egypt in general, see Modrzejewski 1970.

[153] Galsterer 1986 and Garnsey 2004.

or other, we should expect considerable variations in interpretation from region to region. It was standard legal advice to Roman administrators to allow local conditions to influence the outcome of trials.[154] That made sense. Instruments of legal enforcement were not developed as elaborately as the imperial law. Essentially Roman law left it to private initiative to execute the rulings of the court in civil law cases.[155] In that situation, as was also later realised by Mughal judges, it would often be crucial to accommodate provincial sentiments and secure the backing of the local community.[156] Such considerations are even more pertinent in evaluating cases where locals, such as the magistrates and jurors in the small Spanish town with Latin rights, Irni, most of whom would have had only a rudimentary knowledge of Roman law, began to conduct their legal business according to its complicated rules; it goes without saying that results must at times have been idiosyncratic, at least for a fairly long period.[157] Thus the situation was above all characterised by some institutional fluidity caused by the co-existence of imperial law with many locally or regionally varying practices.[158]

An illustration of how the co-existence and clash of different legal practices might at times have caused uncertainty and confusion in the trading world, is provided by a letter written in early medieval Cairo where a Jewish merchant community had to handle both Jewish and Muslim law: "So-and-so confided to me one and a third qintárs of indigo . . . This was done without any specification. I did not know whether the merchandise was given to me as a commenda or a shipment, and if it was a commenda,

---

[154] Several instances can be found in the *Digest*, e.g. 25.4.1.15.

[155] Nippel 1995: 100–112.

[156] See Hasan 2004, chapters 5 and 6 for some case studies of Mughal Gujarat showing how the administration of the *shar'iya* law of the empire was often adjusted or put aside to suit local predilections and power relationships.

[157] *Lex Irnitana*, chapter 93 (Gonzáles 1986) dictates the use of Roman civil law among the inhabitants of this small Latin *municipium*. All the confidence in strong "Romanisation" this newly found law has inspired needs to be tempered by recognising that legal instruction is not the same as practice. Jacques and Scheid 1990: 232 note rightly that even the prescription to use Roman law still seems to expect the inhabitants to complement it with local practices.

[158] See Jakab 1997, 165–220 for examples of the intermingling of local and Roman law regarding the sale of slaves. The spread of Roman law was accompanied by flexible adaptation and adjustment.

whether it was according to Muslim or to Jewish law."[159] In times
of disagreement such questions could be crucial. A ruling in a
case by the emperors Severus and Antoninus (Caracalla) from AD
204 reveals a clash of Roman and Jewish commercial customs.
Roman law espoused the principle that a stolen piece of property
could always be reclaimed from the current possessor by the original owner. This held irrespectively of how many times the object
had been sold or resold or of whether it had been bought in good
faith. Among legal scholars, incidentally, this state of affairs has
generally been considered an impediment to trade. It was difficult
for buyers to be sure that there was no theft in the past history of
goods and hence to be assured of ownership. Not all aspects of
Roman law worked automatically to the benefit of trade, it is well
to remember. But this is not what interests us here. Jewish law
took a more even-handed view of the legal problem. It recognised
the right of the original possessor to vindicate his property, but
was also concerned to protect the innocent buyer. The good was
only to be returned against payment of the sum for which it had
been bought. In the case at hand, a group of Jewish merchants had
attempted to assert this principle when some of their merchandise
had been recognised by the original owner as stolen. The emperors,
however, were unyielding in imposing the Roman law view. "See
to it, therefore, henceforth to be more careful in your dealings, lest
you may incur not only losses of this nature but also the suspicion
of criminal activity", the merchants were reprimanded.[160]

The world of bazaars in the tributary empire

Imperial coinage and law did undoubtedly facilitate market transactions, especially by bringing coinage and written law to areas that

[159] Quoted from Goitein 1967, 183. In his analysis of legal conditions in the Moroccan Suq, Clifford Geertz 1979, 192–197, too, offers a comparative example of the co-existence and mixture of local, Muslim and French colonial law.
[160] *CJ* VI, 2, 2: "Impp. Severus et Antoninus AA. negotiatoribus. Incivilem rem desideratis, ut agnitas res furtivas non prius reddatis, quam pretium fuerit solutum a dominis. Curate igitur cautius negotiari, ne non tantum in damna huiusmodi, sed etiam in criminis suspicionem incidatis." The case was ingeniously analysed by Daube 1980, 56–57, whose translation has been used above. See further Yaron 1964 for examples of differing commercial principles in Roman and Jewish law. In general, see Goodman 1983, chapter 10.

had only a rudimentary pre-conquest experience of those instruments. But it would be far too modernising to depict them as providing a unified institutional foundation for trade in the Roman world. The Empire did not create a homogeneous and solidly generalised market sphere; institutionally, considerable heterogeneity remained. Some enduring residual fragmentation of law and coinage in the empire, however, is only one aspect of the question of the continuous vitality of local and regional trading practices. But it does provide a good starting point, even if we are never likely to see more than the tip of the iceberg. Gaius, in his treatment of contracts in the *Institutes* (a manual of Roman law) includes some observations on the differences between Roman and Greek forms of contract.[161] This can probably be taken as a sign that the cultural divide between east and west in the empire also found an expression in the organisation of trade. In the papyri found at Dura Europos contracts composed according to Greek law continue to be predominant for a considerable number of years after the Roman conquest. The same goes for Egypt, where Roman influence in commercial law was very modest – in fact considerably less so than in family law – and a local variety of Greek forms of contract prevailed.[162] Talmudic literature combined with various Roman rulings (one of them is cited above) indicate the existence of particular Jewish–Semitic forms of commercial practice.[163] Various scattered comments in the ancient sources also give an impression of the existence of different customs for conduct at sea and the ownership of wrecked goods washed up on the coasts. We have, for instance, references by name to both Rhodian and Pontic sea laws.[164]

But trading practices include more than formal laws. In a ruling of the emperors Antoninus and Verus on buying and selling, the

---

[161] Gaius *Inst.* 3.93–141 (especially 133–134). On Greek commercial law see generally Pringsheim 1950.

[162] See Taubenschlag 1955: 50 on the strength of local commercial law in Egypt; Wolff *et al.* 1978 for a detailed discussion of the various forms of contract in Hellenistic and Roman Egypt; Bradford Welles, Fink and Gilliam 1959: 20–22 on the papyri contracts of Dura Europos.

[163] Yaron 1964.

[164] Rougé 1966, part 3, chapters 1 and 5 offers a good survey of the evidence, even if I do not share his conclusions in all details.

judge is advised to take into account whether price and measure have been established in accordance with the local custom.[165] The type of measure shows strong variations between regions. The picture can be filled out in greatest detail for the eastern part of the empire. The provinces of Asia Minor, Syria and Egypt each had their own predominant standards, none of them identical with the main Roman measures.[166] Locally a regional standard might vary quite considerably. In the preserved papyri, the Egyptian grain measure, the artaba, appears in three widely used forms with minor variations and a substantial number of additional local forms.[167] A curious work by a fourth-century Cypriote bishop, Epiphanius, adds to this image by depicting a world with a bewildering variety of measures and their variations. On Cyprus, for instance, two kinds of medimnoi were in use. In the coastal area around Gaza and Ashkalon a local wine measure, the sapation, could contain from 14 to 22 xestai. The xestes was again a very common measure but known in many varieties. Epiphanius lists Italic, Alexandrian, *castrensis*, Pontic and Nicomedian types.[168] The picture can be complicated further. Weighing and filling is not an unambiguous, objective and purely formal process. It involves many socially negotiable choices. Therefore knowledge of the "formal" standard was insufficient. The trader had to be familiar with the prevailing measuring habits in a particular region. According to Epiphanius, a metrétes of wine on Cyprus contained 100 xestai, but would normally be filled with 104 xestai from the press, the 4 being discounted as dregs. Another example was whether a measure was filled to the brim or with a heap on top. A gratuitous discount might also often apply as a matter of course, either in favour of the buyer or seller according to the prevailing custom and balance of power.[169]

[165] *Dig.* 18.1.71.
[166] Harl 1996: 315–318 offers a convenient overview. Hultsch 1882, especially part 5, provides a detailed survey of different standards.
[167] Duncan-Jones 1979 and Rathbone 1983a provide the best treatments of variations in grain measure.
[168] Epiphanius *De mensuris et ponderibus* (ed. J. E. Dean 1935), chapters 59c, 39, 41. See Kruit and Worp 1999 for the bewildering variety of Egyptian liquid measures.
[169] Epiphanius *De mensuris et ponderibus*, chapters 28 and 72b. See also chapter 26 for a distinction between filling the measure either by pressing down or shaking. *P. Oxy.*

We must imagine the world of the Roman trader as steeped in local and regional traditions. It would have been a regionally fragmented world not quickly penetrated by the outsider. This was partly a reflection of the great difficulties that stood in the way of creating standardisation. Even when weights clearly approach the same standard, it is often possible to observe considerable deviations; a cargo of lead ingots from the first century AD reveals fluctuations in the Roman pound between 319 and 330 g.[170] Tampering with weights seems to have been an endemic problem. Contracts therefore often specify in detail the specific set of weights to be used and where the weighing was to take place, in order to ensure some sort of control over the process.[171] The precise time for the weighing or filling would often be of crucial importance. Most products originated in agricultural processes requiring little or no processing by modern standards.[172] Organic products are highly susceptible to change. Levels of moisture in a product, for instance, fluctuate with the season and distance from harvest. Such changes greatly affect the actual volume of a given product received by the merchant. Products also show considerable geographical and inter-annual variations, due to differences in growing conditions. Grain is a good example. As Pliny informs us in his *Natural History*, a measure of grain differed widely according to its region of origin in terms of weight and baking capacity. Balearic wheat would, for example, produce 35 pounds of bread to the modius as compared with the Egyptian producing 20 pounds or less.[173] Qualities

2125 specifies that the grain has been measured with a total discount of 1.5 artabai. Duncan-Jones 1979 is excellent on all this. De Romanis 1998 is a recent, interesting attempt, inspired by Kula 1986, to go beyond traditional metrology and combine the analysis of variations in measure with social processes, even if too rationalising in its attempt to fit the disparate information into an elaborate theory of changes in bargaining power in the levy of customs on the Egyptian trade on the Indian Ocean.

[170] Based on the table on p. 16 in Domergue and Liou 1997. Such small deviations add up. In the Cabrera 6 wreck, a lead ingot of 32–33 kg might be up to almost 1 kg under weight as a result of the minor deviations (no. 14 in the table). Duncan-Jones 1982, appendix, conducts similar tests on weights found in Italy.

[171] Falsification of weights, e.g. *Dig.* 19.1.32. Control of weighing process and specification of measures, *P. Yadin* 21–22; *P. Mich.* 245.

[172] Hopkins 1978b: 50–52 is a rare attempt to take this aspect into consideration.

[173] Plin. *Nat.* XVIII, 67. See also Plin. *Nat.* VIII, 189–197 for geographical variations in wool and 19, 9–15 for flax. Wine of course is the classic example of a regionally varying commodity.

were difficult to control and prone to variations. It was not without reason that Roman lawyers discussed how wine that had gone sour should be treated in sales law.[174] As a consequence of this general condition, adulteration of goods was endemic. Wheat, for instance might be mixed with small quantities of barley and earth, sometimes even with grain which had gone rotten in the storehouses. Expensive spices or frankincense could be blended with lookalike substitutes etc. Pliny again offers a sobering catalogue of methods.[175]

The merchant had to keep his eyes open and be familiar with every trick of the trade. In this respect close knowledge of local conditions was crucial. For most areas of the empire we cannot reconstruct regional practices in any detail or assess the degree of fragmentation. But the distribution and production patterns revealed by some of the major amphorae types may serve as a pointer. Truly global productions are not found; amphorae typologies differ distinctly between east and west. Both production and distribution seem to a large extent dominated by regional and in a few cases superregional patterns.[176] Dressel 6, for instance, was firmly based in the Adriatic with exports finding an outlet in Rome, and to a smaller extent in the nearby Aegean. Dressel 2–4 was linked with the coastal regions of the north-western Mediterranean (Tyrrhenian Italy, Provence and eastern Spain). These containers, to a larger or smaller extent, all entered long- or more often mid-range networks of exchange. But they never lost their regional character.[177] It is telling that the Baetican oil amphora, Dressel 20, was never assimilated to the distinct types of Africa Proconsularis, even though the latter had a much higher carrying capacity (oil per

---

[174] *Dig.* 18.9.2.

[175] See Plin. *Nat.* book XII. On adulteration of wheat, see e.g. *P. Oxy.* 708 and 2125. Not even the emperor refrained from such practices. *Codex Theodosianus* XI, 14, 1 orders fresh wheat to be mixed with stale grain from the state granaries before distribution.

[176] The catalogue of types in Peacock and Williams 1986 clearly reveals a very regional production pattern for amphorae. For more detail, see Empereur and Garlan 1986; *Amphores romaines* 1989; Whitbread 1995, Eiring and Lund 2004. Kruit and Worp 1999 convincingly confirm the regional character of transport containers from analysis of papyri.

[177] This is not to deny the existence of cross-regional fertilisation and borrowings, such as Rhodian amphorae, influencing production styles in Italy or the production of Dressel 2–4 in Egypt. On the latter, see Empereur 1999.

kg clay). This suggests that we should model the trading world, not as a generalised market sphere, but as weak and patchily integrated system consisting of a number of segmented and compartmentalised circuits, some of only regional extent, others crossing a number of regions.[178]

The world of the Roman trader was an uneven, rough and heterogeneous place. Imbalances, asymmetries and bottlenecks in transport, goods, information and social institutionalisation, were a chronic feature. This made for relatively low transparency and high unpredictability. It was a high-risk, high transaction-cost environment.[179] Correspondingly, it was characterised by large numbers of relatively small traders and consignments of goods. Better not put all your eggs in one basket; a typical, medium-sized ship's cargo of say 50–75 tonnes contained a considerable mixture of products in relatively small quantities. There would also normally be more than one merchant behind such a shipment. From inscriptions found on the remains of cargoes in ancient shipwrecks, it is occasionally possible to gauge some minimum numbers. The Pecio Gondolfo wreck, for instance, contained small consignments of fish sauce belonging to at least four different merchants. Another example is the Sud-Lavezzi 2. Here we find the name tag of Appius Iunius Zethus on both a group of lead ingots and the ship's anchor. Shipowner and merchant are here one and the same. But inscriptions on some 235 copper bars found in the wreck reveal that the ship catered for other merchants as well, not unlike the Phoenician merchant captain described in Heliodorus' *Ethiopian Tales*; the captain owned the main part of the cargo in his charge. But the ship catered for a number of other merchants as well. The captain, so to speak, brought his own competitors along to market.[180]

[178] See Duncan-Jones 1990, chapter 3, using the distribution patterns of stamped terracotta lamps for a similar argument.
[179] On the scale set out in North 1990 the Roman Empire would have had the institutional weaknesses of markets in the least successful developing countries and most complex historical societies before the development of capitalism in the early modern European world-system.
[180] Heliodorus *Aethiopica* V, 13–15 and 19. For Pecio Gondolfo, see Liou and Rodríguez Almeida 2000. For Sud-Lavezzi 2, see Domergue 1998. On the basis of some 1,200 ancient wrecks, Parker 1992 concludes that most had more than one kind of article on board; and this is based only on the visible remains. Most organic material has long since perished and must be included in our analysis to produce a fuller image.

Students of traditional trade in the early modern Levant and Indian Ocean have referred to this sort of sociological profile of the marketplace as the pedlar-market.[181] That has been strongly challenged, with some justification.[182] Even among relatively small merchants it is possible to detect significant differences. There is, after all, a considerable contrast between the small trader riding with his donkey bringing a few goods from village to village and a merchant taking several tonnes of grain, wine or fish sauce to the market of a major city. Some large merchants surface in the main markets of that world, too. In the Mughal Empire, Surat, a nodal point in the Indian Ocean trade, boasted a small group of great merchant princes. The Roman Empire can parallel the experience, for example with inscriptional evidence from the city of Palmyra, which played a central role in the long-distance trade in Oriental luxuries: "This statue of Marcus Ulpius Yarhai, son of Hairan son of Abgaros, was erected in his honour by the caravan led by his son Abgaros from Spasinou Charax because he helped it in every possible way."[183]

Pointing out the existence of these differences within the universe of the pedlars may appear a trifling matter, easily brushed aside.[184] It is tempting only to focus on the many market imperfections of this world and reduce the merchants to powerless atoms in a seeming chaos being thrown from side to side by the elements

The small scale of many consigments of goods characteristic of pre-industrial trade is also documented by custom receipts and accounts found in Roman Egypt. Sijpesteijn 1987, appendix 1 and *O. Berenike*, published by Bagnall, Helms and Verhoogt 2000, nos. 1–117, show goods respectively leaving and arriving in peasant villages and passing the customs station in the coastal city of Berenike as part of long-distance trade. In both cases, however, goods are shipped in small quantities which could be carried by a few donkeys or camels.

[181] Most brilliantly, but also most controversially, Steensgaard 1973a, building on van Leur 1955 and Lane 1966, followed by Das Gupta 1979.

[182] Chaudhuri 1979 and Bayly 1983, chapter 11 are the best-developed critiques. But neither van Leur, nor Steensgaard claimed that there were no big traders in Asia or that there were no attempts at local monopolies. They also noted the many imperfections of early modern European trade. Steensgaard's point, however, was that the monopolies enjoyed by the chartered companies paradoxically did not distort, but began to stabilise and integrate markets.

[183] *Inventaire des inscriptions de Palmyre* X, 107. See Das Gupta 1979 for Surat; Tchernia 2000; and Curtis 1991: 152–158 for stratification among Roman traders in wine and fish sauce, garum.

[184] As Finley 1985a: 33 and 136 and Whittaker 1993, chapter 15: 5 tend to.

and occurrences beyond their influence. The observation of Clifford Geertz placed at the beginning of this chapter epitomises the dilemma. Even if the merchants lacked the social power to begin radically to transform the prevailing irregularities, they cannot be described as passive victims. The enterprising spirit and shrewdness of the traditional trader is proverbial. A central point in the new institutional economics is that high transaction costs do not only create market imperfections, they also foster different approaches to the market. They generate distinct patterns of behaviour and give rise to commercial strategies designed to cope with the many uncertainties. This is why attention to social differences between the merchants is important. They show the existence of a hierarchy and thus of a particular social system replete with institutionalised forms of behaviour and specialisation of functions. The markets of traditional trade should not be seen in terms only of one of its players, the pedlar, they constituted an entire social universe – the bazaar.

I use the concept of the "bazaar" advisedly. As a type, the bazaar describes the form of trade characteristic of complex agrarian societies; it is not identical with the cluster of petty retailers and face-to-face bargaining experienced by tourists travelling the Middle East today. These are only the sad, if sometimes still exotic and colourful, remains of a formerly vibrant trading world – a backwater now bypassed by the main currents of trade which have all been subsumed under the institutions of modern capitalism. In pre-capitalist societies, the bazaar represents the main commercial system, in the colonies of European empires, the indigenous sector. Historically, long-distance and wholesale trade, brokers and auctions have all formed part of commercial life in the bazaar.[185] Understood as a system and a hierarchy, the bazaar has involved much more than a mere cluster of shops in an urban centre. It also reached out to the periodic fairs and markets of peasant society, whose schedules, as both the ancient historian and anthropologist can confirm, were

---

[185] Failure to include such phenomena in the analysis is an important weakness of Geertz 1963, largely remedied in 1979. For these activities in India, see Chaudhuri 1978 and Bayly 1983, chapters 10 and 11. For Rome, see Talamanca 1955; Andreau 1974 and 1987; Rauh 1989; and Ankum 1972, who on p. 377 made the important observation that auction sales acquired their importance in Roman society precisely because of the absence of many modern market institutions.

frequently coordinated with market days in nearby cities. Stretching back to its rural hinterland, the bazaar also projected outwards to enter wider urban networks of exchange.[186] But in comparison with the capitalist institutions gradually evolving in seventeenth- and eighteenth-century Europe, the bazaar represented a distinct form of trade. Institutionally it had not so much begun to transform the basic uncertainties of pre-industrial trade, as it had learned to live with its asymmetries and irregularities. As a trading environment, the bazaar is distinguished by low transparency. The combination of solid roots in peasant economies, some trade over longer distances and a considerable degree of uncertainty, makes the bazaar an attractive model for the functioning of markets in the Roman Empire.

Clifford Geertz has developed the bazaar as an ideal-type and given it theoretical coherence.[187] He identifies a number of defining characteristics. Key among these are poor information, fragmented organisation and low standardisation: the features described above as central for our understanding of Roman trade. In comparison to modern markets, bazaars had few institutions collecting and disseminating generalised information, such as, for instance, price statistics. The Roman and Mughal trading world did not know the development, following in the wake of the introduction of the printing press, of widely published price information in newspapers and other media.[188] Instead merchants had to rely to a greater extent on personal connections and correspondents. The bazaar was a place rife with rumours. In terms of commercial organisation, the bazaar represents a fragmented environment. Prices differed, as we have seen, considerably, both inside and between markets and, as shall be examined more fully in Chapter 5, business was situated within a household context. Finally, there was significant variation in the

---

[186] Geertz 1979: 188–189 (for local as well as higher-level connections); de Ligt 1993 is now fundamental on fairs and rural markets in the Roman Empire; Shaw 1984 remains valuable; further discussion of the Roman and Campanian evidence is provided by the contributions of Andreau, Marino and Ziccardi in Lo Cascio 2000a.

[187] The following ideal-type summarises the analysis and description of Geertz 1979, two key sections are pp. 124–125 and 197–217.

[188] The practice of including among other omens the prices of central commodities in astrological records as signs of divine favour or disaffection could hardly have filled a similar role and there is no evidence to suggest that, *pace* Andreau 1997.

standards of goods and commercial customs. Taken together these features put a high premium on the phenomenon which Geertz in another context has deemed "local knowledge", close and detailed understanding of conditions in a specific locale. As a consequence, Geertz explains, success in commerce was less a question of generally assessing the situation across a wide number of markets and then weighing your options than it was about getting it right in your own particular market. "Sampling", of course, did take place; but the coordination of activities in separate markets was less important than in a more closely integrated system: What does it help you that you can get a cheaper consignment of cloth in a distant competing market, if you cannot be sure of its quality? The widespread higgling and haggling, which more than anything else has come to symbolise the bazaar in common perceptions, is a reflection of this problem. A prolonged period of intensive negotiation enables the parties to examine and reach agreement on all the intricate details and conditions relating to the particular set of goods on offer. It is mastery of the specifics which ensures success.[189]

This has significant implications for the conduct of trade. The bazaar should not be understood as a failed attempt to transform the many uncertainties of its environment. Instead the pervasive risks and imbalances had been domesticated, as it were. They were to some extent reproduced and perpetuated by the institutions of the bazaar. Rather than removing the endemic irregularities, the merchants of the bazaar had developed commercial strategies that allowed them to co-exist with the risks and often to turn them to their advantage.[190] A good illustrative example can be found in the report, mentioned above, made by Francisco Pelsaert, the Dutch factor stationed in Mughal Agra. Pelsaert recommended spreading and coordinating activities between different markets in order to be less dependent on the varying individual local situations and create greater continuity. In contrast, the strategy pursued by a

---

[189] See Geertz 1979: 221–229 for the logic of intensive bargaining as distinct from extensive sampling.

[190] Van Leur 1955; Goitein 1967; Stoianovich 1974; Bayly 1983, chapters 10–11; Chaudhuri 1985; Ray 1988; Yang 1998; and Datta 2000 provide a good impression of the functioning of these kinds of market.

small group of Pelsaert's Indian competitors sought to profit rather from the irregularities of the indigo trade. Instead of aiming at permanent control of the market situation, a number of Muslim and Hindu merchants, resident in the production area, bought a portion of the indigo harvest from the peasants some months in advance, sufficient to put them in a favourable position in years with a bad harvest. As a result, they controlled the local market in years of low yield and were able to pocket a temporary monopoly profit in selling to the Dutch. In good years, however, the Dutch were able to do without them.[191] Indian history is full of such, often locally entrenched, groups of traders aiming to take advantage of and increase the market imbalances in order to secure temporary, short-lived local monopolies.[192] They are not foreign to the Roman world either. One thinks of the food crisis in Syrian Antioch, treated above; or that stock character of classical moralising, the grain-speculating merchant. Often mistakenly portrayed as the quintessential capitalist relying on superior organisation to tie markets together, he represents the epitome of bazaar trade, always on the lookout to make a profit from irregular and excessively high prices in some locality.[193] Instead of integrating markets closely, the approach of the bazaar would often have been more opportunistic or speculative, with the merchant constantly seeking to bring himself in a situation where he could benefit from a market imbalance.

Such commercial opportunism was one of the strategies widely employed by merchants to navigate the rough waters of the bazaar. A second, no less important, aspect was the organisation of protection. If bazaar traders were not generally the beneficiaries of

[191] Pelsaert 1925: 15–16.
[192] Datta 2000, especially 208–220, provides abundant evidence of speculative, destabilising local monopoly strategies pursued by merchants in late Mughal/early colonial Bengal. Datta, p. 325, correctly insists that these practices were crucial for the commercialisation process in the first place.
[193] Philostratus *Vita Apollonii*, 4, 32 offers an example of the grain speculator. *SB* 7242 (= Johnston 240), is a business letter seeking to use "insider-knowledge" to create a temporary local monopoly in peaches. Rougé 1966, part 3, chapter 6, mistakes such activities for the capitalist speculator. See Kudlien 1994 for several valuable observations on the particular mixture of freedom and monopolies which made up ancient trade; Giardina 1986 for an interesting analysis of the secretive mentality of the ancient merchant.

mercantilist-style privileges, they still had to obtain a level of protection from political authorities. Customs dues can, in fact, be
understood as a kind of protection money, with all the ambiguities
this implies. Chapter 4 will explore how the price of protection
was negotiated between merchants and the "protection selling"
authorities. How this relationship was worked out, provided one
of the underpinnings of commercial life. A third mechanism which
is of great importance to the bazaar merchant is the formation of
personal relations of trust and communal ties. These will be the
object of Chapter 5. If uncertainty is high, then one way to tackle
this is to forge specific alliances. You do not as a rule do business
with all merchants, you prefer to trade with your personal connections or members from your own group, people who can be trusted
to a greater degree and who may be willing to bail you out in times
of trouble. Clientelisation and formation of group solidarities, as
Geertz explains, serve to cushion the insider against uncertainty.
But this is achieved by making the market situation less transparent and more impenetrable for the outsider. To the individual
agent, the market never presented itself as a generalised sphere
of commercial activity, a level playing field, it was only acessible
through a "limited set" of concrete relations.[194] Combined then,
the next two chapters will explore some of the distinct strategies
and mechanisms which enabled Roman merchants to cope with the
ubiquitous uncertainties and market asymmetries of a bazaar environment. If I am allowed a metaphor from epidemiology, they will
try to show how uncertainty went from being virulent to endemic.

---

[194] Geertz 1979: 217–220 (clientelisation and market fragmentation); 188–189 (the market
as a specific set of concrete limited relations); 154–172 (communal organisations);
137–138 (the relationship between protection and passage toll as underpinning trade).

4

A THIN LINE: *PORTORIUM*, PROTECTION AND PREDATION

Should you wish to abuse a tax farmer, you might try saying: oppressor, burden, garrotter, raiding plunderer, shark, fiercer than the sea, wilder than a winter storm, oppressor of the down-trodden, inhuman, burdensome, insatiable, immoderate, sleazy money grubbing sod, violator, strangler, crusher, burglar, strip-Jack-naked, snatcher, thief, overcharger, reckless, shameless, unblushing, pain in the neck, savage, wild, inhospitable, brute, reef, sharp rock, wreckage, pure animal, and all the other vile terms you can find to apply to someone's character.

Pollux, *Onomasticon*, IX, 30–31

He [the tax official] must assess accurately the value of the goods that the merchants of those mahals bring in so that no future investigation will reveal any discrepancy. Thereby the officers of that place according to the valuation may collect the proper revenues from that (merchandise) for the exalted state. Apart from the established rate, he must not take anything from the merchants.

Richards, *Document Forms for the Official Orders of Appointment in the Mughal Empire*, 224b

In his description of the route taken by the caravans importing frankincense from southern Arabia to Gaza on the Mediterranean littoral, Pliny observes how the costs of various local levies and tolls accumulated to a grand total of 688 denarii per camel load even before customs were exacted by Roman publicans.[1] Roughly speaking, this amount was equal to the annual salary of three Roman legionaries or the average per capita income of some twelve persons in the Empire.[2] This is a powerful, if admittedly extreme, reminder that one of the most important expenses in pre-modern trade was the payment of customs duties. Often it would have been

---

[1] Pliny *Nat.* XII, 32. On the Arabian trade, see Young 2001, chapter 3. The translation of Pollux is heavily modified from Meijer and Nijf 1992: 82.

[2] The ordinary annual pay of a legionary around the time of Pliny (second half of first century AD) was 225 denarii. The quantitative model presented in Chapter 2 suggested a per capita income of approximately 57.5 denarii (HS 230).

far greater than or at least similar to the costs of transport.[3] In the last chapter, for instance, we saw how excise duties quite possibly burdened even the low-value, high-bulk grain trade in the province of Arcadia in late Roman Egypt as much as or more than transport costs.

Attention is too easily focused on the high-profile phenomena of pirates and bandits when assessing the problems of ancient merchants. In everyday experience, the merchant would on average have had to deal with customs officials much more frequently. That could be bad enough. The Empire was not a *Rechtsstaat*. A routine encounter with a customs official could be a harrowing experience. At times there would not have been much to set him apart from the common bandit. As the rich vocabulary of Pollux, the second-century author of a Greek thesaurus, shows the distinction was in popular perception commonly seen as a question of semantic power rather than of real facts.[4] "There is no one who does not know how great is the audacity and recklessness of the bands of publicans", the king of Roman jurisprudence, Ulpian, added.[5] Imperial governments might on occasion, as illustrated by the Mughal set of norms for good conduct issued to its customs collectors, attempt to curb the worst excesses. But in practice it was only a thin line separating protection and predation in the trading world of the Roman and Mughal Empires. This chapter will attempt to examine the process of customs collection as a balance of power between state fiscalism, local elites and commercial agents. That balance was never primarily struck in favour

---

[3] This point has been made most strongly by F. C. Lane 1966, *passim*, and later developed by Steensgaard 1973a, 60–68 and 1981. Rougé 1966, 450–451 followed by De Salvo 1992, 317–321 recognise the important part played by customs but nevertheless speculate that the technical costs of transport and handling would have been much higher. That view is not justified, as a general rule. A papyrus may provide further illustration (*BGU* III, 697). A camel driver has transported alum for merchants in the village of Soknopaiou Nesos. The distance covered is relatively short, yet he had to pass one customs station. That already brought the payment of customs to half the transport costs.

[4] It is interesting to note that according to Ulpian it was generally agreed among Roman lawyers that a wronged party could sue the customs collector both under the special title regulating collection of tolls and under the title for simple theft and robbery, cf. *Dig.* (Ulpian) 39.4.14.

[5] *Dig.* 39.4.12.pr.: "Quantae audaciae, quantae temeritatis sint publicanorum factiones, nemo est qui nesciat."

of the merchant. The imperial peace, it will appear, may well have benefited trade; but traders were also made to pay.

Predation

Abuse of power, confiscations, racketeering and overcharging were frequently complained of in connection with the exaction of tolls. An instructive example is provided by an edict issued by the prefect of Egypt in the mid second century AD: "I [the prefect of Egypt] am informed that the customs collectors have employed fraudulent and clever tricks against those who are passing through the country and that they are, in addition, demanding what is not owing to them and are detaining those who are in urgent haste, in order that some may pay for a speedier release."[6] This is not a phenomenon which was unique to the Roman world. It seems to have been a general problem in pre-modern societies. From the many trading records, descriptions and governmental orders surviving from the Mughal Empire a similar picture emerges.[7] In a segmentary imperial formation, as discussed in Chapter 2, offices invested their holders with a personal share, as it were, in state power. Officials could and did normally expect to profit from their entrusted positions. Hence the widespread practice of state auctioning of offices, rights and perquisites. The profit nexus was never clearer than in the field of tax-farming where the state delegated part of its sovereignty, the right to collect taxes, to private contractors in return for a fixed sum of money or a proportion of the tax proceeds. Most customs and excise duties in the Roman Empire were collected by tax-farmers or, to use another term, publicans (*publicani*).[8] Naturally they would try to make their investment

[6] *P. Princ.* II, 20, col. 1 with Reinmuth 1936.
[7] Hasan 2004, 34–40 (revenue farming) and chapter 7 (customs collection); Das Gupta 1979, e.g. 164 and 206–207. For examples from sources, see the Mughal *farmans* (imperial edicts) preserved in e.g. chapters 105 and 117 of the *Mir'at-i Ahmadi* and the description by Tavernier 1889, vol. 1, chapter 2 of the payment of customs in Surat.
[8] De Laet 1949, followed by Vittinghof 1953: 384–394 and lately in part by France 2001: 433–438, argued that large parts of the Empire during the reigns of Marcus Aurelius and Septimius Severus saw a transition to direct state collection of customs. Brunt 1990, chapter 17 convincingly demonstrated that the epigraphic evidence far from supports this

pay. Thus in the system of customs collection there was a built-in propensity towards squeezing the merchants as much as possible. Abuse was never just a question of the occasional corrupt official falling prey to the temptations offered by a position of power; it was structural. [9] Even in cities where commercial interests could be expected to enjoy better representation than on average, confrontation between the collectors of customs and the traders was inevitable. The surviving customs law of Palmyra, the Roman caravan city in the Syrian desert, was precisely the product of such a conflict.[10] Not that the relationship was always a matter of brute force, confiscation or overt overcharging. The squeezing mechanism could take many forms. The customs officials had several more subtle tools at their disposal.

Often customs duties were levied at a percentage rate charged on the value of the goods carried by the traders. This required the customs collector to make a (subjective) judgement on their value. That left plenty of discretionary scope to the publican for increasing his intake by going for an estimate in the higher ranges of the normal price band. Customary practices also played a considerable role in collecting the duties. By appealing to tradition publicans were often able stealthily to introduce a host of extra administrative charges on the traffic passing through their station.[11] Egyptian papyri show how, in addition to the actual tax, a sometimes very significant number of surcharges applied as well.

interpretation. There is no evidence of a general shift to direct state collection. In any case, if such a transition did occur, it never comprised the entire empire and it would have been short-lived. From the beginning of the fourth century the evidence unequivocally shows the predominance of tax-farming. A more likely interpretation would link the changes observable in the late second-century epigraphic record to a gradual transition in some provinces from the use of large tax-farmer companies to a decentralised system of more localised contractors. While response to Brunt has varied in the detail, his broader picture seems very widely accepted, cf. Cottier 2003; France 2003; and Lo Cascio 2003a.

[9] *Pace* the apologetic and unanalytical comment by Sijpestein 1987: 90–91: "That they [the customs officials] misbehaved on occasion is only human." This simply fails to take account of the social context of the phenomenon. The widespread use of auctions to delegate the right of collection heavily favoured the interests of state and publicans over those of the tax payer, as argued by Malmendier 2002 in her study of the auctions for the Roman companies of *publicani* during the Republic.

[10] Matthews 1984.

[11] Overestimation of goods: (Ps)-Quint. *Declam.* 340 with Vittinghof 1953: 395–397; For the role of custom, e.g. *Dig.* (Paul) 39.4.4.2: "In omnibus vectigalibus fere consuetudo spectari solet" and *Codex Justinianus* IV.62.4. Gradual introduction of extra charges,

Here is an account dating from around the turn of the first century AD for the payment of the Memphis harbour toll:[12]

550 artabae of wheat, customs, 44 dr.; wharfage (?), 6 dr.; tax, 4 dr.; examination dues, 4 dr.; to the banker, 1 dr.; administration, 5 dr.; exchange, 1 dr.; to an interpreter, 2 dr.; rudder (possibly a pilot's fee), 14 dr. 4 ob.; a guard and boat, 4 ob.; for the clerks, 4 dr.; to Artemis, 1 dr.; affidavit, 1 dr.; receipt, 4 ob.; on account of libation fee to examiner, 2 dr.; total, 91 dr.

It is noteworthy how an extra 47 dr. is added to the proper duty of 44 dr., to cover various administrative charges, thus doubling the amount to be paid. The surcharges would not always have been at quite this level. Other accounts show them comprising a smaller, though still significant, proportion. A shipment of some 400 wine jars had 118 dr. added to the excise duty proper of 300 dr., including 30 dr. in *additional charges* ("προσδιαγραφόμενα").[13] In a list covering a month's collection of duty and examination fees at a small customs station in a village of the Fayum the final account is drawn up by adding to the accumulated sum of 959 dr. 3.5 ob. a further 8.5% for administration ("χειριστικόν") and exchange ("ἀλλαγή").[14] Taken together the papyri provide telling evidence of the considerable ability of publicans and administrative personnel to manipulate or influence the effective rate for the exaction of customs.[15]

The imperial states did try to constrain the activities of the customs collectors within certain bounds. Mughal and Roman emperors alike occasionally reprimanded customs officials and admonished them not to charge more than their due. But one may legitimately question how efficient these initiatives were. One cannot quite escape the impression that most were rather irregular, remote, ineffective and recommendatory in character – to

Tac. *Ann.* XIII, 51. The Palmyrene tax law (*CIS* II, 3, 3913; translation in Matthews 1984), section 1a (preamble) indicates how the flexible framework of custom gave rise to conflicts between merchants and publicans.
[12] *P. Oxy.* 1650, col. 1. See especially de Laet 1949: 317–321 for an analysis of this and related documents.
[13] *P. Oxy.* 1651. The editors wrongly published the papyrus as "account of freight".
[14] *SB* 7365, dating to AD 104. A translation is provided by Johnston 1936, no. 347.
[15] See also the express exemption, recorded by Bean 1954: 102, of the merchants from having to pay a surtax "in the name of Aphrodite or as any kind of 'declaration fee'" during a festival suspension of the regular customs dues in Caunos.

paraphrase Farhat Hasan's recent analysis of the Mughal system.[16] The British and Dutch chartered companies trading in seventeenth-century Mughal India had by imperial order been exempted from all levies inland and would only have to pay the imperial duty on exports and imports exacted at entry or exit to the Empire in the coastal regions of Bengal and Gujarat. That was imperial law. Reality proved quite different. The companies had repeatedly to defend their exemption. Occasionally the Great Mughal would issue a *farman* (edict) enjoining customs officials to refrain from exacting the illegal duties from the British and Dutch. That might help, briefly. After a short while the old ways returned and the companies again found themselves pressed to pay inland duties, irrespective of the ruling of the Mughal court.[17]

The story does not read very differently as told by Tacitus commenting on Nero's attempt to curb the most excessive abuses of Roman publicans. At the end of a list of Nero's countermeasures Tacitus makes the following sobering remark: "and there were other very fair rulings which were observed for a time and then allowed to lapse. The abolition, though, of the 'fortieth', 'fiftieth' and the other illicit (sur)charges the publicans had invented, is still in force."[18] Considering the evidence we have just seen for the collection of excise duties in Egypt, some of which was contemporary with Tacitus, it is clear that the modest success of the Neronian reform did not consist in the eradication of the demand for surcharges across the Roman Empire. If Tacitus is right, as he may well be, the lasting influence of the reform would have to be seen as limited to specific sets of customs, such as for instance the Asian *portorium*. More probably, Tacitus' observation meant no more than that the emperors periodically simply repeated the ban in judging legal disputes only to see it lapse again during the everyday practice of regular commercial life.

---

[16] Cf. Hasan 2004: 119: "Direct imperial intervention in the management of the fiscal system did take place, but it was irregular, remote, recommendatory and usually ineffective."

[17] See Hasan 2004: 116–118 and 124–125 for a translation of a *farman* by the emperor Aurangzeb dating to 1667 regarding the trade of the companies from Surat in Gujarat. See also the *farman* from 1665 contained in chapter 106 of the *Mir'at-i Ahmadi* (p. 235). See Prakash 1972 on the precarious hold of the European companies on the privileges they enjoyed in the trade from Bengal.

[18] Tac. *Ann.* XIII, 51.

The impression of relatively feeble state constraints on customs collectors receives confirmation from the legal prescriptions
and rulings preserved mainly in the *Digest*.[19] The Roman jurists
introduced a special title/action to regulate the activities of publicans.[20] The basic principle seems to have been that they were
liable for double the sum they had unlawfully taken. As observed
by the jurists, the paradoxical result was that the tax collectors
were generally in a better position than normal persons illegally
appropriating the property of others; they faced a penalty of the
quadruple amount. Therefore the jurists do not seem entirely to
have excluded the possibility that a wronged party could choose
to sue for simple theft instead.[21] But that does seem more of a
theoretical option than a reflection of the day-to-day running of
things. Why else should the jurists ever have bothered about developing and commenting upon the special title? A ruling, attributed
to the Severan jurist, Paulus, tried to lessen the gap slightly by
beefing up the penalty, if violence had been involved, to triple the
exacted amount with the added possibility of extraordinary punishments – the latter measure for the sake of "public discipline".[22]
However, generally the current seems to have run in the opposite
direction. There was a broad consensus among the jurists that an
accused publican could free himself of all further liabilities simply by returning the wrongfully exacted objects or money. Some

---

[19] In the late Empire, from the time of Constantine, the state approach towards abusive
publicans does formally seem to have become significantly tougher, in line with the
general tendency in penalties. Failure to recognise immunities or overcharging were
now sometimes ordered to be punished by death or exile (*C. Th.* IV, 13, 1 and 3; *CJ* IV,
61, 5; 62, 4). The old more lenient procedures, however were still included in the legal
codifications (*Codex Justinianus* IV, 62, 3; *Dig.* 39.4 *passim*). Thus it is questionable
whether the harsher imperial punishments ever translated into a coherent new regime
(de Laet 1949, 475–482 also emphasises the co-existence of new and old measures).
More importantly, if anything the need to resort to extreme actions such as the death
penalty is probably rather an indication of weakness than strength – the limited ability
of the government to regulate daily practice. Capital punishment is not a very flexible
tool. On balance, it would probably have become more difficult for people of moderate
status to obtain a judgement against quasi state officials such as publicans because
the penalty was so drastic and potentially much more disruptive to social peace. With
persons of influence it was a different matter. Publicans would now have found it even
more difficult to challenge such people.

[20] De Laet 1949: 444–445 for a basic, though not very analytical, treatment.

[21] *Dig.* (Ulpian) 39.4.1.2–4.

[22] *Dig.* 39.4.9.5 (excerpted from the *Sententiae Pauli,* a late third-century collection of
rulings ascribed to Paulus, but certainly not all of which were genuine).

maintained that this still applied even after a Roman magistrate had granted a trial against the culprit.[23] This, of course, would have opened an avenue for a last-minute "amicable" settlement where the obviously wronged merchant could have his goods returned without having to go through with the trial. But this has to be set against the much greater leeway such a measure granted the publicans in their negotiations with dissatisfied merchants. The possibility of returning with impunity enabled them to hold on to goods for longer, draw things out and test the stamina, determination and social clout of the opposing merchants. Given the seasonal nature of much trading, and the time and effort required to seek out a court, sometimes far away, this concession must have worked to the distinct advantage of the publicans.[24]

The relative leniency shown in the legal rules against the collectors of customs duties is in stark contrast to the uncharitable attitude towards the possessors of imperfectly declared or undeclared goods.[25] The responsibility for declaring the goods rested solely with the merchant. The publican had no duty to be of assistance with instructions or advice. Only, one reads chillingly, "care

[23] *Dig.* (Ulpian) 39.4.1.4 : "et restituendi facultas publicano vi abreptum datur, quod si fecerit, omni onere exuitur et poenali actione ex hac parte edicti liberatur." *Dig.* 39.4.5.pr., a preserved comment of Gaius, starts off by denying the right of restitution after trial has been granted. In the next sentence, he nevertheless ends up concluding the opposite. This indicates that the text might have been interpolated. But when and how, it is difficult to say. It might just be an abbreviation of a longer argument eventually leading to a less rigorous interpretation of the edict of the urban praetor. To judge from Ulpian's very general statement, there is no compelling reason to take the opinion as a post-classical invention.

[24] On a similar note, the expectation of Cottier 2003: 226 that a decision from AD 5 to remove cases concerning the Asian *portorium* from the governor's court to the *praetor peregrinus* in Rome would have enabled a more equitable administration of justice, cannot be taken for granted. The Roman *publicani* would have been well connected in the imperial capital. So that would not have prevented the working of influence. What is certain, however, is that the threshold for seeking redress via the courts would have been raised substantially. The merchant would now have to go all the way to Rome, a much more time-consuming and costly enterprise. Taking on the publicans had become more difficult, cf. Engelmann and Knibbe 1989: 120.

[25] See de Laet 1949: 437–444 for a basic treatment. It is symptomatic of the asymmetrical legal position of publicans and merchants that de Laet could make do with less than two pages for actions against publicans, whereas he spends seven pages paraphrasing the titles in the *Digest* against smugglers. See Klingenberg 1977 for a more thorough, but juridically over-systematic analysis.

should be taken that he does not mislead those who are willing to declare".[26] Falsely declared or undeclared goods were, as a general rule, simply confiscated.[27] If an error in declaration had resulted in the tax collector getting more than his due, it was apparently even necessary for the emperors Severus and Antoninus (Caracalla) to specify that the merchant should have the excess amount returned.[28] There were other modest concessions granted in the name of equity. Had bad weather forced a merchant to unload his goods from a ship without declaring them at customs first, he was not to suffer confiscation. Equally, a fragment of an Egyptian customs law states, if the tax collector had ordered a cargo to be unloaded without finding any goods not declared, he should carry the costs of unloading himself. But such mitigating measures were

---

[26] *Dig.* (Marcian) 39.4.16.5–6. According to Tacitus (*Ann.* XIII.51), Nero declared that all customs laws should be made public so people could at least read them. To what extent this happened it is difficult to say, but the very need to promulgate such a reform speaks volumes. The inscription with the *Asian Customs Law*, dating from AD 62 and found in Ephesos, shows that some inscriptions certainly were set up following the Neronian decision. But, considering the great scarcity of finds of customs laws from all over the Empire, it is doubtful whether the reform was generally implemented. The *Asian Customs Law* was published by Engelmann and Knibbe 1989. A revised version is available in Merola 2001, appendices 1–4. A new edition is now in preparation.

[27] *Asian Customs Law (MonEph.)*, lines 45–56 with Dreher 1997: 89–91. See also (Ps)-Quint. *Declam.* 359: "Quod professus non fuerit, perdat" and *P. Oxy.* 36. Klingenberg's attempt (1977: 62–65) to introduce a distinction between non-declaration and false declaration where only the former would lead to confiscation can now safely be rejected on the basis of the *Asian Customs Law*, pace Dreher 1997: 89, n.45 who attempts to rescue the interpretation by seeing it as a later legal development. There is no good reason to take such a view. Klingenberg's interpretation was based on a priori reasoning with no basis in the legal evidence. In fact, his own discussion forced him to recognise that a falsely declared quantity fell under the right of confiscation. That left only the false declaration of quality. In that case, Klingenberg maintained, declaration had actually been made and the goods would therefore not have been subject to confiscation. I doubt Roman customs officials would have been much impressed by such an argument. A merchant attempting to pass off some bales of precious silk as a few bundles of coarse, inexpensive cloth would surely, on detection, have seen his goods confiscated for smuggling. The *Asian Customs Law* confirms this. The act of making a declaration (*professio/apographē*) is treated as requiring a statement of kind, value, weight and number (*Asian Customs Law (MonEph.)*, § 18, and line 50 in particular). The problem raised by Klingenberg, however, is a real one: when could the obligation to declare be held to have been met? Some legitimate disagreement among the parties over estimates of value, for instance, must have been allowed for. It is symptomatic of the favourable position accorded by the law to the publicans that the legal material practically left open the question of when the duty to declare had been fulfilled.

[28] *Dig.* (Marcian) 39.4.16.14.

few and yielded only cautiously.[29] Favour remained firmly on the side of the customs collector. In a case concerning false declaration of some slaves, the emperors Marcus and Verus "gracefully" conceded that the poor wretch could get away with paying double customs, if the failure to declare was unintentional, by mistake rather than fraud.[30] Though certainly far preferable to outright confiscation, this was still a harsh penalty. Double duty was the sanction imposed on people who failed to defray the customs after declaration had been made.[31] But in this case, it was to be paid on some slaves who would have been exempt had the "error" not occurred. As far as one can tell from the context, the slaves were for personal use and could thus normally have been passed free of charge.[32] Confiscated goods were, as a rule, auctioned off with the profits accruing to the tax collectors and the authorities. The previous owner might even be offered the opportunity to buy back his lost property. It does not require much imagination to see how the right of confiscation and the practice of selling back the goods to the original owners might sometimes have been turned into a profitable system of abuse where people were forced to "ransom" their own property.[33]

The wronged party could of course always attempt to get his case heard in the court of the often distant Roman provincial authorities. This did undoubtedly happen, as the legal *responsa* preserved in the *Digest* testify. But litigation was and still is a slow and burdensome way of resolving conflicts. In addition it could

---

[29] *Dig.* (Marcian) 39.4.16.8; *P. Oxy.* 36. Klingenberg 1977: 70–82 makes the most of these few concessions.

[30] *Dig.* (Marcian) 39.4.16.10. De Laet 1949: 443, followed to some extent by Vittinghof 1953: 395–397, is not justified in making this a general principle. Both scholars ignore the character of the judicial pronouncements in the *Digest*. The pronouncements often represent judgements in concrete cases and far from always add up to a coherent system without internal contradictions.

[31] *Asian Customs Law (MonEph.)*, § 38.

[32] *Dig.* (Marcian) 39.4.16.10 follows in close connection with 39.4.16.9 concerning an error made by a minor in declaring the slaves for his personal use. The slaves to be returned against double duty are thus best seen to belong to the same category. Cf. *Codex Justinianus* IV.61.3 exempting soldiers from suffering confiscation of duty-exempt goods. In general, however, goods exempt from duty still risked confiscation if wrongly declared, see Klingenberg 1977: 70.

[33] *Dig.* (Paulus) 39.4.11.4, cf. 39.4.16.pr. Klingenberg 1977: 115–116 treats this as an issue of whether the *dominus* had a right to buy back his property. This is beside the point.

be fairly risky to complain about an abusive tax collector. First of all, it was far from unlikely that the provincial authorities were in collusion with the publicans.[34] Second, many customs officials would have had a relatively sizeable staff of slaves and other servants at their disposal. These came in handy during situations of conflict. The *familia publicanorum* constituted a ready instrument of power which might expediently convince dissatisfied "customers" to hold their tongue, pay up and move on. One guard, for instance, reporting about fraudulent customs collection in an Egyptian village, was delivered a severe beating by the local publicans in return for his efforts. A central concern in the section of the *Digest* dealing with publicans is how to treat abusive conduct of their slaves and other dependants.[35] Not all publicans, of course, need to be seen as equally powerful. There is a great distance separating the big and notorious Roman companies farming some of the imperial customs across large districts and the small contractors collecting dues at the gates of Egyptian villages. But whether big or small, the publicans had to be sufficiently wealthy to pledge property to the state in guarantee of the contract. They would have had to be men of at least some substance in their communities, though far from always members of the political elite.[36] Thus, whether a specific incident was ever reported to the courts might come down to a question of the power and influence possessed by the persons involved and a consideration of the cost and trouble of judicial proceedings set against the sum required to strike a deal with the publican. The balance must often have come out in favour of bending and putting up with the publicans.

---

[34] Cicero's Verrine orations are essentially a catalogue of the various ways this could happen. The phenomenon has been dealt with in Chapter 2 above.

[35] *P. Amp.* 77 = Wilcken, *Chr.* 277 = Johnston 1936, no. 348 for the attack on the guard reporting irregularities. *Dig.* 39.4.1.5–39.4.3 and 39.4.12 deal with the *familia publicanorum*.

[36] *Lex Irnitana* (Gonzáles 1986), chapters 63–64 forbids members of the local council (as well as their close kin and dependants) to contract for local *vectigalia*. This practice, however, was not observed empire-wide. See Andreau 1974 for a study of a man of middling wealth contracting for some *vectigalia* in Pompeii. On the other hand, rich councillors might on occasion bid for the collection of *vectigalia* outside their home town. A member of Antioch's council is known to have contracted for the collection of the imperial customs on Eastern luxuries passing through Palmyra, *Inv. Palm.* X, 29 (R. Drexhage 1988, no. 29).

Parasitical fiscalism

If legal regulations were heavily tilted in favour of the customs officials, it was because the interests of the imperial state had more in common with those of the tax collectors than of the merchants. Customs duties were not, as they later became in mercantilist strategies, an important tool which the government used to shape and promote economic activity in the empire. The main interest of the state in the exaction of customs was fiscal.[37] Trade was to a large extent viewed as a flow of resources which could be tapped into for the sake of revenue. Hence, in order to maximise their proceeds, neither the Romans nor the Mughals did much which would lessen the appeal of handling the levy of duties. This has made the two tributary empires look very strange indeed to modern commentators. Customs were not something mainly charged on exports, and especially imports, in order to work as an economic barrier between a state and the outside world. The imperial systems taxed the internal movement of goods as well as of those crossing their external boundaries almost indiscriminately. The empires did not totally abstain from graduating the customs and excise rates. But it happened for very different reasons and along quite different lines. In general terms, provisioning policies and consumer interests were more prominent in shaping policies. Tributary elites put greater store on well-supplied markets, to the equal advantage of urban consumption and taxation potential, than on guarding the interests of any specific group of merchants.

The sharpest illustration of this is the concessions granted by the Great Mughals to some of the European chartered companies trading on India in the seventeenth century. These enabled European traders to participate more or less on equal terms with the native population in commercial pursuits. Indeed, from a mercantilist point of view, the privileges had the absurd result that in some periods the European merchants even seem to have enjoyed some advantages in comparison to their Indian colleagues,

---

[37] Originally propounded by Cagnat 1882, the view has largely been confirmed by later research such as de Laet 1949 (with some exeptions); Vittinghof 1953; and France 1994 and 2001.

particularly with respect to road tolls and sales taxes.[38] The lack of external customs barriers is a slightly more contentious issue in the Roman case. Though convincingly criticised when it was first aired, Sigfried de Laet's hypothesis of the creation of an external customs barrier, especially on the eastern frontier of the Empire, has refused to die out and is occasionally cited with some approval in scholarly discussions.[39] The basis of this theory is the imperial levy of 25% *ad valorem* charged on the import of Eastern luxuries in the provinces of Egypt, Syria and Arabia. There is, however, not one scrap of evidence in support of the view that this very high duty was imposed to impede commercial exchanges with the East. Some three decades ago Paul Veyne demonstrated the absence of a mercantilist ideology in the Empire.[40] There is, too, the unequivocal testimony of Strabo, the geographer. In his portrait of Egypt the high duty on Eastern luxuries is treated as part of a discussion of the large proceeds generated by the Roman administration in the province. The rich trade with the East is singled out by Strabo for its revenue-generating qualities: "as far as India and the extremities of Aethiopia, from which the most valuable cargoes are brought to Egypt, and thence sent forth again to the other regions; so that double duties are collected, on both imports and exports; *and on goods that cost heavily the duty is also heavy.*"[41] If customs were exacted at an onerous rate on Eastern luxuries, it was because the trade could support them. The imperial state, motivated by fiscal concerns, took advantage of this condition and squeezed the merchants all the more tightly to exploit to the

---

[38] Prakash 1998: 119–134 and Hasan 2004: 113–119 and 124–125 for the different sales tax, road toll and customs rates in seventeenth-century Mughal India. More generally, Pearson 1991: 96–98 and 110–113 and Richards 1993a: 203.

[39] Especially France 1994: 142. See Dreher 1997: 85 for a more reserved endorsement. For the original critique of de Laet, see Étienne 1952 and Vittinghof 1953: 378–384.

[40] Veyne 1979.

[41] Strabo XVII, line 13 (my emphasis). There are other examples of increased customs to take advantage of an unusually rich trade. One such is the attempt to tap into the wine trade with Gaul in the last century of the Republic, reported by Cicero in *Pro Flacco* 9, 19–20 ("*pecuniam permagnam* ratione ista cogi potuisse confiteor", my emphasis). The highest rate was charged on wine leaving the Empire as a luxury intended for *barbaricum*. Yet another instance is the taxing of purple shells at twice the normal rate in the *Asian Customs Law* (*MonEph.*, line 20).

full the revenue-generating potential of this particular branch of trade.[42]

In the absence of a strong, systematic mercantilist impulse in the tributary empires, the fiscally dominated approach to the exaction of customs did nonetheless on occasion give way to other objectives.[43] In both empires we find examples of the state extending customs privileges to some groups or activities.[44] But concessions were rarely, if ever, granted with a strong wish to remould the economic system. The motives were different, mainly political or ideological in nature. In the Mughal Empire this is brought out clearly by the attempt of the last great Mughal emperor, Aurangzeb (1658–1707) to favour Muslims over Hindus with regard to the payment of imperial excise duty, the *zakat*. In a *farman* of 1665 he set the rate for Hindus at 2/40 and for Muslims at 1/40. Two years later he went even further and abandoned the duty for Muslims altogether. This happened as part of a policy to boost Muslim imperial primacy. The policy, however, had unexpected consequences. In the eyes of the emperor Muslim merchants abused their newly acquired privilege. They began to handle the goods of their Hindu colleagues on payment of a commission fee. That way the Hindus avoided the imperial excise duties and the Muslims made an extra profit. The loser was the Mughal treasury, which saw the income from customs dwindle. This was not what the government had in mind. The exemption was intended as a political and ideological symbol of the religious supremacy of Islam – "that the Muslims may be distinguished with obligation and kindness from vicious unbelievers", as an imperial order stated. The privilege had not been granted with a view to creating a Muslim commercial dominance in the Empire. Hence in 1681, after a little more than a

---

[42] For an analysis, looking at archaeological traces of customs exaction on the eastern frontier, also emphasising the predominance of fiscal motives, see Young 2001: 66–74 and the general discussion in chapters 5 and 6.

[43] Ørsted 1985: 288–289 tries to detect a protectionist dimension in the fiscally motivated exaction of customs. This is unconvincing and is based purely on speculation. All exaction of customs tends to make the movement of goods more expensive. This is an inevitable effect of tolls and cannot be seen in itself as the result of protectionism.

[44] France 1994: 143–144 is right to insist that Roman customs cannot be entirely reduced to a fiscal question. But admitting this does not commit one to go searching for mercantilist measures. Political and ideological objectives should not too readily be brushed aside.

decade, the exemption was cancelled and imperial excise duty was reintroduced for Muslims.[45]

The same concern with limiting the fiscal effects of politically motivated concessions occurs frequently in Roman policies. The *Asian Customs Law* recently found on an inscription in Ephesos contains several examples. Among the privileges granted to the colony of Augusta Troas, (re)founded by Augustus, was the grant of the right to the imperial customs on goods imported or exported from its territory. However, goods which were passing through in transit, still fell under the rights of the publicans appointed by the Roman state.[46] The aim, in other words, was to grant an economic privilege to a politically favoured community, not to make Augusta Troas a dominant emporium. The same goes for the exemption from customs for thirty days granted on imports, but not exports, to the territory of most probably Pergamon and its harbour city Elaea, in order to facilitate supplies for the politically important festival of the Romaia Sebasta.[47] If we change our perspective from individual grants of privileges to general imperial policies, the impression is confirmed.

The Roman state did exempt some groups and activities from duty across the Empire. This comprised, among other things, all transports of state-owned "goods", and goods belonging to

---

[45] *Mir'at-i Ahmadi* contains the Mughal *farmans* dealing with the gradation in the rate of duties. See chapter 121 and the following for the cancellation of Muslim customs exemption (citation in chapter 121); chapters 104, 108 and more broadly 97 and 120 for the introduction of Muslim privilege, cf. Hasan 2004: 117. For a broader treatment of Muslim religious privilege, see chapters 97 and 120 of *Mir'at-i Ahmadi*; Richards 1993a: 171–177; and for some modern treatments, see Hodgson 1974, vol. 3: 92–98.

[46] *Asian Customs Law (MonEph.)*, lines 103–105 with Engelmann and Knibbe 1989: 114–115.

[47] *Asian Customs Law (MonEph.)*, lines 128–133 with analysis in Engelmann and Knibbe 1989: 125–129. See de Ligt 1993: 42–48 and particularly 222–234 for the dominance of symbolical and consumerist motives involved in the granting of festive *ateleia* combined with a strong continued imperial fiscal interest. This, of course, does not rule out that such privileges may also occasionally have turned out to be of benefit to transit trade as well. But it was not normally the main purpose. The elevation of Delos, by the Roman authorities in the second century BC, to the status of a free harbour to harm the central position of Rhodes in the eastern Mediterranean trade may be thought to constitute evidence to the contrary. But not even here was trade the motivating force. The action was taken as punishment for wavering Rhodian support during the Third Macedonian War and included stripping the island state of her Anatolian dependencies as well, Scullard 1980: 287.

military personnel and veterans.[48] Such exemptions were used, no
doubt to some extent successfully, as we would expect from our
Mughal parallel, to gain commercial advantages.[49] Private contractors transporting state goods, for instance, attempted to mix
their own goods with the official cargoes to avoid paying customs.
Soldiers would engage in trade and exploit the exemption to gain
the edge in the competition with private merchants. These were
inevitable consequence of political privilege. In the view of the
imperial state, they were also unfortunate, causing an unintended
loss of revenue. Repeatedly the state tried to contain these practices
and diminish its economic loss.[50] The emperor Hadrian instructed
provincial governors, legionary commanders and their procurators
when they dispatched people to buy things for their personal use
to write a memorandum for the customs collectors indicating the
exact amount ordered "so that anything brought in excess can be
subject to duty".[51] In the *Asian Customs Law* we read generally
that the exemption for state transports also included the people
who operated them. But only on items for their own use. This was
similar to the arrangement for soldiers. Their freedom from excise
was limited to items for personal use. If the goods were intended
for trading, customs were due according to normal rules.[52] When
the tributary state granted customs privileges it was not in pursuit
of a general economic policy. The goal was more limited. Privilege was awarded in a more narrow trade-off that jealously sought

---

[48] De Laet 1949: 427–431 and 432–435 for a broad survey of the material. Normally the
instruments of travel were exempt for all persons.
[49] As pointed out by Whittaker 1994a, chapter 4.
[50] In addition to the following examples, *Dig.* 39.4.9.8, excerpted from the spurious
Sententiae Pauli, deserves mentioning. It states that while the imperial fiscus is free
from all duties, the merchants who market imperial goods cannot claim any general
exemption from customs.
[51] *Dig.* (Gaius) 39.4.5.1.
[52] *Asian Customs Law (MonEph.)*, lines 58–66. Tac. *Ann.* XIII, 51. The privilege of soldiers
is later mentioned in *Codex Justinianus* IV 61, 7 (discussing a late imperial sales tax)
and again they are not exempt in matters of buying and selling. Constantine introduced
immunity for all *navicularii*, the transporters serving the state, even for goods they
intended to sell (*C. Th.* XIII, 5, 5 with de Laet 1949: 480 and De Salvo 1992: 259).
But the title of *navicularius* was connected with obligations and it is symptomatic that
the Roman state, just as the Mughal, did not look favourably upon the habit of some
navicularii to carry the goods of others. Hence *C. Th.* XIII, 5, 24 specifies: "navicularii
are exempt when it is proved that they do business for their own account (cum sibi rem
gerere probabuntur)".

to safeguard the state fiscal interests while giving recognition to groups and individuals that for one reason or another were deemed important to the political order, be it, for example, as soldiers, governmental transporters or as those involved in significant religious activities.

The imperial state did not have much incentive for changing the predominantly fiscal approach to the commercial sector. Neither in the Roman nor in the Mughal Empire had expansion ever been closely tied to collaboration with commercial groups. Therefore the tributary state had no compelling reasons to forgo revenue in the short-term by favouring specific groups of traders. As the empires grew and the amount of trade inside the boundaries expanded to ever greater dimensions, compared to exchange with the world on the outside, this became even more the case. From the perspective of the treasury there was not much to be gained, except loss of revenue, from helping one group of merchants to capture a greater share of a largely internal commerce at the expense of other traders in the empire.[53] Instead, the exaction of customs was directed to take profit on existing trade flows irrespective of their direction. Hence excise and other trade-related dues were regularly levied in nodal points or on traffic arteries where many goods more or less had to pass, such as at city gates, harbours, highways, river crossings, bridges and in the bazaars.[54] Customs were in the Roman world to a very large extent passage tolls.[55] It was not uncommon to levy the tax on the same goods both on entry

---

[53] The first European mercantilist "economists" saw the global economy as a zero sum game too (Anderson 1974). However, as the states were much smaller the advantage to be gained from capturing a greater share of the international economy at the loss of foreign competitors was all the more apparent. Only later, particularly in the eighteenth century, did the notion of real growth develop on the basis of these ideas. Though it would be wrong to claim any automatic link between full-blown mercantilism and small states in a partly internationalised economy, it still seems clear that commercial interests could be better heard in such systems. Thus without developing real mercantilist policies, the Mughal successor states in eighteenth-century India did give more attention to commercial groups than their imperial predecessor (Bayly 1988: 1–78).

[54] *P. Oxy.* 1439–1440; *ILS* 375 (collection at city gates); *Asian Customs Law (MonEph.)* chapter 21 (customs office close to the landing of ships); *P. Oxy.* 1650 (Memphis harbour tax, excise at administrative district border); *OGIS* 674 (road tax); *AE* 1975: 413 (riverbank); *Dig.* 19.2.60.8 (bridge crossing); *P. Lond. Inv.* 1562 verso (market tax).

[55] Now again confirmed by France 2001, summarised in the conclusion. However, France seems to me to underestimate the possibility of double customs payment, cf. note 57 below.

and exit through a customs district or station.[56] Consignments of goods travelling beyond the confines of their nearest region would also normally have had to pay several tolls, sometimes at a considerable number of stations. Customs multiplied with the distance travelled.[57] The tendency for excise duties to accumulate is aptly illustrated by some tax receipts found among the Egyptian papyri.

[56] De Laet 1949 and Vittinghof 1953: 375–378, and now confirmed by the *Asian Customs Law*, which applied to both imports and exports, cf. Dreher 1997. However, the notion is difficult to reconcile with modern sentiments and doubts continue to be voiced without any good reasons, e.g. France 1994: 138–139. A letter from Cicero (*Att.* II, 16, 4) reveals that the Asian *publicani* even tried to make merchants pay the Asian import duty again when they moved from one city to another inside the province. It may also be noted that the *Asian Customs Law* (*MonEph.*, lines 16–20) exempts people from paying imports or exports twice on the same goods, in the same year, at the same customs station. Thus, if a merchant had taken his goods to a city in the province of Asia and paid the import duty, if he then left again with some of his goods and returned later in the year he would not have to pay customs on the same items again. The publishers (Engelmann and Knibbe) typically prefer to take this to mean that the merchant was exempted from paying re-export duty on goods already paid for at entry. This is not supported by the inscription which clearly deals with exports and imports separately. On Egypt, see also Sijpesteijn 1987, chapter 5, who accepts the principle but believes some goods to be exempt, especially wine, which he takes to be taxed only on entry. But a look at Sijpesteijn's data makes it clear that his conclusion is more likely to be a reflection of the prevailing flow of goods in the villages whose records have been preserved than evidence of avoidance of double payment. Thus wine was imported in small quantities, whereas oil was sent out. Hence wine is documented in relation with imports and oil with exports from the villages.

[57] Rougé 1966: 450, emphasising the accumulative burden of excise dues. See further Ørsted 1985: 285–289, followed by De Salvo 1992: 317–321 and France 1994: 140. Drexhage 1994 and Drexhage, Konen and Ruffing 2002: 145–147 underestimate the number of customs exacted. They strangely ignore the evidence from Egypt, where customs receipts reveal the district duty of the Memphis harbour tax being added on top of city customs (cf. n.59). Purcell 2005 insists, to my mind rightly, on the ubiquity of local customs, yet maintains they did not accumulate (pp. 220–222). That seems counter-intuitive, not to say a contradiction in terms. The customs inscription from Caunos (*SEG* XIV: 639), cited as evidence, does not prove that customs were never paid on goods in transit. Quite the reverse, the inscription (very fragmentary) describes a regime of exemptions paid for by a local benefactor, propably as a suspension to encourage imports in connection with a periodically recurring religious festival (cf. Schwarz 2001b: 288–289). Other customs laws, such as the regulations concerning the *portorium* collected in Asia, do not as a rule mention a specific exemption of transit goods. Indeed, both the customs regulations preserved from the Lycian *koinon* and the province of Asia envisage taxing transit goods. Augusta Troas and Myra each had the right to collect these respective customs on goods sold within their own districts. Those just passing through, however, had to defray duty to the collectors of the province and the *koinon* (*MonEph.*, lines 103–105; Schwartz 2001a). Equally, Purcell refers to the transit dues collected by Massilia at the mouth of the Rhone (Strabo 4.1.8). But merchants also had to pay the imperial customs on entering the Gallic provinces. Dues would have been accumulating with distance.

By chance, several receipts have survived documenting the payment of different customs on the same consignments of goods. Thus we find small amounts of wheat, travelling a fairly short distance northwards from the village of Philadelphia, paying three separate duties: one for leaving the nome, one for using the desert road and one for the so-called Memphis harbour tax.[58]

It is noteworthy, too, how the different Egyptian tolls tend to be connected with different levels in the state system. The Memphis harbour tax was charged on goods crossing between the larger administrative districts, the so-called *epistrategia*, while there was also a more local tax for leaving the primary administrative unit, the nome. This is a typical feature of segmentary state systems. They consisted of many parts which both tried and had to be allowed to tap into the economy and get their share of the tribute. An analysis of the structure of Mughal customs collection in the province of Gujarat makes the principle clearer. The central state exacted a customs-cum-sales tax on all movement of goods in the province. In addition to this there were numerous local tolls of various kinds. These were controlled by the various aristocratic groups that together made up the state on the ground. The central Mughal state did formally claim to exercise authority over the local levies. Some of them were even gradually being drawn into the orbit of the imperial system, as they became part of the revenue assignments of Mughal nobles, the so-called *jagirdars*. But that was as far as it got. When the state attempted to exercise closer control, for instance by outlawing local dues or reducing their number, it encountered stiff opposition. The *Mir'at-i Ahmadi* – a history of Gujarat – reports how on one occasion aristocrats demanded economic compensation if they were to accept such an abolition. In that situation there were essentially two options open to the state to defend its policy, neither of which was very attractive. It might try to hold its own and compel the noblemen to agree to respect the ban. In the long-term this was bound to be ineffectual. Aristocrats were not generally inclined to accept having their incomes reduced, especially not when they were running

---

[58] P. *Customs*, list 1, nos. 139–141, see also nos. 184–186, 355–356, 362–363 and 419–421 with Sijpesteijn 1987: 19.

things on the ground. Alternatively the state might grant the aristocrats compensatory incomes. As a general solution, however, this
was equally problematic in the eyes of the imperial government;
it was expensive and diverted scarce resources from other activities. So either way, the government tended to back away from
the abolition of local dues and allow their continued collection
or silently tolerate their reintroduction after a short term of suppression. The revenue pressure exerted by the different segments
of the Mughal polity consolidated the existence of a customs and
excise regime with frequent collection points and the co-existence
of many separate dues.[59]

This mechanism can be seen at play in the Roman Empire, too.
During the high Empire most regions of the realm were divided
into a number of large, separate customs districts where toll was
collected in the name of the Roman state on entry or exit. The exact
nature of these districts is not entirely clear, but they bore some
relation to provincial divisions, without necessarily being strictly
identical. The Asian *portorium*, for instance, was clearly arranged
around the core of the old Attalid kingdom that made up the bulk
of the province of Asia Minor. But to this were added, among
other things, the customs collected in the strait of the Bosporus,
even though this area was outside the provincial boundaries of
Asia.[60] Beneath the umbrella of imperial excise duties the existence of a system of locally based tolls and levies is attested by our

[59] *Mir'at-i Ahmadi*, chapter 117. See Hasan 2004, chapter 7, for the customs system in
Gujarat. Pp. 114–121 are particularly relevant for the analysis presented here. In general
about the many tolls in the Mughal Empire, see Habib and Raychauduri 1982: 186–189.
The East India Company after the conquest of Bengal attempted the cancellation of such
tolls but ultimately found the resistance from local elite groups too strong (Chatterjee
1996, chapter 5).

[60] *Asian Customs Law (MonEph.)*, lines 22–28 defines the Asian customs district; see lines
8–11 and 13–15 for exaction of customs in the strait of the Bosporus, cf. Nicolet 1993:
945–951. Some customs districts seem to have comprised several provinces, though
without losing all relation to the administrative framework, as in the cases of Gaul and
Illyricum, cf. de Laet 1949 for these larger circumscriptions. France 2001 treats the
Gallic *portorium* anew. He rejects the notion of circumscription and concludes that the
quadragesima Galliarum was a passage toll separating Italy from the north-western
provinces. I am not entirely convinced. He seems to be misled by the chance preservation of evidence in the Alpine regions. See Ørsted 1985: 251–347 for an interesting,
but speculative and over-complex analysis of the material pertaining to the Illyrian
portorium.

sources.[61] To some extent this has militated against the preconceptions of modern researchers expecting to find a rigorously defined legal, coherent administrative system in the Empire. They have therefore suggested various ways around this so-called problem. For instance, it has been claimed that these tolls were primarily collected by communities that in legal terms were outside the imperial system, the so-called *civitates liberae ac foederatae*.[62] There is no strong evidence in support of that proposition. One of the best-preserved inscriptions with an example of a local customs law was found in Palmyra. The inscription was erected in the reign of Hadrian. At that time the city had formally been part of the province of Syria for more than a century.[63]

Another way out of the "predicament" has been to claim that local tolls were a feature of the Greek east, whereas the Latin west was largely without this phenomenon.[64] That is unconvincing. An *octroi* was collected at the very gates of Rome, the capital.[65] It is undeniable that in terms of sheer wealth of epigraphic testimony local dues are far better attested in the eastern provinces than elsewhere, but this is more likely to be a function of the epigraphic record than anything else. It is worth reminding ourselves that the sources are fragmentary traces rather than a direct reflection of

[61] France 1999 admirably updates the material first gathered by de Laet 1949: 351–361. See Schwarz 2001b, III, 4 for an excellent treatment of local customs exaction in Anatolia. Outside the province of Egypt, the large rabbinic literature connected with Judaea has yielded some of the best evidence for the density of customs collection, cf. Goldschmid 1897: 199–202.

[62] France 1999: 99–100 (and more broadly France 2001) surprisingly reverts, it seems, to the notion of Rostovtzeff 1902: 390 (and, it would seem Frank 1933–40, vol. I: 255) that the right to collect local *portoria/vectigalia* was restricted to *civitates liberae ac foederatae*. This view had already been exploded by de Laet 1949: 90 and 351 (and now confirmed by Schwarz 2001b: 338–406), who observed that formal legal status was not decisive. Quite the reverse, we even find attempts to levy the imperial *portorium* in "free" communities, e.g. Byzantium.

[63] Young 2001: 137 summarises the evidence on the status of Palmyra: "the city should accordingly be understood as a tributary city of the province of Syria". Within modern Palmyrene studies, the notion has gained currency that the city became a *civitas libera* following a visit of Hadrian, during which the city changed its name to Hadriana Tadmor. This does not affect our argument since the tax law, as is clear from the inscription, also existed during the first century of Roman rule. However, as observed by Fergus Millar (1993: 325), this modern assertion is completely baseless and may safely be discarded. Under Septimius Severus, the city was made a Roman *colonia*.

[64] De Laet 1949: 353 and France 2001: 278–283, who essentially restricts the phenomenon for all Gaul to Massilia.

[65] *CIL* VI, 1016a = *ILS* 375 with de Laet 1949: 347–349.

the ancient reality. The challenge is to interpret the nature of the lacunae in the material. If positive evidence is scarce in the western Empire, there are nevertheless indications that local excise duties were as much a part of life there as they were in the Greek-speaking east. Cities across the Empire were expected to possess their own *vectigalia* – taxes accruing, for example, from the leasing of communal lands, pasturage and, not least, various dues on commercial traffic. It seems improbable that cities in the western provinces should, en bloc as it were, have abstained from levies of different kinds on the movement of goods.[66]

Imperial conquest, in other words, did not eradicate the existence of locally administered dues on trade. The conquerors tolerated their continuance. As in the Mughal Empire, local government needed financing and the provincial aristocracies did not bear the entire burden themselves. Formally, the Roman state did claim some sort of sovereignty over these tolls. At the time of inclusion in the imperial fabric, the local community would normally have received the right to continue or begin the collection of some such taxes. In the eyes of the Roman state the post-conquest settlement could not be changed without its express permission. The introduction of new dues required imperial sanction based on the recommendation of the provincial governor, as Vespasian made clear in reply to a request from the Baetican community Sabora.[67] Gradually the "hunger" for tribute led the Roman state to confiscate and absorb more and more of these tolls into the imperial revenues. This happened slowly and piecemeal, apart from in Egypt where the state had already successfully come to control local dues before the Roman annexation.[68] In the rest of the Empire, the development culminated in the fourth century when different emperors made several attempts to clear the table and include all local *vectigalia* in the imperial taxes.[69]

---

[66] For *vectigalia*, see *Lex Irnitana* (Gonzáles 1986), chapter 76; Sabora (*CIL* II, 1423). See Rougé 1966: 449 for a similar point of view.

[67] *CIL* II, 1423, confirmed by *Dig.* (Hermogenian) 39.4.10.pr.

[68] Cf. some of the scattered comments in different historians about the usurpation of local *vectigalia* by emperors. For example, Suet. *Tib.* 49.2; *Vesp.* 16.

[69] Jones 1964: 732–733, who dates the general confiscation of local *vectigalia* to the reigns of Constantine and Constantius II. After its initiation, the fortunes of this policy fluctuated considerably. Julian abandoned it. Then it was reinstated. Then the cities

That was far too ambitious. Even when the imperial *fiscus* had achieved some sort of control, it was still forced to recognise local claims on these taxes, both in Egypt and the rest of the Empire. This normally happened in the form of allocations to local institutions of a proportion of the proceeds from a given tax.[70] Julian, in a temporary setback for the expansive policy, went further and simply restored the old *vectigalia* to the communities.[71] His successors reversed this decision. But it is doubtful if they ever achieved more than partial success. Some local dues continued to evade imperial authority as they had in the preceding centuries. From the first through to the fourth century AD the emperor and his administration repeatedly found it necessary to enjoin local councils that they were not allowed to institute new customs and excise dues of their own accord without imperial sanction.[72] For the most part, imperial control, when it worked at all, is likely to have been relatively lax and discontinuous. The customs law found in Palmyra offers a fascinating glimpse into this. The surviving version, inscribed on stone in AD 137, set out to revise the regulations for the local collection of tolls. However, it also preserved the older version and a few rulings by Roman officials in former disputes. What is particularly interesting to note is that a Roman governor had apparently been present when the old version was agreed upon. The new law, on the other hand, appears to be entirely the work of the local council acting independently of the Roman provincial authorities.[73] In the light of this, it is difficult to speak of a unified customs policy in the Empire. Roman hegemony did not lead to the creation of a single customs regime. The central state only partially

were granted a proportion of the customs proceeds. Then these were again confiscated and later granted yet again. I doubt if we should take this narrative as a reflection of how things worked out on the ground. Rather the line of events suggests only partial or limited implementation of the imperial enactments. For similar scepticism about the success of these measures, see de Laet 1949: 462.

[70] For grants of part of the customs to the city councils, see *C. Th.* IV, 13, 5 and 7 and *Codex Justinianus* IV, 61, 13. The market tax of the Serapeum in Oxyrhynchus (*P. Lond. Inv.* 1562 verso) was quite possibly allocated to the temple (Rea 1982).

[71] Amm. Marc. XXV, 4, 15. A very important element in Julian's measure was the restitution of temple property.

[72] *CIL* II, 1423; *Dig.* 39.4.10.pr; and *Codex Justinianus* IV, 62, 1–4.

[73] Compare the decree of the council of Palmyra, which introduces the tax law, with the heading of the old law given later in the text. In Matthews 1984 this would be section 1a with 2a. See further Rougé 1966: 448 in a similar direction.

controlled the exaction of tolls; it had to recognise or silently tolerate a probably very significant number of additional local titles to tax existing trade flows. If tributary empires did not generally erect tall customs barriers between their subjects, they did not do much to promote long-distance trade by abolishing internal tolls either. Instead, the fiscal interests of the different segments of the imperial system were allowed to dominate and the movement of goods was slowed by the need to defray the costs of a potentially considerable number of duties.

Merchant response and bargaining power

Yet, commerce did not grind to a halt. The publican had to balance his short-term interest in squeezing the merchant against future loss of revenue if the continuation of commerce was jeopardised. This gave the merchants a far from insignificant bargaining power vis-à-vis the customs collector. The imperial state did not only find it hard to exert a tight control over customs exactions; in addition its representatives experienced similar difficulties in monitoring and regulating trading activities. Merchants were not always easy prey. Both they and their goods were mobile. This made them difficult to tax.

Should the imperial authorities happen to forget, the lesson was regularly repeated. In the late seventeenth century the Mughal state attempted to change the procedure for the collection of a sales tax, *zakat*. Whereas merchants had formerly paid the tax at the time of purchase, they were now ordered to pay at the time of sale. The chronicler of the *Mir'at-i Ahmadi* explains:

the collection of tax at places of sale was decided upon because the price of an article is higher at that place than at that of purchase. It thus means an increase in revenue. But as the merchants sold many commodities at places where collection of taxes was not regular, the government suffered losses. An order was, therefore, issued a second time for its collection at places of purchase.[74]

The problems encountered by the Mughal authorities in raising the sales tax mirror the experience of the Roman state in the

[74] *Mir'at-i Ahmadi*, chapter 126 (p. 284 in the translation of Lokhandwala).

collection of the so-called *collatio lustralis* or *chrysargyron*, a tax instituted by Constantine to be collected every five years from merchants and other businessmen. The emperors, Theodosius and Valentinianus prescribed "that no more should furtive commerce render the merchant rare in the glorious cities and the throng of traders hide in obscure and secluded places to the loss of public revenue".[75] The reach of public power, always a precarious thing in the agrarianate world, was particularly weak outside cities and the main traffic routes. The world of Mughal and Roman merchants alike was not only one of traditional abuse, it was also one of equally traditional freedom, to paraphrase the late Ashin Das Gupta.[76] Merchants, therefore, were often tempted simply to circumvent taxation by conducting business in some remote village or bay far away from the toll station and hungry glances of customs officials. Quantification is out of the question, but smuggling is bound to have been rife and to have gone largely undetected.[77]

Relocating business to more remote areas did, of course, have some drawbacks. The traders would lose the central-place services offered by cities, such as a greater concentration of buyers and sellers. They would also be outside the protection of the law and hence more vulnerable to predation by bandits and powerful landowners. Smuggling carried risks, but it offered enough of an alternative to be a serviceable defence against new taxes or unusually abusive or frequent customs exactions. In practice, the flexibility of the merchant did impose some restrictions on the conduct of customs officials. It did not prevent arbitrary predation but in the aggregate it would have exercised a moderating influence, both on the conduct of officials and on the total tax burden; hence the generally relatively low official customs rates, most lying between 2% and 5% in the Roman and Mughal Empires.[78]

---

[75] *C. Th., N. Val.* 24: "ne ulterius furtiva negotiatio et claris urbibus rarum faciat mercatorem et obscuris ac reconditis locis in damnum publicae functionis lateat turba mercantum".

[76] Das Gupta 1987: 136; Hasan 2004: 117–118 treats the episode in the *Mir'at-i Ahmadi*.

[77] See also Faroqhi 1984: 54–55 for an instructive description of the difficulties in detecting smuggling in Ottoman Anatolia, complemented by pp. 66–69 on the ready distribution of stolen goods.

[78] See de Laet 1949 on Roman customs rates. On Mughal customs rates, see e.g. Tavernier 1889, vol. 1: 7; *Mir'at-i Ahmadi*, chapter 104 (between 1/40 and 2/40); Hasan 2004:

They were intended to tap into trade flows, not force them underground or out of business. It was not only a question of smuggling. The merchant could often choose between different itineraries to bring his goods to market. The most reckless publicans or the most heavily and frequently taxed routes might find that they were being passed by to the advantage of revenue takers on alternative, but less expensive routes.[79]

The relationship between merchant and customs official should not be seen as one-sided. Rather it was based on a tenuous balance of power. A game of cat and mouse was played out where the rules were subject to constant renegotiation according to concrete circumstances. The result was the establishment of a fragile modus vivendi.[80] Some trades and merchants possessed more leverage than others. According to the situation, particularly attractive "customers", as it were, sometimes managed to wring smallish or moderate privileges and concessions from the customs authorities. Among such "fiscal" rebates we find the practice, in which familiar merchants passing a customs station on a regular basis were in some cases allowed to postpone the payment of toll till their return when they could settle the bill out of the profits derived from selling their wares.[81] The large and valuable export of slaves from Anatolia was taxed at a slightly lower rate than slave imports.[82]

113–117; and Richards 1993a: 175 and 203. The similarity of range is surely more than coincidental.

[79] The extreme example of this phenomenon is of course when bandits ruthlessly descend on traders. In his Roman history (XIV, 2, 2–4) Ammianus Marcellinus describes how Isaurian brigands, after having plundered a number of merchant craft, found that their source of "revenue" dried up as ships simply avoided the coastal stretch under their control. Mughal sources allow us to follow this in greater detail than Roman. From Surat a letter survives from a governor trying to persuade traders, especially the European companies, to return to Surat by promising to stop overtaxing and provide better protection for caravans, cf. Hasan 2004: 35 and 50–51.

[80] Sijpestein 1987: 44, for instance, documents how Egyptian peasants/traders, known to the village customs collector, were able to pay their taxes in advance.

[81] *Dig.* (Marcian) 39.4.16.12 provides evidence of the practice of postponing payment. On a similar arrangement for the English East India Company in Surat, see Hasan 2004: 116.

[82] It is customary to interpret the higher import rate (*Asian Customs Law (MonEph.)*, § 41, l. 98) as an attempt through customs to discourage imports of slaves to Asia (Drexhage 1994: 6; Dreher 1997: 85). However, the difference only amounts to a few sesterces per slave. With slaves often priced at several hundred HS, the extra duty cannot have been even moderately prohibitive. Therefore, I see the smaller export duty as a courtesy discount granted to a particularly valuable export.

In Palmyra a camel-load of unguents imported in alabaster vessels was taxed at 25 denarii. But when the merchant left the town again he was only charged 13 denarii. This was probably a kind of rebate intended to encourage traders to bring the merchandise to the city in the first place; unsold goods would be charged less than the normal fare on departure.[83] Luxury goods from India passing through Egypt were perhaps weighed with favourable scales when paying some minor, local dues on their way to Alexandria.[84] In the same context, some merchants might secure the patronage of persons of power inside the tributary system. This could provide such merchants with preferential treatment and perhaps even sometimes, tax concessions.[85] That would be a plausible explanation of the discount on exported slaves in the Asian customs law. Merchants supplying the Roman elite with much wanted slaves presumably used their connections to have the concession written into the law. However, patronage rarely comes gratis. Bribes or other reciprocating services would often have had to be paid as a kind of compensatory tribute. The profits from such discounts would thus have re-entered the tributary system to a considerable extent. This is presumably what was taking place when a group of ferrymen put up, probably in consecutive years, inscriptions and statues honouring the customs collectors of Chios "for their virtuous conduct towards them". The "honorific monuments", as suggested by Onno van Nijf, "may have been the public face of

---

[83] *Palmyrene Tax Law*, *CIS* II, 3, 3913, panel 3a, lines 19–31. Again I am certain that this should not be seen as a customs barrier to imports. The practice of occasionally granting a discount to goods being re-exported in order to attract them to the market in the first place is also known from the inscription recording a local toll in Caunos in Lycia (*SEG* XIV, 639 with the comments of Bean 1954). There a benefactor set up a foundation to pay for a number of exemptions from the regular customs regime. See now Schwarz 2001b: 385–394. Purpura 1985 unconvincingly argues that the Caunos prescriptions were regular rather than exemptions from the generally established practice.

[84] *P. Vindob.* G 40822 (second column). For analysis of the discount in the weighing process see Casson 1990. De Romanis 1998 is an interesting if ultimately too speculative attempt to make something out of these discounts. Rathbone 2001 now challenges this interpretation and substitutes a scenario with surcharges accruing to the customs officials.

[85] In the law codes it is often observed that merchants connected with great households managed to escape taxation (*C. Th.* XIII.1.5; 15 and 25). However, the phenomenon should not be seen as restricted to late antiquity. Cicero (*Fam.* 13.75) shows aristocratic patronage securing privileges in dealing with the authorities for a grain transporter/trader.

personal corruption".[86] Generally, however, fiscal rebates were relatively fragile. Based on the concrete balance of power they were permanently under pressure, subject to renegotiation and, if the Mughal evidence is anything to go by, constantly subject to erosion.[87]

The toll of the *Pax Romana* – drawing up a balance sheet

So far my discussion has focused on the parasitic dimension of customs exaction. But the tributary system can, to some extent, be seen as offering the merchants something in return for the payment of dues: a modicum of social order, protection from brigandage and piracy. The Roman emperor claimed to have brought *Pax* to the subject populations of the Empire; in the process roads and seas had allegedly been cleared of pirates and bandits and made safe for merchants and travellers. The imperial propaganda of the *Pax Romana* has been accepted by most generations of classical scholarship. The notion of an imperial peace has also occasionally found its way into Indian history. The *Pax Mogulica* has been used to describe a "golden" age before the fall of the great Empire and political chaos of the eighteenth century, by Indian historians to boost national confidence and by British colonialist historians to justify the Raj as a benevolent attempt to re-establish order among the Orientals.

Broadly speaking, however, Mughal historiography has paid more attention to the brittle foundations and fragile nature of the so-called peace established by tributary empires. Not only large-

---

[86] See van Nijf 1997: 92–93 on *IK* I, 74. Robert 1969: 545–548 published this and a more fragmentary but similar inscription which suggests that the practice was repeated over several years.

[87] The European chartered companies "just as some prominent indigenous merchants" managed to secure discounts through patronage. Such privilege came at a high price and doubts were often voiced as to whether they might not have done just as well by simply paying the unmodified rate. The diary of the Surman embassy to the Mughal court in 1714–1716, *The Oriental and India Office Records (London), Home Miscellaneous Series*, vol. 69, provides very instructive evidence on the high costs and the numerous complications and intrigues arising out of attempts to obtain fiscal exemptions. The fiscal privileges were also often ignored on the ground. Entangled in the shifting ties of patronage networks, they were frequently being undermined and needed permanent defence. See in general Hasan 2004, chapter 7 and Prakash 1985: 41–45.

but also small-scale local rebellions and other forms of low-level violence hold a more prominent position in the history of the north Indian Empire than they do in most periods of Roman history.[88] It would be foolhardy to claim categorically that there were no differences between the two empires in the respective levels of violence. So many factors of culture, social organisation and geography affect the scope for successful banditry that one could never expect exact similarity. Even so the difference can to a large extent be explained with reference to separate historiographical traditions rather than genuine contrasts between past worlds. In the last couple of decades Roman historians have become increasingly aware of the ideological nature of the claim of the Roman emperors and the indications of persistent violent disorder in the empire. Though successful for centuries, small-scale rebellions, occasionally growing to significant proportions, violent disputes or even minor wars between local communities and raids by mountain people, nomads and "barbarians" were part of the empire in the best of times. The Roman world was only relatively pacified.[89]

Banditry and piracy continued to constitute a real menace for merchants and other travellers, even in Italy.[90] This was a fact of life acknowledged by all, including the imperial state. Roman law prohibited the build-up of stores of arms intended for rebellion or social disturbance, but its subjects were still allowed to retain weapons for their own defence. Merchants and travellers were to a large extent expected to be able to take care of themselves and defend their possessions from violent attackers.[91] The relationship between the level of taxation and the quality of protection was not necessarily very close. An extreme illustration of this is the caravan trade bringing luxuries from India through the Syrian desert to Palmyra and from there further on into the Empire. The

---

[88] The fragile foundation of the Mughal peace was already a main theme in Habib 1963. See Hintze 1997 for some historiographical overviews.

[89] Woolf 1993 and Brunt 1990, chapter 11.

[90] Cf. Pliny *Ep.* 6.25 reporting the disappearance of a Roman knight during travel in Italy. See Shaw 1984; Hopwood 1989; Grünewald 1999; and Wolff 2003 (though empiricist, rather than analytical) for the continuation of banditry. For piracy, Braund 1993 and De Souza 1999, chapter 6. De Souza and Wolff though, seem too impressed with the claims of the imperial ideology of *Pax*.

[91] *Dig.* 48.6.1 with Brunt 1990: 257–259.

imperial state claimed the 25% customs duty on this traffic. Still, the Roman army does not appear to have been conspicuously active in ensuring the safety of the caravans. That was a task mainly left to semi-private initiative and the city council of Palmyra. The rich inscriptional evidence from the Syrian oasis city informs us about the need for local grandees, commanding influence among the desert tribes, to step in and ensure the safe passage of the caravans. In addition to this, the city seems to have maintained a local militia which patrolled and stationed the desert routes, and fought off the occasional bedouin attack on city territory.[92]

Much has been made of the proximity of Parthia and the political inability of the Roman army to act in the frontier zone without increasing the risk of provoking war, to explain the role of Palmyra in patrolling the desert. There may be a grain of truth in this, especially when the laxity on the Syro-Parthian route is contrasted with the heavier state control exercised in the Egyptian desert on the roads carrying Eastern luxuries. But the importance of such considerations can easily be exaggerated. Even in the Egyptian desert, the state presence seems to have been as much a question of keeping an eye on the valuable goods to reduce smuggling as providing protection. The merchants were still expected to hire their own guards and pay a road tax on them as well.[93] If anything, it is rather the relatively heavy presence on the Egyptian desert roads that constitutes the exception. The Roman army normally left it to local initiative to maintain law and order around the empire.[94] In that respect there is nothing surprising about Palmyra's semi-autonomous policing of the desert. An inscription from the early third century shows the Rhodians organising a

---

[92] Sommer 2005: 202–213 (on the complex interrelationship between Palmyra and the nomadic tribes of its hinterland, based on cooperation, intermittently disrupted by armed confrontation). See further Teixidor 1984; R. Drexhage 1988; Will 1992; and Young 2001, chapter 4.

[93] *OGIS* 674, line 12 (though emended) for duty payable on accompanying guards. *P. Vindob.* G 40822, recto column 2 for the use of private guards in commercial transports in Egypt. Young 2001: 69–74 analyses the desert roads. Faroqhi 1984: 52–55 offers comparative confirmation from Ottoman Anatolia that imperial surveillance might happen as much to avoid smuggling as to provide protection.

[94] Liebenam 1900: 357–359 long ago noted the sparing involvement of the imperial government in the policing of its territory. See Wolff 2003, chapter 8 for a recent discussion.

quasi-military expedition to teach bandits and pirates a lesson.[95]
The emperor Commodus praised the city of Bubon as a model
worthy of emulation by other communities because "you hastened
with such great enthusiasm to the arrest of the bandits, overcoming
them, killing some, and capturing others".[96] Much of this locally
organised protection will have been rather amateurish, sometimes
ad hoc in character and often of doubtful value. This, for instance,
was the experience of a pair of pig merchants returning from
the village of Philadelphia to Arsinoe in second-century Egypt.
Though the locally employed guard came to their rescue, this did
not deter the bandits from attacking. On the contrary, the guard
simply received the same treatment as the unfortunate traders, who
were tied, given a good beating and had a pig stolen.[97]

Protection offered by the different segments of the imperial system often left much to be desired. A relatively high degree of
low-level violence was tolerated. Not infrequently one gets the
impression that gangs of bandits were harboured by members of
the local elite, the very group supposed to underwrite local order.[98]
The exaction of customs cannot, in other words, simply be seen
as payment for protection. Anyhow, this is not something which is
peculiar to tributary empires. A pacified civil society is only a relatively recent phenomenon. The important but elusive question is
how the Roman imperial system compares to other pre-industrial
societies. In the sharpest attempt so far to conceptualise the process
of customs exaction in agrarianate societies, the American historian F. C. Lane suggested that customs dues be seen as comprising
two elements: the costs of producing protection, and a further tribute, a monopoly profit exacted by threat of using military force.

[95] *BE* 1946–1947: 337–338, no. 156.III with De Souza 1999: 218–219.
[96] *AE* 1979 no. 624 (translation quoted from Lendon 1997: 137) with Wolff 2003: 118–121, 196–197.
[97] *P. Fay.* 108. Alston 1995: 86–96 observes that the Roman state was involved in these local arrangements. We possess papyri showing district centurions ordering local com-munities to man watchtowers with guards. But the same papyri attest the crucial role left to the initiative of local communities in executing imperial orders and the huge scope for local "negligence". None of this is to deny the occasional imperial assistance to local policing units, but Alston 1995: 81–86 is too optimistic in his assessment of the scope of this, as is Wolff 2003, chapter 9. The available manpower resources were simply inadequate, as is clear from the convenient and still valuable surveys of Sherk 1955 and 1957.
[98] Shaw 1984; Hopwood 1989.

The stronger the position of the customs exactor, the greater the proportion of tribute. In other words, fewer protection-producing rivals would lessen the opportunities open to merchants for taking their goods by a different route. The result would be to weaken their negotiating power vis-à-vis the tribute takers and the cost of protection, taxation that is, would increase.[99]

The large tributary empires had been created by conquering tributary rivals and absorbing them into the same system. As we have seen repeatedly above, it would be wrong to describe these empires as unitary entities exercising a strong, centralised monopolistic power in society. The emperors' reach fell far short of that. But the alliance between the different segments of the imperial state did in some ways reduce, not, I emphasise, eradicate, competition and strengthen the position of tribute takers in the body politic. The result, as argued in Chapter 2, was an intensification of surplus extraction or, to use the language of Lane, rising monopolistic profits in the sale of protection. Essentially these could be realised in two ways, raising the price and cutting costs. It is possible to argue that both methods occurred in the Roman Empire, not least in the sphere of customs collection.

The need to accommodate the revenue demands both of the central imperial state and of local aristocratically ruled communities would probably have worked towards increasing the total burden of customs and other dues on trade.[100] This did not happen overnight. The process would have been slow, piecemeal and very gradual. Nonetheless, over time from the consolidation of imperial rule under Augustus until the fourth century, such a trend does seem to make itself discernible. The central imperial government gradually attempted to confiscate more and more local tolls, as we have already seen. It also occasionally introduced new dues, for instance on particular roads and, in the fourth century, the so-called *chrysargyron* tax to be paid by trades people, among others.[101] The local aristocratic segments of the imperial state would have sought

---

[99] Lane 1966: 383–428; Steensgaard 1981.
[100] Incidentally Purcell 2005: 222 is open to the possibility of rising customs under the Romans.
[101] We know, for instance, that Tiberius confiscated many local *vectigalia* (Suet. *Tib.* 49.2). Galba remitted some. This was annulled by Vespasian who needed money. He even added new and heavier ones (Suet. *Vesp.* 16.1). See further Herodian II, iv, 7,

compensation for some of the lost *vectigalia* by introducing new excise duties. Such tolls remained important for financing local government.[102] Taken together, the combined pressure for revenue exerted by the (competing) demands of central government and local elite groups, one may hypothesise, would have created a trend towards slowly increasing the tax burden on trade.[103] There were countercurrents too. Occasionally the emperor remitted or cancelled *vectigalia*. He also tried to impose some kind of control on the number of locally exacted dues. However, as already argued above, these actions were of relatively limited extent and usually only marginally successful; the emperor could always do with more money and he also had to placate local allies. The sporadic attempts to reduce the burden can therefore best be seen as precautionary and limited measures intended to counter the risk of over-burdening and thus of killing off the trade flows. They did not reverse the general trend, and were not even intended to; rather it was a question of safeguarding the fiscal interest.[104]

At the same time, the imperial system probably benefited from reduced military costs, though only for a period. Conquering and incorporating many of its neighbours reduced the incidence of full-scale war drastically in core areas of the Empire, such as Italy, southern France, Asia province, and the Mediterranean Sea. This meant that the effort of the army could be concentrated in the frontier regions, whereas internal policing, as we have seen, was left very much to the cheaper, irregular "troops" used by local communities. They were normally sufficient to keep violence at a tolerable

who mentions new tolls as one way forward for a princeps in need of extra money. One senses a pattern of ever-widening imperial customs exaction. This culminated with Constantine, who laid claim to most local tolls. At around the same time, the *chrysargyron* or *collatio lustralis* was introduced too, cf. Jones 1964: 431–432 and 871–872.

[102] See Schwarz 2001b: 338–406 for a clear demonstration of the continued importance of customs in city finances.

[103] Liebenam 1900: 359–360 points in this direction, too. But he had too much confidence in the ability of the central government to regulate municipal taxation.

[104] As de Laet 1949: 463–467 remarked we know much less about the formal customs rates in late antiquity than during the Principate. A mysterious *octava* hovers in the background, though it was probably a sales tax rather than a customs duty. Be that as it may, in general the late Roman state seems to have increased taxation. There is little reason to think that this did not also affect trade. The introduction of the *chrysargyron* confirms this expectation.

level, that is to prevent it from erupting into full-scale war or open rebellion where tribute extraction would become endangered. As a result, Roman conquest probably effected a reduction in the over-all military burden in the Mediterranean region. Long ago Gibbon remarked upon the relatively modest size of the imperial army. Thus the Roman state was able to cash in a peace dividend from lowered costs of producing protection in the Mediterranean world. This lasted roughly for the period normally associated with the heyday of the *Pax Romana*. By the reign of Marcus Aurelius the barbarians at the frontiers were beginning to catch up with Roman military superiority.[105] This made the defence of the Empire more difficult and military expenditure was again under pressure to rise. Gradually the peace dividend was eaten up in the coming centuries by growing costs of the military.

This scenario for the *Pax Romana* collides head on with tradi-tional interpretations which have normally focused entirely on the many benefits of peace accruing to the free movement of goods around the Empire. But the aim is not to deny that trade would have benefited from a reduction in the incidence of disruptive wars in the Mediterranean. The merit of the model, however, is to draw our attention to the process of how the benefits of empire were distributed and thus question the automatic, economic textbook assumption of a straightforward link between peace and grow-ing interregional trade. Against the benefits of imperial law and coinage, must also be set the disruptive influences of the activities of the Roman state and its personnel. As one business representa-tive observed in a letter to "Athenodoros, the merchant", he could not send the requested grain unless a new boat was sent down to him because his boats had been requisitioned by the army and were not available for commercial transport at that moment.[106]

The significant point to appear from the model outlined above is that merchants were far from the first in line to benefit from the imperial order. Here the imperial states really seem to part company with early modern capitalism. Competition for "shares of trade" between the emerging nation states of Europe forced them into a different process (see Chapter I). They had to continue to invest

---

[105] Whittaker 1994a.   [106] *BGU* XVI, 2644 (26 June, AD 4).

more of their income in steadily improving the basic conditions of traders by offering them better protection, first through mercantilist privileges, later through firm support for the "free" movement of goods in the face of local resistance, and finally by effecting a gradual pacification of their civil societies from the seventeenth until the nineteenth centuries.[107] The gains from the *Pax Romana*, by contrast, were not invested in steadily improving the conditions of trade still further after its initial establishment. On the contrary, the tributary state was content to accept the continued existence of considerable low-level violence.[108] Indeed, its personnel often contributed to everyday brutality and abuse, as we have seen in this chapter. Instead, the central government and landed elites pocketed the profits from the reduced costs of organising protection and were probably even able slowly to increase the price the merchants had to pay for this service. In spite of appearances, the conditions of trade during the high Empire were not nearly as favourable as they are often imagined to have been. In the crucial area of protection, transaction costs, if anything, probably experienced a slow rise from the consolidation of the Empire under Augustus until the fourth century AD.[109]

The question still remains, however, whether this slow rise in protection costs ever outweighed the benefits deriving from the initial reduction in large-scale violence in the Mediterranean brought about by the consolidation of Roman rule. There is no simple answer to that; we cannot make useful quantitative estimates of the different forces and balance them off against each other. Only broad impressions are possible. The key issue is just how much of a burden on regular trade were war and the concomitant plundering, often referred to as piracy by the ancient authors, before the coming of the so-called Roman peace. The size of this burden

---

[107] In general Lane 1966, chapters 22–25; Hont 2005 for European state-building and commercial competition; Persson 1999 links the creation of national markets under the banner of laissez-faire with absolutist governments.

[108] Strabo's stray remark (11.2.12) about the negligence of Roman governors in comparison to local chieftains in combating brigandage in the more remote corners of the Black Sea seems no less relevant for conditions in general under Rome than the ideological celebration of the fruits of peace.

[109] Bang 2007 attempts to develop this argument to model the macro conditions of the Roman political economy from the Republic until late antiquity.

in the Hellenistic period is easily exaggerated. Contemporary discussions of war and large-scale piracy were embroiled in a heavily
ideologised discourse about the true representatives and defend-
ers of civilisation. Military enemies were habitually branded as
pirates and destroyers of civilised order. The Roman conquerors
adopted this symbolic language to set themselves apart from the
alleged unruly chaos of the preceding period of the Hellenistic
monarchies. One should therefore be wary of making the contrast too stark. The centuries preceding Augustus saw considerable
commercial developments. Activity in the western Mediterranean
expanded significantly, if we can trust the statistical increase in
the number of shipwrecks which have been discovered, dating to
this period.[110] In the eastern Mediterranean Alexandria, Rhodes,
Delos and the opening up of trade with India all suggest the vitality of commercial activity. Taken together this calls for caution in
estimating the initial improvement in the conditions of trade created by the *Pax Romana*. A revolution in transaction costs would
clearly be much too strong a description of what happened. At
most one can hypothesise moderate improvements which would
then have been subject to gradual erosion by rising tax payments
over the following centuries. In general, the tributary empire only
brought about a moderate reduction in protection costs. It did not
fundamentally alter the basic conditions of the bazaar.

If the Roman "peace" nevertheless did lead to an expansion
in the intercity movement of goods, the explanation, as argued
in Chapter 2, can be found in the area of tribute extraction. The
reduction in the incidence of large-scale violence inside the empire
meant that the process of tribute extraction became less subject to
disruptions. At least for a period, tribute extraction experienced
greater stability and, as a consequence, achieved greater intensity.
The result was an increased demand for the services of the Roman
bazaar. The Empire gave it a greater and, for a long period, more

---

[110] Parker 1992. The wreck evidence does unmistakably show a rise in activity during
the last two centuries BC. The changes in the following centuries, however, need not
necessarily be taken as evidence of stagnation or decline. Both Egyptian and African
ships sailing the Mediterranean are underrepresented in the material, though trade and
transport from these regions picked up precisely when the material begins to indicate
contraction, cf. Whittaker 1989.

stable flow of resources to handle.[111] Such an interpretation finds support in developments in north India during the dissolution of the Mughal Empire in the eighteenth century. In areas where the surplus extracting apparatus remained intact, or even intensified, trade continued in spite of the increased level of violence. On the other hand, in regions where the aristocratic, fiscal system disintegrated, demand collapsed and trade dwindled away.[112]

This chapter has examined one aspect of uncertainty in the world of the bazaar: protection costs. The problem of security was larger than that ensuing from the high-profile phenomena of piracy and banditry; it embraced also the no less important element of fiscally motivated customs exactions. However, the merchants and traders of the bazaar were not as defenceless in the face of corrupt and abusive customs officials as they are often portrayed. Rather, a balance of power existed between merchant and customs collector; traders were able to establish a modus vivendi, however fragile, with the authorities. Their ability to circumvent the toughest collection points limited the room for manoeuvre left to the individual customs official. Too much brutality would undermine his income in the long term.[113] Mechanisms were in place then that enabled trade to take place in what to modern sentiments was a "rough" environment. The next chapter will explore the character of such mechanisms further.

[111] Cf. Wickham 2005.   [112] Bayly 1983, chapters 1–4.
[113] Cf. Dirlmeier 1987 on the frequent collection points of transit dues along the Rhine in medieval times. If the many customs collected did not kill off trade, it was because the collectors were interested in its continuance. But this does not mean, *pace* the optimistic, but unfounded assertion of Purcell 2005, that customs did not burden or limit trade. They did add significantly to the costs and hence limited potential consumption.

5

COMMUNITY: CULT, COURTS, CREDIT AND
COLLABORATION IN THE BAZAAR

Poor men of humble birth sail the seas and come to places which they have never seen before and where they are strangers to the people they meet and where they do not always have people to vouch for them. Yet they count on being safe only by putting trust in their Roman citizenship.

Cicero, *Second Speech Against Gaius Verres*, V, 167

Banarasidas and his friend Narrotamdas went to Banaras for business. First they offered prayers to Parsvanath and took a vow to observe the usual religious practices. They kept all the fasts, gave up green vegetables, and the company of prostitutes. In the bright half of Baisakh (April), Samvat 1671 (AD 1614), they completed the vow and offered worship.

Banarasidas, *Ardha-Kathanak* (Sharma 1970), p. 107

The first of the epigraphs above is normally cited as proof of the low social standing of Roman merchants. I am interested in a slightly different aspect of Cicero's rhetorical figure: the question of security and uncertainty in the world of the trader, habitually travelling between different communities. In the preceding chapter, the customs collector was used as the ideal-typical example of how the tributary state did not manage unambiguously to make conditions of trade secure. A *dirigiste* state might be expected to have exercised strong controls on the movement of goods through all branches of economic life. But that was not primarily the cause of commercial uncertainty in the agrarian empires. Firm command of the market sector or the bazaar in its entirety was completely beyond the means of the imperial state. In fact, it was unable even to curb its own officials.[1] The inability of the state to control commercial life, therefore, is not to be mistaken for the existence of a de facto regime of laissez-faire. The tributary

---

[1] The price edict of Diocletian is a telling if unintentional demonstration of how unrealistic such control was under Roman conditions; its grandiloquent tone and sheer abundance of detail are signs of weakness, not strength.

239

state simply was not strong enough to provide the level of guaranteed security and predictable administration implied by Adam Smith when he coined his influential advice for optimum economic performance.

Telling confirmation of this can be found in Pliny's Bithynian correspondence with Trajan. The city of Juliopolis in the province suffered from difficulties with looting and assault on civilians by passing army contingents. Hence the city had applied to the governor to have military personnel stationed to protect it from the abuses of troops on the march. Apparently Pliny was inclined to grant the city this favour which was already enjoyed by Byzantium. But Trajan said no on the grounds that it would set a dangerous example to the rest of the cities in the province. The guards in Byzantium were to remain the absolute exception, a carefully guarded privilege, not a right. If another city was to receive imperial guards, others would soon follow with the same demands. The result would be an intolerable increase in the administrative burden of the province. Instead, Trajan preferred to direct his governor to do his best to see to it that breaches of military discipline were punished. This was effectively a decision to leave things be. Pliny must already have been aware that he could not contain the military abuses with the normal means available to him. In practice, benign foresight and care, those much praised qualities in the emperor, turned out to make little difference to the subjects on the ground. Even Trajan, generally celebrated as *optimus princeps* by an admiring posterity, had to allow a certain level of abuse to continue unchecked.[2] Roman peace did not come with the night watchman demanded by classical economics. The tributary empire lacked both the will and the capacity to fulfil the role.

The main problem of the bazaar trader was not too much governmental control, but too little.[3] Mixing in a foreign community or

---

[2] Plin. *Ep.* X, 77–78. *Pace* Wolff 2003: 203–204 who cites these letters as reflecting a process of improving imperial security arrangements for the population. But that means ignoring the negative answer to Pliny's request. In this case, that is ill advised. The letters were published and circulated as representing a standard worthy of emulation.

[3] See Jones 1988, chapter 8 for the relatively low degree of social organisation of the market sector created by the empires. See further Geertz 1963, chapter 3, modified by Geertz 1979.

engaging with persons of superior status or official rank posed all sorts of physical as well as financial risks. Merchants and traders, however, should not be seen as helpless in the face of these challenges. In the last chapter, their ability to vote with their feet, so to speak, was seen to have worked as a counterbalance against overtaxation. But merchant response was not restricted to individual acts of smuggling and avoidance. Instead the people of the trading world set about creating *their own* social institutions, back-up mechanisms as it were, to compensate for the relatively weak guarantees provided by the state system. If at all possible most traders preferred to have "people to vouch for them".[4] Certainly, those who could do so would not as a general rule have been content to venture forth into the great unknown only trusting in the protective powers of their Roman citizenship, as Cicero boasted. Instead, merchants all over the Roman world, just as in other pre-industrial societies, attempted to forge personal links and construct social networks of various kinds which, to some extent, would cushion them against the vicissitudes of commercial life, the process Geertz referred to as clientelisation. Two key components of the social fabric of the bazaar were communal associations and the household. This chapter examines the role of the former in creating ties of community and trust among traders and of the latter in providing basic capital and credit to finance commerce.

Communal association – the power of religious conviviality

The copious epigraphic record surviving from the Empire contains numerous inscriptions revealing the existence of a rich texture of communal merchant organisations and other professional bodies in many cities.[5] These records, incised in marble and put on display, mainly inform us about the public life of the professional associations, or guilds. They bear witness to the religious and social

[4] Cic. II *Verr.* V, 167.
[5] Waltzing 1895–1900 remains unsurpassed and collects most of the evidence for professional associations in the Roman Empire in vols. 3–4, including those of merchants. Other central works are Mickwitz 1936, De Robertis 1971; Ausbüttel 1982; De Salvo 1992; van Nijf 1997. Mommsen 1843 is a seminal contribution.

rituals performed by the trader confraternities, *collegia* in Latin.[6] Students familiar with medieval guilds have been struck by the general absence in their Greco-Roman predecessors of formally recognised powers to regulate and define the rules of the trade, such as number of practitioners, prices etc. Compared to medieval guilds, the professional associations of the ancient world appear not to have been greatly concerned with economic objectives. Their focus was on community matters, such as ensuring a proper burial of deceased "brethren" or providing a setting for convivial gatherings or cultic activities. The distinction between socio-religious clubs and economic guilds, however, can easily be overdrawn. Absence of a securely established monopoly on economic regulation, and predominance of "cultural" functions, should not, as is the case for instance in Finley's work, be equated with economic impotence per se, let alone lack of an economic function for these merchant societies in general.[7] Once more, comparison with Mughal India may prove illuminating.

In many respects, discussions of the role of religious caste in India resemble the arguments of classicists over the exact nature of professional associations in the ancient economy. Caste has been portrayed as a religiously ordered division of labour in society. The clearest expression of this view was offered by the French ethnographer Louis Dumont in his *Homo Hierarchicus* (1966). In his version caste is seen as a rigid, unchanging system which, since time immemorial, has organised Indian society into a large number of hereditary, functionally specialised groups, so-called castes. Each caste would ideally comprise the members of a specific occupation; the salt-merchants' caste, the barbers' caste etc. But caste has in fact never been able to hold Indian society in such

---

[6] Patterson 1994 and van Nijf 1997 treat the public, ritual life of Greco-Roman civic associations.

[7] See van Nijf 1997, chapter 1 for a tentative critique of Finley's analysis. Rauh 1993 shows the economic function of the religious aspects of trading guilds at Delos. Finley's analysis (1985a: 81 and 137–138) of the non-economic character of Greco-Roman *collegia* was based on Waltzing 1895–1900 via Mickwitz 1936. Waltzing, however, was more nuanced than Finley. He also argued that *collegia*, though different from medieval guilds, did fulfil important economic functions: "L'influence et l'utilité des collèges au point de vue économique furent-elles donc nulles? Certes non... les négociants et les ouvriers... s'associaient afin de mieux défendre leurs intérêts communs" (1895–1900, vol. 1: 188–189).

an iron grip. Paradoxically, to the extent that the very hardened, static and stylised version of the caste system has ever had any social reality, this seems to have been the result of the changes Indian society went through after the fall of the Mughal Empire and in particular during British colonial rule. During this period, organisation along caste lines was intensified. Caste was increasingly employed by different groups as a means to defend, carve out and assert their position in a struggle over access to resources and privilege in a rapidly changing social order. As a result divisions between different segments of society became more clearly defined and caste boundaries hardened. Before this period, during Mughal rule, caste seems to have been much less dominant, far more flexible and not nearly as highly articulated as was later to be the case.[8]

The family history of the seventeenth-century Bania trader and Jain guru, Banarasidas, provides illustration. Originating from a clan of so-called Hindu Rajputs, probably peasants, the family converted to Jainism (a sect bordering on Hinduism) and joined the caste or sub-caste Srimal. But throughout the history, we find Banarasidas and members of his family still embracing more traditional Hindu beliefs and engaging in business partnerships with members of other creeds and sub-castes. Banarasidas' father Karagsen, though himself a Jain, collaborated in the jewel trade with a Siva worshipper and member of the Oswal sub-caste. Uniting these different socio-religious groups was a "vague" notion of the Bania community. The Banias were a very broad and loosely defined group of Jain and Hindu commercial people (traders, bankers etc.).[9] Add to this the co-existence of other similarly broad commercial groupings, such as Parsis, the Khattris, particularly in the central part of the Empire, and powerful Muslim groups of merchants, for instance at the hub of the commercial network radiating from Surat using Banias as assistants, and the image of a clearly defined caste system begins to fall apart. The social reality appears much more fluid and far less tidy than the traditional view allows. In economic terms this means it would

[8] Bayly 1999 is fundamental.
[9] Banarasidas, *Ardha-Kathanak*, in Sharma 1970: 52 and 56 and Habib 1990: 382–383.

be wrong to see the different merchant castes as identical in function with medieval guilds. They were more social and religious in nature. They did not as a general rule constitute clearly formalised bodies regulating their trades. Only in cases where a particular caste came to monopolise a trade locally did it establish control of commercial practices in ways more closely resembling medieval guilds. More often castes formed rather loose conglomerates of numerous locally co-existing sub-castes, usually of an ad hoc nature, which could also combine to form cross-caste councils of merchants.[10]

None of this deprived castes of economic significance. Though not strongly corporate in character, local caste bodies did usually still influence conditions in the bazaar in many ways and provided some of the underpinnings and social architecture of commercial life. The common religious identity produced by local caste gatherings could often be mobilised by merchants when needed to defend their interests. In 1669 the *qazi* (local law-and-order officer) initiated the destruction of Hindu temples in Surat, the great trading port, following an order from the Mughal emperor Aurangzeb. The Bania community answered by closing their shops and leaving the city en masse. The consequence, as reported by the English factor, was that "the people of Surat suffered great want... there was not any provisions to be got, the tanksall and customs house shut; no money to be procured; soe much as for home expenses; much less for trade, which was wholy at a stand."[11] Only when the *qazi* agreed to disregard the imperial order and abandon the policy of religious persecution did the Banias return and city life was restored to its former level of activity. Religious power was no trifling matter in the tributary empires. It was a powerful rallying point. The shared experience of cultic rituals, meals and festivals created a sense of community among the participants, which could be mobilised in social conflicts.

Greco-Roman *collegia* were not hereditary castes of course. But they did seek to create a communal identity around common participation in regular religious and convivial activities. Time

[10] Ashin Das Gupta 1979: 14–15 and 74–88.
[11] *The English Factories*, vol. 13: 190–192, cited in Singh 1972: 224. See further Hasan 2004: 40–43 and 60–65.

and time again the sources allow us a glimpse of their potential for social mobilisation. In his speech against the governor Flaccus, the Jewish-Alexandrine intellectual Philo describes how the notorious Isidorus roused the membership of several Alexandrine confraternities against Flaccus.[12] The potential power of private associations centred on religious ritual and conviviality should not be underestimated.

This lesson was not lost on the imperial authorities. Their attitude towards private associations always remained ambiguous. Though far from identical in their policies, both Mughal and Roman emperors looked with suspicion on the capacity of various religiously organised, autonomous groups to turn rebellious, riot and disrupt the established social order.[13] One of the Great Mughal Aurangzeb's imperial *farmans* (edicts), for instance, declares that "men and women visit shrines of saints on their anniversary days, Friday nights and nights of the last days of the months. This fact is a cause of disturbance. It should be arranged that none should crowd at the tombs."[14] A few lines above in the same *farman* the emperor makes a similar-sounding complaint about a Hindu festival. In the Roman law codes under a title concerning private associations we find the jurist Marcianus opining that religious gatherings should be tolerated as long as they do not evolve into illegal activities.[15] This concern is mirrored in Tertullian's late second-century defence of Christianity directed to the Roman authorities. It is telling that he chose to argue that the Church should be considered legitimate by the Empire because it did not present a threat to the political and social order, in contrast to many other associations.[16] Furthermore, in strict law professional organisations may quite

---

[12] Philo *In Flac.* 136–138 and Seland 1996.

[13] See Veyne 1979 for the "disciplinary" attitude of the Roman authorities designed to uphold the moral and social order of society.

[14] *Mir'at-i Ahmadi*, 233.

[15] *Dig.* 47.22.1.1. The suspicion that religiously organised bodies might turn rebellious and go against the state is a constant of Greco-Roman history, from the Bacchanalian affair in early second-century BC Roman Italy right down to the imperial juristic writings of the Antonine and Severan period. Good examples of the suspicious attitude are Philo *In Flaccum* 4 and Trajan's comment to Pliny (*Ep.* X, 34): "whatever name we give them and for whatever reason, if people assemble for a common purpose they soon turn into brotherhoods". See Cotter 1996.

[16] Tertullian *Apol.* 38.1–3.

possibly have been required to obtain an imperial authorisation.[17] But that was imperial hyperbole. In practice, many associations of merchants and other commercial people continued to exist without imperial blueprint and without interference from the authorities as long as they did not actually disturb the social order. The government had to tolerate their existence, outside the law as it were, since it had neither the intention nor the ability to take on the functions performed by these bodies.[18]

In fact, the imperial state and local authorities on occasion actually needed the cooperation of some of the many associations. These were of course granted the right to meet. But more than that, through involvement with state institutions some of these professional bodies did develop a more consolidated corporate character *of sorts* with a formally recognised position in society. In early imperial Egypt, local groups of merchants bought the right to administer the state-imposed monopoly in the salt trade in their areas.[19] The municipal fire brigades formed on the basis of builders' associations in Italy and some cities in other parts of the Empire are a prominent example.[20] A further instance is the payment of sales taxes and fulfilment of other officially imposed obligations via the agency of some of the professional associations.[21] However, the development of more consolidated corporate bodies was, as far as the sources allow us to judge, slow, uneven and predominantly, though not exclusively, a feature of the late Empire. It was the product of the expansion of the administrative apparatus

[17] *Dig.* 47.22.3.1 supported by *Dig.* 47.22.1.pr. This explains the habit of some professional *collegia* of announcing in inscriptions that they had permission to meet, e.g. *CIL* VI, 4416. Waltzing 1895–1900, vol. 1: 114–132 is still the best treatment.
[18] A clear indication of this is the admission by Marcianus (*Dig.* 47.22.1.pr.) that people of small means should be allowed to form burial societies without formal authorisation as long as they do not meet more than once a month. In practice, however, many more colleges were tolerated. Waltzing 1895–1900, vol. 1: 132–140 clearly brings out the discrepancy between formal law and administrative implementation. De Robertis 1971, vol. 1: 323–395 and de Ligt 2000, argue against Waltzing, but unconvincingly. They suggest that the right of association granted to the *tenuiores* should be seen as a general permission to form *collegia* for any purpose they wished, including professional. Waltzing 1896, vol. 1: 142–153 correctly rejected this theory.
[19] *P. Mich.* V, 245 with van Nijf 1997: 13–14 and Alston 1998: 175.
[20] In Sentinum they were referred to as the *tria collegia principalia*, *CIL* XI, 5749. Cf. Royden 1988 and Patterson 1994.
[21] *P. Lond. Inv.* 1562 verso (second century) reveals some groups, e.g. the vegetable sellers, being taxed with a lump sum payable by the "guild" (line 13).

and the concomitant deepening of its reach. Until quite recently, there was a tendency to exaggerate the general extent of the process, with historians trusting imperial claims of omnipotence more than they do at present. But the most pronounced crystallisation of corporate features happened primarily in connection with colleges involved with imperial supply systems, such as the *annonae* of Rome, and the armies in the provinces. None of these associations were ever allowed to take on a strong independent identity. Their functions were too important to the state. It kept them subdued as its servants and transformed them in the process. The shippers, *corpora naviculariorum*, serving the *annona* of Rome and Constantinople were, for instance, changed into an association of landowners, possessing specifically designated lands which carried the obligation to supply ships for the *annona*. Hence the famous hesitations of St Augustine as to whether to accept the inheritance of one of those properties on behalf of the Church.[22]

Thus, even if the tributary empire was never favourable, and often even inimical, to the formation of strong corporations, it both had to accept the existence of numerous communal groupings within the bazaar and at times actually promoted some corporate features in order to serve its own ends. In the commercial centre of late Mughal Surat, the need of the state for the active cooperation of merchants in the administration of local society does seem to have invested some merchant bodies with more corporate characteristics.[23] Roman professional associations, therefore, were not necessarily without a measure of bargaining power. Occasionally the sources allow us a glimpse of commercial groups applying their collective muscle to some perceived wrong, much in the style of caste groups and merchant councils in the Mughal Empire. An inscription records the decision by a high-ranking official, probably the *praefectus annonae*, seeking to accommodate the complaint of the five corporations of shippers from Arles serving the

---

[22] Augustine *Serm.* 355, 5 with Jones 1964: 827–828; De Salvo 1992 treats the *corpora naviculariorum*. *Collegia* reporting commodity prices, as we encountered in chapter 3, would also have sharpened corporate profiles. In general, see Mickwitz 1936, chapter 5. See further Waltzing 1895–1900, vol. 2; De Robertis 1971, vol. 2, parts 4–5, and Ruggini 1973.

[23] Hasan 2004: 43–49 (should be balanced by the account of trouble and division in Das Gupta 1979).

annona, over some unspecified abuse. A local imperial procurator is ordered to address and correct the injury in order to ensure the continued operation of state transports.[24] One should not, however, see this exclusively as a phenomenon restricted to *corpora* involved in state service. To be sure, it is the area best attested in the sources. But that seems largely due to the character of what has survived from antiquity. The "private" sector has not left us many detailed records of collective commercial life. Most inscriptions, our main source, are very short, concise and predominantly informative about "public ritual". On the other hand, the activities of the semi-official *corpora* are primarily known from various law texts, imperial rulings and administrative decisions. It is only to be expected that such texts would tend to reflect the main areas of direct state involvement in economic life.

Even so, a few examples do survive in the records of collective action taken by professional groups not strongly integrated into the administrative apparatus. A damaged inscription, probably late second century, found near Magnesia but most probably from Ephesos, informs us about a conflict with the bakers in the city. Apparently a deadlock had been reached: "The people are plunged into disorder and tumults." As a last resort, a high-ranking imperial official was made to intervene by the city council and bring "the seditious groups of bakers in the market" to order.[25] A set of council minutes from Egypt treats of merchants complaining of and in effect negotiating about the price they are offered for spinning yarn to be used for a consignment of cloth requisitioned by the imperial government.[26] Other examples include linenworkers in Tarsus, weavers in Oxyrhynchus and builders in late antique Sardis.[27] Though not amounting to the solid privileges enjoyed generally by many guilds in medieval Europe, these examples do

---

[24] *ILS* 6987 (second or early third century) with Höbenreich 1997: 97–115.

[25] *CIG* 2374, translation cited from Broughton in Frank 1933–40, vol. 4: 847. Finley (1985a: 226 n. 57) was unduly dismissive of the text. But he was clearly right in arguing against the vision of Rostovtzeff (1957: 178–179) of a capitalist system with an urban labour class on strike against its capitalist exploiters.

[26] *P. Oxy.* 1414 (late third or early fourth century).

[27] Dio Chrysostomus *Or.* 34.21–23 (weavers of Tarsus); van Minnen 1986 (Egyptian weavers); Garnsey 1998b, chapter 5 (builders of Sardis). In general van Nijf 1997: 82–107.

bespeak the existence of collective organisational power and the use of communal association by professional groups to defend their economic interests. This might sometimes even have taken the form of tacit collective agreements on prices.[28] The ambition to defend and promote their collective interests, however, is also reflected in the widespread habit of such societies to elect patrons from among their most prominent members and not least from various strata of the political elite (local and imperial according to circumstances).[29] The relationship of patronage cannot be reduced to a question merely of finding rich contributors to cult and convivial activities. Patrons could be asked to intervene in commercial disputes, offer protection in social conflicts and soften the attitude of the authorities.[30] Likewise colleges might, for example, be employed in various ways to support their patrons in political contests and conflicts.[31]

A web of ties – building community

It is possible, however, to focus too much on the exterior role of collective organisations in the bazaar. Their function was not simply that of defending the members against the outside world. Their nature was dual. They were at least as important in serving as centres of community, assisting the formation and reproduction of social ties. The shared identity constructed around common participation in cultic commensality created a sense of community among the membership. It provided a social environment where

[28] Thus a small set of imperial rulings, collected in the *Codex Justinianus* under number 4.59, forbid the collusion of commercial bodies on matters of price. I see little reason to restrict the possibility of such informal agreements among groups of merchants and other professionals to late antiquity.

[29] *CIL* XIII, 1688 (an equestrian patron for a guild of shippers); 1900, 1911 and 1916 (municipal councillors as patrons of *collegia*); 1954 (a wine merchant, *sevir* and patron of the *equites Romani* as well as his *collegium*); *ILS* 7490 (an equestrian oil trader from Baetica and wine merchant from Lugdunum and patron of the latter corporation). In general, see Clemente 1972 and De Salvo 1992: 265–287.

[30] Van Nijf 1997: 82–111. The material from Ostia, treated best by Meiggs 1973, chapter 14, is particularly good. *CIL* XIV, 4144 (second century); *CIL* VI, 1759 (AD 389) and 1872 (AD 206) all show patrons actively defending the interests of their *collegia*.

[31] As in Pompeii, Mouritsen 1988: 65–68 and 175; Jongman 1988, chapter 7.

business could take place. Here traders would forge contacts and find "people to vouch for them". Nothing illustrates this better than the habit of merchants, trading in foreign cities, of forming and using communal associations, frequently structured around their native identities, in their host societies. These not only provided shelter in a foreign environment, but also furnished traders with social connections.[32] Banarasidas, the Mughal Jain merchant mentioned above, settled in several different cities to do business during his career. But it is characteristic that most of the time he was moving within a network of relatively closely connected sub-castes of the wider Bania community. It was, for instance, in this social setting that he found his frequently changing business associates.[33]

The networks of traders between as well as within cities cannot be mapped with nearly the same precision in the Roman as in the Mughal Empire. The epigraphic record, our main source, is simply too fragmented and contains too many gaps. Alexandrian merchants might certainly be expected to figure prominently in the corpus of extant inscriptions. Several literary sources confirm their commercial significance. Yet they hardly appear at all.[34] Nonetheless, there is sufficient material to allow us occasionally to follow the community-building strategies pursued by Roman merchants in some detail. Rome and its harbour city Ostia, the greatest market in the Empire, has produced some illuminating evidence, most importantly in the famous Piazzale delle Corporazioni in Ostia of the early to high Empire. There, a number of different "ethnic" groups of merchants and shippers each possessed a small section of a large portico surrounding a temple. The surviving pavement mosaics give the names of some of these associations: "The Shippers and Merchants of Karales; Station of the Sabratensians" and so on. Thus we see merchants from distant places "building" a social

[32] *Per. Mar. Eryth.* 16, first century AD, provides a clear demonstration of the principle. Merchants from Muza in Arabia maintained trade links with East Africa by employing other Arab captains who had acquired a base in the foreign community.

[33] See Habib 1990: 382–383 on Banarasidas. Markovits 2000 studies one such caste network from the eighteenth to the twentieth centuries.

[34] It is tempting to see many of them lurking among the worshippers of the Egyptian cults (e.g. Isis) which spread across the Empire. See Noy 2000: 245–251, though too cautious, for a discussion regarding the city of Rome.

(a)

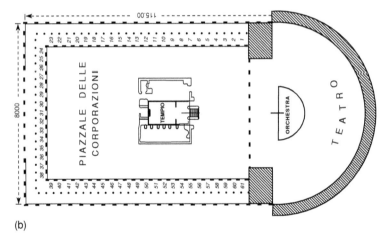

(b)

Fig. 5.1 Piazzale delle Corporazioni
(a), top, view of Piazzale delle Corporazioni from the theatre in Ostia
(b), bottom, plan of the complex (from CIL XIV, suppl. Ostiense: 662)

(c)

(d)

Fig. 5.1 (*cont.*)
(c), top, close-up of the small temple in the centre of the complex
(d), bottom, floor mosaic from the section of the portico belonging to the
navicul(arii) et negotiantes Karalitani (*CIL XIV*, 4549, 21 = no. 21 on the plan)

environment in the port city of the imperial capital, structured around their geographical and cultural origin, but also participating in a wider business community, perhaps centred on the cult of the (unidentified) temple situated in the middle of the architectural complex (Fig. 5.1).[35]

A different way of organising the business community is attested in Lugdunum.[36] In this nodal point of the main commercial arteries in the Gallic provinces, we find *collegia* admitting practitioners of a particular line of trade in the city whatever their geographical or ethnic background, such as "the wine merchants living in Kanabis" (a neighbourhood in Lugdunum).[37] In that way, merchants and commercial people from other areas of Gaul were able to acquire a social base irrespective of their point of origin. Among the *utricularii Lugduni consistentium* there was room for Iliomarus Aprus of the Veliocasian tribe alongside G. Libertus Decimanus from the city of Vienne.[38] Another example would be the *navicularius marinus* Q. Capito Probatus, who managed to enter the order of the *seviri Augustales* – a club of well-to-do typically, but not invariably, ex-slaves, often active in business – both in Lugdunum and Puteoli (the "second" harbour of Rome).[39]

One of the best-attested merchant communities, however, and certainly the best-documented network is that of Palmyra, the oasis city in the Syrian desert very roughly midway between the Euphrates and Damascus.[40] During the first three centuries AD, there were resident groups of Palmyrene merchants in Vologesias and Spasinou Charax, both on the route down the Euphrates

---

[35] *CIL* XIV, 4549 (nos. 21 and 14). See De Salvo 1992: 391–396 and Meiggs 1973: 283–288 and 329–330. See also Noy 2000, chapters 7 and 8 on foreign communities in the city of Rome.

[36] See Jacobsen 1995 for Gaul. Lugdunum is treated on pp. 112–122.

[37] *CIL* XIII, 1954. Waltzing 1895–1900, vol. 2: 181–182 is still fundamental.

[38] *CIL* XIII, 1998 and 2009. The Lugdunese variety of communal organisation could well be a result of close links between the shippers, wine traders and the state. Many will have been employed in supplying the army at the frontier (Middleton 1983 and Whittaker 1994a). Hence the state might have promoted corporations based on state service rather than geographical origin.

[39] *CIL* XIII, 1942. Duthoy 1976 collects the evidence. Abramenko 1993 treats the group in Italy.

[40] Most inscriptions are published in *Inventaire des inscriptions de Palmyre* I–XIII, 1930–75 and *Corpus Inscriptionum Semiticarum* II, 3. R. Drexhage 1988 surveys the material. See further, Will 1957; Teixidor 1984; Will 1992; Young 2001, chapter 4; Yon 2002; Sommer 2005: 202–213.

towards the Persian Gulf and India. In addition, Palmyrene communities did at some point exist in, among other places, Seleucia,
Babylon and Dura Europos, Coptos and Denderah in Egypt as well
as in Rome (Fig. 5.2).[41] The vitality of this network was supported
by a rich communal life centred on the religious and civic institutions of the "mother" city. Temples of their native gods were
established by the Palmyrenes when temporarily or permanently
resident away from home in the foreign cities.[42] Even as far away
as Coptos an inscription records the existence of what appears to
be a religious community building belonging to the Palmyrene
merchants plying the waters of the Red Sea.[43] The impressive
catch of inscriptions recovered at Palmyra offers illuminating evidence of the workings of a moral economy inside this widespread
merchant network. Several inscriptions found in the desert city's
grandiose temple of Bel honour euergetists for their benefactions
towards or on behalf of Palmyrenes living in the diaspora. One
Aqqia was commemorated for erecting a temple in Vologesias.
Another inscription shows the Palmyrene and Greek merchants in
Seleucia setting up a statue to their leader, who had made benefactions to the temple of Bel. Civic and religious ritual, securely
anchored in the institutions of the "home" city, was used as a
medium for maintaining and expressing social relationships inside
the merchant community even across different localities.[44]

The practices of Indian merchants of the seventeenth and eighteenth centuries may help further to elucidate the significance
of such activities. Cultic and social ritual did not just offer a
focal point for establishing contacts and bringing people together.

[41] Young 2001: 140 and R. Drexhage 1988, chapter 4. See Noy 2000: 234–245 for the Palmyrene presence in Rome.
[42] Dirven 1999 has studied this phenomenon for Dura.   [43] Young 2001: 80–81.
[44] *Inv. Palm.* IX, 6a (Palmyrene and Greek merchants in Seleucia); *CIS* II, 3, 3917 (the tribe of Gadiboli honour Aqqia for a temple erected in Vologesias). See also *CIS* II, 3, 3916 and *Inv. Palm.* IX, 11. The practice should not be dismissed as a Palmyrene exception. Another example of such communal ties inside diasporas is provided by an inscription from Puteoli (*OGIS* 595, AD 174). It records the attempt by the Tyrians in Puteoli to exploit their connections with Tyre on the Phoenician coast to receive financial support from its city council. Normally the Puteolan station of the Tyrians had been subsidised by the branch of the diaspora residing in Rome. But this had come to an end. The Tyrian city council, however, refused the request and decided that an appeal should be directed to the Roman community to resume support of their Puteolan brothers.

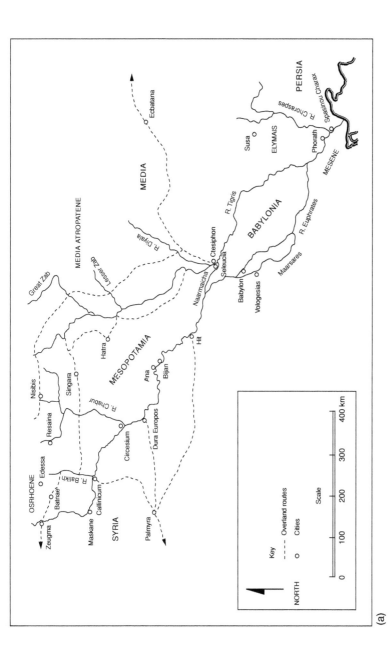

Fig. 5.2 Palmyra and its trading world

(a), map of the central part of Palmyra's trading network (from G. Young 2001: 140)

(b)

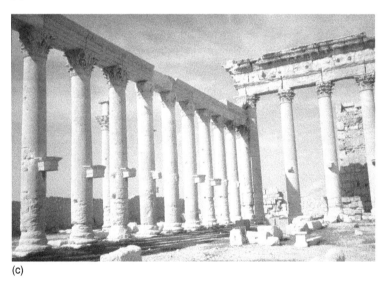

(c)

Fig. 5.2 (*cont.*)
(b), top, view of the central *cella* (to the right) and the courtyard of the
enormous temple of Bel in Palmyra
(c), bottom, section of the Bel temple's portico

(d)

Figure 5.2 *(cont.)*
(d), close-up of one of the statue bases with bilingual inscription

Its effect was much more profound and penetrating. It allowed the commercial household a means of asserting or improving its position within the business community. For the ambitious merchant this "meant", to cite C. A. Bayly, "above all, playing an active and steady part in the temple as well as the bazaar."[45] Life around "the temple" provided a context for merchants to express, (re)shape and cement social hierarchies within the world of the bazaar. It was important in stabilising relations and adding symbolic form to an otherwise fluent and opportunistic trading environment. The universe of the temple offered a vision of hierarchy in the world of the bazaar. It was, so to speak, a re-enactment and statement in socio-religious terms of the shape of life in the business community.

Such a model seems to capture well the epigraphic habit of the Palmyrene traders. In the inscriptions of the Bel-temple, the colonnaded streets and the agora, a very clear sense of hierarchy

---

[45] Bayly 1983: 373.

among the traders emerges.[46] At the bottom, groups of merchants, most commonly the members of the caravans, pose as grateful honorants, thanking benefactors for services rendered. Towards the other end of the spectrum a select group of commercial leaders stand out as patrons of the smaller merchants. They receive public honour for assisting the caravans "in every way possible".[47] Thereby their commercial primacy received a symbolic recognition, on occasion even supported by declarations of the local senate. They were not merely wealthy men in the market. They were cast in the mould of community leaders, pillars of merchant society. This is a role they seem readily to have accepted and reinforced. The grandees of Palmyra's long-distance trade even undertook to organise military expeditions to combat intrusive bedouins, who harassed the caravans. Thus they conformed to patterns commonly linked with Greco-Roman euergetism. Office holding in the city, for instance, does not seem to have been beyond the reach of the top-ranking merchants. Not only did they command local militias, they also held other civic magistracies in the city. In addition we

---

[46] How to interpret the hierarchy in the inscriptional record has been a concern of several scholars during the last century. Rostovtzeff 1932b saw it as evidence of a group of "merchant princes" in Palmyra. For Will 1957 the merchant princes were not really merchants. They were more like desert sheikhs using their finances and their control of vast pastures to supply the merchants travelling in caravans with funding and transport animals. Though free from the modernising connotations of Rostovtzeff's analysis, the distinction seems very artificial. The merchant princes of the Italian Renaissance, it should be remembered, also combined capitalist activities with aspects of the world of the knights, as the viewer of Donatello's famous, first statue of St George in Florence will know. Young 2001: 149–157 is a rather confusing and at times muddled critique. But he rightly insists that the material does not warrant a clear separation of traders and patron sheikhs. His own interpretation, however, almost eliminating the group of "patrons" and making the caravan leader *the* most central commercial figure, is unconvincing. It is also improbable on comparative grounds. It was normal in "rich" trades that the leading, financing merchants would be sedentary while their apprentices, smaller merchants and people on the rise would be travelling (van Leur 1955: 62–71; Goitein 1967: 156–160; and Das Gupta 1991: 355–356). This is the arrangement we encounter in Palmyra. *Inv. Palm.* X, 107 shows Akgar, son of the prominent merchant Marcus Ulpius Yarhai, conducting a caravan while his father provides assistance from his base in Palmyra. The role of caravan leader seems a sort of junior leadership position: the culmination of a career for some; for others a stepping stone on the way to the very top. The merchant princes, as re-emphasised by Yon 2002, must be placed in the context of a complex interrelationship between steppe and city – they had a foot in each camp.

[47] *Inv. Palm.* X, 44, 107, 111.

have already seen how they paid for temples or for the performance of sacrifices.[48]

No other, or perhaps almost no other, group of merchants within the orbit of Greco-Roman civilisation ever managed to achieve such a prominent position, including complete integration in city government. That was a function of the uniquely important role of the rich Oriental luxury trade in Palmyra's economy. However, on a more modest scale similar claims to social leadership in the trading world were made by the wealthier merchants across the Empire. The inscriptions present them acting as benefactors and patrons of professional associations, and in particular as *seviri Augustales*, of the *polis* at large. We see them investing in munificence, paying for temples, festivals and dinners to the greater good of the bazaar.[49] In that way, as has recently been remarked, commercial groups and especially their leaders were able to claim a publicly recognised role within the social hierarchy of Roman cities.[50] This motive was even more prominent in the status-seeking strategies of Indian merchants in the Mughal and especially early colonial era. But the comparison also invites us to look for the economic significance of such behaviour. In the world of Indian merchants the financial credit and the social prestige enjoyed by a commercial household were not easily separable. Failure in "the temple" could easily lead to serious damage in the bazaar.[51]

Such an experience would probably not have been foreign to merchants in the Roman world. The Latin word for credit was *fides*. *Fides*, however, was also a function of the trust and authority one was able to command in the sphere of personal relations. The word was one of the key concepts used to describe the relationship between patron and client.[52] It was a social, as well as economic,

---

[48] A prominent example is the commercial and civic leader Soadu; R. Drexhage 1988, nos. 15 and 16 with pp. 101–102. See also *CIS* II, 3, 3942.

[49] *Seviri Augustales*: *CIL* XIII, 1960, 1966, 1972; *CIL* XIV, 318 and 397; patrons, benefactions and handouts: *CIL* XIII, 1954; *CIL* XIV, 4142, 4620–4622; payment for temples and other public structures *CIL* VI, 814, 1035 (with Andreau 1987: 122–123) and XIV, 2793; Rauh 1993: 289–338.

[50] Van Nijf 1997, chapters 4–6.   [51] Bayly 1983: chapter 10.

[52] Skydsgaard 1976 on *fides* in relation to the conduct of business and credit. A crisis of *fides* might therefore be a "financial" crisis, the collapse or narrowing of credit, Caes. *BC* 3.1.2; Cic. *De Imp. Cn. Pomp.* 19. See further Bang 1997b and Verboven 2002: 170–182, 287–330 and 349–351.

measure of the pulling power and attractiveness of the household in interpersonal engagements of all sorts. In their epitaphs Roman merchants can therefore be found describing themselves as *fidelissimi*. Some emphasise how they had always been open to help friends in need and generous in extending hospitality. Complaints about the failure of friends to honour their moral obligations are also voiced. It is in the same context that one should understand claims that merchants had led blameless, spotless (*sine macula*), frugal (*frugi*) or "pure" (*castus*) lives or that they had lived together with their wives *sine ulla animi laesione*, "without damage to the soul". This was a way of indicating that the household had been a healthy and well-administered "enterprise"; its members would make for reliable business associates.[53] Honour was integral to the conduct of trade.[54]

Investment in social standing cannot, therefore, be dismissed as wasteful conspicuous consumption. It was sound business. Maintaining a prominent position in the ritual and social life of the business community served to safeguard or improve the *fides*, the credit and honour, of the merchant household. From this perspective, as remarked by C. A. Bayly, "the distinction between bad moral and bad economic conduct disappears".[55] The communal activities of the merchants take on importance as a means of providing the bazaar with all the trappings of a social system proper. It was not merely a market. It became a social universe fostering a sense of hierarchy and promoting norms of proper conduct between individual traders.[56] The principle can be seen at work very clearly in the autobiography, referred to earlier, of the Mughal Jain trader Banarasidas. In the quotation at the start of this chapter, he tells how he initiated a new business venture together with a

---

[53] See *ILS* 7480, 7518, 7519, 7530, 7531, 7542 for a selection of expressions used by merchants to describe the moral worth of their households. The link between moral worth, social status and sound management of the household is a central theme in Greco-Roman moralising, Cicero *Off.* 2, 52–64 and 86–87; Plutarch *Comparison of Aristeides and Cato*, Horace *Serm.* 1, 2; 2, 3, 166–181 and *Ep.* 1, 6, 15–42.

[54] Plaut. *Merc.* 418–424 and *Tab. Vindol.* II, 343 connect failure to honour an agreement with loss of *fides* and shame. In the Vindolanda letter the gloss *erubescam* (I will blush) is used.

[55] Bayly 1983: 385.

[56] See *P. Mich.* 243. As emphasised by Hasan 2004: 62, collective organisations combined economic and social roles.

partner by performing sacrifices and beginning to observe his religious duties more strictly. Conduct of business and ritual acts are overlapping. Thus, he succeeds in depicting himself and his partner as sound, responsible people who could be trusted not to waste others' money on enjoyments (prostitutes and the like) instead of making profitable investments.

The world of Roman traders also knew such edifying tales. The cult of Hercules was popular among traders. A short story about the Roman merchant Marcus Octavius Herrenus and his relationship to the cult of Hercules has been preserved for us in late antique commentaries. Macrobius relates how Herrenus, after having had success in trade, failed to deliver on his promise of paying a tithe of his profits to the temple of Hercules. During a voyage Herrenus encounters a violent storm but escapes miraculously. Afterwards Hercules reveals to him in a dream that it is he who saved Herrenus and conquered the storm. Hence Herrenus dedicates a temple in Rome to Hercules with the epithet "victorious".[57] Long-term success in business required proper conduct in the world of religious and civic ritual. The popularity of the cult of the goddess Fides (Pistis among Greeks) within Greco-Roman bazaars is another very visible demonstration of this.[58] The collective life of traders in the empire performed an important function in serving as a vehicle for the dissemination of norms and the reproduction of social order and discipline among the participants. This can also be seen from the fact that professional associations were normally organised as miniature replicas of a city state with popular assembly and magistrates. It was common that members of such societies would refer to each other as "friends" or occasionally even as "brothers".[59]

[57] Macrob. *Sat.* 3.6.11. For discussions, see Rauh 1993: 116–120 and Coarelli 1988: 185–204. The catch of inscriptions and altars found at Colijnsplaat at the mouth of the Rhine in the modern-day Netherlands is a good illustration of such activities. These were dedications by Roman merchants and sailors to the goddess Nehalenia in the second/third century AD thanking her for safe passage and return; see Stuart and Bogaers 2001 for a catalogue.

[58] Rauh 1993: 111–112.

[59] Waltzing 1895–1900, vol. 1: 322–333. Kloppenborg and Wilson 1996 *passim*. The organisation of professional associations along city state lines should therefore not be seen entirely in terms of adherence to the city state, as van Nijf 1997: 68–69 and chapters 4–6 does. It was also a matter of creating a parallel society.

Members who failed to live up to the societal ideals of the clubs risked being fined or in the worst case faced expulsion.[60]

Courts, arbitration and witnesses

The ancient professional associations, in other words, constituted small parallel societies. In that respect they shared many of the functions of Indian castes. Both helped to give shape to commercial society and create social institutions. One important task was the administration of justice. Castes served as judicial bodies of the first instance. They would normally seek to regulate legal disputes internally. Only when caste groups failed to re-establish social consensus and mediate between litigants was the local Mughal court approached.[61] Any judiciary role of Greco-Roman *collegia* was never formally recognised to quite the same extent. The corporate character of the city state was far more clearly articulated in Greco-Roman society than in India. Every *polis* had its own local court and guarded its political rights within the imperial framework. Only rarely, such as in the case of Jewish diaspora communities, were resident subgroups officially granted the privilege of using their own internal courts, though only grudgingly.[62] Even so, the city state and the imperial government left much room for semi-private administration and implementation of justice, indeed, depended upon it. Both state institutions had fairly weak instruments of enforcement available for the resolution of private disputes. In most cases it was left to the winning side of an argument to bring a favourable verdict into effect. Self-help was always a crucial element in ancient justice. This made involvement of the "closest" community in most legal disputes inevitable. Its support was all but indispensable to the litigants and a key factor in making solutions last.[63] The expectation of Plato in *The Laws* that an attempt would

---

[60] *P. Mich.* 243 and Waltzing 1895–1900, vol. 1: 378. See Alston 2002: 207–212 for an excellent analysis of the intertwined social, cultural, religious and economic functions performed by urban "guilds" in the cities of Roman Egypt.

[61] Hasan 2004: chapter 6; Bayly 1983, chapter 10.

[62] Josephus *Ant. Jud.* XIV, 185–267 and XVI, 160–178 with Cotter 1996: 86.

[63] Finley 1983: 1–49 and 118–121. Gelzer 1912 is still unsurpassed on this, and is no less relevant for the Empire than the Republic (Wallace-Hadrill 1989). See further Lintott

be made to settle commercial disagreements through mediation by neighbours or arbiters before approaching the official courts, remained relevant for all of antiquity (and beyond).[64]

As social hierarchies grew steeper and internal coherence within the numerous *poleis* weakened during Roman rule, one may legitimately surmise that the need for private legal arbitration increased.[65] But very little is known of these practices. Our evidence tends to overemphasise the role of the state because its activities produced a significant body of legal writings and juridical documents. The bishops of early Christianity, it is clear, attempted, as part of the care of their congregations, to play the role of mediator and arbiter among quarrelling members of their flock.[66] The very few ordinances of professional associations surviving from Roman antiquity, however, leave us very much in the dark about their part in conflict resolution, and any judgement must remain conjectural.[67] But there are some strong indications that professional associations played a far more active role in the private adjudication of conflicts than is usually thought. If "guild" ordinances were not normally very detailed, it is still clear that the general assembly did, at least occasionally, hear and decide on complaints raised by the membership. One ordinance, for instance, prescribed that members must not raise grievances about one another during communal dinners. Festive occasions were to be kept free of internal skirmishes. Those should be reserved for treatment by the monthly assemblies.[68] The regulations of an unknown association from the village of Tebtunis in Roman Egypt, dating to the reign of Tiberius, add more flesh to the bones. There a fine is imposed on one who takes legal action against any co-member

---

1968; Garnsey 1970; Gagos and van Minnen 1994; and Nippel 1995. See Galanter 1981 for an analysis pointing out the critical importance of arbitration, even for the functioning of modern judiciary systems. With fewer tools of state enforcement, the relevance can only have been greater in antiquity.

[64] Plato *Leg.* 920c–d.
[65] Cf. Ziegler 1971: 161–163; Garnsey 1970 is fundamental.
[66] See Harries 1999, chapter 10 for how this role continued to shape the character of episcopal justice even after it had been granted some official recognition during the fourth century.
[67] See Waltzing 1895–1900, vol. 1: 368–378 for a basic discussion of the general assemblies of these associations where members would consider "toutes les affaires".
[68] *ILS* 7212: "si quis quid queri aut referre volet, in conventu referat".

of the confraternity.[69] The *collegium* tried to ensure that conflicts would be settled internally within the collective rather than in a court setting outside its immediate control.

The aim of such measures was to contain conflicts and prevent them from escalating to a level where they threatened the social order among the membership; the prohibition of prosecuting co-members is mentioned together with a ban on defaming, intriguing against or corrupting the households of other members. To judge from Indian examples, such internally organised maintenance of the social consensus normally reinforced the established order of things. Lower-ranking members and people on the fringes of the community found it difficult to stand up against more prominent merchants.[70] The episode set in the marketplace, which Petronius included in his novel, the *Satyricon*, suggests that this experience was not foreign to the ancient world. The three travelling fictional heroes get embroiled in a commercial dispute with a peasant and his wife involving a fine gown and an old rag. As things get heated the wider bazaar community interferes in the conflict. A prominent member takes command of the situation. He takes custody of the disputed objects until a judge can rule in the case, knowing well that the three foreigners, lacking support in local society, would probably not risk showing up at the trial. In that way, he hopes to keep the objects for himself. This is slapstick comedy of course. But the comedy does not arise out of a deliberate misrepresentation of the social mechanisms involved. Indeed, Petronius depends on exploiting these to produce the constant and incredible reversals of fortune which underpin the burlesque humour of the scene. Just as the main characters of the novel believe that the old tunic, hiding a valuable treasure only they know about, is again within their grasp, chaos erupts. The unsuspecting peasant couple suddenly realise that the gown put on sale by the three (anti)heroes has been stolen from the wife in the first place. Immediately they start shouting

---

[69] *P. Mich.* 243, lines 7–8 with the editor's commentary. *P. Mich.* 245, the ordinances of a guild of salt merchants, also indicates internal regulation of disputes.

[70] Pearson 1976: 147–149 and Hasan 2004: 95–99.

that they have found the thieves and put the three outsiders in a rather awkward position.[71]

Lifting a conflict out of the immediate community and bringing it to a magisterial court carried risks of its own, not necessarily to be taken lightly. However unfair and hierarchically skewed mediation within the bazaar might occasionally become, it was still often preferable to the courts. Mediation allowed greater scope for negotiation and the adoption of flexible solutions to conflicts. By comparison a formal trial was a blunter instrument. With few tools of enforcement available, an official judge might well handle the conflict roughly.

> Why do you not judge for yourselves what is right? Thus, when you go with your accuser before a magistrate, on the way make an effort to settle the case, or you may be dragged before the judge, and the judge hand you over to the officer, and the officer throw you in prison. I tell you, you will never get out until you have paid the very last penny.

So the faithful are admonished in the Gospel of Luke.[72] Private settlement, as it aimed to restore social consensus, though far from "fair", normally offered a more lenient solution; the prospect of reaching a successful conclusion improved significantly if an agreement, at least in some sense, acceptable to all parties could be found. Court trials, on the contrary, were the result of failure or breakdown in the conflict-solving mechanisms of the social networks in which the combatants were enmeshed. They represented an escalation of strife. Harsher means were required to restore peace in the community.[73]

The stakes and the risks were higher in a court trial. But on average the chances of successfully challenging the reigning distribution of power in a community probably did not increase correspondingly. Local courts, staffed by judges and juries drawn

---

[71] Petr. *Sat.* 12–15, 7. See also *P. Oxy.* 3814 on the importance of local power to assert one's rights within the community.

[72] Luke 12:57–59 cited from Gagos and van Minnen 1994: 44; further pp. 30–48. Their analysis, though about late antiquity, is equally valid for the Principate.

[73] As rulings usually still required the active collaboration of the community to remain in force, the judge would often tend to reinforce the already dominant party but now more harshly in order to ensure his continued predominance. See Hinton 1966, chapters 3–4 for a comparative demonstration of this principle.

from the ruling groups of a city, could more often than not be supposed to reflect prevailing patterns of influence. The courts of governors and other imperial administrators were less entangled in local intrigue, but also more distant and with an interest, generally, in maintaining amiable relations with local ruling groups since imperial administration depended on the active collaboration of these. Add to this that the ancient notion of justice required courts in reaching their decisions to take into account the general status, standing and character of litigants and the witnesses appearing for or against them. Lawyers were even expected to play on matters of hierarchy and influence in presenting a case.[74] From an individualist perspective, this may seem harsh and unjust, but in a society where the enforcement of rulings usually required the active collaboration of communities, finding in favour of established relations of power nevertheless represents a form of justice: societal justice.[75]

The last point deserves emphasis. Even if courts generally tended to favour and reinforce existing relations of power, they still did so within the context of a discussion of right and wrong. There was thus a chance that occasionally a David might defeat a Goliath. Greco-Roman justice was not simply a "done deal".[76] Not all contestants, moreover, would have been unevenly matched. So courts were used, and sometimes to a surprising extent.[77] Private administration of justice with its inclination towards the status quo was vulnerable to silent obstruction and the forces of inertia. In such cases, an indication of the willingness of one of the parties to up the stakes and take the conflict to another level might be just the thing required to break a deadlock. Courts, therefore, need

---

[74] See Saller 1982, chapters 2 and 5 for patronage; Crook 1995 for the importance of rhetoric in the practice of Greco-Roman law; Jongman 1988, chapter 6 for an attempt, perhaps overly schematic, to argue that witnesses to documents were normally listed according to rank and status.

[75] Geertz 2000, 175–195 for an example and discussion of similar phenomena.

[76] Harries 1999: 181–184 makes this point even for the more hierarchical late antique world.

[77] Some papyri indicate a remarkable number of grievances being presented to governors. Often, however, decisions of higher courts consisted in little more than returning the case to a local forum. This kind of litigiousness, as Harries 1999: 184 observes, needs to be understood in the context of the complex strategies pursued by local networks of power in a system of communally administered justice.

not merely be seen as an alternative to private adjudication. Frequently, they seem to have been used to reinforce it. Indeed, the filing of lawsuits often served to scare an opponent into accepting private arbitration.[78] Among the Murecine wax tablets are some documents pertaining to a business dispute between the banker Caius Sulpicius Cinnamus and his sometime companion Caius Julius Prudens. The case was brought in front of a judge in February AD 55. A document shows the parties agreeing to transfer the case to private arbitration. Next in the dossier comes a number of pronouncements of their chosen arbiter Marcus Barbatius Epaphroditus, setting time, date and location for hearing the case. Arbitration could be a rather prolonged affair. The dispute had not yet been finally settled by March 56. But communications clearly had not broken down completely. The process of mediation probably enabled slow negotiations to go on in order to explore the ground for reaching a compromise.[79]

These documents remind us that when we think of mediation administered by the merchants themselves we need not necessarily and certainly not primarily focus on the more formal aspects of life inside the business community such as the assemblies of *collegia*. The writings of the Roman jurists discuss the arbiter in relation to the concept of a *vir bonus*, a "good man". It was standard to agree on a person of some standing and moral authority within the community to act as mediator.[80] To judge from the onomastic features of Barbatius' *cognomen*, he belonged to the same libertine business circles in which the bank of the Sulpicii operated. The formal structure of the social and religious associations of the bazaar would most probably not have played any direct role in the actual proceedings. *Collegia* and other communal bodies should rather be seen as providing an environment that enabled "good

---

[78] Hasan 2004: 106 shows this for Mughal Surat. Harries 1999, chapter 9 makes this point forcefully for the late Roman world. But her argument applies equally well to the Principate.

[79] *TPSulp.* 25, 34–39 and 48 with Camodeca's (1999) editorial comments. Another illustration of this strategy can be found in the dossier of documents compiled over a number of years by the Jewish woman Babatha in the conflict regarding her son's inheritance. Petitions for a court hearing are drafted to cajole the unwilling guardians to enter into negotiations, cf. *P. Yadin* 13–15 with Cotton 1993.

[80] *Dig.* 17.2.6 and 17.2.76.

men" to stand out and be identifiable. The same considerations are equally applicable to witnesses. Witnesses who enjoyed a high reputation in the bazaar would have been an important asset in judicial disputes. Their word carried greater weight and people of low standing in the community would have found it more difficult to get such persons to support their case.[81] Symbolic capital which arose out of life in the communal associations of the bazaar played an important part in the organisation and maintenance of the commercial order and hierarchy.

The structure of credit in the community

In their provision of contacts, symbolic capital, trust and credit, social hierarchy, rules of behaviour, arbitration and witnesses, the communal associations of the bazaar made a significant contribution towards the production of "services" necessary to the activities of merchants. These would also have included prospective partners in business and a network for the provision of extra capital.[82] Communal organisation enabled the merchant to access a larger pool of resources, social as well as economic, than was under his immediate command. But ties of community were far from alone in creating the social foundations of business; they overlapped and intersected with other forms of institutions. The most important of these was the family and (extended) household. The *oikos* was the basis of merchant operations.

While social and religious clubs provided an outer shell, so to speak, for business activities, family and household constituted the core. Banarasidas, our Mughal ideal-typical merchant, turned repeatedly to family and relatives to raise his trading capital.[83] Banks and money lenders were certainly present in the bazaars

---

[81] See Bayly 1983: 375 on how merchants with a low standing found it difficult to get access to arbitration; Hasan 2004, chapter 6 in general for the social bias of courts of the Mughal *qazi*. Garnsey 1970 has treated this for the Roman Empire.

[82] Such activities are, for instance, envisaged by the provisions of the *SC de Bacchanalibus* (S. Riccobono *et al.* (eds.) 1941, *Fontes Iuris Romani Antejustiniani*, vol. 1, Florence, pp. 240–241), cf. the perceptive analysis of lines 10–14 by Rauh 1993: 254. See further his chapter 6 and Gabrielsen 2001.

[83] Banarasidas, *Ardha-Kathanak*, in Sharma 1970: 67–68 and 72–73.

of India.[84] But their capital was normally of modest proportions, confined as they were to household organisation, just as with the merchants. Deposit banking was far from unknown. The small scale of the overall enterprise, however, imposed strict limits on the capacity of the banks to turn such deposits into working capital. They were always vulnerable to insolvency. Most loans from banks, though far from unimportant, were therefore short-term. They can perhaps better be described as financial services together with money assaying and changing, giro transfers and bills of exchange, which constituted the core operations of Indian banks and money lenders in relation to the trading world. Such services were not at all peripheral. They eased the workings of commercial life considerably, for instance by facilitating money transfers between localities. But they did not constitute the foundation of trading capital. That came from the more or less extended household.[85]

One common procedure, also practised by Banarasidas and his father, was to devolve a portion of the household fortune onto a young member of the family or poorer business relation in a sort of partnership. With few means of his own, the contribution of the junior partner consisted of his work. He was expected to increase the capital outlay by conducting business, frequently on long trading voyages. The profits were then to be shared in some way specified by custom and personal agreement. Such asymmetrical business partnerships were well suited to the uncertainties and irregularities of the bazaar world. By parcelling out the capital, the household spread its risks. It also acquired a convenient and above all fairly reliable means of setting up branches of the family business in different cities. By employing persons who would regularly be dependent on the family, and furthermore, by giving them a stake in the financial outcome, the household tried to ensure that its representative would remain loyal to its interests. This avenue also opened an outlet for surplus capital otherwise

---

[84] Indian banking is the most complex example of a pre-modern banking system. It is therefore a useful benchmark for Roman banking. See Jain 1929; Habib 1972; Goldsmith 1987; Goody 1996: 72–74 and 94; and Haider 1997, chapter 4.

[85] Goitein 1967: 161–185 and 229–266, though dealing with the medieval Jewish trading community in Cairo, provides a useful description of the structure of credit in the bazaar.

stored in the bountiful coffers of the Mughal elite. Members of the imperial aristocracy sometimes invested or speculated in trade through merchants connected with their great households. But it is important not to exaggerate the significance of this. Aristocratic involvement never amounted to commercial dominance. One can probably better describe it as a process whereby tentacles spreading outwards from the larger households occasionally penetrated the world of the bazaar without ever taking it over.[86] Instead a picture emerges of a market sphere with many small individual units, comprising poorer and junior members – often travelling – of the merchant community. A considerable portion of these would have been connected with larger, more established households consisting of senior merchants, richer financiers and the odd aristocrat.[87]

A different but equally asymmetrical form of credit extended by the financing segment of the trading world was the bottomry loan, used to finance trading voyages. In return the borrower had to put up the cargo or sometimes the ship as security. If the ship was lost at sea the money was lost too. Thus the main risk was borne by the lender who received very high interest payments on a successfully completed journey. Rates of 15, 20 or 30% cover the normal range. Often such loans would be accompanied by quite detailed instructions for the trip regarding destination, route and duration. It was also common for the lender to send a representative to accompany the borrower and keep an eye on the investment. In effect the bottomry loan was another way of expanding the business of the household without actually having to increase the size of the firm. Instead, the financier relied on semi-independent agent households. Merchants of more equal means also regularly, when need arose, pooled their resources in partnerships where risk and profit were shared more equally. Though sometimes of long duration, most of these were only short-term and frequently changing engagements. They never really effected a separation of the trading capital and the individual households.[88]

---

[86] Blake 1991: 109–110 and 117–118, modified by Chatterjee 1996: 66.
[87] Das Gupta 1991 and Raychaudhuri 1991.
[88] Banarasidas, *Ardha-Kathanak*, in Sharma 1970: 71, 107–110, illustrates the transient nature of partnerships.

The pattern of credit outlined above is sometimes loosely referred to, with a phrase borrowed from the Italian Middle Ages, as a *"commenda"*-system.[89] *Commenda* was the term used to designate a particular form of partnership where one entrant provided the capital and the other the work while profits were shared on a three-quarter to one-quarter basis. In a common variation of the arrangement, funds were contributed two-thirds to one-third, with the junior partner providing the work and receiving half the profits.[90] Ever since Weber devoted a now classic study to this phenomenon, *commenda* has been closely linked to an evolutionary story about the rise of capitalism in northern Italy. In Weber's analysis *commenda* was treated as a first step towards achieving a separation of household funds and business capital. The legal form given to *commenda* contributed to a development which eventually enabled jurists to conceptualise the trading capital of merchants as a fund distinct from and independent of the household, in other words as a firm in the modern understanding of the word.[91]

One needs to make a distinction here. Weber was interested in how the various specific legal formulas, which developed in the Italian city states, were gradually manipulated and shaped by jurists to form the modern concept of the trading firm. In that sense *commenda* may have become part of a process that eventually saw the first institutional shoots of capitalism appear in Italy. But in itself there was nothing intrinsically modern or "developed" about the commercial practice of *commenda*, as Weber was the first to admit.[92] The researches of Udovitch and Goitein in the 1960s identified varieties of *commenda* in Jewish, Byzantine and especially Islamic law that pre-dated the Italian practices.[93] Used as a convenient shorthand for the flexible, and frequently asymmetrical forms of finance described above for India, *commenda*-style financing seems to be a common and very old expression of the household-based economy of the bazaar. Our steadily expanding database on ancient Mesopotamian trade leaves little doubt that

[89] Van Leur 1955: 62–73. See further Goitein 1967: 170–183.
[90] Lopez and Raymond 1955: 174–184 for a convenient list of illustrative examples of medieval Italian *commenda* contracts in translation.
[91] Weber 1924c. [92] Weber 1924c: 335–339.
[93] Udovitch 1962 and further Udovitch 1970 and Goitein 1967.

the familiar medieval repertoire of partnerships, bottomry loans and *commenda* had strong roots in remote Middle Eastern history. These forms of finance were not in themselves the first step in a development away from the *oikos*, but rather reflected its needs for spreading risks and flexible adaptation to a shifting environment.[94] The Roman world seems to offer confirmation of this; and the story of Greco-Roman commercial credit needs to be fitted into this broader picture. The structure of Roman commercial capital provides a fairly accurate reproduction of the main features of the pattern outlined above based on the bazaars of Mughal India.[95]

Commercial loans were generally short-term, rarely extended for more than the duration of a single operation. The archive belonging to a group of Sulpicii freedmen bankers resident in Puteoli, serving as a harbour for Rome under the Julio-Claudians, offers a glimpse of the situation in what must have been one of the busiest markets in the Empire.[96] Two grain traders, Caius Novius Eunus and Lucius Marius Iucundus, are attested raising money on the security of a couple of medium-sized shipments of mainly Alexandrian wheat. Eunus secured a loan of some 13,000 sesterces to be repaid immediately on the request of the lender, but only by handing over control of goods at least 3–4 times the value. Iucundus obtained 20,000 sesterces for a two-month period by giving a consignment of goods probably worth twice or three times as much into the custody of the lender.[97] Short timespan and high securities are two of the features which are already familiar from the foregoing discussion of the character of credit in early modern India. They are a reflection of the close interrelationship between

---

[94] Van Leur 1955: 73; Trolle Larsen 1967 and 1976; Goody 1996: 64–69 (in spite of the modernist emphasis); Renger 2003.

[95] Cf. the reflections offered by Andreau 1999: 151. What follows runs counter to Temin and Kessler 2007, but they mistake the *societates publicanorum*, the companies of tax-farmers, for merchant companies and ignore the fact that these *societates* were exceptional and to a large extent phased out with the advent of monarchy; they cannot do service as a Roman version of the chartered joint stock companies of early modern capitalism.

[96] See Camodeca 1999 and 2003 for an edition and analysis of the archive. Though descriptive and mainly derivative of Camodeca's work, Jones 2006 provides a useful introduction and survey of the evidence.

[97] *TPSulp.* 45 and 51–52 (Eunus), 46; 53 + 79 (Iucundus).

the need for a flexible and opportunistic approach to business and the concern to reduce the risks so characteristic of bazaar households.

Another common feature is the high number of actors and the relatively circumscribed nature of individual commercial capitals. A good illustration is provided by a second-century letter sent from the Alexandrian banker Marcus Claudius Sabinus to two merchants from Askalon.[98] The document records the payment of a loan of 7 talents 5,160 dr. on behalf of two Roman citizens to the two merchants together with their two further companions and joint shipowners. The sum total is far from negligible, about half the minimum census for a city councillor in a wealthy community and enough to procure some 150 tonnes of wheat – an above-average grain cargo, but somewhat less than the capacity of the large Alexandrian grain freighters plying the route to Rome. The merchants presumably had more valuable goods in mind since their ship was a relatively small merchantman. Whatever the precise nature of the trading venture, it is highly revealing that the funding of such a mid-range operation still saw two lenders sharing the risk and required four merchants to combine their resources to carry the burden.

Family and extended household partake as important elements in all of the above examples from Roman business life. The Sulpicii bank of Puteoli was based on a succession of freedmen relationships. Caius Novius Eunus, the freedman trader, maintained relations to his old master, Caius Novius Cypaerus, who ran a warehouse where his former slave stored his goods.[99] Of the four merchants from Askalon, two were brothers. The painted inscriptions on Spanish oil amphorae recovered from Monte Testaccio in Rome offer some of the best evidence on the household dynamics of merchant enterprises in the Roman Mediterranean.[100] Frequently one

[98] See Casson 1986 for an edition, translation, commentary and analysis. See further the discussion by Rathbone 2003: 217–219.
[99] *TPSulp.* 45.
[100] It matters little whether the state was ultimately behind these imports. Private personnel conducted the actual transports of oil, at least until the third century. The material is published in *CIL* XV and updated in Rodríguez-Almeida 1984: 222–233. De Salvo

encounters partnerships based on a shared connection to the same household, such as "Corneliorum" or "Fadiorum".[101]

Occasionally it is possible to follow the operation of such "business families" in greater detail. Take for example the "DD. Caeciliorum".[102] In AD 149 potsherds document D. Caecilius Maternus operating on his own. D. Caecilius Hospitalis is also on record trading individually. But in AD 154 the two appear in partnership. At this point it is necessary to introduce a feature particularly prominent in Roman society – slavery. One might speculate that both or perhaps one of the two were former slaves. In that case, we seem to be faced with a situation where the one or both as slaves were provided with capital to set up individual branches of the household. As they proved their worth, they were eventually set free. But it is clear that they still kept close contacts with the "mother" household, as evidenced by their business collaboration. However, both the *cognomina*, Maternus and Hospitalis, were only rarely used of slaves. Maternus in particular seems to have been common in the Spanish provinces, while the chance of Hospitalis being used to designate a slave is marginally bigger.[103] Another possibility, therefore, is that we are looking at the collaboration of two freeborn male members of the same family, or a mixture of statuses. At any rate, freeborn or libertine, the combination of members working individually with occasional collaboration in partnerships between branches of the extended household is characteristic of the flexible patterns produced by a *commenda*-type system. The presence of slavery modifies, but does not fundamentally alter the basic principle. Sometimes, of course, such collaboration also included business contacts from outside the household.

1992: 183–225 and 255–256 shows the fluidity of partnerships in the Monte Testaccio material. See further Liou and Tchernia 1994.

[101] *CIL* XV, 3844, 3874.

[102] *CIL* XV, 3764–3795 for the DD. Caeciliorum. Hospitalis in 3764, Maternus in 3765–3766 and jointly in 3768–3781.

[103] De Salvo 1992: 219–222 and 251 thinks of traders like Hospitalis and Maternus as belonging to the Spanish municipal aristocracy. Liou and Tchernia 1994 puncture much of the prosopographical guesswork which has attempted to identify the traders appearing on Dressel 20 amphorae with members of the landed elite in Baetica. The names Maternus and Hospitalis are discussed by Kajanto 1965: 79–80.

Another inscription sports a business partnership of "DD. Caecil-iorum et Aelii Optati".[104]

The provisions of Roman law add confirmation of the validity of the impression gained from the Spanish oil amphorae. They recognise several varieties of the asymmetrical and parcellised form of capital provision characteristic of *commenda* and related commercial instruments.[105] First, there is the business partnership proper, the *societas*. This was conceived as a very flexible instrument by the Roman jurists.[106] The partnership might be comprehensive or merely cover a single business venture. It was not generally treated as giving rise to an independent economic entity, except in exceptional circumstances, but was seen mainly as regulating relations between partners rather than with the "outside" world. Therefore it was consensual. If consent was withdrawn, the partnership ceased to exist. By the same token, the death of a partner saw the dissolution of the partnership. From a modern perspective, this kind of partnership looks like a fleeting and transient entity. But from a bazaar perspective, what meets the eye is the adaptability of the instrument which allowed economic actors to adjust quickly to the hazards and opportunities offered by a shifting market. One year it might prove expedient to be on your own, while in the next, greater advantages were to be had from pooling resources with one of your business connections, as we saw the Caecilii do above. This kind of partnership also facilitated diversification of risks. One might explore opportunities in one line of trade or market together with one partner, while perhaps employing another part of the household capital in a completely different range of products with other partners or on your own.

---

[104] *CIL* XV, 3795; further 3951–3952 and 3973. Another example of business household and branches is given by Curtin 1991: 90–96 and 167–169 in his discussion of the Pompeian producer and merchant of fish sauce, Umbricius Scaurus.

[105] Verboven 2002, part 3 is an excellent attempt to understand the institutions of Roman "business law" as reflecting the honour and trust-based personal relationships of the household, rather than the needs of proto-modern commercial firms. Crook 1967, chapters 6–7, is still useful on commercial life and the institutions of law.

[106] Gaius *Inst.* 3.148–154 and *Dig.* 17.2. For some modern discussions of Roman *societas* see Johnston 1999: 106–107; Zimmerman 1990, chapter 15. Arangio-Ruiz 1950 is a classic.

The Roman *societas*, in other words, corresponds quite well with the flexible patterns we have come to expect from our comparisons and shares many of the formal properties characteristic of partnership in other *commenda*-type systems. It also spans a wide spectrum of social relations ranging from complete equality to stark hierarchy. Among the many possible varieties, it should by now be unsurprising that the jurists recognised something akin to a clear example of *commenda*. It is stated that a partnership can exist between people where one brings the capital and the other the work. Additionally, profits may be shared by agreement while loss is wholly borne by the capital investor.[107] In other words, the arrangement described by the jurists is a *commenda* in all but name. The only thing missing is that the contract has not been severed from the general law of partnership and treated under a separate heading. But that is a matter of legal formalism, not commercial practice.[108]

Roman law elaborated in greater detail a number of other legal instruments which, like the unequal partnership, enabled the master to diversify his interests and devolve part of his capital onto junior members or associates of the household. Most important of these were the regulations concerning agency or business managers and the so-called *peculium*.[109] The *peculium* denoted a share of the household resources given over as a personal fund to people in the power of the head of the household, for instance sons and daughters or slaves. This could be used much like a *commenda*

---

[107] *Dig.* 17.2.29.pr.–1; 17.2.5.1; 17.2.30 and Gaius 3.149. Santucci 1997 has recently emphasised the importance of this institution. Reinhardt 1968: 24–68 presents a discussion of how Roman law came to recognise unequal partnerships. He portrays it in gradual evolutionary terms from Republic to high Empire. This seems to me mistaken. The principle is clearly attested already from the late Republic. If jurists continue to discuss it, this is due precisely to the unequal social relationship underlying the practice. The more powerful partner would inevitably be tempted in some cases to challenge the equality of his junior partner. Similar conflicts appear in discussions of *commenda* by Muslim jurists, cf. Udovitch 1962: 205 and more extensively 1970, chapters 3–6.

[108] Cf. Andreau 1999: 151.

[109] Gaius *Inst.* 4.69–74 remains an exemplary introduction to these instruments. The relevant text in the *Digest* are: Book 14 for agency and business managers, *Dig.* 14.1 (*actio exercitoria*); 14.3 (*actio institoria*); 14.5; Book 15 deals with the regulations concerning the *peculium*. Some modern surveys and discussions: Kirschenbaum 1987; Aubert 1994, chapter 2; Wacke 1994; Johnston 1999: 99–108. The relevant chapters of Buckland 1908 are still useful.

arrangement. In Plautus' comedy *The Merchant*, the father invests his son with a *peculium* for a trading voyage. On his return the son is to render accounts, pay back the principal and a share of the profits. The remainder is for him to keep.[110] Many of the basic characteristics of *commenda* are clearly present here.

Nevertheless, the *peculium* is more frequently discussed as a way of achieving the limited liability of modern companies and separating the business from the household. By making his dependants do business on the basis of a *peculium* the master would not be responsible for more than the size of this fund, it is claimed.[111] That is not quite what was envisaged by the Roman jurists. They distinguished clearly between cases where the *pater familias* had either ordered his dependants to conduct a particular business transaction or put them in charge as managers of a shop or business enterprise, and cases where their dependants acted on their own. Only in these latter cases would the liability of the household be restricted to the size of the *peculium*, otherwise liability was for the full amount, *in solidum*. As Gaius explained in his introduction to Roman law, if a person had entered into a transaction with a dependent person authorised by his master, he could certainly always sue him on the *peculium*. "But no one would be that stupid", he went on, because the master was liable for the full amount irrespective of the current holdings of the *peculium*.[112] A ruling by the emperor Alexander Severus upheld this view. Even if a person was liable up to the amount of a *peculium*, the emperor observed, he would still be liable for any enrichment he had drawn from the transaction or for the full amount if he had put his dependant in charge of the business.[113]

---

[110] Plaut. *Merc.* 80–97. At least this interpretation seems the most economical. Plautus describes the arrangement in terms of the father equipping the expedition and counting out money to the son and giving him instructions about the minimum sale price. The excess profit is described as a gain to the son's *peculium*. But the original capital should undoubtedly be seen as having entered his *peculium* as a debt to the father. It was through the *peculium* that a son *in potestate* was enabled to participate in business, cf. Johnston 1999: 99–101.

[111] E.g. Johnston 1999: 101–105; Zwalve 2002.

[112] Gaius *Inst.* 4.74, cf. *Dig.* (Gaius) 14.5.1.

[113] *Codex Justinianus* IV, 25.2. Cf. *Dig.* (Ulpian) 14.1.1.22. A slave forming part of the *peculium* of a son in power, still renders the *pater familias* liable in full if the latter had authorised the business management of the slave. Business pursued with a *peculium*, in other words, did not per se limit the liability of the master to the extent of its contents.

The logic of the relationship between the head of the household and his agents appears with particular clarity from a case discussed by the jurist Paul. A slave had been put in charge of lending out money against security by his master. On his own volition the same slave had also begun to offer his services to grain merchants. He would take over their payment obligations towards their suppliers. Only now, the slave had run away and one of the suppliers demanded payment from his master as liable for the conduct of his business manager. The master denied responsibility since he had not authorised the line of business giving rise to the dispute. During the trial, however, it emerged that the master had underwritten the activities of his slave in a range of other areas. The prefect of the Roman grain supply, therefore, decided in favour of the claimant. On the appeal, however, the legal councillors were inclined to find in favour of the defendant *pater familias* since he had not given a mandate for this particular line of business. But in the end, the emperor decided to uphold the sentence because the master had seemed "in everything to have regarded the slave as acting in his name".[114] There is no question here of regarding the conduct of business through slave agents in general as based on a legally sanctioned form of limited liability.[115]

The limited liability of the *peculium* must be placed in a different context. It was an attempt to protect the master from receiving harm from his slaves. One of the advantages of *commenda* proper is that it gives the agent a stake in a positive outcome of the business. As shown by the Plautine example a similar result could also be achieved directly through the primary activities connected with the *peculium*. A complementary method was to allow the slave, next to his main operation, to do a little business on the side that would enable him to earn money with which eventually to obtain his freedom. This seems to be the phenomenon underlying the

---

[114] *Dig.* (Paul) 14.5.8.

[115] The inadequacy of the focus on limited liability also emerges from Andreau's work. On several occasions he has discussed the cause célèbre involving the future pope Calistus. According to Hippolytus (*Ref. Omn. Haes.* 9.12.1–12) the imperial freedman Carpophorus had set up his slave Calistus in banking. When Calistus defaulted and fled, his creditors came to the master Carpophorus. In 1999: 67–68 Andreau took this as a case of the limited liability of the *peculium*. But now (2006: 205–208) he has changed his mind and takes it as a case of full liability for the business manager.

Pauline case. But when the slave was acting on his own initiative, it was important to protect the master from people trying to exploit the situation and thereby inflicting a loss on him.[116] That is how the limited liability of the *peculium* fits into economic practice, not as a generalised means of investment with limited liability. This is not to say, of course, that during conflicts masters would not sometimes manipulate the rules to their advantage and try to claim limited liability. Inevitably they would, as is clear from the claims which sparked the two imperial rulings just treated. But such claims had no secure backing in law, nor in business practice, it would seem. That is the very clear impression conveyed by the documents in the archive belonging to the Sulpicii bankers. They provide some of our richest information on the employment of slave agents and managers in business. A recurrent feature is the specification that a particular activity takes place at the master's command or authorisation.[117] The rules governing the use of business agents and the *peculium* reflected the need of households for a flexible set of instruments through which to delegate the management of

---

[116] *Dig.* (Gaius) 50.17.133 states the general principle that masters should benefit from their slaves, not receive harm. The jurists had little sympathy for those who inflicted loss on other people by exploiting, colluding with or taking advantage of their slaves. Instead they emphasise the duty to act responsibly and with circumspection in dealing with other people's slaves active in business, cf. *Dig.* 14.1.1.pr; 14.1.7; 14.1.9. Slaves acting on a *peculium*, therefore, could not give give away presents or stand surety unless it was clearly in the interests of their master, cf. *Dig.* (Ulpian) 15.1.3.5–9. For an analysis, see Kirschenbaum 1987: 27–28 and Buckland 1908: 213–216.

[117] E.g. *TPSulp.* 45, 46, 48, 51, 78. Cf. the discussion in Jones 2006: 138–142; the evidence for authorisation is much clearer and more copious than the vague tit-bits he can assemble for independent action with liability limited to the *peculium*. The last practice can only be hypothesised (not more than that) in a few instances, often of doubtful interpretation. Thus *TPSulp.* 25 contains the record of a hearing in front of a Puteolan judge between the Sulpicii and one of their business associates Gaius Julius Prudens concerning an unpaid debt. In the record Sulpicius asks Prudens to confirm that he is the owner of two named slaves. Some years before, Prudens had mandated the Sulpicii to transact with these slaves in his own name (*TPSulp.* 48). Now from his reply has been stricken the addition that the said slaves were in his power "suaque im [*sic*] potestate". This was to avoid a "noxal action", that is a criminal trial, Jones explains, with the commentary provided by the editor of the tablets, Camodeca, and ensure that the case was treated as a civil suit, e.g. an ordinary action on the *peculium*. The *actio de peculio*, however, is not the sole alternative, some of the other middleman institutions could equally well be implied. But here Jones strangely ignores Camodeca's commentary: "Sempre nello stesso ordine di idee di progressi rapporti commerciali fra le parti si è pero preferito piuttosto pensare all' *actio quod iussu* o all' *actio institoria*" (1999: 86). Avoiding the noxal action might equally well lead to Prudens being sued for the full amount, *in solidum*.

its different economic activities/branches to junior members and dependants (children, slaves and freedmen). In that respect, they served some of the same functions as a *commenda* arrangement proper.[118]

Finally, the bottomry loan was a well-established practice in Roman commerce, too; and the form it took fits well the argument advanced here about a generalised asymmetrical, *commenda*-style pattern of finance for the bazaar.[119] It was common practice for the lender to have a representative accompany the borrower on the trading voyage, thus reducing the latter almost to the level of a junior partner. One case discussed in the *Digest* by Scaevola, an advisor to Marcus Aurelius, saw a slave representative situated in Berytus advancing a maritime loan to a merchant for a trip to Brundisium and back again. A slave, Eros, was sent to accompany and supervise the borrower on the journey to make sure he abided by the terms of the agreement. If for some reason, the merchant was unable to start his return trip before the end of the sailing season, the loan was to be repaid immediately. Eros, the accompanying slave, would then bring the money to Rome where, presumably, the master of the two slaves was living. Behind this operation stood a financier sufficiently rich to maintain a branch of his household in a foreign harbour.[120]

It is worthwhile emphasising the flexibility and adaptability of these instruments. Bottomry loans were employed to finance commercial ventures of very varying scale. The 47,160 dr. advanced to the four merchants from Askalon was given as a bottomry loan. In that case, the lenders do not seem to have had representatives

---

[118] The suggestion by Johnston 1999: 102–108 that masters essentially left the initiative to their slaves as to how to invest the household resources, in order to enjoy limited liability from a position of passivity, is implausible. Roman morality prescribed that the *pater familias* did not neglect his household and kept a firm hold on the activities of his subordinates (e.g. Cato *Agr.* II and IV). A master unable to control his slaves and freedmen was an object of condemnation and of ridicule (e.g. Sen. *Apocolocyntosis*); he was one of the stock characters of Roman comedy. Roman jurisprudents expected masters to take care when setting up slaves in business. Thus Ulpian (*Dig.* 14.3.11.4) insisted that responsibility remained with the master if an *institor*/agent had intentionally damaged the owner in conducting business with an unsuspecting third party.

[119] Plutarch *Cato Maior* 21, 6 and the so-called Muziris Papyrus (Casson 1990; Rathbone 2001).

[120] *Dig.* 45.1.122.1. Two recent discussions, Sirks 2002; Rathbone 2003: 216.

to monitor the movements of the borrowers. Credit on an entirely different scale is attested by a papyrus detailing the specific conditions of another bottomry loan; it was extended to a merchant, probably in Alexandria, for a round-trip to Muziris in India to procure highly prized Oriental luxuries. The value of the cargo which served as security for the loan amounted to some 7 million sesterces, 6–7 times the minimum census requirement of a Roman senator. To safeguard the investment, the lender had agents stationed at several nodal points along the route in Egypt. The terms specify that the borrower place the goods under the seal of either the lender or his agents at the warehouse in Coptos while awaiting shipment down the Nile and again on arrival in Alexandria. In the preceding damaged section of the papyrus, there may be mention of further representatives located in the Red Sea harbour where the cargo would arrive from India and of a camel driver to take the goods through the desert. With that sort of economic and organisational muscle, it should have been possible for the lender to conduct the trade on his own account. However, by financing the venture of another, he gained one important advantage: he ensured that the man actually travelling to a foreign and far distant location had a significant interest in a successful outcome. The travelling merchant, on the other hand, gained the advantage of having someone with stronger shoulders carry the ruinous and very real risks of losing the capital outlay on the way, to pirates, bad weather or some other accident.[121]

Thus, allowing for small culture-specific variations, the structure of Roman commercial capital can be seen as an example of a general bazaar pattern which the path-breaking historian of trade in the Indian Ocean, J. C. van Leur, described for the Indian Ocean in the sixteenth and seventeenth centuries and saw stretching back

---

[121] Some basic analyses (with varying emphasis) and text: Casson 1990 and Rathbone 2001. Further Rathbone 2003: 220–221; Young 2001: 54–58 and De Romanis 1996, chapter 4. The suggestion by Rathbone that the papyrus describing the terms of the loan is a general master contract, a generic document which would then serve as basis for drawing up loan agreements for specific trading voyages, is no more than a possible hypothesis. The fact that an account of the specific cargo was written up on the verso after the completion of the journey, seems to me to speak against the interpretation of the recto as a "generic" rather than a specific document.

at least to Hellenistic times.[122] It was a pattern characterised by the predominance of household organisation, fragmentation of capital in various *commenda*-like arrangements and transient partnerships, but also by the presence of some very substantial and wealthy financiers.[123] This, of course, also opened an avenue for occasional aristocratic involvement at the financing level, as in India. There has been much debate about the precise extent of such activities.[124] Many contributions have been ill guided. Considerable aristocratic involvement in commerce has been claimed by the critics of Finley as a sign of the economic modernity of the Roman world.[125] But no plausible level of aristocratic interests in trade could possibly call into question his main point, the predominance of agricultural

[122] Rathbone 2003: 214–215 and 225–227, on the contrary, postulates a decisive break with Hellenistic practices, in spite of the institutional continuities, and prefers to place the Roman phenomena in a context comparable to the joint stock companies of the seventeenth and eighteenth centuries. That seems excessive and based on an argument from exceptions. The anecdote told by Plutarch of Cato the Elder (*Cato Maior* 21.6) who is alleged to have grouped fifty merchant borrowers together in a partnership before lending them money, should not be seen as the norm. Quite the reverse. The number fifty is a round number, chosen for effect rather than verisimilitude, and is used by Plutarch to illustrate Cato's excessive and extraordinary zeal in moneymaking. The other piece of key evidence adduced, a ruling preserved in the *Digest* on a bottomry loan (22.2.6), is misunderstood by Rathbone. The attempt by the lender to claim security in goods financed by other lenders on other ships does not reflect the existence of a partnership (and no partners are mentioned). The point is that the borrowing merchant had spread his risks by sending his goods on different ships financed by different lenders. Now, the present lender had claimed what remained after repayment of these other loans as an additional security. When the cargo offered as primary security to him was lost, he tried to reclaim his money by arguing that the loss of the cargo, in effect, only amounted to a *diminution* of its value and that the borrower therefore had to make up the shortfall from the other pledged securities. This, however, was rejected by the jurisprudents since the cargo had been lost under the terms of the sea loan and the risk accordingly rested wholly with the lender. Neither of the bottomry loans attested in the papyri, incidentally, support Rathbone's view. That involving the partnership of four merchants only represented a very modest concentration of capital, while the enormous, and exceptional, wealth implied by the document concerning the commercial trip to India only involved one lender and one borrower. It is not an important distinction that some Roman financiers of bottomry loans had representatives travelling with the lenders; that practice remained common also in the Middle Ages and in the Indian Ocean trade before the joint stock companies.

[123] The last point merits emphasis since it is often wrongly claimed that van Leur denied the structural importance of big financier merchants (cf. his analysis 1955: 191–227). See Colin 2000 for a discussion of sedentary and travelling merchants in the Roman world.

[124] See Garnsey 1976; see Wallace-Hadrill 1991 for some of the best contributions. See further D'Arms 1981; Pleket 1983 and 1984; and Schleich 1983 and 1984.

[125] D'Arms 1981.

COMMUNITY

wealth in the composition of elite incomes. In fact, the dominant
trend within Indian studies has been going in the exact opposite
direction. Here most scholars have been keen to downplay the
extent of involvement by the vast households of the political elite
in commercial activities. They prefer to portray it as a marginal
phenomenon precisely in order to assert the vitality, strength and
potential modernity of the traders of pre-colonial India.[126] That
is a curious contrast in the strategies of argumentation. The same
phenomenon is ascribed the opposite meaning within each field
of scholarship in order to make similar claims about the relative
modernity of commercial life. The contrast cannot be explained
merely as a reflection of a real difference between the worlds of
the Roman and Mughal lords. In neither empire does the evidence
permit a sufficiently solid and detailed reconstruction of the phenomenon to enable such precise comparison. The contrast, in short,
is a product of different historiographical traditions.

   This is an indication that the terms of the discussion are
wrong. Occasional aristocratic commercial investments, the extent
of which must in any case be supposed to have varied significantly with the opportunities offered by widely different local
circumstances, do not represent a departure from the general
shape of the bazaar.[127] Indeed, the great concentration of economic resources in the hands of the aristocracies in each empire
makes some level of involvement almost inevitable. Wealth on a
scale implied by the cargo from Muziris could be mustered by
only few men within the Roman Empire; and of those, the over-
whelming majority will have belonged to the political elite. In
the archive of the Sulpicii freedmen bankers, one can actually
observe a trickle-down of wealth from the imperial household into
the business community of the harbour city of Puteoli.[128] On the
other hand, the Indian comparison may serve as a warning against
exaggerating the level of aristocratic dominance within the commercial life of the Empire. The Muziris cargo, after all, cannot

---

[126] Chatterjee 1996, chapter 3 contra Blake 1991: 117–118.
[127] See Bayly 1983: 391–393 for the ability of the bazaar to absorb the involvement of the
   political elite.
[128] E.g. *TPSulp.* 49, 67, 69; Camodeca 2003. See Rathbone 2003: 219–223 for the almost
   certain elite context of the Muziris cargo.

easily be taken as representative of trade in general. The sheer concentration of monetary value represented by this transaction necessarily implies that there would have been very few of these in any given year. Even so, some very wealthy merchants, rather than landed aristocrats, are likely to have existed in the centres for the richest and busiest trades. One thinks of the small group of merchant princes known from Palmyra. Below these heights there would have been many more operating at a relative distance from the households of the political elite.[129] The same banker's archive which shows money finding its way into business from the emperor's patrimony, also indicates the existence of a commercial community by no means generally dominated by aristocratic masters.[130] The most likely scenario, therefore, would see aristocratic investments going into commercial activities next to those conducted by various more independent groups consisting of richer merchants and financiers – the majority of whom would have been of middling wealth.[131] Such involvement, in fact, blends in rather well with the commercial patterns of uncertainty and opportunistic distortions by local monopoly groups established in Chapter 3.[132] Merchants and commercial ventures of the great Roman households would have been able to exploit the political muscle of the supporting aristocrat to gain special advantages. They might, for instance, have been more difficult to tax than their competitors who lacked the support of a grandee; or they might have found it easier momentarily to corner a specific line of trade by mobilising

---

[129] Some inscriptional examples of very rich and merely wealthy merchants: *CIL* VI, 29722; X, 1872; XIII, 1942, 1954, 1960, 2448; XIV, 4142, 4620–4622 (possibly); *AE* 1973, 646. D'Arms 1981, 140–148 recognised that for a large number among the wealthiest freedmen, the so-called *seviri Augustales*, it was not possible to claim aristocratic backing. Abramenko 1993 takes this too far; it is inconceivable that hardly any freedmen *Augustales* would have owed their privileged position to their connection with an aristocratic household. These households were the major slave owners, therefore also the main manumitters in Roman society and potentially provided slaves with better opportunities for enrichment.

[130] E.g. *TPSulp.* 13–14, 53, 78, 80. See the balanced treatment of Camodeca 2003 (the Sulpicii, for instance, may have had some distant connections to one of the great aristocratic families, but as we meet them, they seem to have been operating independently).

[131] See also Andreau 1999, chapter 6 for a discussion of such intermediary groups of independent entrepreneurs and financiers.

[132] See Prakash 1985: 29–34 and 232–234 and Ali 1997, chapter 6 for Mughal nobles using their political muscle to gain from trade.

the great political and financial power of the noble household to achieve their end.[133]

Thus far the basic structure of trading capital in the Roman world appears to correspond with our image of the household-*commenda* pattern of the bazaar with many individual actors, fragmentation of capital and a restricted layer of richer financiers. In terms of financial services, however, the Roman system does not appear to have developed quite the same array of instruments as existed in the bazaars of Mughal India. The availability of forms of insurance was greater in India. But in particular the Indian merchant had access as a matter of routine to an institutionalised system of bills of exchange and cheques known as *hundis*. These were negotiable, in principle. In practice many obstacles reduced the extent to which this was the case. The most important function of the *hundi* was to enable cash-free paper transfers of money between localities.[134] Along the most frequented trading routes the *hundi*-system operated quite well. Roman bankers and money lenders never established so routinely institutionalised a system as this.[135]

Nonetheless, the contrast can be exaggerated. Our sources for Roman banking operations leave many gaps. Much is simply unknown about the detailed activities of Roman bankers. But from more recent research it is becoming increasingly clear that bankers may have been of greater service to traders than is often thought.[136] For instance, payment not infrequently happened via a bank account. Thus traders were able, though absent, to receive and effect payment through their bank representative. Giro transfers are also a possibility one should not dismiss out of hand. Many banks seem to have been local, but some bankers had correspondents or branches outside their home base which enabled them to conduct credit and money transactions across geographical locations without necessarily having physically to move coin.[137]

[133] *C. Th.* XIII. 1, 5, 7, 15, 21. Whittaker 1993, chapter 12.
[134] Haider 1997: 185–189; Habib 1972.
[135] De Ligt 2002, though he much exaggerates the capacity of the Mughal system, cf. Richards 1981.
[136] Contra Bürge 1987 and Finley 1985a: 141. Andreau 1987 is fundamental.
[137] The insistence by Rathbone 2003 and Harris 2006 on the importance of various kinds of non-cash transfers in the Roman economy is surely correct. But their observations

Finally the evidence from Roman Egypt, recently treated by Hiderato, deserves mentioning. A fair number of papyri document the use of a sort of non-negotiable bill of exchange or cheque, a so-called *epitheke*, to create short-term credit and effect paper transfers of money between different locations in the province.[138] It would be rash to elevate this into a widely used system of bills of exchange. However, it does remind us that we risk underestimating the intercity transfer of money by credit instruments in the Roman world. Though clearly unable to match the Indian *hundi*, the Roman financial instruments do not belong on an entirely different planet. Perhaps they are better viewed as an earlier example of a system which gradually reached maturity and became more institutionalised during the Middle Ages and early modern period across Eurasia.[139]

Compartmentalised networks of trade

This chapter has focused on the social relationships of Roman traders, in particular those shaped by the household and communal associations. The aim has been to demonstrate how the commercial order depended on the ability of its members to form ties of community. These, both inside or outside the household, were of crucial importance to the success of the individual merchant. Wherever he went, the merchant would try to use his personal network in order to safeguard and promote his interests. A business letter, dating to second- or third-century Roman Egypt, illustrates the point:

Ammon to Dionysius his brother, greetings ... Provided you know that we could find a letter of credit at your place in order to pay the money there, I am willing to come to you to pay the wool. I think the other dyers, too, will go there for this purpose. When they come, please deal with them on my behalf and write (and tell me) which one you want me to remit the money to. Many salutations from your mother Plousias and your sister Hermione and Amoitas your father

need to be balanced by the evidence which suggests a more limited role, cf. de Ligt 2002. For some cautious observations, see Andreau 1987, chapter 18; Andreau 1999: 42–44; Bogaert 2000; Camodeca 2003.

[138] Hiderato 1999–2000 developing Preisigke 1910.

[139] Van Leur 1955: 71–73; Abu-Lughod 1989; and Goody 1996, chapters 2 and 3.

and Pathermuthis your brother and Pallas. Salutations to the father from myself and the aforesaid. We pray for the health of yourself and all your household all your life long.[140]

A dyer, Ammon, contacts his business partner living in a different location about possibly travelling to the latter's place to buy wool. However, to do so, he needs to know whether he would be able to obtain an *epithéke*, the Egyptian letter of credit, with which to make payment. Furthermore, Ammon requires his partner Dionysius to handle his dealings with other dyers coming to the market and inform him to whom he needs to transfer money. Thus we see Ammon mobilising his personal connections to forward his business venture in another place. Without such connections, he would not be able to conduct business there, or only at much greater risk. Note, therefore, how the relations with the partner are invested with greater and more enduring meaning by the use of affectionate metaphors to create a sense of family, even though the two were not "brothers", strictly speaking.

Personal contacts, or clientelisation as Geertz called it, were all-important in the world of the bazaar. They helped to shelter the merchant in an uncertain and risky market environment. But such contacts worked through exclusion as well as inclusion. Traders outside the social network of personal contacts were at a disadvantage or even excluded. In economic terms, the various personal and communal networks served to lower the transaction costs of insiders while creating higher barriers to entry in the market by outsiders. Thus communal ties and clientelisation operated to turn the uncertainties and risks of the bazaar to the advantage of the traders by reinforcing the fragmentation of business. The result was a tendency towards the compartmentalisation of commerce. Trade would often have been conducted within relatively closed circles and goods would regularly move in separate or parallel channels.[141]

---

[140] *P. Oxy. Hels.* 48 (trans. the editors). Hiderato 1999–2000: 94–95 treats the letter in relation to *epithéke*.
[141] Greif 1993. Cf. Geertz 1979.

This is a phenomenon which can sometimes be documented to a surprising extent from the archaeological record.[142] Italian *terra sigillata*, that is mould-made and stamped red-slip pottery from the late Republic and early Empire, may serve as illustration. Surviving in substantial quantities, enjoying a wide distribution and with finds having recently been collected in a database of more than 35,000 entries, the distribution patterns of this type of pottery can be examined in unusual detail and enable us to go beyond the merely impressionistic.[143] The evidence points to the importance of different networks for the distribution of the products of different potters and production centres. A good example is provided by two of the larger manufacturers of Italian *terra sigillata*, P. Cornelius and L. Gellius. Both enjoyed a roughly equal distribution in Italy. The products of Cornelius, however, were exported in much greater quantities to Spain and Morocco, whereas Gellius figures far more prominently in north Italy and along the Danube.[144] Likewise, the products bearing the stamp of MURRIUS, a potter tentatively located in Pisa, are found particularly in Narbonese Gaul, Hispania Tarraconensis and Africa Proconsularis. By contrast, the contemporary Pisan products of Cn. Ateius Euhodus also find their way in substantial numbers to the provinces of Germania Inferior and Superior.[145] Euhodus was one of a number of Ateii potters, most of them Pisa-based. Together they make up one of the most prolific groups of producers. Yet their products are not particularly prominent on Italian sites whereas they seem to have been exported in large quantities, not least to the Germanic provinces. This points to a more general difference between productions in Pisa and Arezzo further inland. The former seem to have been part of a commercial network focused on the north-west Mediterranean littoral, the Gauls and the Germanies. Arretine products, on the other hand, dominated the Italian scene, but were also exported,

---

[142] See Reynolds 1995: 139 and Lund 1999 for some examples of the cellular movement of goods. Bounegru 2006: 86–88 indicates different domains for different Roman commercial groups in the Danubian and Pontic area.

[143] Kenrick 2000.   [144] Kenrick 2000: 46–49.

[145] See Kenrick 2000 for statistics for potter 292 (Ateius Euhodus) and 1202 (Murrius). However, even with 143 and 122 attested finds respectively, the level of statistical uncertainty in the analysis of individual potters is still quite high. A single big find could influence the overall shape of distribution patterns significantly.

presumably via different channels, to a large number of provincial locations.[146]

In the case of the Pisan productions, the legions stationed on the northern frontier will have been an important market. Similarly closed and separate circuits of supply have been suggested in relation to deliveries made of Spanish olive oil to the Rhine army and as a model more generally for how military units procured their supplies.[147] In the analysis presented here, such activities need not necessarily be taken as anomalous, state-induced deviations from proper markets. As strategies they were not exclusive to the state.[148] Rather, they blend well into the broad weave of personalised ties and social networks which have been described as crucial for the functioning of trade in general. In a bazaar environment, lacking the institutional supports developed by capitalism, the use of such strategies was an expression of how markets worked.

[146] The difference, therefore, cannot simply be explained in terms of geography and the easier transport afforded by the location of Pisa much closer to the sea. Arretine products also travelled widely. Geography and social networks interacted to produce specific patterns. That phenomenon has also been documented for the distribution of the various provincial productions of *sigillata* in the Gauls and Germanies of the second and third centuries AD, see Rapsaet 1987 and Rapsaet-Charlier 1988.

[147] Remesal-Rodríguez 1997 (though the evidential base is weak; the numbers are too small to make the statistical analysis certain) and Whittaker 1994a: 104–113.

[148] Cf. Lo Cascio 2006 insisting that the state was not simply standing outside "the market". As the biggest landowner, it would have engaged in markets as one, albeit very powerful, seller of agricultural produce among others.

EPILEGOMENA
TAKING STOCK – THE WORLD OF GOODS

A French missionary who had viewed these palaces found "it incredible how rich this sovereign [i.e. the Chinese emperor] is in curiosities and magnificent objects of all kinds from the Occident". Yet the foreign treasures were only part of an assemblage that aimed to make the imperial retreats complete with every imaginable creation of nature as well as humanity. As Granet says, even things that no collector could find nevertheless figured there, sculpted or drawn: it was a universal collection of "evocative singularities". Such diversity was directly linked to the ruler's power,

Marshall Sahlins, *Cosmologies of Capitalism*, p. 432

Here is brought from every land and sea all the crops of the seasons and the produce of each land, river, lake, as well as of the arts of the Hellenes and barbarians, so that if someone should wish to view all these things, he must either see them by travelling over the whole world or be in this city [Rome]. It cannot be otherwise than that there always be here an abundance of all that grows and is manufactured among each people . . . Whatever one does not see here neither did nor does exist.

Aelius Aristeides, *To Rome, Or.* XXVI, 11–13[1]

The blatant flattery and undisguised hyperbole of the second-century Greek orator, Aelius Aristeides' eulogy to Rome and her Empire jar with modern sentiments. Students of the Roman world are now increasingly convinced that Aristeides could not in earnest have subscribed to his rosy image of empire. They have started searching for chinks in the rhetorical armour of the Greek master: anything to suggest the resistance of a cultured Hellene to his Roman oppressors.[2] Nonetheless, to generations of Roman historians the image conveyed by Aristeides' speech has come to embody their view of the second-century Empire.[3] The

---

[1] Translation adopted from Charles Behr (Aristeides, *The Complete Works*, vol. II, 1981) and J. H. Oliver (1953).

[2] See Swain 1996: chapter 8 for a balanced discussion of Aristeides.

[3] Schiavone 2000, chapters 1 and 2 draws attention to the central place of Aristeides' speech in Roman historiography.

290

Aristeidean paradigm, so to speak, reached its fullest fruition in the work of Rostovtzeff, for whom it was the story of the creation of a liberal, enlightened monarchy that unified the Mediterranean into one vast economic space – a world market and cosmopolitan bourgeois, capitalist society. Rostovtzeff's construction was a fragile one. Even in his own analysis the bourgeois order was constantly threatened by collapse into oppressive and destructive despotism. Our notion of empire has been caught up in this duality. A 'primitivist' conception focuses on the exploitative and predatory character of empire.[4] 'Modernists', on the other hand, have conjured up a sort of ideal Smithian market economy.[5]

Both dimensions in our image of empire are, in fact, present in Aristeides' speech. If the Roman Empire appears as an agent of economic integration, it is not exactly in the liberal, laissez-faire sense, which Rostovtzeff envisaged. It is rather as the omnipotent commander of the world's resources. The city of Rome is presented as an irresistible magnet gathering all the globe's variety in the imperial centre. If it is not to be found there, it does not exist, as Aristeides hyperbolically claims. This is Rome as ruler of the *oecumene*, a universal empire commanding, collecting and consuming the world's diversity. Such is the Empire's resourcefulness and strength that whole regions are laid bare by its demands. In one of Aristeides' oratorical flourishes, the Arabs are depicted as having to travel to Rome and beg for incense should they wish to enjoy a share of that luxurious product of their own country.[6] In the universe of the Greek orator market trade becomes an expression of imperial submission and tributary obligations. The character of Roman trade is Janus-faced. Both aspects of the imperial experience, greater flow of resources and exploitative command, must be accommodated within the same framework in order to achieve a satisfactory understanding of markets, trade and the economy of the Roman Empire.

---

[4] See Finley 1985a: 182–183 for instance emphasising pure exploitation in response to Keith Hopkins' taxes-and-trade model.

[5] See Persson 1988, chapter 5 for an interesting example of an economist suggesting parallels between Rome and the later integration of the European economy.

[6] A different variation of this ideological theme is developed in Pliny's *Panegyric to Trajan* 29–32. There it appears in the claim that even Egypt has come to depend on Rome for its grain. The flow of economic resources is perceived within a context of tribute.

It has been the aim of this study to construct such a framework – not, however, in the form of a simple middling compromise. A portrait of the Roman world as either a "failed" version of modernity or an agrarian economy approaching modernisation would be entirely unsatisfactory. Either of these unconvincing alternatives would leave us with an unattractive conglomerate, neither this nor that, and would fail to bring us past the current deadlock in the debate about the Roman economy in general and trade in particular. We need to rid our discussions of the implicit and sometimes explicit modernisation narrative undergirding much of the current disagreement. To escape our conceptual impasse we need to turn to comparative history, and what is more, a kind of comparative history which has never before been attempted. We need to identify different analytical contexts which resemble the Roman situation more closely than the early modern European world that is normally used as point of reference (cf. Chapter 1). Mughal India is one such possibility. Other pre-industrial empires would lend themselves to the same exercise. But the historiography of the Indo-Muslim empire is particularly well suited to our purposes. The image of the Great Mughals presiding over a vast and expanding empire based on the floodplains of India has many features in common with the way Roman hegemony has been understood. However, whereas the liberal, benevolent conception of Rome has been slow to die, Mughal studies have had to struggle with an equally persistent hardcore vision of an exploitative, Oriental despotism. The notion of a possible modernity has only rarely possessed the same plausibility to Mughal historians as it has enjoyed with students of Rome. Their task has therefore been slightly different. It has been a question of finding an appropriate characterisation for a society in which a considerable transfer of economic resources between regions takes place within an assuredly, or at least more assuredly, non-modern context. This has produced an understanding of trade and markets that is of use to us.

In Chapters 2 to 5 I have attempted to use examples from the Mughal Empire, occasionally with the inclusion of additional material from other places, to suggest ideal-types or models for the shape and character of markets and particularly intercity trade in the Roman Empire. Rather than observing Rome in the traditional perspective of later European developments, I have been looking at the Empire through a Mughal-Indian lens. Perhaps in the process Rome has come to look more like seventeenth-century India and seventeenth-century India more like Rome than was actually the case. This may well provoke some classicists and historians of India alike. It is a widespread misperception that the individual characteristics of a particular culture are always to be considered paramount. But cross-cultural similarities should not a priori be seen as any less real than differences. Differences and similarities must be handled pragmatically. Whether to emphasise one or the other depends on our questions and the problems we examine. The first chapter argued that, in spite of the obvious cultural contrasts, the political economy of the Roman and Mughal as well as a number of other tributary empires differed in the same fundamental way from the developing world/state system of early modern Europe.

This shared difference in the political economy of the two empires has been made the basis of the analysis. Comparisons with Mughal India have enabled the identification of a number of key processes, developments and characteristics which similarly shaped the economy of the Roman Empire in important ways. This is not to deny that there were important differences between the Indo-Muslim and Greco-Roman worlds. There obviously were. But it suggests that in relation to the fundamental economic processes examined here, such differences are better treated as factors creating variations in the common pattern rather than as the foundations of entirely different social systems. Greco-Roman as well as Indo-Muslim civilisation have, in other words, not been individually reified as absolute, all defining entities, but rather treated as similar kinds of imperial high culture which developed in response to a shared condition – a social technology designed or employed to handle related problems arising out of the need to mobilise the surplus of the peasant masses.[7]

In Chapter 2, the Mughal parallel suggested that the economic impact of the Roman Empire should be seen both in terms of elite

---

[7] See Gellner 1988b for such an approach, using the term agro-literate society.

building and taxation. When that is done, it becomes clear that the economic integration created by the formation of empire in the Mediterranean happened as a consequence of tribute extraction. It was not a market-driven process, *Ricardo-style*, based on a steadily deepening interregional division of labour. A hypothetical quantitative model helped to demonstrate that there could hardly have been room for such a development. The existence of a world empire, to borrow Wallerstein's term, did not so much prevent economic integration per se as create a different interregional flow of the limited agricultural surplus. The function of the market was here rather that of serving as a transformer of the politically extracted agricultural surplus. In that role market trade greatly facilitated the capacity of the political elite to consume the surplus outside its production area.

The second part of the study, "Imperial Bazaar", examined how this different function of Mughal and Roman traders alike affected the shape of the market world in institutional terms. A key concept was the organisational capacity of merchants. Neither Mughal nor Roman traders acquired as solid and influential a position in the political order of their respective societies as early modern European traders did. The consequences of this were brought out in Chapter 3 by an analysis of the clash of European and Indian trading institutions that occurred within the Mughal Empire. The more limited social power of Indian merchants made for a lesser ability, on average, to integrate markets. Individual markets in the Mughal Empire were therefore more prone to violent short-term fluctuations and were characterised by considerable fragmentation. It was a less predictable trading environment than gradually began to emerge in the Dutch and later British-led European world-system. This model was tested, to the extent that was possible, with positive results on Roman material, including price series from the province of Egypt. From here the parallel with Mughal India was expanded to include consideration of the ability of the imperial apparatus to homogenise coinage, laws and measures. Often the Roman Empire has been seen as creating an institutionally unified economic space in the lands surrounding the Mediterranean. The Mughal comparison helped bring out the clear limits to what was achieved by the tributary empires on that account. Though a homogenising influence, the trading world of the Roman Empire remained steeped in local and regional practices.

The many local variations and irregularities, however, must not be mistaken for complete chaos and fragmentation. Instead Mughal India suggests that the merchants developed a market form with a particular shape of its own. It is normally referred to as the bazaar. But it is not the "castrated" phenomenon, sidelined by modern developments, of petty retailers we meet as tourists in poor Middle Eastern countries today. These are only the sad remains of a formerly vibrant commercial universe. The larger bazaars of the agrarianate world included long-distance trade, wholesalers, brokers, auctions and specialised money lenders. However, if modern capitalist markets have been characterised by a drive to integrate separate markets, stabilise and homogenise trading conditions, increase security and reduce irregularities of trade, the bazaar operated at a more modest level of ambition. Its ability to transform the commercial environment and provide more generally stable conditions was much less. But, as argued by Clifford Geertz, the bazaar merchant was not reduced thereby to the level of a powerless victim of irregularity. Instead he developed strategies to manage or possibly even take advantage of the situation. The bazaar was a world of many impenetrable, tightly knit groups seeking to profit from local, most often short-term, monopolies. The much discussed famine in Antioch during the visit of the emperor Julian presents us with precisely this form of commercial speculation. The chapter therefore concluded by suggesting the bazaar as a general model for the workings of Roman commercial life.

The mechanisms and strategies developed by the bazaar merchants in the face of irregularity were explored further in the two following chapters. Chapter 4 examined the relationship between bazaar and state through the process of customs collection. On the basis of the Mughal comparison it was portrayed as a balance of power. In spite of the customs collector's proverbial abusiveness, the ability of merchants to go elsewhere did impose some limits on his exactions. Though far from satisfying modern notions of security this balance of power did provide a fragile order that enabled trade to take place. If the imperial state did not provide the level of guarantees offered by the bourgeois state, the merchants of the bazaar compensated by developing private forms of order and organisation. This was treated in Chapter 5, which explored community building and social networks among the merchants in the bazaar. The focus was on communal structures and the household. By comparing Indian caste with Roman *collegia* it was suggested that a significant economic role underlay the often-noticed predominantly socio-religious character of Roman professional associations. Those associations were important in creating or supporting structures of community among the merchants; social norms were disseminated, private judicial arbitration and credit possibly made available. The household, too, was an important source of social support. It provided the basis of commercial capital and fitted into a hierarchical pattern of *commenda*-style financing. However, by fostering clientelisation, to use Geertz' expression, both sets of institutions reinforced the fragmented shape of the bazaar. They benefited insiders while making it very difficult for outsiders to penetrate markets. This would have created a tendency for goods to be channelled into compartmentalised and separate circuits of distribution.

This study has aimed to provide a different context for our understanding of market trade in the Roman Empire. The prolonged battle of the modernists and primitivists has tended to descend into a quarrel over quantities: much or little, important or unimportant? This is beside the point. Clearly large quantities of goods did move about in the Roman Mediterranean and markets served an important function in the empire. But the aristocratic and tributary order had very different needs from capitalism. Those needs fashioned the shape of the world of market trade in a particular way and promoted distinct commercial patterns which differed from the evolving capitalism of early modern Europe in significant ways. Roman trade was not bourgeois or capitalist. It took the form of market exchange characteristic of the civilised societies of the agrarian world: *the bazaar.*

The bazaar, however, does not only represent a particular way of organising trade. Institutions have been the focus of this study. But the concept of the bazaar is far from exhausted by that approach. It can be developed in other directions, too. In the popular perception the bazaar is primarily a world of a bewildering variety of exotic rarities and enticing luxuries, a universe speaking to and stimulating the senses through fine, expensive cloths, delicate handcraft and aromatic, colourful spices. That reputation is well earned and is closely connected with sumptuous forms of imperial expenditure. The dominance in societies such as the Roman and Mughal of consumption by the patrimonial households of the landed elite and the emperor had more than institutional effects on the imperial bazaar. It also shaped the world of goods in fundamental ways.

It is often stated that only with the advent of capitalism did trade across longer distances in ordinary commodities, staple goods that is, become important;[8] in the preceding aristocratic world, trade was only a question of luxuries. Outside the European Middle Ages, though even here there are grounds for hesitation, this view is in need of substantial revision. Both the Roman Empire and Mughal India knew large flows of staple goods – not, however, of the generalised production and marketing of goods aimed at the expanding mass-market of the middle classes that came to fruition during the seventeenth and particularly eighteenth centuries in, for example, Holland and England.[9] But the consumption of elite income and imperial tribute did intensify patterns of urbanisation and increase demand for staple goods. The Mughal and Roman emperor or grandee were in public view, their power constantly displayed in lavish expenditure on pageantry, public buildings (temples, markets etc.), private "palaces" and large numbers of servants and retainers to provide

---

[8] Israel 1989 attempts to counter the exclusive focus on staple goods in many descriptions of Dutch capitalism.

[9] Described by McKendrick, Brewer and Plumb 1982. See Kloft 1996 and Morley 2007: 39–46 for a discussion of ancient forms of consumption. Yet, while it is important not to write ancient luxury consumption off as a trivial economic phenomenon, we still need concepts to distinguish different cultures of consumption, instead of simply elevating modern middle-class consumption to the universal model. Pomeranz 2000, chapter 3, for instance, finds greater similarity between early modern Chinese and European patterns of consumption, with India having a much steeper hierarchy of consumers. However, with the consolidation of the Ch'in dynasty, the Chinese pattern becomes more "imperial", less egalitarian and "bourgeois".

a suitable backdrop for the grand spectacle of aristocratic life.[10] If
the vision of empire claimed command of the world's diversity that,
too, included the availability of men and women in abundance –
as servants, craftsmen, entertainers, producers or just audience.
All this increased the size of urban populations. The top end of the
urban hierarchy, in particular, saw the creation of some very big
conurbations swelled by the enormous expenditure of the emperor
and leading aristocrats. The luxury of imperial culture necessitated
the mobilisation of large urban populations to serve its needs and
hence created a demand for substantial staple imports to the imperial capitals and some other cities that had outgrown the production
capacity of their hinterlands.[11]

The ideal of universal empire was acted out in the lifestyle of the
emperor, closely emulated by the different strata of the landed elites
to the best of their varying financial capacities. Around the imperial
court and the great households of the leading nobles an extremely
elaborate culture of luxurious consumption evolved. It was based
on abundance and artistic refinement in art, handicrafts and haute
cuisine, not to mention love-making and eroticism as well as philosophical reasoning. Of course there were differences in emphasis
between the two courtly cultures. Not every register was played to
the same extent or in the same way. The art of calligraphy, as any
visitor to the Taj Mahal will testify, was far more important to the
Muslim Mughals than to Roman emperors who on the other hand
promoted human sculpture to a much larger extent, to the benefit
of later European museums. But both cultures set great store by the
availability of the most valuable, prized and exotic luxuries such
as precious stones and metals, expensive colours, rare materials,

[10] See Blake 1991 on Mughal courtly consumption. Friedländer 1921–3 *passim* pioneered the study of Roman styles of consumption, e.g. vol. 1: 33–35; vol. 2, chap. xi,
and attempted to sever it from the realm of moralistic condemnation and fantasy. An
important point of his was that modern capitalist consumption had exceeded Roman.
Veyne 1976b is the classic treatment of public munificence in the Hellenistic and Roman
worlds. For modern analyses, see Garnsey 1994, chapters 8–9 (food); Toner 1995
(leisure); Edwards and Woolf 2003 (the various aspects of imperial Rome). Weeber
2003; 2006 is a useful, but mainly descriptive, survey of Roman luxury consumption.
[11] See Habib & Raychaudhuri 1982: 170–171 and Richards 1993a: 28 on the main Mughal
cities and strongholds. On Mughal urban hierarchies and revenue flows: Moosvi 1987,
chapters 12–13; Blake 1987; Richards 1987 (contributions of Blake and Richards); on
Roman: Woolf 1997.

animals and spices frequently imported from afar and even beyond the confines of the empires.[12] Palmyrene grave goods provide ample documentation for the import of Chinese silks into the Roman Empire via India. Spices and incense were other products which the Romans imported from the East.[13]

The notion of the marvellous and the singular was central to this kind of consumption. Monarchs and aristocrats delighted in the presentation of wonderful and sensational specimens of animals and objects. Scattered across the memoirs of the Mughal emperor Jahangir are many expressions of satisfaction prompted by the reception of such objects:

This day Dilawar Khan's son came from Patan . . . and paid homage, presenting a Kachhi horse. It was extremely well formed and easy to ride. No horse this good had been presented since I came to Gujarat . . . On this day my son Shahjahan showed me a pomegranate and a quince he had been brought from Farahabad. Until now nothing this big had ever been seen.[14]

Ostentatious expenditure by the aristocrat was meant to impress and to dazzle not only the common folk but also, and more importantly, his peers. Roman and Mughal nobles joined in competition over who could stage the most impressive, surprising and extraordinary displays. The fashions of luxury were driven by the agonistic impulse of the political elite. Occasionally one would see attempts to curb this competitive urge to consume. Sumptuary laws and moralising discourse, harping on the corruption of manners or the frenzy of fashion and teaching personal restraint, served intermittently to reinforce cohesion among the aristocracies and to protect their members from committing financial suicide in a kind of gigantic imperial potlatch. True nobility, that was the message, depended on more than the mere ability to spend.[15]

---

[12] Dalby 2000: 1 aptly notes that "a geography of luxury runs though the literature of imperial Rome". Unfortunately his book is mainly descriptive rather than analytical, a catalogue of ancient literary references.

[13] Schmidt-Colinet, Stauffer and Al-As'ad 2000.

[14] *The Jahangirnama*, trans. Wheeler M. Thackston, Oxford, 1999, p. 251. Phlegon's *Book of Marvels* (conveniently translated by William Hansen, Exeter, 1996) is a good example of Greco-Roman fascination with the strange and extraordinary.

[15] On these aspects of elite consumption, see Edwards 1993, in particular chapter 5.

Since Sombart wrote his now classic work on *Luxury and Capitalism*, it has become customary to see modern middle-class consumption as emerging out of the tension between the democratic force of fashion and the rearguard actions of aristocratic groups trying to limit competition by making key status markers their legal preserve. As the Middle Ages gave way to the early modern era in Europe, old styles of aristocratic living became obsolete. Where feudal nobles had gloried in the size of their retinues, early modern elites placed a growing emphasis on refinement in housing, dining and courtship. At the end of this process, aristocratic privilege gave way to bourgeois spending. Consumption became increasingly shaped by the middle classes and access to the market.[16] In theoretical terms, this represented a shift in the culture of consumption from a coupon- to a fashion-regulated system. Access to prestige goods was not reserved to groups with particular privileges and entitlements (coupons). Instead the ability to follow the changing dictates of fashion came to define high status.[17]

However, there is a danger of imposing too teleological a view on these developments. While the rule of fashion may in some contexts serve to break down established hierarchies and widen participation to include broader groups, there is nothing inevitable or automatic about this outcome, not even in the European context. The possession of vast retinues remained central to the Roman and Mughal nobles as they diversified their habits of consumption.[18] The dichotomy of stable coupon and dynamic fashion systems seems too crude to do justice to the Roman and Mughal experience. Both imperial societies were far too complex and dynamic to rely primarily on law and established convention to regulate

[16] This view of the history of European consumption was anticipated by Ferguson in his *Essay on the History of Civil Society* of 1767, part sixth, section III (1995: 238–241).
[17] Cf. Appadurai 1986: 32. But as his own discussion, pp. 23–41, indicates, the operation of fashion does not necessarily undermine aristocratic dominance. The polar distinction between coupon and fashion may usefully capture the difference between many simple societies known from anthropology and modern consumption; it is less well suited to understand differences between complex agrarian, or as I prefer to call them, agrarianate, societies.
[18] Horace, *Serm.* I, 100–130, by literary conceit, considered himself fortunate that he was sufficiently unimportant to be able to travel without a huge retinue. Yet, Horace, the 'simple-living' poet of high equestrian substance, still took his modest meal served by three(!) slaves. See Blake 1991, chapters 2–4 on the importance of the great noble households in the Mughal Empire.

aristocratic entitlement to prestige goods, though they did that too. Their aristocracies mobilised markets successfully to obtain access to a widened range of luxuries to adorn their dwellings and grace their ambience. The elaboration of the culture of consumption did not, in their cases, lead to any notable middle-class challenges to their hegemony. It is true that Roman satirists never seem to tire of lampooning the unworthy upstart. Pride of place is taken by Petronius' famous literary portrait of the stupendously wealthy freedman Trimalchio who, in spite of his riches, fails miserably to win respect in the eyes of the aristocratic readership; his social pretensions are held up to ridicule and terminate in farce. But, as Paul Veyne argued long ago, the fleeting class of freedmen could hardly represent a serious social challenge to the Roman elite.[19] It did, however, provide a convenient target of scorn against which to reaffirm elite identity. There is nothing intrinsically "democratic" about fashion-driven consumerism. The Roman and Mughal version served, rather, to consolidate the position of the imperial aristocracies and increase the hierarchical gradient in society.[20] Adam Ferguson, one of the Scottish Enlightenment philosophers, understood clearly that the emerging commercial society of his own day was something different from the Roman past. "The manners of the imperial court, and the conduct of succeeding Emperors will scarcely gain credit with those who estimate probabilities from the standard of modern times", he commented of Rome.[21]

Here again the bazaar, with its emphasis on the irregular, seems a useful prism through which to observe the imperial styles of consumption rather than treating them in an analytical framework derived from the emerging middle-class consumer revolution of the seventeenth, eighteenth and nineteenth centuries. One aspect of the repertoire of goods in the bazaar is the relatively low degree of standardisation. But merchants could also turn this characteristic into a virtue by stressing the unique properties and particular quality of their products. That enabled them to respond to and

[19] Veyne 1961. Cf. Nicolet 1980 on the lack of a middle-class "challenge" to the Roman aristocracy.
[20] See Qaisar 1967 for the steep economic hierarchy of the Mughal Empire. Garnsey 1970 remains fundamental on the intensification of social hierarchies under the Roman imperial monarchy.
[21] Ferguson 1799, vol. 5: 404 (with Pocock 2003: 410–411).

cultivate the demand of the imperial courts and aristocracies. The ideological principle underlying this form of consumption is neatly captured by C. A. Bayly:

Whereas modern complexity demands the uniformity of Levis and trainers, the archaic simplicity of everyday life demanded that great men prized difference in goods... and sought to capture their qualities. Modern "positional" goods are self-referential to themselves and to the markets that create demand for them; the charismatic goods of archaic globalization were embedded in ideologies which transcended them. In one sense archaic lords and rural leaders were collectors rather than consumers. What they did, however, was more than merely to collect because people, objects, foods, garments and styles of deportment thus assembled changed the substance of the collector... [the archaic lord aimed] strategically to consume diversity.[22]

The collection and consumption of exotic rarities and novel products was, like Pliny's *Historia Naturalis*, a cultural manifestation of the wide reach of imperial might.[23] As such this activity formed an important part of the self-fashioning of Roman and Mughal nobles as gentlemen and as men of power who were free of ordinary constraints and could realise the full potential of human life in all its aspects.[24] "Clothes maketh the man", as the expression goes. Luxury goods were thus imbued with certain charismatic, mystical or even magical properties; they were culturally invested with transformative capacity. Expensive spices and other rare natural substances were regularly used in medicine, much of it based on humoral theories of balancing bodily elements. Equally, precious goods were used extensively in religious ritual. The burning of incense, and other fragrant substances, was a staple of solemn ceremony.[25]

While such esoteric goods – "evocative singularities" as Marshall Sahlins called them in the epigraph to these epilegomena

[22] Bayly 2002: 52–53.
[23] See Beard and Henderson 2001: 96–105 and chapter 4 for some observations on power and the art of collecting in ancient Rome.
[24] See Finley 1985a, chapter 2 for the relevance of the gentlemanly ideal for ancient economic history; Blake 1991, chapter 5 and Richards 1984 on gentlemanly aristocratic culture in the Mughal Empire.
[25] As Miller 1969, chapters 1–2, made clear, much of our evidence for the ancient spice trade is derived from medical treatises, e.g. Galen's *De Antidosis*. For the central position of humoral theories of the body to the consumption of food, drink and medication, see further Galen, *On the Properties of Foodstuffs* and *On the Natural Faculties* II, 8.

– facilitated the creation of public authority and the cultivation of elevated character, they also served as a test of nobility. These rare, often foreign and always ruinously expensive products were surrounded by a dangerous aura; they were difficult to manage and control. Only the truly noble character knew how to master them, that was the claim. This belief was preached among the elites to bolster their confidence and preserve their sense of exclusivity. Therefore the use of prestige goods was enveloped in complex rituals and civilisational codes. Intricate and many of them tacit, the rules of decorum were all important: "Let no one rashly claim as his the art of dining."[26] These words Horace, the protégé of the arbiter of taste at the Augustan court, Maecenas, with double-edged irony put into the mouth of one of his satirical characters who is exposed as having failed himself to grasp the true content of what he was admonishing. Money was only a prerequisite to participation in polite society. Exterior possession of knowledge of the proper manners and rituals of consumption was a "give-away" and socially inhibiting in higher circles. Horatian satire mercilessly exhibits the failings of the trite big spender who, for all his display of luxuries, falls far short of the civilisational idiom and therefore comes across as vulgar and embarrassing. A host who bores his guests with long lectures on the splendours of the dinner he is serving them, instead of trusting their refinement and ability to appreciate the delicacies on their own, is trying too hard to impress.[27] The secret to social success was the effortless mastery of the art of consumption which came from an internalisation of the proper manners, acquired through long exposure. The great man was no mere commoner who had become rich. He was a connoisseur surrounding himself with all the trappings of high culture and knowing how to put them to their proper and balanced use, the true embodiment of their spirit.[28]

---

[26] Hor. *Serm* II, 4, 35: "nec sibi cenarum quivis temere arroget artem" (trans. Frances Muecke, Warminster, 1993). Decorum is a key concept in Cicero's *De Officiis*, a manual on the proper gentlemanly conduct. An example of a Mughal gentleman's manual is provided by Husain 1913 (with the analysis of Blake 1991: 130–132).

[27] Hor. *Serm*. II, 8.

[28] As Veblen remarked in his *Theory of the Leisure Class* (1899: 47): "the gentleman must consume freely", "of the right kind" and "in a seemly manner".

The patterns of consumption developed by the aristocratic leaders were emulated by local elites across the empires and in some
areas trickled even further down the social hierarchy. Trade in fine
food grains and fruits, Kashmiri shawls, Bengali muslins, silks
from Gujarat and other prestige goods catered to the demand of
the households of Mughal noblemen, *zamindars*, rural leaders and
service gentry of the small towns.[29] In the Roman Empire, the
ruins of Pompeii document how the "high" styles of decoration
were emulated by middling urban households, though of course in
a modified version.[30] In the Gaulic provinces Roman-style goods,
in a limited range, also made their way to the more prominent
peasants such as village leaders.[31] The dissemination, portrayed
by Paul Zanker, of imagery and styles related to the imperial court
across Roman provincial societies was perhaps, rather than the
result of propaganda, an expression of the wish by local grandees
to participate in this culture of consumption, acquire the substance
of universal hegemony.[32] As courts and aristocracies set new standards for prestige objects, the range and diversity of material culture expanded, as archaeologists will testify, in both empires.

Thus, the imperial bazaar does not only offer a different institutional context for our understanding of markets, it also opens a
window to a different world of goods, a distinct culture of consumption. Under the Romans, this is what unites the marketing
of large quantities of the mould-made terracotta tableware known
as *terra sigillata*, one of the most common artefacts of Roman
archaeology, and the imports of spices, cloths and ivory from the
greater region of the Indian Ocean described in the *Periplus Maris
Erythraei*.[33] As a concept, the bazaar is broad enough to accommodate both the peddling of small batches of ornamented, red-slip
tablewares by traders travelling with a few pack animals between
the rural fairs and numerous villages of the Roman countryside,

---

[29] Bayly 1983, introduction and chapter 1; 1986b: 297–302.
[30] Wallace-Hadrill 1994, chapter 7.   [31] See Woolf 2001 for this suggestion.
[32] See Zanker 1988 on dissemination of styles; Morley 2007: 46–49 on the importance of
imitation.
[33] As a concept the bazaar allows us to steer clear of some of the modernising connotations
implied by using the modern notion of globalisation – as does Hingley 2005 – to
understand the Roman Empire. There were some significant differences between the
two processes. See Casson 1989 for the modern standard edition of the *Periplus*.

and the considerably fewer merchants traversing the Middle East and Indian Ocean to bring back each year a fairly limited number of more valuable cargoes.[34] In the latter case, the increased demand created by the development of imperial styles of consumption marks a conjuncture in the history of old-world long-distance trade. It is in the Roman period that the pattern familiar from later ages of precious metals flowing eastwards in return for Oriental spices, incense and cloth really takes shape and matures. From India as well as other foreign locations, these goods and many more arrived in the Roman world, particularly through Egypt and Syria, with Alexandria and the caravan city of Palmyra as important commercial hubs.[35]

This basic system was to endure for centuries, though the fortunes of individual centres fluctuated. By the sixteenth century, Palmyra had long since slipped back into obscurity and stopped playing any role in long-distance trade. That function was now served by Aleppo while Cairo had eclipsed Alexandria as the main market in Egypt. Since Roman times, this trade had gone through several ups and downs. But underneath the movement of ebb and flow, the system had continued to develop and expand, not least under the aegis of the creation of a vast Muslim ecumene stretching from North Africa into Central Asia and India.[36] With the consolidation of the strong imperial monarchies of the Ming dynasty in China, the Ottomans in the Mediterranean, the Safavids in Persia and the Mughals in India, the pace and size of old-world long-distance trade received new stimulus from increased demand during the fifteenth and sixteenth centuries. It was to tap into the wealth of this trade in general and to cut into the profits earned by the Venetians in their capacity as the leading middlemen in the Levantine trade in particular that Europeans, spearheaded by

---

[34] The enormous values concentrated in relatively small quantities of Eastern prestige goods are best documented by the so-called Muziris Papyrus which records a single cargo worth almost HS 7 million (7 times the minimum fortune requirement for a Roman senator). For edition and translation see Casson 1990 and Rathbone 2001.

[35] Raschke 1978 surveys much of the evidence and provides a sceptical antidote to the most optimistic speculations and wildest guesses hazarded about this emerging trade. See Tchernia 1992 and 1995; De Romanis 1996; Yong 2001 for a selection of more recent work on Rome's Oriental trade.

[36] Chaudhuri 1985 and 1990; Abu-Lughod 1989; Curtin 1984.

the Portuguese, circumnavigated Africa and stumbled on America. Neither of these events, as used to be thought, brought down the old system which, after some initial disruption, continued to function.[37] But the establishment of commercial empires in the Indian Ocean, notably by the Portuguese, the Dutch and the English, combined with the arrival of American silver, did begin to modify the contours of the pre-existing pattern. From the late seventeenth century, this process intensified and European traders began to subject and transform the old system more deeply.[38] That spelled the end of the "imperial bazaar". The Mughal Empire thus stands at the end of a historical conjuncture which, irrespective of some earlier preliminaries, came into its own for the first time under the Romans. This adds historical depth to our comparison. For these were two tributary empires whose trade and markets followed similar patterns; they shared the world of the imperial bazaar.

---

[37] Das Gupta and Pearson 1987; Prakash 1997, introduction. See Perlin 1993 for some further, if perhaps occasionally too grand, observations on this world.

[38] Bayly 2004, chapters 1–2 are now fundamental. Steensgaard 1973a remains the best structural analysis, and further 1987. This also expanded the quantities involved enormously. In Zosimus' account of Alaric's first siege of Rome (V, 41, 4), a ransom was agreed involving the payment of 3,000 pounds of pepper. By implication this was supposed to represent a very substantial consignment of the spice in late antiquity. By the end of the seventeenth century, the combined annual imports to Europe of the Dutch and English East India Companies amounted to some 7 million pounds, see Steensgaard 1990a: 120. Obviously, these figures are not directly comparable. But there is no way to estimate total annual Roman pepper imports, so we are left with impressions. They suggest a change in the orders of magnitude; the Roman ransom would not have made a huge impression in the eighteenth century. As Gibbon concluded (1993, vol. 3: 277 and chapter 31): "the improvement of trade and navigation has multiplied the quantity and reduced the price [of pepper]".

BIBLIOGRAPHY

Abramenko, A. 1993, *Die Municipale Mittelschicht in kaiserzeitlichen Italien*, Frankfurt.

Abu-Lughod, J. 1989, *Before European Hegemony. The World System A.D. 1250–1350*, Oxford.

Adams, C. E. P. 1995, "Supplying the Roman Army: O. Petrie 245", *Zeitschrift für Papyrologie und Epigraphik* 109, pp. 119–124.

2007, *Land Transport in Roman Egypt. A Study of Economics and Administration in a Roman Province*, Oxford.

Adams, J. 1994, "Trading States, Trading Places: The Role of Patrimonialism in Early Modern Dutch Development", *Comparative Studies in Society and History* 36, pp. 319–355.

Adanir, F. 1997, "Der Zerfall des Osmanischen Reiches", in A. Demandt (ed.), *Das Ende der Weltreiche. Von den Persern bis zur Sowjetunion*, Munich, pp. 108–129.

Ain-i Akbari, by Abu'l-Fazl Allami, translated into English by H. Blochmann, ed. D. C. Phillott, 3 vols., 2nd edn, Calcutta, 1939.

Akerlof, G. 1970, "The Market for 'Lemons'", *Quarterly Journal of Economics* 84, pp. 488–500.

Alam, M. 1986, *The Crisis of Empire in Mughal North India*, New Delhi.

Alam, M. and Subrahmanyam, S. (eds.) 1998, *The Mughal State 1526–1750*, Delhi.

2000, "Witnessing Transition: Views on the End of the Akbari Dispensation", in Panikkar, Byres and Patnaik, pp. 104–140.

Alcock, S. 1993, *Graecia Capta. The Landscapes of Roman Greece*, Cambridge.

1997a, "Greece: A Landscape of Resistance?", in Mattingly 1997a, pp. 103–115.

(ed.) 1997b, *The Early Roman Empire in the East*, Oxford.

Alcock, S., D'Altroy, T., Morrison, K. D. and Sinopoli, C. M. (eds.) 2001, *Empires. Perspectives from Archaeology and History*, Cambridge.

Alföldy, G. 1977, *Konsulat und Senatorenstand unter den Antoninen. Prosopographische Untersuchungen zur Senatorischen Führungsschicht*, Bonn.

Ali, M. A. 1975, "The Passing of Empire: The Mughal Case", *Modern Asian Studies* 9, pp. 385–396.

1985, *The Apparatus of Empire. Awards of Ranks, Offices, and Titles to the Mughal Nobility, 1574–1658*, Delhi.

1986–7 "Recent Theories of Eighteenth Century India", *Indian Historical Review* 12, 1–2, pp. 102–110.

1997, *The Mughal Nobility under Aurangzeb*, Delhi (1st edn, 1966).

Alston, R. 1995, *Soldier and Society in Roman Egypt*, London.

1998, "Trade and the City in Roman Egypt", in Parkins and Smith, pp. 168–202.

2002, *The City in Roman and Byzantine Egypt*, London and New York.

Amin, S. 1973, *Le Développement inégal*, Paris.

Amouretti, M. C. and Brun, J. P. (eds.) 1993, *La Production du vin et de l'huile en Méditerranée* [*Oil and Wine Production in the Mediterranean Area*], Actes du Symposium International organisé par le Centre Camille Julian et le Centre Archéologique du Var, Aix-en-Provence et Toulon, 20–22 novembre 1991, Athens and Paris.

Amphores romaines et histoire économique. Dix ans de recerche. Collection de l'École Française de Rome 114, Rome 1989.

Anderson, A. C. and Anderson, A. S. (eds.) 1981, *Roman Pottery Research in Britain and North-West Europe. Papers Presented to Graham Webster*, Vols. 1–2, BAR International Series 123, Oxford.

Anderson, P. 1974, *Lineages of the Absolutist State*, London.

André, J.-M. and Baslez, M. F. 1993, *Voyager dans l'antiquité*, Paris.

Andreau, J. 1974, *Les Affaires de Monsieur Jucundus*, Rome.

1980, "Réponse à Yvon Thébert", *Annales ESC*, pp. 912–919.

1987, *La Vie financière dans le monde romain. Les métiers de manieurs d'argent (IVe siècle av. J.-C.–IIIe siècle ap. J.-C.)*, Rome.

1994a, "La cité romaine dans ses rapports à l'echange et au monde de l'échange", in Andreau, Briant, Descat *et al.*, pp. 83–98.

1994b, "L'Italie impériale et les provinces: déséquilibre des échanges et flux monétaires", in *L'Italie d'Auguste à Dioclétien*. Collection de l'École Française de Rome 198, Rome, pp. 175–203.

1995, "Vingt ans aprés *L'Économie Antique* de Moses I. Finley", *Annales. Histoire, Sciences Sociales* 50, pp. 947–960.

1997, "Deux études sur les prix à Rome: les "mercuriales" et le taux d'intérêt", in Andreau, Briant, Descat, *et al.*, pp. 105–120.

1999, *Banking and Business in the Roman World*, Cambridge.

2003, "Les commerçants, l'élite et la politique romaine à la fin de la république (IIIe–Ier siècles av. J.C.)", in Zaccagnini, pp. 217–243.

2006, "Roman Law in relation to Banking and Business: A Few Cases", in Bang, Ikeguchi and Ziche, pp. 201–214.

Andreau, J., Briant, P., Descat, R. *et al.* (eds.) 1994, *Économie antique. Les echanges dans l'Antiquité: le rôle de l'Etat*, Saint-Bertrand-de-Comminges.

Andreau, J., Briant, P., Descat, R. *et al.* (eds.) 1997, *Économie Antique. Prix et formation des prix dans les économies antiques*, Saint-Bertrand-de-Comminges.

Andreau, J., France, J. and Pittia, S. (eds.) 2004, *Mentalités et choix économiques des Romains*, Bordeaux.

Andreau, J. and Hartog, F. (eds.) 1991, *La città antica? La Cité antique, Opus* 6–8, 1987–9.

Ankum, H. 1972, "Quelques problèmes concernant les ventes aux enchères en droit Romain classique", *Studi in Onore de Gaetano Scherillo* I, Milan, pp. 377–394.

Aperghis, M. 2001, "Population – Production – Taxation – Coinage. A Model of the Seleukid Economy", in Archibald *et al.*, pp. 69–102.

2004, *The Seleukid Royal Economy. The Finances and Financial Administration of the Seleukid Empire*, Cambridge.

Appadurai, A. (ed.) 1986, *The Social Life of Things. Commodities in Cultural Perspective*, Cambridge.

Arangio-Ruiz, V. 1950, *La società in diritto romano*, Naples.

Arasaratnam, S. 1986, *Merchants, Companies and Commerce on the Coromandel Coast 1650–1740*, Delhi.

1990, "Recent Trends in the Historiography of the Indian Ocean", *Journal of World History* 2, pp. 225–248.

Archibald, Z. H. *et al.* (eds.) 2001, *Hellenistic Economies*, London.

Atsma, H. and Burguière, A. (eds.) 1990, *Marc Bloch aujourd'hui: Histoire comparée et sciences sociales*, Paris.

Aubert, J.-J. 1994, *Business Managers in Ancient Rome. A Social and Economic Study*, Leiden.

(ed.) 2003, *Tâches publiques et entreprise privée dans le monde romain*, Geneva.

2004, "De l'usage de l'écriture dans la gestion d'entreprise à l'époque romaine", in Andreau, France and Pittia, pp. 127–148.

Aubert, J.-J. and Sirks, B. (eds.) 2002, *Speculum Iuris. Roman Law as a Reflection of Social and Economic Life in Antiquity*, Ann Arbor, MI.

Ausbüttel, F. M. 1982, *Untersuchungen zu den Vereinen im Westen des römischen Reiches*, Kallmünz.

Autour de Coptos. Actes du colloque organisé au Musée des Beaux-Arts de Lyon (17–18 mars 2000). Topoi. Orient-Occident 3, Supplément, Lyon, 2002.

Aymard, M. (ed.) 1982, *Dutch Capitalism and World Capitalism*, Cambridge.

1990, "Histoire et comparaison", in Atsma and Burguière, pp. 271–278.

Baechler, J., Hall, J. and Mann, M. (eds.) 1988, *Europe and the Rise of Capitalism*, Cambridge.

Bagnall, R. S. 1993, *Egypt in Late Antiquity*, Princeton, NJ.

2000, "Governmental Roles in the Economy of Late Antiquity", in Lo Cascio and Rathbone, pp. 86–91.

Bagnall, R. S. and Frier, B. W. 1994, *The Demography of Roman Egypt*, Cambridge.

Bagnall, R. S., Helms, C. and Verhoogt, A. 2000, *Documents from Berenike*, vol. 1: *Greek Ostraka from the 1996–1998 Seasons*, Papyrologica Bruxellensia 31, Brussels.

Bairoch, Paul 1993, *Economics and World History. Myths and Paradoxes*, New York.

Bajekal, M. 1990, "The State and the Rural Grain Market in Eighteenth Century Eastern Rajasthan", in Subrahmanyam 1990a, pp. 90–120.

Balasz E., 1964, *Chinese Civilization and Bureaucracy. Variations on a Theme*, New Haven, CT.

Banaji, J. 2001, *Agrarian Change in Late Antiquity*, Oxford.

Banerjee, K. K. 1990, "Grain Traders and the East India Company: Patna and its Hinterland in the Late 18th and Early 19th Centuries", in Subrahmanyam 1990a, pp. 163–189.

Bang, P. F. 1997a, *Antiquity between "Primitivism" and "Modernism"*, Arbejdspapirer Center for Kulturforskning, Aarhus Universitet, no. 57, Aarhus, www.hum.au.dk/ckulturf/pages/publications/pfb/antiquity.htm.

1997b, "Aristokrati og handel i status-modellen – et clientela-perspektiv", *Historisk Tidsskrift* 97, 1, pp. 1–28.

2002a, "Romans and Mughals – Economic Integration in a Tributary Empire", in De Blois and Rich, pp. 1–25.

2002b, "Trade and Industry", *Classical Review*, n.s., 52, 1, pp. 97–100.

2004, "The Mediterranean: A Corrupting Sea? A Review-essay on Ecology and History, Anthropology and Synthesis", *Ancient West and East* 3, 2, pp. 385–399.

2006, "Imperial Bazaar: Towards a Comparative Understanding of Markets in the Roman Empire", in Bang, Ikeguchi and Ziche, pp. 51–88.

2007, "Trade and Empire – In Search of Organising Concepts for the Roman Economy", *Past and Present* 195, pp. 3–54.

Bang, P. F. and Bayly, C. A. (eds.) 2003, "Tributary Empires in History: Comparative Perspectives from Antiquity to the Late Medieval", *Medieval History Journal* 6, 2, special issue.

Bang, P. F., Ikeguchi, M. and Ziche, H. G. (eds.) 2006, *Ancient Economies, Modern Methodologies. Archaeology, Comparative History, Models and Institutions*, Bari.

Bang, P. F. *et al.* (eds.) 1999, *Agrarimperier mellem Marked og Tribut. Den Jyske Historiker* 86/87, Aarhus.

Barbour, V. 1966, *Capitalism in Amsterdam in the 17th Century*, Ann Arbor, MI.

Barker, G. and Mattingly, D. (eds.) 1996, *Farming the Desert: The UNESCO Libyan Valleys Archaeological Survey*, vols. 1–2, Tripoli and London.

Bay, A. 1972, *Den Romerske Finansadministration fra Augustus til Hadrian*, vols. 1–2, Horsens.

Bayly, C. A. 1983, *Rulers, Townsmen and Bazaars. North Indian Society in the Age of British Expansion 1770–1870*, Cambridge.

1986a, "The Middle East and Asia during the Age of Revolutions, 1760–1830", *Itinerario* 10, 2, pp. 69–84.

1986b, "The Origins of Swadeshi (Home Industry): Cloth and Indian Society, 1700–1930", in Appadurai, pp. 285–321.

1988, *Indian Society and the Making of the British Empire*, The New Cambridge History of India 2, 1, Cambridge.

1989, *Imperial Meridian*, Harlow.

2000, "South Asia and the 'Great Divergence'", *Itinerario* 24, pp. 83–103.

2002, "'Archaic' and 'Modern' Globalization in the Eurasian and African Arena, c. 1750–1850", in A. G. Hopkins (ed.), *Globalization in World History*, London, pp. 47–73.

2004, *The Birth of the Modern World 1780–1914. Global Connections and Comparisons*, Malden, MA and Oxford.

Bayly, C. A. and Bayly, S. 1988, "Eighteenth-Century State Forms and the Economy", in Dewey, pp. 66–90.

Bayly, C. A. and Subrahmanyam, S. 1990, "Portfolio Capitalists and the Political Economy of Early Modern India", in Subrahmanyam 1990a, pp. 242–265.

Bayly, S. 1999, *Caste, Society and Politics in India from the Eighteenth Century to the Modern Age*, The New Cambridge History of India 4, 3, Cambridge.

Bean, G. E. 1954, "Notes and Inscriptions from Caunus", *Journal of Hellenic Studies* 74, pp. 85–110.

Beard, M. and Henderson, J. 2001, *Classical Art. From Greece to Rome*, Oxford.

Bekker-Nielsen, T. 2004, *The Roads of Ancient Cyprus*, Copenhagen.

Beloch, K.-J. 1886, *Die Bevölkerung der griechisch-römischen Welt*, Leipzig.

Berktay, H. 1991, "Three Empires and the Societies They Governed: Iran, India and the Ottoman Empire", *Journal of Peasant Studies* 18, 3/4, pp. 242–263.

Bharadwaj, K. 1985, "A View on Commercialisation in Indian Agriculture and the Development of Capitalism", *Journal of Peasant Studies* 12, 1, pp. 7–25.

Bitterli, U. 1991, *Die "Wilden" und die "Zivilisierten"*, Munich.

Bjørkelo, A. 1999, "Noen karakteristiske trekk ved økonomisk virksomhet i Det osmanske riket", in Bang *et al.*, pp. 121–143.

Blake, S. P. 1979, "The Patrimonial Bureaucratic Empire of the Mughals", *Journal of Asian Studies* 39, pp. 77–94.

1987, "The Urban Economy in Pre-Modern Muslim India: Shahjahanabad, 1639–1739", *Modern Asian Studies* 21, 3, pp. 447–471.

1991, *Shajahanabad. The Sovereign City in Mughal India*, Cambridge.

Blázquez Martínez, J. M. and Remesal Rodríguez, J. (eds.) 1999–2001, *Estudios sobre el Monte Testaccio (Roma)*, vols. 1–2, Barcelona.

Bloch, M. 1934, "Une étude régionale: géographie ou histoire?", *Annales d'Histoire Économique et Sociale* 6, pp. 81–85.

1967, *Land and Work in Medieval Europe. Selected Papers by Marc Bloch*, trans. J. E. Anderson, Berkeley and Los Angeles.

Blois, L. de and Rich, J. (eds.) 2002. *The Transformation of Economic Life under the Roman Empire. Proceedings of the Second Workshop of the*

International Network Impact of Empire (Roman Empire, c. 200 B.C.–A.D. 476), Amsterdam.

Bogaert, R. 2000, "Les opérations des banques de l'Égypte romaine", *Ancient Society* 30, pp. 135–269.

Boserup, E. 1965, *The Conditions of Agricultural Growth. The Economics of Agrarian Change under Population Pressure*, London.

1981, *Population and Technology*, London.

Bounegru, O. 2006, *Trafiquants et navigateurs sur le Bas Danube et dans le Pont Gauche à l'époque romaine*, Wiesbaden.

Bradford Welles, C., Fink, R. O. and Gilliam, J. F. (eds.) 1959, *The Excavations at Dura-Europos* final report, 5, pt. 1: *The Parchments and Papyri*, New Haven, CT.

Brady, T. A., Jr. 1991, "The Rise of Merchant Empires, 1400–1700: A European Counterpoint", in Tracy, pp. 117–160.

Braudel, F. 1972, *The Mediterranean and the Mediterranean World in the Age of Philip II*, vol. 1, London.

1981, *The Structures of Everyday Life. Civilization and Capitalism*, vol. 1, trans. S. Reynolds, London.

1982, *The Wheels of Commerce, Civilization and Capitalism*, vol. 2, trans. S. Reynolds, London.

1984, *The Perspective of the World, Civilization and Capitalism*, vol. 3, trans. S. Reynolds, London.

Braudel, F. and Spooner, F. 1967, "Prices in Europe from 1450 to 1750", in E. E. Rich and C. H. Wilson (eds.), *The Cambridge Economic History of Europe*, vol. 4, chapter 7, pp. 374–486.

Braund, D. 1993, "Piracy under the Principate and the Ideology of Imperial Eradication", in Rich and Shipley, pp. 195–212.

Breckenridge, C. A. and Veer, P. van der (eds.) 1993, *Orientalism and the Postcolonial Predicament. Perspectives on South Asia*, Philadelphia, PA.

Bresson, A. 2000, *La Cité marchande*, Bordeaux.

2003, "Merchants and Politics in Ancient Greece: Social and Economic Aspects", in Zaccagnini, pp. 139–164.

Brimnes, N. 1997, "Traditionaliseringen af Indien", *Den Jyske Historiker* 77/78, pp. 13–29.

Bruhns, H. 1985, "De Werner Sombart à Max Weber et Moses Finley: La Typologie de la ville de consommation", in Leveau, pp. 255–274.

Bruhns, H. and Nippel, W. (eds.) 2000, *Max Weber und die Stadt im Kulturvergleich*, Göttingen.

Brunt, P. A. 1990, *Roman Imperial Themes*, Oxford.

Bücher, K. 1911, *Die Entstehung der Volkswirtschaft*, 8th edn, Tübingen (first published 1893).

1922, "Zur griechischen Wirtschaftsgeschichte", in K. Bücher, *Beiträge zur Wirtschaftsgeschichte*, Tübingen, pp. 1–97.

Buckland, W. W. 1908, *The Roman Law of Slavery. The Condition of the Slave in Private Law from Augustus to Justinian*, Cambridge.

Bürge, A. 1987, "Fiktion und Wirklichkeit: Soziale und rechtliche Strukturen des römischen Bankwesens", *Zeitschrift der Savigny-Stiftung für Rechtsgeschichte. Romanistische Abteilung* 104, pp. 465–558.

Burke, P. 1988, "Republics of Merchants in Early Modern Europe", in Baechler, Hall and Mann, pp. 220–233.

Burton, G. P. 1975, "Proconsuls, Assizes and the Administration of Justice under the Empire", *Journal of Roman Studies* 65, pp. 92–106.

Butcher, K. 1988, *Roman Provincial Coins. An Introduction to the "Greek Imperials"*, London.

Byres, T. J. 2000, "Pre-Capitalist Economic Formations and Differential Agricultural Productivity: A Tentative Hypothesis", in Panikkar, Byres and Patnaik, pp. 239–275.

Byres, T. J. and Mukhia, H. (eds.) 1985, *Feudalism and Non-European Societies*, London.

Cagnat, R. 1882, *Étude historique sur les impôts indirects chez les Romains jusqu'aux invasions des barbares d'après les documents littéraires et épigraphiques*, Paris.

Calder. W. M. and Demandt, A. (eds.) 1990, *Eduard Meyer. Leben und Leistung eines universal Historiker*, *Mnemosyne* 112, Supplementum, Amsterdam.

Camodeca, G. 1999, *Tabulae Pompeianae Sulpiciorum (TPSulp.): Edizione critica dell'archivio puteolano dei Sulpicii*, 2 vols., Rome.

2003, "Il credito negli archivi campani: il caso di Puteoli e di Herculaneum", in Lo Cascio, pp. 69–98.

Capogrossi Colognesi, L. 1990, *Economie antiche e capitalismo moderno*, Bari.

1995, "The Limits of the Ancient City and the Evolution of the Medieval City in the Thought of Max Weber", in Cornell and Lomas, pp. 27–37.

Carandini, A. 1981, "Sviluppo e crisi delle manifatture rurali e urbane", in Giardina and Schiavone, vol. 2, pp. 249–260.

1983a, "Columella's Vineyard and the Rationality of the Roman Economy", *Opus* 2, pp. 177–204.

1983b, "Pottery and the African Economy", in Garnsey, Hopkins and Whittaker, pp. 145–162.

1988, *Schiavi in Italia. Gli strumenti pensanti dei Romani fra tarda repubblica e medio impero*, Rome.

1989, "Italian Wine and African Oil: Commerce in a World Empire", in Klaus Randsborg (ed.), *The Birth of Europe*, *Analecta Romana Instituti Danici*, Supplementum 16, Rome.

Cartledge, P., Cohen, E. E. and Foxhall, L. (eds.) 2002, *Money, Labour and Land. Approaches to the Economies of Ancient Greece*, London.

Casson, L. 1968, Review of Rougé 1966, *American Journal of Philology* 89, pp. 359–364.

1974, *Travel in the Ancient World*, London.

1984, *Ancient Trade and Society*, Detroit, MI.

1986, "New Light on Maritime Loans: P. Vindob G. 19792 (=SB VI 9571)", in R. S. Bagnall and W. V. Harris (eds.), *Studies in Roman Law in Memory of A. Arthur Schiller*, Leiden, pp. 11–17.

1989, *The Periplus Maris Erythraeie*, ed., trans. and commentary by L. Casson, Princeton, NJ.

1990 "New Light on Maritime Loans: P. Vindob. G 40822", *Zeitschrift für Papyrologie und Epigraphik*, 84, pp. 195–206.

Cerati, A. 1975, *Caractère annonaire et assiette de l'impôt foncier au bas-empire*, Paris.

Chastagnol, A. 1992, *Le Sénat romain a l'époque imperiale. Recherches sur la composition de l'assemblée et le statut de ses membres*, Paris.

Chatterjee, K. 1996, *Merchants, Politics and Society in Early Modern India*, Leiden.

Chaudhuri, K. N. 1978, "Some Reflections on Town and Country in Mughal India", *Modern Asian Studies* 12, pp. 77–96.

1979, "Markets and Traders in India during the Seventeenth and Eighteenth Centuries", in K. N. Chaudhuri and C. Dewey (eds.), *Economy and Society*, New Delhi, pp. 143–162.

1981, "The World System East of Longitude 20: The European Role in Asia 1500–1750", *Review* 5, 2, pp. 219–246.

1985, *Trade and Civilization in the Indian Ocean. An Economic History from the Rise of Islam to 1750*, Cambridge.

1990, *Asia Before Europe. Economy and Civilisation of the Indian Ocean from the Rise of Islam to 1750*, Cambridge.

Chaudhuri, S. 1983, "The Surat Crisis of 1669: A Case Study of Mercantile Protest in Medieval India!", *Calcutta Historical Journal* 5, pp. 129–146.

Chayanov, A. V. 1986, *On the Theory of Peasant Economy*, with a foreword by Teodor Shanin, Madison, WI.

Chevalier, R. 1988, *Voyages et déplacements dans l'empire romain*, Paris.

Christensen, A. E. 1941, *Dutch Trade to the Baltic about 1600. Studies in the Sound Toll Register and Dutch Shipping Records*, Copenhagen.

Christiansen, E. 1982, "Marx, Slaver og Antikken", *Historisk Tidsskrift* 82, 1, pp. 63–94.

1988, *The Roman Coins of Alexandria*, Aarhus.

1995, *A History of Rome*, Aarhus.

2004, *Coinage in Roman Egypt. The Hoard Evidence*, Aarhus.

Cipolla, C. M. (ed.) 1970, *The Economic Decline of Empires*, London.

Çizakça, M. 1985, "Incorporation of the Middle East into the European World-Economy", *Review* 8, pp. 353–377.

Clark, C. and Haswell, M. 1970, *The Economics of Subsistence Agriculture*, 4th edn, London.

Clemente, G. 1972, "Il patronato nei collegia dell'impero romano", *Studi Classici e Orientali* 21, pp. 142–229.

Coarelli, F. 1988, *Il Foro Boario*, Rome.

Colin, X. 2000, "Commerçants itinérants et marchands sédentaires dans l'Occident romain", in Lo Cascio 2000a, pp. 149–161.

Corbier, M. 1991, "City, Territory and Taxation", in Rich and Wallace-Hadrill, pp. 211–239.

Cornell, T. and Lomas, K. (eds.) 1995, *Urban Society in Roman Italy*, London.

Cotter, W. 1996, "The Collegia and Roman Law: State Restrictions on Voluntary Associations, 64 BCE–200 CE", in Kloppenborg and Wilson, pp. 74–89.

Cottier, M. 2003, "Le ferme des douanes en Orient et la *lex portorii Asiae*", in Aubert, pp. 215–228.

Cotton, H. 1993, "The Guardianship of Jesus Son of Babatha: Roman and Local Law in the Province of Arabia", *Journal of Roman Studies* 83, pp. 94–108.

Coulton, J. J. 1987, "Opramoas and the Anonymous Benefactor", *Journal of Hellenic Studies* 107, pp. 171–178.

Crawford, D. J. 1971, *Kerkeosiris. An Egyptian Village in the Ptolemaic Period*, Cambridge.

Crawford, M. (ed.) 1986a, *L'impero romano e le strutture economiche e sociali delle province*, Como.

1986b, "The Monetary System of the Roman Empire", in Crawford 1986a, pp. 61–70.

Crone, P. 1989, *Pre-Industrial Societies*, Oxford.

Crook, J. A. 1967, *Law and Life of Rome, 90 B.C.–A.D. 212*, Ithaca, NY.

1995, *Legal Advocacy in the Roman World*, Ithaca, NY.

Crow, B. 1999, "Researching the Market System in Bangladesh", in Harris-White 1999a, pp. 115–150.

Curtin, P. D. 1984, *Cross-Cultural Trade in World History*, Cambridge.

Curtis, R. I. 1991, *Garum and Salsamenta. Production and Commerce in Materia Medica*, Leiden.

Dalby, A. 2000, *Empire of Pleasures*, London.

D'Arms, J. H. 1977, "M. I. Rostovtzeff and M. I. Finley: The Status of Traders in the Roman World", in D'Arms and Eadie (eds.), *Ancient and Modern. Essays in Honor of G. E. Else*, Ann Arbor, MI, pp. 159–179.

1981, *Commerce and Social Standing in Ancient Rome*, Cambridge, MA.

D'Arms, J. H. and Kopff, E. C. (eds.) 1980, *The Seaborne Commerce of Ancient Rome. Studies in Archaeology and History*, Memoirs of the American Academy in Rome 36, Rome.

Das Gupta, A. 1979, *Indian Merchants and the Decline of Surat, c. 1700–1750*, Wiesbaden.

1987, "India and the Indian Ocean in the Eighteenth Century", in Das Gupta and Pearson, pp. 131–161.

1991, "Changing Faces of the Maritime Merchant", in Ptak and Rothermund, pp. 352–362.

1998, "Trade and Politics in Eighteenth Century India", in Alam and Subrahmanyam, pp. 361–397.

Das Gupta, A. and Pearson, M. N. (eds.) 1987, *India and the Indian Ocean, 1500–1800*, Calcutta.

Datta, R. 2000, *Society, Economy and the Market. Commercialisation in Rural Bengal, 1760–1800*, New Delhi.

Daube, D. 1980, "Jewish Law in the Hellenistic World", in B. S. Jackson (ed.), *Jewish Law in Legal History and the Modern World*, Leiden, pp. 45–60.

Davies, J. K. 1998, "Ancient Economies: Models and Muddles", in Parkins and Smith, pp. 225–256.

De Robertis, F. M. 1971, *Storia delle corporazioni e del regime associativo nel mondo romano*, vols. 1–2, Bari.

De Romanis, F. 1996, *Cassia, cinnamono, ossidiana. Uomini e merci tra Oceano indiano e Mediterraneo*, Rome.

1998, "Commercio, Metrologia, Fiscalità", *Mélanges de l'École Française de Rome. Antiquité* 110, pp. 11–60.

De Salvo, L. 1992, *Economia privata e pubblici servizi nell'impero romano. I corpora naviculariorum*, Messina.

De Souza, P. 1999, *Piracy in the Graeco-Roman World*, Cambridge.

Demougin, S. 1988, *L'ordre équestre sous les Julio-Claudiens*, Rome.

Demougin, S. and Devijver, H. (eds.) 1999, *L'ordre équestre. Histoire d'une aristocratie (IIe siecle av. J.C –IIIe siecle ap. J.C.)*, Collection de l'École Française de Rome 257, Rome.

Dewey, C. 1988, *Arrested Development. The Historical Dimension*, Riverdale, MD.

Dietz, S., Ladjimi Sebai, L. and Ben Hassen, H. (eds.) 1995, *Africa Proconsularis. Regional Studies in the Segermes Valley of Northern Tunisia*, vols. 1–2, Aarhus.

Dirlmeier, U. 1987, "Mittelalterliche Zoll- und Stapelrechte als Handelshemmnisse", in H. Pohl. (ed.), *Die Auswirkungen von Zöllen und anderen Handelshemmnissen auf Wirtschaft und Gesellschaft vom Mittelalter bis zur Gegenwart*. Vierteljahrschrift für Sozial- und Wirtschaftsgeschichte, suppl. 80, pp. 19–39.

Dirven, L. 1999, *The Palmyrenes of Dura-Europos. A Study of Religious Interaction in Roman Syria*, Leiden.

Disney, A. (ed.) 1995, *Historiography of Europeans in Africa and Asia 1450–1800. An Expanding World*, vol. 4, Aldershot.

Dmitriev, S. 2005, *City Government in Hellenistic and Roman Asia Minor*, Oxford.

Domergue, C. 1994, "L'état romain et le commerce des metaux à la fin de la République et sous le Haut-Empire", in Andreau, Briant and Descat *et al.*, pp. 99–113.

1998, "A View of Baetica's External Commerce in the 1st c. A.D. based on its Trade in Metals", in Keay, pp. 201–215.

Domergue, C. and Liou, B. 1997, "L'apparition de normes dans le commerce maritime romain", *Pallas* 46, pp. 11–30.

Dreher, M. 1997, "Das *Monumentum Ephesenum* und das römische Zollwesen", *Münstersche Beiträge zur antiken Handelsgeschichte* 16, 2, pp. 79–96.

Drexhage, H. J. 1988, "... Scimus quam varia sint pretia rerum per singulas civitates regionesque ... Zu den Preisvariationen im römischen Ägypten", *Münstersche Beiträge zur Antiken Handelsgeschichte* 7, 2, pp. 1–11.

1991, *Preise, Mieten/Pachten, Kosten und Löhne im römischen Ägypten*, St Katharinen.

1994, "Einflüsse des Zollwesens auf den Warenverkehr im römischen Reich – handelshemmend oder handelsfördernd?", *Münstersche Beiträge zur antiken Handelsgeschichte* 13, 2, pp. 1–15.

Drexhage, H.-J., Konen, H. and Ruffing, K. 2002, *Die Wirtschaft des Römischen Reiches (1.–3. Jahrhundert)*, Berlin.

Drexhage, R. 1988, *Untersuchungen zum römischen Osthandel*, Bonn.

Dreyer, E. L. 2007, *Zheng He. China and the Oceans in the Early Ming Dynasty, 1405–1433*, New York.

Drinkwater, J. F. 2001, "The Gallo-Roman Woollen Industry and the Great Debate: The Igel Column Revisited", in Mattingly and Salmon, pp. 297–308.

Droysen, J. G. 1977, *Historik*, ed. Peter Leyh, vol. 1, Stuttgart-Bad Cannstatt.

Dumont, L. 1980, *Homo Hierarchicus. The Caste System and Its Implications*, rev. English. edn, Chicago.

Duncan-Jones, R. 1976, "The Price of Wheat in Roman Egypt under the Principate", *Chiron* 6, pp. 241–262.

1979, "Variation in Egyptian Grain Mesure", *Chiron* 9, pp. 347–375.

1982, *The Economy of the Roman Empire. Quantitative Studies*, Cambridge.

1990, *Structure and Scale in the Roman Economy*, Cambridge.

1994, *Money and Government in the Roman Empire*, Cambridge.

2003, "Roman Coin circulation and the Cities of Vesuvius", in Lo Cascio 2003b, pp. 161–180.

Duthoy, R. 1976, "Recherches sur la répartition géographique et chronologique des termes sevir augustalis, augustalis et sevir dans l'empire romain", *Epigraphische Studien* 11, pp. 143–214.

Eck, W. (ed.) 1999, *Lokale Autonomie und römische Ordnungsmacht in den kaiserzeitlichen Provinzen vom 1. bis 3. Jahrhundert*, Munich.

2000, "The Growth of Administrative Posts", in *The Cambridge Ancient History*, vol. XI, 2nd edn, Cambridge, pp. 238–265.

Edhem, E., Goffman, D. and Masters, B. 1999, *The Ottoman City between East and West. Aleppo, Ismir and Istanbul*, New York.

Edwards, C. 1993, *The Politics of Immorality in Ancient Rome*, Cambridge.

Edwards, C. and Woolf, G. (eds.) 2003, *Rome the Cosmopolis*, Cambridge.

Eiring, J. and Lund, J. (eds.) 2004, *Transport Amphorae and Trade in the Eastern Mediterranean. Acts of the International Colloquium at the Danish Institute at Athens, September 26–29, 2002. Monographs of the Danish Institute at Athens* 5, Athens.

Eisenstadt, S. 1963, *The Political Systems of Empires*, London.

Eisenstadt, S. and Schluchter, W. (eds.) 1998, *Early Modernities, Daedalus* 127, 3, special issue, Cambridge, MA.

Elvin, M. 1973, *The Pattern of the Chinese Past*, Stanford, CA.

Empereur, J.-Y. (ed.) 1999, *Commerce et artisanat dans l'Alexandrie hellénistique et romaine. Actes du colloque d'Athènes, organisé par le CNRS, le laboratoire de Céramologie de Lyon et l'École Française d'Athènes, 11–12 decembre 1988*, Athens.

Empereur, J.-Y. and Garlan, Y. (eds.) 1986, *Recherches sur les amphores grecques*, Paris.

Engelmann, H. and Knibbe, D. 1989, "Das Zollgesetz der Provinz Asia. Eine neue Inschrift aus Ephesos", Epigraphica Anatolica 14, pp. 1–206.

Engels, D. 1990, *Roman Corinth*, Chicago.

Epigrafia della produzione e della distribuzione, Collection de l'École Française de Rome 193, Rome, 1994.

Epigrafia e ordine senatorio=Atti del Colloquio Internazionale AIEGL su Epigrafia e Ordine Senatorio (1981: Roma), Tituli 4–5, Rome 1982.

Erdkamp, P. 2001, "Beyond the Limits of the 'Consumer City'. A Model of the Urban and Rural Economy in the Roman World", *Historia* 50, pp. 332–356.

2002, "A Starving Mob has No Respect: Urban Markets and Food Riots in the Roman World, 100 B.C.–A.D. 400", in de Blois and Rich, pp. 93–115.

2005, *The Roman Grain Market*, Cambridge.

Erslev, K. 1911, *Historieskrivning. Grundlinier til nogle kapitler af historiens Theori*, Copenhagen.

Étienne, R. 1952, "Rome eut-elle une politique douanière?", *Annales ESC* 7, pp. 371–377.

Étienne, R. and Mayet, F. 1998, "Les 'mercatores' de saumure hispanique", *Mélanges de l'École Française de Rome. Antiquité* 110, pp. 147–165.

Faroqhi, S. 1984, *Towns and Townsmen of Ottoman Anatolia. Trade, Crafts and Food Production in an Urban Setting, 1520–1650*, Cambridge.

1991, "In Search of Ottoman History", *Journal of Peasant Studies* 18, 3/4, pp. 211–241.

Fawaz, L. and Bayly, C. A. (eds.) 2002, *Modernity and Culture. From the Mediterranean to the Indian Ocean*, New York.

Ferguson, A. 1995, *An Essay on the History of Civil Society*, ed. F. Oz-Salzberger, Cambridge (first published 1767).

1799, *The History of the Progress and Termination of the Roman Republic*, a new edn, revised and corrected, 5 vols., Edinburgh.

Fikhman, I. F. 1991–2, "State and Prices in Byzantine Egypt", *Scripta Classica Israelica* 11, pp. 139–148.

Finkielkraut, A. 1988, *The Undoing of Thought*, London.

Finlay, R. 2000, "China, the West and World History in Joseph Needham's Science and Civilisation in China", *Journal of World History* 11, 2, pp. 265–303.

Finley, M. I. 1954, *The World of Odysseus*, New York.

1965, "Technical Innovation and Economic Progress in the Ancient World", *Economic History Review*, 2nd ser., 18, pp. 29–45.

1970, "Aristotle and Economic Analysis", *Past and Present* 47, pp. 3–25.

1975, *The Use and Abuse of History*, London.

(ed.) 1976, *Studies in Roman Property*, Cambridge.

1977, "The Ancient City: From Fustel de Coulanges to Max Weber and Beyond", *Comparative Studies in Society and History* 19, pp. 305–327.

1980, *Ancient Slavery and Modern Ideology*, London.

1983, *Politics in the Ancient World*, Cambridge.

1985a, *The Ancient Economy*, 2nd edn, London.

1985b, *Ancient History. Evidence and Models*, London.

Fischer, W., McInnis, R. M. and Schneider, J. (eds.) 1986, *The Emergence of a World Economy 1500–1914*, Papers of the IXth International Congress of Economic History, 2 vols., Wiesbaden.

Foraboschi, D. 1994, "Economie plurali e interdipendenze", in *L'Italie d'Auguste à Dioclétien*, Collection de l'École Française de Rome, Rome, pp. 215–218.

2000, "The Hellenistic Economy: Indirect Intervention by the State", in Lo Cascio and Rathbone, pp. 37–43.

France, J. 1994, "De Burmann à Finley: les douanes dans l'histoire économique de l'empire romain", in Andreau, Briant and Descat *et al.*, pp. 127–153.

1999, "Les revenues douanières des communautés municipales dans le monde romain", in *Il capitolo delle entrate nelle finanze municipali in Occidente ed in Oriente*, Collection de l'École Française de Rome, 256, pp. 95–113.

2001, *Quadragesima Galliarum. L'organisation douanière des provinces Alpestres, Gauloises et Germaniques de l'empire Romain*, Collection de l'École Française de Rome 278, Rome.

2003, "La Ferme des douanes dans les provinces occidentales et l'empire romain", in Aubert, pp. 193–214.

Frank, A. G. 1998, *ReOrient. Global Economy in the Asian Age*, Berkeley and Los Angeles.

Frank, A. G. and Gills, B. K. (eds.) 1993, *The World System. Five Hundred Years or Five Thousand?* London and New York.

Frank, T. (ed.) 1933–40, *An Economic Survey of Ancient Rome*, vols. 1–6, Baltimore, MD.

Frayn, J. M. 1993, *Markets and Fairs in Roman Italy*, Oxford.

Frederiksen, M. 1975, "Theory, Evidence and the Ancient Economy", *Journal of Roman Studies* 65, pp. 164–171.

Freyberg, H.-U. von 1989, *Kapitalverkehr und Handel im römischen Kaiserreich (27 v. Chr.–235 n. Chr.)*, Freiburg.

Frezouls, E. 1985, "Les ressources de l'euergetisme: le cas d'Opramoas de Rhodiopolis", in Leveau, pp. 249–254.

Friedländer, L. 1921–3, *Darstellungen aus der Sittengeschichte Roms in der Zeit von Augustus bis zum Ausgang der Antonine*, vol. 10, ed. Georg Wissowa, 4 vols., Leipzig.

Frier, Bruce W. 2000a, "Demography", in *The Cambridge Ancient History*, vol. XI, 2nd edn, pp. 787–816.

2000b, "More is Worse: Some Observations on the Population of the Roman Empire", in Scheidel, pp. 139–159.

Fulford, M. 1987, "Economic Interdependence among Urban Communities of the Roman Mediterranean", *World Archaeology* 19, 1, pp. 58–75.

Fülle, G. 1997, "The Internal Organization of the Arretine *Terra Sigillata* Industry", *Journal of Roman Studies* 87, pp. 111–155.

Gabba, E. 1988, *Del buon uso della ricchezza. Saggi di storia economica e sociale del mondo antico*, Milan.

Gabrielsen, V. 1997, *The Naval Aristocracy of Rhodes*, Aarhus.

2001, "The Rhodian Associations and Economic Activity", in Archibald *et al.*, pp. 215–244.

Gagos, T. and van Minnen, P. 1994, *Settling a Dispute. Toward a Legal Anthropology of Late Antique Egypt*, Ann Arbor, MI.

Galanter, M. 1981, "Justice in Many Rooms: Courts, Private Ordering, and Indigenous Law", *Journal of Legal Pluralism* 19, pp. 1–47.

Galsterer, H. 1986, "Roman Law in the Provinces – Some Problems of Transmission", in Crawford 1986a, pp. 13–27.

1996, "The Administration of Justice", in The *Cambridge Ancient History*, vol. X, 2nd edn, pp. 397–413.

1997, "Neues zu den römischen Stadtgesetzen", *Zeitschrift der Savigny-Stiftung. Romanistische Abteilung*, pp. 392–401.

Garnsey, P. 1970, *Social Status and Legal Privilege in the Roman Empire*, Oxford.

1976, "Urban Property Investment", in Finley, pp. 123–136.

1978, "Rome's African Empire under the Principate" in Garnsey and Whittaker, pp. 223–254.

1983a, "Famine in Rome", in Garnsey and Whittaker, pp. 56–65.

1983b, "Grain for Rome", in Garnsey, Hopkins and Whittaker, pp. 118–130.

1988, *Famine and Food Supply in the Graeco-Roman World*, Cambridge.

1991, "The Generosity of Veyne", *Journal of Roman Studies* 81, pp. 164–168.

1994, *Food and Society in Classical Antiquity*, Cambridge.

1996, "Prolegomenon to the Study of the Land in the Later Roman Empire", in J. H. M. Strubbe, R. A. Tybout and H. S. Versnel (eds.), *Energeia*: Studies on Ancient History and Epigraphy Presented to H. W. Pleket, Amsterdam, pp. 135–153.

1998a, *Cities, Peasants and Food in Classical Antiquity*, Cambridge.

1998b, *Food and Society in Antiquity*, Cambridge.

2000, "The Land", in *The Cambridge Ancient History*, vol. XI, 2nd edn, Cambridge, pp. 679–709.

2004, "Roman Citizenship and Roman Law in the Late Empire", in S. Swain and M. Edwards (eds.), *Approaching Late Antiquity. The Transformation from Early to Late Empire*, Oxford, pp. 133–155.

Garnsey, P., Hopkins, K. and Whittaker, C. R. (eds.) 1983, *Trade in the Ancient Economy*, London.

Garnsey, P. and Humfress, C. 2001, *The Evolution of the Late Antique World*, Cambridge.

Garnsey, P. and Saller, R. 1987, *The Roman Empire. Economy, Society and Culture*, London.

Garnsey, P. and Whittaker, C. R. 1978 (eds.), *Imperialism in the Ancient World*, Cambridge.

1983 (eds.), *Trade and Famine in Classical Antiquity*, Cambridge.

1998, "Trade, Industry and the Urban Economy", in *The Cambridge Ancient History*, vol. XIII, 2nd edn, Cambridge.

Geertz, Clifford 1963, *Peddlers and Princes. Social Development and Economic Change in Two Indonesian Towns*, Chicago.

1979, "Suq: The Bazaar Economy in Sefrou", in C. Geertz, H. Geertz and L. Roan, *Meaning and Order in Moroccan Society*, Cambridge, pp. 123–313.

2000, *Local Knowledge. Further Essays in Interpretive Anthropology*, New York.

Gellner, E. 1988a, "Introduction", in Baechler, Hall and Mann, pp. 1–5.

1988b, *Plough, Sword and Book*, Chicago.

Gelzer, M. 1912, *Die Nobilität der Römischen Republik*, Berlin.

Giardina, A. 1986, "Le merci, il tempo, il silenzio: Ricerche su miti e valori sociali nel mondo Greco e Romano", *Studi Storici*, 27, 2, pp. 277–302.

(ed.) 1989, *L'uomo romano*, Rome and Bari.

1997, *L'Italia Romana. Studi di storie di un'identità incompiuta*, Rome.

Giardina, A. and Schiavone, A. (eds.) 1981, *Società romana e produzione schiavistica*, vols. 1–3, Bari and Rome.

Gibbon, E. 1993, *The Decline and Fall of the Roman Empire*, introduction by Hugh Trevor-Roper, vols. 1–6, London.

Gibson, A. J. S. and Smout, T. C. 1995, "Regional Prices and Market Regions: The Evolution of the Early Modern Scottish Grain Market", *Economic History Review* 48, 2, pp. 258–282.

Glamann, K. 1958, *Dutch-Asiatic Trade, 1620–1740*, Copenhagen.

1977, "The Changing Patterns of Trade", in *The Cambridge Economic History of Europe*, vol. V, Cambridge, chapter 4.

Goethe, J. W. von 1907, *Maximen und Reflexionen*, ed. Max Hecker, Weimar.

Goitein, S. D. 1967, *A Mediterranean Society. The Jewish Communities of the Arab World as Portrayed in the Documents of the Cairo Geniza*, vol. 1, Berkeley and Los Angeles.

Gokhale, B. G. 1979, *Surat in the 17th Century*, London.

Golden, M. and Toohey, P. (eds.) 1997, *Inventing Ancient Culture*, London.

Goldschmid, L. 1897, "Les impôts et droits de douane en Judée sous les Romains", *Revue des Études Juives* 34, pp. 192–217.

Goldsmith, R. W. 1987, *Pre-Modern Financial Systems. A Historical Comparative Study*, Cambridge.

Goldstone, J. 1991, *Revolution and Rebellion in the Early Modern World*, Berkeley, CA.

1998, "The Problem of the 'Early Modern' World", *Journal of the Economic and Social History of the Orient* 41, pp. 249–284.

2002, "Efflorescences and Economic Growth in World History: Rethinking the 'Rise of the West' and the Industrial Revolution", *Journal of World History* 13, pp. 323–389.

Gommans, J. 2002, *Mughal Warfare. Indian Frontiers and High Roads to Empire, 1500–1700*, London and New York.

Gonzáles, J. 1986, "The Lex Irnitana: A New Copy of the Flavian Municipal Law", *Journal of Roman Studies* 76, pp. 147–243.

Goodman, M. 1983, *State and Society in Roman Galilee, AD. 132–212*, Totowa, NJ.

Goody, J. 1990, *The Oriental, the Ancient and the Primitive*, Cambridge.

1996, *The East in the West*, Cambridge.

1998, *Food and Love. A Cultural History of East and West*, London.

Goody, J. and Whittaker, D. 2001, "Rural Manufacturing in the Rouergue from Antiquity to the Present: The Examples of Pottery and Cheese", *Comparative Studies in Society and History* 43, 2, pp. 225–245.

Gordon, S. 1990, "*Burhanpur: Entrepot and Hinterland, 1650–1750*", in Subrahmanyam 1990a, pp. 48–65.

Goudineau, C. 1974, "La céramique dans l'économie romaine", *Dossiers d'Archéologie* 6, pp. 103–109.

Granger, C. W. J. and Elliott, C. M. 1967 "A Fresh Look at Wheat Prices and Markets in the Eighteenth Century", *Economic History Review* 20, pp. 257–265.

Greene, K. 1986, *The Archaeology of the Roman Economy*, London.

1994, "Technology and Innovation in Context: The Roman Background to Medieval and Later Developments", *Journal of Roman Archaeology* 7, pp. 22–33.

2000, "Technological Innovation and Economic Progress in the Ancient World: M. I. Finley Re-considered", *Social and Economic History Review* 53, 1, pp. 29–59.

Greif, A. 1993, "Contract Enforceability and Economic Institutions in Early Trade: The Mahgribi Traders' Coalition", *American Economic Review* 83, pp. 525–548.

Gren, E. 1941, *Kleinasien und der Ostbalkan in der Wirtschaftlichen Entwicklung der römischen Kaiserzeit*, Uppsala Universitets Årsskrift 1941: 9, Uppsala.

Grenier, J.-Y. 1997, "Économie du surplus, économie du circuit", in Andreau, Briant and Descat *et al.*, pp. 385–404.

Grover, B. R. 1966, "An Integrated Pattern of Commercial Life in the Rural Society of North India during the 17th and 18th Centuries", *Proceedings of the 37th Session of the Indian Historical Records Commision* 38, New Delhi.

Grünewald, T. 1999, *Räuber, Rebellen, Rivalen, Rächer. Studien zu Latrones im römischen Reich*, Stuttgart.

Guarino, A. 1972, "Societas consensu contracta", *Atti della Accademia di Scienze Morali e Politiche della Società Nazionale di Scienze, Lettere ed Arti di Napoli*, 83, 261–359.

Gungwu, W. 1990 "Merchants Without Empire: The Hokkien Sojourning Communities", in Tracy, pp. 400–421.

Habib, I. 1963, *The Agrarian System of Mughal India*, Bombay.

1969, "Potentialities of Capitalistic Development in the Economy of Mughal India", *Journal of Economic History* 29, pp. 32–78.

1972, "The System of Bills of Exchange (*Hundis*) in the Mughal Empire", *Proceedings of the Indian History Congress, (33rd session, Muzaffarpur)*, pp. 290–303.

1985, "Classifying Pre-Colonial India", in Byres and Mukhia, pp. 44–53.

1990, "Merchant Communities in Precolonial India", in Tracy, pp. 371–399.

1999, *The Agrarian System of Mughal India*, 2nd rev. edn, Oxford and Delhi.

Habib, I. and Raychaudhuri, T. (eds.) 1982, *The Cambridge Economic History of India*, vol. 1: *c. 1200–c. 1750*, Cambridge.

Hackens, F. and Miro, M. 1990 (eds.), *Le commerce maritime romain en Méditerranée occidentale*, PACT 27, Strasbourg.

Hackl, K. 1997, "Der Zivilprozess des frühen Prinzipats in den Provinzen", *Zeitschrift der Savigny-Stiftung, Romanistische Abteilung* 114, pp. 141–159.

Haider, S. N. 1997, *The Monetary System of the Mughal Empire*, D. Phil. thesis, University of Oxford.

Haldon, J. 1993, *The State and the Tributary Mode of Production*, London.

Halfmann, H. 1979, *Die Senatoren aus dem östlichen Teil des Imperium Romanum bis zum Ende des 2. Jahrhunderts n. Chr.*, Göttingen.

Hall, J. 1985, *Powers and Liberties*, Oxford.

Hammond, M. 1957, "Composition of the Roman Senate AD 68–235", *Journal of Roman Studies* 47, pp. 74–81.

Harl, K. W. 1996, *Coinage in the Roman Economy, 300 B.C.–A.D. 700*, London.

Harries, Jill 1999, *Law and Empire in Late Antiquity*, Cambridge.

Harris, B. 1987, "Merchants and Markets of Grain in South Asia", in Shanin, pp. 205–220.

Harris, W. 1980, "Roman Terracotta Lamps: The Organisation of an Industry", *Journal of Roman Studies* 70, pp. 125–145.

1993, "Between Archaic and Modern: Problems in Roman Economic History", in (ed.) *The Inscribed Economy: Production and Distribution in the*

Roman Empire in the Light of Instrumentum Domesticum, Journal of Roman Archaeology Supplementary Series 6, Ann Arbor, MI, pp. 11–29.

1999, "Demography, Geography and the Sources of Roman Slaves", *Journal of Roman Studies* 89, pp. 62–75.

2000, "Trade and Transport", in *The Cambridge Ancient History*, vol. XI, 2nd edn, Cambridge, pp. 710–740.

2003, "Roman Governments and Commerce, 300 B.C.–A.D. 300", in Zaccagnini, pp. 275–306.

2006, "A Revisionist View of Roman Money", *Journal of Roman Studies* 96, pp. 1–24.

Harris-White, B. (ed.) 1999a, *Agricultural Markets From Theory to Practice. Field Experience in Developing Countries*, London.

1999b, "Power in Peasant Markets", in Harris-White 1999a, pp. 261–286.

Hartwell, R. 1962, "A Revolution in the Chinese Iron and Coal Industries During the Northern Sung, 960–1126 A.D", *Journal of Asian Studies* 21, pp. 153–162.

1966, "Markets, Technology and the Structure of Enterprise in the Development of the Eleventh-century Chinese Iron and Steel Industries", *Journal of Economic History* 26, pp. 29–58.

Hasan, F. 2004, *State and Locality in Mughal India. Power Relations in Western India, c. 1572–1730*, Cambridge.

Hassall, M. 2000, "The Army", in *The Cambridge Ancient History*, vol. XI, 2nd edn, pp. 320–343.

Haswell, M. 1967, *Economics of Development in Village India*, London.

Hatzfeld, J. 1919, *Les trafiquants italiens dans l'Orient hellénique*, Paris.

Heberdey, R. 1897, *Opramoas. Inschriften vom Heroon zu Rhodiopolis*, Vienna.

Heberdey, R. and Kalinka, E. 1896, *Bericht über zwei Reisen im südwestlichen Kleinasien*, Vienna.

Hegel, G. W. 1996, *Vorlesungen über die Philosophie der Weltgeschichte*, ed. K. H. Ilting, K. Brehmer and H. N. Seelmann, Hamburg.

Herz, P. 1988, *Studien zur römischen Wirtschaftsgesetzgebung. Die Lebensmittelversorgung*. Historia Einzelschriften 55, Stuttgart.

Hiderato, I. 1999–2000, "The Transfer of Money in Roman Egypt", *Kodai* 10, pp. 83–104.

Hingley, R. 2005, *Globalizing Roman Culture. Unity, Diversity and Empire*, London and New York.

Hinton, W. 1966, *Fanshen. A Documentary of Revolution in a Chinese Village*, New York and London.

Hintze, A. 1997, *The Mughal Empire and its Decline. An Interpretation of the Sources of Social Power*, Aldershot.

Hitchen, R. B. 2005, "'The Advantages of Wealth and Luxury': The Case for Economic Growth in the Roman Empire", in Manning and Morris, pp. 207–222.

Hitchner, R. B. and Mattingly, D. 1995, "Roman Africa: An Archaeological Review", *Journal of Roman Studies* 85, pp. 165–213.

Höbenreich, E. 1997, *Annona. Juristische Aspekte der Stadtrömischen Lebensmittelversorgung in Prinzipat*, Graz.

Hobsbawm, E. 1987, *The Age of Empire, 1875–1914*, London.

Hodgson, M. 1974, *The Venture of Islam. Conscience and History in a World Civilization*, vols. 1–3, Chicago.

1993, *Rethinking World History*, ed. Edmund Burke III, Cambridge.

Hont, I. 2005, *Jealousy of Trade. International Competition and the Nation-state in Historical Perspective*, Cambridge, MA.

Hopkins, K. 1978a, *Conquerors and Slaves*, Cambridge.

1978b, "Economic Growth and Towns in Classical Antiquity", in P. Abrams and E. A. Wrigley (eds.), *Towns in Societies. Essays in Economic History and Historical Sociology*, Cambridge, pp. 35–77.

1980, "Taxes and Trade in the Roman Empire 200 B.C.–A.D. 400", *Journal of Roman Studies* 70, pp. 101–125.

1983a, *Death and Renewal*, Cambridge.

1983b, "Models, Ships and Staples", in Garnsey and Whittaker, pp. 84–109.

1983c, "Introduction", in Garnsey, Hopkins and Whittaker, pp. ix–xxv.

1995–6, "Rome, Taxes, Rents and Trade", *Kodai. Journal of Ancient History* 6/7, pp. 41–75.

2000, "Rents, Taxes, Trade and the City of Rome", in Lo Cascio 2000a, pp. 253–268.

Hopwood, K. 1989, "Bandits, Élites and Rural Order", in Wallace-Hadrill, pp. 171–189.

Horden, P. and Purcell, N. 2000, *The Corrupting Sea. A Study of Mediterranean History*, Oxford.

Howgego, C. 1992, "The Supply and Use of Money in the Roman World", *Journal of Roman Studies* 82, pp. 1–31.

1994, "Coin Circulation and the Integration of the Roman Economy", *Journal of Roman Archaeology* 7, pp. 5–21.

1995, *Ancient History from Coins*, London.

Huang, R. 1974, *Taxation and Governmental Finance in Sixteenth-Century Ming China*, Cambridge.

Hultsch, F. 1882, *Griechische und römische Metrologie*, 2nd rev. edn, Berlin.

Huntington, S. P. 1996, *The Clash of Civilizations and the Remaking of World Order*, New York.

Hurst, H. 1993, "Cartagine, la nuova Alessandria", in A. Schiavone (ed.), *Storia di Roma*, vol. 3, 2, Turin, pp. 327–337.

Husain, M. M. H. (ed.) 1913, "The Mirza-Namah (The Book of the Perfect Gentleman) of Mirza Kamran with an English Translation", *Journal of the Asiatic Society of Bengal* 9, pp. 1–13.

Inalcik, H. 1969, "Capital Formation in the Ottoman Empire", *Journal of Economic History* 29, pp. 97–140.

Inalcik, H. and Quataert, D. (eds.) 1994, *An Economic and Social History of the Ottoman Empire*, vol. 2: *1600–1914*, Cambridge.

Inden, R. 1990, *Imagining India*, Oxford.

Irvine, W. 1962, *The Army of the Indian Moghuls. Its Organization and Administration*, New Delhi.

Islamoglu-Inan, H. (ed.) 1987, *The Ottoman Empire and the World-economy*, Cambridge.

Israel, J. I. 1989, *Dutch Primacy in World Trade 1585–1740*, Oxford.

Jacobsen, G. 1995, *Primitiver Austausch oder Freier Markt? Untersuchungen zum Handel in den gallisch-germanischen Provinzen während der römischen Kaiserzeit*, St Katharinen.

Jacques, F. and Scheid, J. 1990, *Rome et l'intégration de l'empire (44 av. J.C.–260 ap. J.C.)*, Paris.

Jain, L. C. 1929, *Indigenous Banking In India*, London.

Jakab, É. 1997, *Praedicere und Cavere beim Marktkauf. Sachmängel im griechischen und römischen Recht*, Munich.

2003, "Fixierte Preise für die Vermarktung des Weins im Heroninos-Archiv?", *Münstersche Beiträge zur Antiken Handelsgeschichte* 22, 1, pp. 1–26.

2006, "Vertragsformulare im Imperium Romanum", *Zeitschrift der Savigny-Stiftung für Rechtsgeschichte, Romanistische Abteilung* 123, pp. 71–101.

Jeannin, J. P. 1982, "Les interdépendances économiques dans le champ d'action européen des Hollandais (XVIe–XVIIe siécle), in Aymard, pp. 147–170.

Johnston, A. C. 1936, *Roman Egypt to the Reign of Diocletian*, Baltimore, MD.

Johnston, D. 1999, *Roman Law in Context*, Cambridge.

Jones, A. H. M. 1940, *The Greek City from Alexander to Justinian*, Oxford.

1964, *The Later Roman Empire 284–602. A Social, Economic and Administrative Survey*, vols. 1–2, Norman, OK.

1974, *The Roman Economy*, ed. P. A. Brunt, Oxford.

Jones, D. 2006, *The Bankers of Puteoli. Finance, Trade and Industry in the Roman World*, Stroud.

Jones, E. L. 1981, *The European Miracle*, Cambridge.

1988, *Growth Recurring. Economic Change in World History*, Oxford.

Jongman, W. 1988, *The Economy and Society of Pompeii*, Amsterdam.

2000a, "Hunger and Power: Theories, Models and Methods in Roman Economic History", in H. Bongenaar (ed.), *Interdependency of Institutions and Private Entrepreneurs*, MOS Studies 2, Leiden, pp. 259–284.

2000b, "Wool and the Textile Industry of Roman Italy: A Working Hypothesis", in Lo Cascio 2000a, pp. 187–198.

2006, "The Rise and Fall of the Roman Economy: Population, Rents and Entitlement", in Bang, Ikeguchi and Ziche, pp. 237–254.

Kajanto, L. 1965, *The Latin Cognomina*, Societas Scientiarum Fennica, Helsingfors.

Kaser, M. 1996, *Das römische Zivilprozessrecht*, 2nd edn, rev. by K. Hackl, Munich.

Katzoff, R. 1972, "Precedents in the Courts of Roman Egypt", *Zeitschrift der Savigny-Stiftung, Romanistische Abteilung* 89, pp. 256–292.

Kautsky, J. H. 1982, *The Politics of Aristocratic Empires*, Chapel Hill, NC.

Keay, S. J. 1984, *Late Roman Amphorae in the Western Mediterranean. A Typology and Economic Study: The Catalan Evidence*, BAR International Series 136, Oxford.

(ed.) 1998, *The Archaeology of Early Roman Baetica, Journal of Roman Archaeology*, Supplementary Series 29, Ann Arbor, MI.

Kehoe, D. 1993, "Economic Rationalism in Roman Agriculture", *Journal of Roman Archaeology* 6, pp. 476–484.

1997, *Investment, Profit and Tenancy. The Jurists and the Roman Economy*, Ann Arbor, MI.

Kennedy, P. 1988, *The Rise and Fall of the Great Powers. Economic Change and Military Conflict from 1500 to 2000*, London.

Kenrick, Philip 1993, "Italian Terra Sigillata: A Sophisticated Roman Industry", *Oxford Journal of Archaeology* 12, 2, pp. 35–42.

2000, *Corpus Vasorum Arretinorum*, 2nd edn., Bonn.

Kessler, D. and Temin, P. 2005, "Money and Prices in the Early Roman Empire", *MIT Department of Economics Working Paper No. 05–11*, Cambridge, MA.

Keyder, C. 1997, "The Ottoman Empire", in K. Barkey and M. von Hagen (eds.), *After Empire*, Boulder, CO.

Kirschenbaum, A. 1987, *Sons, Slaves and Freedmen in Roman Commerce*, Washington, DC.

Klein, P. W. 1965, *De Trippen in de 17e eeuw. Én studie over het ondernemersgedrag op de Hollandse stapelmarkt*, Assen.

Klingenberg, G. 1977, *Commissum. Der Vervall nichtdeklarierter Sachen im römischen Zollrecht*, Graz.

Kloft, H. 1996, "Überlegungen zum Luxus in der frühen römischen Kaiserzeit", in J. H. M. Strubbe, R. A. Tybout and H. S. Versnel (eds.), *Energeia: Studies on Ancient History and Epigraphy Presented to H. W. Pleket*, Amsterdam, pp. 113–134.

Kloppenborg, J. S. and Wilson, S. G. (eds.) 1996, *Voluntary Associations in the Graeco-Roman World*, London and NewYork.

Kneissl, P. 1998, "Die Berufsvereine im römischen Gallien", in P. Kneissl and V. Losemann (eds.), *Imperium Romanum. Festschrift für Karl Christ*, Stuttgart, pp. 431–449.

Kobes, J. 1999, "Fremdes Getreide: Beobachtungen zum Problem der Getreideversorgung in der kaiserzeitlichen Provinz Asia", *Laverna* 10, pp. 81–98.

Kokkinia, C. 2000, *Die Opramoas-Inschrift von Rhodiapolis*, Bonn.

Krause, J.-U. 1994, *Witwen und Waisen im römischen Reich*, II: *Wirtschaftliche und gesellschaftliche Stellung von Witwen*, Stuttgart.

1995, *Witwen und Waisen im römischen Reich*, III: *Rechtliche und soziale Stellung von Waisen*, Stuttgart.

Kruit, N. 1992, "Local Customs in the Formulas of Sales of Wine for Future Delivery", *Zeitschrift fur Papyrologie und Epigraphik* 94, pp. 167–184.

Kruit, N. and Worp, A. 1999, "Metrological Notes on Measures and Containers of Liquids in Graeco-Roman and Byzantine Egypt", *Archiv fur Papyrusforschung* 45, pp. 96–127.

Kudlien, F. 1994, "Die Rolle der Konkurrenz im antiken Gesellschaftsleben", *Münstersche Beiträge zur Antiken Handelsgeschichte* 13, 1, pp. 1–39.

1997, "Der antike Makler – ein verleugneter Beruf", *Münstersche Beiträge zur Antiken Handelsgeschichte* 16, 1, pp. 67–84.

Kula, W. 1976, *An Economic Theory of the Feudal System*, London.

Laet, S. de 1949, *Portorium. Étude sur l'organisation douanière chez les Romains*, Bruges.

Landes, D. 1998, *The Wealth and Poverty of Nations. Why Some Are So Rich and Some So Poor*, New York.

Lane, F. C. 1966, *Venice and History. The Collected Papers of Frederic C. Lane*, Baltimore, MD.

Larsen M, T. 1967, *Old Assyrian Caravan Procedures*, Istanbul.

1976, *The Old Assyrian City-State and its Colonies*, Mesopotamia 4, Copenhagen.

Laurence, R. 1998, "Land Transport in Roman Italy: Costs, Practice and the Economy", in Parkins and Smith, pp. 129–148.

1999, *The Roads of Roman Italy*, London.

Lendon, J. E. 1997, *Empire of Honour*, Oxford.

Lepelley, C. (ed.) 1998, *Rome et l'intégration de l'empire (44 av. J.C. – 260 ap. J.C)*, tome 2: *Approches régionales du Haut-Empire romain*, Paris.

Lesger, Clé 2006, *The Rise of the Amsterdam Market and Information Exchange: Merchants, Commercial Expansion and Change in the Spatial Economy of the Low Countries, c. 1550–1630*, Ashgate.

Leur, J. C. van 1955, *Indonesian Trade and Society. Essays in Asian Social and Economic History*, The Hague.

Leveau, P. (ed.) 1985, *L'Origine des richesses dépensées dans la ville antique*, Aix-en-Provence.

Lévi-Strauss, C. 1962, *La Pensée sauvage*, Paris.

Lévy-Bruhl, L. 1910, *Les Fonctions mentale dans les sociétés inferieures*, Paris.

1985, *How Natives Think*, with an introduction by C. Scott Littleton, London (first published 1926).

Lewis, N. (ed.) 1989, *The Documents from the Bar Kokhba Period in the Cave of Letters. Greek Papyri*, Judean Desert Studies, Jerusalem.

Liebenam, W. 1900, *Städteverwaltung im römischen Kaiserreiche*, Leipzig.

Ligt, L. de 1993, *Fairs and Markets in the Roman Empire. Economic and Social Aspects of Periodic Trade in a Pre-Industrial Society*, Amsterdam.

2000, "Governmental Attitudes towards Markets and *Collegia*", in Lo Cascio 2000a, pp. 237–252.

2002, "Tax Transfers in the Roman Empire", in de Blois and Rich, pp. 84–102.

Lintott, A. 1968, *Violence in Republican Rome*, Oxford.

1993, *Imperium Romanum. Politics and Administration*, London.

Liou, B. and Rodríguez-Almeida, E. 2000, "Les Inscriptions des amphores du Pecio Gondolfo", *Mélanges de l'École Française de Rome. Antiquité* 112, 1, pp. 7–25.

Liou, B. and Tchernia, A. 1994, "L'interprétation des inscriptions sur les amphores Dressel 20", in *Epigrafia della produzione e della distribuzione*, pp. 133–156.

Littleton, C. S. 1985, "Introduction", in Lévy-Bruhl, pp. iii–lviii.

Livi-Bacci, M. 1992, *A Concise History of World Population*, trans. Carl Ipsen, 2nd edn, Oxford.

Lo Cascio, E. 1991, "Forme dell'economia imperiale", in A. Schiavone (ed.), *Storia di Roma*, vol. 2, 2, pp. 313–365.

1998, "Considerazioni su circolazione monetaria, prezzi e fiscalitá nel IV secolo", in G. Crifò and S. Giglio (eds.), *Atti dell'Accademia Romanistica Costantiniana. XII Convegno Internazionale*, Naples, pp. 121–136.

(ed.) 2000a, *Mercati Permanenti e Mercati Periodici nel Mondo Romano. Atti degli Incontri capresi di storia dell'economia antica*, Bari.

2000b, *Il Princeps e il suo impero. Studi di storia amministrativa e finanziaria romana*, Bari.

2000c, "The Roman Principate: The Impact of the Organization of the Empire on Production", in Lo Cascio and Rathbone, pp. 77–85.

2003a, "Appaltatori delle imposte e amministrazione finanziaria imperiale", in Aubert pp. 249–268.

(ed.) 2003b, *Credito e moneta nel mondo romano*, Bari.

2003c, "Mercato libero e 'commercio amministrato' in età tardoantica", in Zaccagnini, pp. 307–325.

2006, "The Role of the State in the Roman Economy: Making Use of the New Institutional Economics", in Bang, Ikeguchi and Ziche, pp. 215–234.

Lo Cascio, E. and Rathbone, D. (eds.) 2000, *Production and Public Powers in Classical Antiquity*, The Cambridge Philological Society Supplement 26, Cambridge.

Lopez, R. S. and Raymond, I. W. 1955, *Medieval Trade in the Mediterranean World. Illustrative Documents Translated with Introductions and Notes*, London.

Love, J. R. 1991, *Antiquity and Capitalism. Max Weber and the Sociological Foundations of Roman Civilization*, London.

Lund, J. 1999, "Trade Patterns in the Levant from c. 100 BC to AD 200 as Reflected by the Distribution of Ceramic Fine Wares in Cyprus", *Münstersche Beiträge zur Antiken Handelsgeschichte* 18, 1, pp. 1–22.

MacMullen, R. 1974, *Roman Social Relations, 50 B.C.–A.D. 284*, New Haven, CT.

1990, *Changes in the Roman Empire. Essays in the Ordinary*, New Haven, CT.

Maddison, A. 2001, *The World Economy. A Millennial Perspective*, Paris.

Maine, H. S. 1861, *Ancient Law*, Gloucester.

1871, *Village Communities in the East and West*, London.

Malinowski, B. 1924, *Argonauts of the Western Pacific*, London.

1948, *Magic, Science and Religion and Other Essays*, New York.

Malmendier, U. 2002, *Societas Publicanorum*, Cologne.

Manacorda, D. 1989, "Le anfore dell'Italia repubblicana", in *Amphores romaines et histoire économique. Dix ans de recherche*. Collection de l'École Française de Rome 114, Rome pp. 443–467.

Mann, M. 1986, *The Sources of Social Power. A History of Power from the Beginning to A.D. 1760*, Cambridge.

Manning, J. G. and Morris, I. (eds.) 2005, *The Ancient Economy. Evidence and Models*, Stanford, CA.

Markovits, C. 2000, *The Global World of Indian Merchants, 1750–1947. Traders of Sind from Bukhara to Panama*, Cambridge.

Marsh, G. 1981, "London's Samian Supply and its Relationship to the Development of the Gallic Samian Industry", in Anderson and Anderson, pp. 173–238.

Marshall, A. 1890, *Principles of Economics*, London.

Marshall, A. J. 1980, "The Survival and Development of International Jurisdiction in the Greek World", *Aufstieg und Niedergang der Römischen Welt* 2, 13, pp. 626–661.

Marshall, P. J. 1976, "British Merchants in Eighteenth-Century Bengal", *Bengal Past and Present* 86, pp. 151–163.

1993, "Retrospect on J. C. Van Leur's Essay on the Eighteenth Century as a Category in Asian History", *Itinerario* 17, 1, pp. 45–58.

Marx, K. and Engels, F. 1960, *The First Indian War of Independence*, London.

Masschale, J. 1993, "Transport Costs in Medieval England", *Economic History Review* 46, pp. 266–279.

Masters, B. 1988, *The Origins of Western Economic Dominance in the Middle East. Mercantilism and the Islamic Economy, 1600–1750*, New York.

Matthews, J. F. 1984, "The Tax Law of Palmyra: Evidence for Economic History in a City of the Roman East", *Journal of Roman Studies* 74, pp. 157–180.

Mattingly, D. J. 1988a, "Oil for Export? A Comparison of Libyan, Spanish and Tunisian Olive Oil Production in the Roman Empire", *Journal of Roman Archaeology* 1, pp. 33–56.

1988b, "The Olive Boom: Oil Surpluses, Wealth and Power in Roman Tripolitania", *Libyan Studies* 19, pp. 21–41.

1996, "First Fruit? The Olive in the Roman World", in G. Shipley and J. Salmon (eds.), *Human Landscapes in the Ancient World. Environment and Culture*, London, pp. 213–253.

1997a, "Beyond Belief? Drawing a Line Beneath the Consumer City", in Parkins 1997b, pp. 210–218.

(ed.) 1997b, *Dialogues in Roman Imperialism, Journal of Roman Archaeology* Supplementary Series 26, Ann Arbor, MI.

1997c, "Africa, a Landscape of Opportunity", in Mattingly 1997b, pp. 117–139.

Mattingly, D. J. and Salmon, J. (eds.) 2001, *Economies Beyond Agriculture in the Classical World*, London.

Mattingly, D. J., Stone, D., Stirling, L. and Ben Lazreg, N. 2001, "Leptiminus (Tunisia): a 'Producer' City", in Mattingly and Salmon, pp. 66–98.

Mauro, F. 1990, "Merchant Communities, 1350–1750", in Tracy, pp. 255–286.

McKendrick, N., Brewer, J. and Plumb, J. H. (eds.) 1982, *The Birth of a Consumer Society. The Commercialization of Eighteenth-Century England*, Bloomington, IN.

McNeill, W. H. 1982, *The Pursuit of Power*, Chicago.

1986, *Mythistory and Other Essays*, Chicago.

McPherson, K. 1993, *The Indian Ocean. A History of People and the Sea*, Delhi.

Meiggs, R. 1973, *Roman Ostia*, 2nd edn., Oxford.

Meijer, F. and van Nijf, O. 1992, *Trade, Transport, and Society in the Ancient World. A Sourcebook*, London.

Meilink-Roelofsz, M. A. P. 1962, *Asian Trade and European Influence in the Indonesian Archipelago between 1500 and about 1630*, The Hague.

1980, "The Structure of Trade in Asia in the Sixteenth and Seventeenth Centuries", in *Mare Luso-Indicum*, IV, Paris, pp. 1–43.

Merola, G. D. 2001, *Autonomia locale governo imperiale*, Bari.

Meyer, Eduard 1910, *Einleitung. Elemente der Anthropologie. Geschichte des Altertums*, vol. 1, 1, Berlin.

1924, "Die Wirtschaftliche Entwicklung des Altertums", in E. Meyer, *Kleine Schriften*, vol. 1, 2nd edn, Halle, pp. 79–168.

Meyer Elizabeth, A. 2004, *Legitimacy and Law in the Roman World*, Tabulae *in Roman Belief and Practice*, Cambridge.

Mickwitz, G. 1936, *Die Kartellfunktionen der Zünfte und ihre Bedeutung bei der Entstehung des Zunftwesens*, Helsinki.

1937, "Economic Rationalism in Greco-Roman Agriculture", *English Historical Review* 52, pp. 577–589.

Middleton, P. 1983, "The Roman Army and Long Distance Trade", in Garnsey and Whittaker, pp. 75–83.

Millar, F. 1964, *A Study of Cassius Dio*, Oxford.

1977, *The Emperor in the Roman World*, London.

1981, "The World of the Golden Ass", *Journal of Roman Studies* 71, pp. 63–75.

1993, *The Roman Near East, 31 BC–AD 337*, Cambridge, MA.

1998, "Caravan Cities: The Roman Near East and Long-Distance Trade by Land," in M. Austin, J. Harries and C. Smith (eds.), *Modus Operandi. Essays in Honour of Geoffrey Rickman. Bulletin of the Institute of Classical Studies* 71, Supplement, London, pp. 119–137.

1999, "The Greek East and Roman Law: The Dossier of M. Cn. Licinius Rufinus", *Journal of Roman Studies,* 89, pp. 90–108.

Miller, J. I. 1969, *The Spice Trade of the Roman Empire*, Oxford.

Millett, M. 1990, *The Romanization of Britain. An Essay in Archaeological Interpretation*, Cambridge.

Millett, P. 2001, "Productive to Some Purpose? The Problem of Ancient Economic Growth", in Mattingly and Salmon, pp. 17–48.

Minnen, P. van 1986, "The Volume of the Oxyrhynchite Textile Trade", *Münstersche Beiträge zur Antiken Handelsgeschichte* 5, 2, pp. 88–95.

1987, "Urban Craftsmen in Roman Egypt", *Münstersche Beiträge zur Antiken Handelsgeschichte* 6, 1, pp. 31–88.

Mirat-i-Ahmadi. A Persian History of Gujarat, by Ali Muhammad Khan, trans. M. F. Lokhandwala, Baroda 1965.

Mitchell, S. 1993, *Anatolia: Land, Men and Gods in Asia Minor*, vols. 1–2, Oxford.

Mitteis, L. 1891, *Reichsret und Volksrecht in den östlichen Provinzen des römischen Kaiserreichs. Mit Beiträgen zur Kenntnis des griechischen Rechts und der spätrömischen Rechtsentwicklung*, Leipzig.

Mitteis, L. and Wilcken, U. 1912, *Grunzüge und Chrestomathie der Papyruskunde*, vols. I–II, Leipzig and Berlin.

Modrzejewski, J. 1970, "La règle de droit dans l'Égypte romaine", *Proceedings of the XIIth International Congress of Papyrology*, Toronto, pp. 317–377.

1990, *Droit impérial et traditions locales dans l'Égypte romaine*, Aldershot.

Mommsen, T. 1843, *De collegiis et sodaliciis Romanorum*, Kiel.

1904, *Römische Geschichte*, vol. V, Berlin.

1992, *Römische Kaisergeschichte nach den Vorlesungen – Mitschriften von Sebastian und Paul Hensel 1882–86*, ed. Barbara and Alexander Demandt, Munich.

Montesquieu, C. 1955, *De l'esprit des lois. Texte établi et présenté par Jean Brethe de la Gressaye*, Paris.

Moosvi, S. 1986–7, "The Gross National Product of the Mughal Empire, c. 1600", *Indian Historical Review* 13, 1–2, pp. 75–87.

1987, *The Economy of the Mughal Empire, c. 1595*, Delhi.

2000, "The Indian Economic Experience", in Panikkar, Byres and Patnaik, pp. 328–358.

Morel, Jean Paul 1985, "La Manufacture. Moyen d'enrichissement dans l'Italie romaine", in Leveau, pp. 87–112.

Morley, Neville 1996, *Metropolis and Hinterland. The City of Rome and the Italian Economy 200 B.C.–A.D. 200*, Cambridge.

2000, "Markets, Marketing and the Roman Élite", in Lo Cascio 2000a, pp. 211–223.

2007, *Trade in Classical Antiquity. Key Themes in Ancient History*, Cambridge.

Morris, I. 2002, "Hard Surfaces", in Cartledge, Cohen and Foxhall, pp. 8–43.

Mouritsen, H. 1988, *Elections, Magistrates and Municipal Elite. Studies in Pompeian Epigraphy, Analecta Romana Instituti Danici*, Suppl. 15, Rome.

Nafissi, M. 2005, *Ancient Athens and Modern Ideology. Value, Theory and Evidence in Historical Sciences. Max Weber, Karl Polanyi and Moses Finley*, London.

Needham, Joseph 1954, *Science and Civilization in China*, vol. 1, Cambridge.

Neesen, L. 1980, *Untersuchungen zu den direkten Staatsabgaben der römischen Kaiserzeit (27 v. Chr.–284 n. Chr.)*, Bonn.

Neeve, P. W. de 1985, "The Price of Agricultural Land in Roman Italy and the Problem of Economic Rationalism", *Opus* 4, pp. 77–109.

Nicolet, C. 1980, "Économie, société et institutions au IIe siecle av. J.-C.: De la lex Claudia a l'ager exceptus", *Annales, Histoire, Sciences Sociales*, pp. 871–894.

1988, *Rendre à César. Économie et société dans la Rome antique*, Paris.

1991a, *Geography, Space and Politics in the Early Roman Empire*, Ann Arbor, MI.

1991b, "Le 'Monumentum Ephesenum' et les dîmes d'Asie", *Bulletin de Correspondance Hellénique* 115, pp. 465–480.

1993, "Le 'Monumentum Ephesenum' et la délimitation du *portorium* d'Asie", *Mélanges de l'École Française de Rome. Antiquité* 105, pp. 929–959.

1996, *Financial Documents and Geographical Knowledge in the Roman World. The Sixteenth J. L. Myres Memorial Lecture*, Oxford.

Nijf, O. M. van 1997, *The Civic World of Professional Associations in the Roman East*, Amsterdam.

Nippel, W. 1990, *Griechen, Barbaren und "Wilde". Alte Geschichte und Sozialanthropologie*, Frankfurt.

1995, *Public Order in Ancient Rome*, Cambridge.

Nollé, J. 1999, "Marktrechte ausserhalb der Stadt: Lokale Autonomie zwischen Statthalter und Zentralort", in Eck, pp. 93–114.

Nörr, D. 1998, "Römisches Zivilprozessrecht nach Max Kaser: Prozessrecht und Prozesspraxis in der Provins Arabia", *Zeitschrift der Savigny-Stiftung für Rechtsgeschichte. Romanistische Abteilung* 115, pp. 80–98.

North, D. C. 1977, "Markets and Other Allocation Systems in History: The Challenge of Karl Polanyi", *Journal of European Economic History* 6, 3, pp. 703–716.

1990, *Institutions, Institutional Change and Economic Performance*, Cambridge.

2005, *Understanding the Process of Economic Change*, Princeton, NJ and Oxford.

North, D. C. and Thomas, R. P. 1973, *The Rise of the Western World. A New Economic History*, Cambridge.

Noy, D. 2000, *Foreigners at Rome. Citizens and Strangers*, Swansea.

Nørlund, P. 1920, *Det romerske slavesamfund under afvikling*, Copenhagen.

O'Brien, P. K. 1998, "Inseparable Connections: Trade, Economy, Fiscal State, and the Expansion of Empire, 1688–1815", in P. J. Marschall (ed.), *Oxford*

History of the British Empire, vol. 2: *The Eighteenth Century*, Oxford, pp. 53–77.

Obeysekere, G. 1992, *The Apotheosis of Captain Cook. European Mythmaking in the Pacific*, Princeton, NJ.

Oliver, J. H. 1953, "The Ruling Power: A Study of the Roman Empire in the Second Century After Christ Through the Roman Oration of Aelius Aristeides", *Transactions of the American Philosophical Society* n.s. 43, 4, pp. 871–1003.

1989, *Greek Constitutions of Early Roman Emperors from Inscriptions and Papyri*, Philadelphia, PA.

Osborne, R. 1991, "Pride and Prejudice, Sense and Subsistence: Exchange and Society in the Greek City", in Rich and Wallace-Hadrill, pp. 119–145.

1996, "Pots, Trade and the Archaic Greek Economy", *Antiquity* 70, pp. 31–44.

Paludan, H. 1995, *Familia og Familie. To europæiske kulturelementers møde i højmiddelalderens Danmark*, Aarhus.

1996, "Pots, Trade and the Archaic Greek Economy", *Antiquity* 70, pp. 31–44.

Pamuk, O. 2005, *Istanbul. Memories of the City*, trans. Maureen Freely, London.

Pamuk, S. 2000, "The Ottoman Empire in the Eighteenth Century", *Itinerario* 24, pp. 104–116.

Panella, C. 1981, "La distribuzione e i mercati", in Giardina and Schiavone, pp. 55–80.

1993, "Merci e scambi nel Mediterraneo tardoantico", in A. Schiavone (ed.), *Storia di Roma*, vol. 3, 2, Turin, pp. 613–697.

Panella, C. and Tchernia, A. 1994, "Produits agricoles transportés en amphores: L'huile et surtout le vin" in *L'Italie d'Auguste à Dioclétien*, Collection de l'École Française de Rome 198, Rome, pp. 145–165.

Panikkar, K. N., Byres, T. J. and Patnaik, U. (eds.) 2000, *The Making of History. Essays Presented to Irfan Habib*, New Delhi.

Parker, A. J. 1992, *Ancient Shipwrecks of the Mediterranean and the Roman Provinces*, BAR International Series 580, Oxford.

1996, "Sea Transport and Trade in the Ancient Mediterranean", in E. E. Rice (eds.), *The Sea and History*, Gloucester, pp. 97–109.

Parkins, H. 1997a, "The 'Consumer-city' Domesticated? The Roman City in Élite Economic Strategies", in Parkins 1997b, pp. 83–111.

(ed.) 1997b, *Roman Urbanism Beyond the Comsumer City*, London.

1998, "Time for Change? Shaping the Future of the Ancient Economy", in Parkins and Smith, pp. 1–15.

Parkins, H. and Smith, C. 1998 (eds.), *Trade, Traders and the Ancient City*, London.

Parthasarathi, P. 2002, "Review Article: The Great Divergence", *Past and Present* 176, pp. 275–293.

Paterson, J. 1998, "Trade and Traders in the Roman World: Scale, Structure, and Organization", in Parkins and Smith, pp. 149–167.

Patterson, J. R. 1987, "Crisis: What Crisis? Rural Change and Urban Development in Imperial Apennine Italy", *Papers of the British School at Rome* 55, pp. 115–146.

1991, "Settlement, City and Elite in Samnium and Lycia", in Rich and Wallace-Hadrill, pp. 147–168.

1994, "The *Collegia* and the Transformation of the Towns of Italy in the Second Century AD", in *L'Italie d'Auguste à Dioclétien*. Collection de l'École Française de Rome 198, Rome, pp. 227–238.

2006, *Landscapes and Cities. Rural Settlement and Civic Transformation in Early Imperial Italy*, Oxford.

Pavis d'Escurac, H. 1976, *La Préfecture de l'annone, service administratif impérial d'Auguste à Constantin*, Rome.

1977, "Aristocratie sénatoriale et profits commerciaux", *Ktèma* 2, pp. 339–355.

Peacock, D. P. S. and Williams, D. F. 1986, *Amphorae and the Roman Economy*, London.

Pearson, M. N. 1976, *Merchants and Rulers in Gujarat. The Response to the Portuguese in the Sixteenth Century*, Berkeley, CA.

1985, "Land, Noble, and Ruler in Mughal India", in E. Leach, S. N. Mukherjee and J. O. Ward (eds.), *Feudalism. Comparative Studies*, Sydney, pp. 175–196.

1988a, *Before Colonialism. Theories of Asian–European Relations*, New Delhi.

1988b, "Brokers in Western Indian Port Cities: Their Role in Servicing Foreign Merchants", *Modern Asian Studies* 22, 3, pp. 445–472.

1991, "Merchants and States", in Tracy 1991, pp. 41–116.

1998, *Port Cities and Intruders. The Swahili Coast, India, and Portugal in the Early Modern Era*, Baltimore, MD and London.

Pearson, R. 1993, "Taking Risks and Containing Competition: Diversification and Oligopoly in the Fire Insurance Markets in the North of England During the Early Nineteenth Century", *Economic History Review* 46, 1, pp. 39–64.

Pelsaert, F. 1925, *Jahangir's India. The Remonstrantie of Francisco Pelsaert*, translated from the Dutch by W. H. Moreland and P. Geyl, Cambridge.

Perkins, D. 1969, *Agricultural Development in China, 1368–1968*, Chicago.

Perlin, F. 1978, "Of White Whale and Country-men in the Eighteenth-century Maratha Deccan", *Journal of Peasant Studies* 5, 2, pp. 172–243.

1981, "The Pre-Colonial Indian State in History and Epistemology", in H. Claessen and P. Skalnik (eds.), *The Study of the State*, The Hague, pp. 275–302.

1983, "Proto-Industrialization and Pre-Colonial South Asia", *Past and Present* 98, pp. 30–95.

1993, *The Invisible City. Monetary, Administrative and Popular Infrastructures in Asia and Europe, 1500–1900*, Aldershot.

1994, "Changes in Production and Circulation of Money in Seventeenth and Eighteenth Century India: An Essay of Monetization Before Colonial Occupation", in Subrahmanyam, pp. 276–306.

Persson, K. G. 1988, *Pre-Industrial Economic Growth. Social Organization and Technological Progress in Europe*, Oxford.

1999, *Grain Markets in Europe 1500–1900. Integration and Deregulation*, Cambridge.

Pflaum, H. G. 1950, *Les Procurateurs équestres sous le Haut-Empire romain*, Paris.

1960, *Les Carrières procuratoriennes équestres sous le Haut-Empire romain*, vols. 1–3, Paris.

Pleket, H. 1983, "Urban Élites and Business in the Greek Part of the Roman Empire", in Garnsey, Hopkins and Whittaker, pp. 131–144.

1984, "Urban Élites and the Economy in the Greek Cities of the Roman Empire", *Münstersche Beiträge zur Antiken Handelsgeschichte* 1, pp. 3–36.

1990, "Wirtschaft", in F. Vittinghoff (ed.), *Europäische Wirtschafts- und Sozialgeschichte in der römischen Kaiserzeit*, Stuttgart, pp. 25–160.

1994, "The Roman State and the Economy: The Case of Ephesus", in Andreau, Briant and Descat *et al.*, pp. 115–126.

Pocock, J. G. A. 2003, *Barbarism and Religion*, vol. 3: *The First Decline and Fall*, Cambridge.

Polanyi, K. 1957, "The Economy as Instituted Process", in Polanyi, Arensberg and Pearson, pp. 243–270.

1963, "Ports of Trade in Early Societies", *Journal of Economic History* 23, 1, pp. 30–45.

1977, *The Livelihood of Man*, London.

Polanyi, K., Arensberg, C. and Pearson, H. (eds.) 1957, *Trade and Market in the Early Empires*, New York.

Pollard, N. 2000, *Soldiers, Cities, and Civilians in Roman Syria*, Ann Arbor, MI.

Pollock, S. 1998, "India in the Vernacular Millennium: Literary Culture and Polity", *Daedalus* 127, 3, pp. 41–75.

Pomeranz, K. 2000, *The Great Divergence. China, Europe and the Making of the Modern World Economy*, Princeton, NJ.

Pomey, P. and Tchernia, A. 1977, "Le tonnage maximum des navires de commerce romains", *Archaeonautica* 2, pp. 233–251.

Ponsich, M. 1998, "The Rural Economy of Western Baetica", in Keay, pp. 171–182.

Postan, M. M. 1972, *The Medieval Economy and Society. An Economic History of Britain in the Middle-Ages*, Birkenhead.

Posthumus, N. W. 1946, *Inquiry into the History of Prices in Holland*, Leiden.

Prachner, G. 1980, *Die Sklaven und Freigelassenen im Arretinischen Sigillatengewerbe*, Wiesbaden.

Prakash, O. 1972, "The Dutch East India Company in Bengal: Trade Privileges and Problems, 1633–1712", *Indian Economic and Social History Review* 9, pp. 258–287.

1985, *The Dutch East India Company and the Economy of Bengal, 1630–1720,* Princeton, NJ.

1991, "Precious Metal Flows, Coinage and Prices in India in the 17th and the Early 18th Century", in E. van Cauwenberghe (ed.), *Money, Coins and Commerce. Essays in the Monetary History of Asia and Europe,* Louvain, pp. 55–73.

(ed.) 1997, *European Commercial Expansion in Early Modern Asia. An Expanding World,* vol. 10, Aldershot.

1998, *European Commercial Enterprise in Pre-Colonial India,* The New Cambridge History of India 2, 5, Cambridge.

Preisigke, F. 1910, *Der Girowesen im griechischen Ägypten,* Strasbourg.

Pringsheim, F. 1950, *The Greek Law of Sale,* Weimar.

Ptak, R. and Rothermund, D. (eds.) 1991, *Emporia, Commodities and Entrepreneurs in Asian Maritime Trade, c. 1400–1750,* Stuttgart.

Purcell, N. 2005, "The Ancient Mediterranean: The View from the Customs House", in W. V. Harris (ed.), *Rethinking the Mediterranean,* Oxford, pp. 200–232.

Purpura, G. 1985, "Il regolamento doganale di Cauno e la lex Rhodia in D. 14.2.9", *Annali Seminario Giuridico della Universita di Palermo* 38, pp. 273–331.

Qaisar, A. J. 1967, "Distribution of the Revenue Resources of the Mughal Empire among the Nobility", in *Proceedings of the Twenty-Seventh Session of the Indian History Congress,* Aligarh, pp. 237–243.

Quass, F. 1993, *Die Honoratiorenschicht in den Städten des griechischen Ostens. Untersuchungen zur politischen und sozialen Entwicklung in hellenistischer und römischer Zeit,* Bonn.

Quereschi, J. H. 1966, *The Administration of the Mughal Empire,* Karachi.

Rapsaet, G. 1987, "Aspects de l'organisation du commerce de la céramique sigillée dans le Nord de la Gaule au IIe siècle de notre ère, I: Les données matérielles", *Münstersche Beiträge zur antiken Handelsgeschichte* 6, 2, pp. 1–29.

Rapsaet-Charlier, M.-T. and G. 1988, "Aspects de l'organisation du commerce de la céramique sigillée dans le Nord de la Gaule au IIe siècle de notre ère I: Les données matérielles", *Münstersche Beiträge zur antiken Handelsgeschichte* 7, 2, pp. 45–69.

Raschke, M. G. 1978, "New Studies in Roman Commerce with the East", *Aufstieg und Niedergang der römischen Welt* 2, 9.2, pp. 604–1378.

Rathbone, D. 1983a, "The Weight and Meassurement of Egyptian Grains", *Zeitschrift für Papyrologie und Epigraphik* 53, pp. 265–275.

1983b, "Italian Wines in Roman Egypt", *Opus* 2, pp. 81–98.

1991, *Economic Rationalism and Rural Society in Third-Century A.D. Egypt*, Cambridge.

1997, "Prices and Price Formation in Roman Egypt", in Andreau, Briant and Descat *et al.*, pp. 183–244.

2000, "Ptolemaic to Roman Egypt: The Death of the Dirigiste State?", in Lo Cascio and Rathbone, pp. 44–55.

2001, "The 'Muziris' Papyrus (SB XVIII 13167): Financing Roman Trade with India", in Alexandrian Studies II in Honour of Mostafa el Abbadi, *Bulletin de la Société Archéologique d'Alexandrie* 46, Alexandria, pp. 39–50.

2003, "The Financing of Maritime Commerce in the Roman Empire, I–II AD", in Lo Cascio 2003b, pp. 197–230.

Rauh, N. 1986, "Cicero's Business Friendships, Economics and Politics in the Late Roman Republic", *Aevum* 60, pp. 3–30.

1989, "Auctioneers and the Roman Economy", *Historia* 38, pp. 451–471.

1993, *The Sacred Bonds of Commerce. Religion, Economy, and Trade Society at Hellenistic Roman Delos, 166–87 B.C.*, Amsterdam.

Ray, R. K. 1988, "The Bazaar: Changing Structural Characteristics of the Indigenous Section of the Indian Economy Before and After the Great Depression", *Indian Economic and Social History Review* 25, pp. 263–318.

Raychaudhuri, T. 1991, "The Commercial Entrepreneur in Pre-Colonial India: Aspirations and Expectations: A Note", in Ptak and Rothermund, pp. 339–351.

Rea, J. 1982, "P. Lond. Inv. 1562 Verso: Market Taxes in Oxyrhynchus", *Zeitschrift fur Papyrologie und Epigraphik* 46, pp. 191–209.

Reed, M. 1996, "London and its Hinterland 1600–1800", in P. Clark and B. Lepetit (eds.), *Capital Cities and their Hinterlands in Early Modern Europe*, Aldershot, pp. 51–83.

Reger, G. 1994, *Regionalism and Change in the Economy of Independent Delos*, Berkeley, CA.

2003, "*Aspects of the Role of Merchants in the Political Life of the Hellenistic World*", in Zaccagnini, pp. 165–198.

Reinhardt, F. 1968, *Kapitalaufwendungen der Gesellschafter und Gesellschaftvermögen in der klassischen römischen Societas*, Heidelberg.

Reinmuth, O. W. 1936, "Two Prefecturial Edicts Concerning The *Publican*", *Classical Philology* 31, pp. 146–162.

Remesal Rodríguez, J. 1983, "Ölproduktion und Ölhandel in der Baetica", *Münstersche Beiträge zur Antiken Handelsgeschichte* 2, 2, pp. 91–112.

1986, *La annona militaris y la exportatión de aceite betico a Germania*, Madrid.

1997, *Heeresversorgung und die Wirtschaftlichen Beziehungen zwischen der Baetica und Germanien*, Stuttgart.

1998, "Baetican Olive Oil and the Roman Economy", in Keay, pp. 183–199.

2001, "Politik und Landwirtschaft im Imperium Romanum am Beispiel der Baetica", in Peter Herz and Gerhard Waldherr (eds.), *Landwirtschaft im Imperium Romanum*, St Katharinen.

Renger, J. 2003, "Trade and Market in the Ancient Near East: Theoretical and Factual Implications", in Zaccagnini, pp. 15–39.

Reynolds, P. 1995, *Trade in the Western Mediterranean, AD: 400–700. The Ceramic Evidence*, BAR International Series 600, Oxford.

Ricardo, D. 1996, *Principles of Political Economy and Taxation*, Great Minds Series, Amherst, NY.

Rich, J. and Shipley, G. (eds.) 1993, *War and Society in the Roman World*, London and New York.

Rich, J. and Wallace-Hadrill, A. (eds.) 1991, *City and Country in the Ancient World*, London and New York.

Richards, J. F. 1975, *Mughal Administration in Golconda*, Oxford.

1981, "Mughal State Finance and the Premodern World Economy", *Comparative Studies in Society and History* 23, pp. 285–308.

1984, "Norms of Comportment among Imperial Mughal Officers", in B. D. Metcalf (ed.), *Moral Conduct and Authority. The Place of Adab in South Asian Islam*, Berkeley, CA, pp. 255–289.

1986, *Document Forms for Official Orders of Appointment in the Mughal Empire*, Cambridge.

(ed.) 1987, *The Imperial Monetary System of Mughal India*, Delhi.

1990, "The Seventeenth Century Crisis in South Asia", *Modern Asian Studies* 24, 4, pp. 625–638.

1993a, *The Mughal Empire*, The New Cambridge History of India 1, 5, Cambridge.

1993b, *Power, Administration, and Finance in Mughal India*, Aldershot.

Rickman, G. 1980a, *The Corn Supply of Ancient Rome*, Oxford.

1980b, "The Grain Trade under the Roman Empire", in D'Arms and Kopff, pp. 261–275.

Rizzo, G. 2003, *Instrumenta Urbis I. Ceramiche fini da mensa, lucerne ed anfore a Roma nei primi due secoli dell'impero*, Collection de l'École Française de Rome 307, Rome.

Robert, L. 1969, *Opera Minora Selecta*, vol. 1, Amsterdam.

Roberto, U. 2003, "'Del commercio dei Romani': Politica e storia antica nelle riflessioni del Settecento", in Zaccagnini, pp. 327–361.

Robertson, J. 1997, "Gibbon's Roman Empire as a Universal Monarchy: The Decline and Fall and the Imperial Idea in Early Modern Europe", in R. McKitterick and R. Quinauldt (eds.), *Gibbon and Empire*, Cambridge, pp. 247–270.

Roda, S. 1998, "Il Senato nell'alto impero Romano", in *Il Senato nella storia. Instituto Poligrafico e Zecca Dello Stato*, Rome, pp. 129–221.

Rodger, A. 1996, "Postponed Business at Irni", *Journal of Roman Studies* 86, pp. 61–73.

1997, "Vadimonium to Rome (and Elsewhere)", *Zeitschrift der Savigny-Stiftung. Romanistische Abteilung* 114, pp. 160–196.

Rodinson, M. 1966, *Islam et capitalisme*, Paris.

Rodríguez-Almeida, E. 1984, *Il Monte Testaccio. Ambiente, storia, materiali*, Rome.

Rostovtzeff, M. I. 1902, *Geschichte der Staatspacht in der Römischen Kaiserzeit bis Diocletian, Philologus*, Suppl. 9, pp. 329–512.

1932a, *Caravan Cities*, trans. D. and T. Talbot-Rice, Oxford.

1932b, "Les inscriptions caravanières de Palmyre", in *Mélanges Gustave Glotz*, vol. II, Paris, pp. 792–811.

1957, *The Social and Economic History of the Roman Empire*, 2nd edn, revised by P. M. Fraser, Oxford.

Rothermund, D. 1991, "Asian Emporia and European Bridge-Heads", in Ptak and Rothermund, pp. 3–8.

Rotschild, M. 1973, "Models of Market Organization with Imperfect Information: A Survey", *Journal of Political Economy* 81, pp. 1283–1308.

Rougé, J. 1966, *Recherches sur l'organisation du commerce maritime en Méditerranée sous l'empire romain*, Paris.

1980, "Prêt et société maritime dans le monde romain", in D'Arms and Kopff, pp. 291–303.

1981, *Ships and Fleets of the Ancient Mediterranean*, trans. Susan Frazer, Middleton, CT.

1985, "Droit romain et sources de richesses non foncières", in Leveau 1985, pp. 161–176.

Royden, H. L. 1988, *The Magistrates of the Roman Professional Collegia in Italy. From the First to the Third Century A.D.*, Pisa.

Ruggini, L. C. 1973, "Stato e associazioni professionali nell'età imperiale romana" in *Akten des VI. Internationalen Kongresses für Griechische und Lateinische Epigraphik*, Munich, pp. 271–311.

Ruprechtsberger, E. M. (ed.) 1987, *Palmyra. Geschichte, Kunst und Kultur der Syrischen Oasenstadt*, Linz.

Sabloff, J. A. and Lamberg-Karlowsky, C. C. (eds.) 1975, *Ancient Civilization and Trade*, Albuquerque, NM.

Sahlins, M. 1972, *Stone Age Economics*, Chicago.

1995, *How "Natives" Think About Captain Cook For example*, Chicago and London.

2000, "Cosmologies of Capitalism: The Trans-Pacific Sector of 'The World System'", in M. Sahlins, *Culture in Practice. Selected Essays*, New York, pp. 415–469.

Said, E. 1978, *Orientalism. Western Conceptions of the Orient*, New York and London.

1993, *Culture and Imperialism*, London.

Sallares, R. 2002, *Malaria and Rome. A History of Malaria in Ancient Italy*, Oxford.

Saller, R. 1982, *Personal Patronage under the Early Empire*, Cambridge.

1994, *Patriarchy, Property and the Roman Family*, Cambridge.

2000, "Status and Patronage", in *The Cambridge Ancient History*, vol. XI, 2nd edn, Cambridge, pp. 817–854.

2002, "Framing the Debate over Growth in the Ancient Economy", in Scheidel and von Reden, pp. 251–269. (Also published in Morris and Manning 2005, pp. 223–238.)

Santucci, G. 1997, *Il socio d'opera in diritto romano. Conferimenti e responsabilità*, Padua.

Salmeri, G. 1998, "Per una lettura dei capitoli V–VII Della Storia economica e sociale dell'Impero Romano di M. Rostovtzeff", *Athenaeum* 86, pp. 57–84.

Sarris, P. 2006, *Economy and Society in the Age of Justinian*, Cambridge.

Sartre, J.-P. 1961, "Preface", in Franz Fanon, *Les Damnés de la terre*, Paris.

Sartre, M. 1991, *L'Orient romain. Provinces et sociétés provinciales en Méditerranée orientale d'Auguste aux Sévères (31. avant J.C.–235 aprés J.C.)*, Paris.

Scheidel, W. 2000, *Debating Roman Demography*, Leiden.

2002, "A Model of Demographic and Economic Change in Roman Egypt after the Antonine Plague", *Journal of Roman Archaeology* 15, pp. 97–114.

2007a, "Demography", in I. Morris, R. Saller and W. Scheidel (eds.), *The Cambridge Economic History of the Greco-Roman World*, Cambridge, pp. 38–86.

2007b, "A Model of Real Income Growth in Roman Italy", *Historia* 56, pp. 332–346.

(ed.) 2008, *Rome and China: Comparative Perspectives on Ancient World Empires*, New York.

Scheidel, W. and von Reden, S. 2002, *The Ancient Economy*, Edinburgh.

Schiavone, Aldo 2000, *The End of the Past*, Cambridge, MA.

Schleich, T. 1983, "Überlegungen zum Problem senatorischer Handelsaktivitäten. Teil 1. Senatorische Wirtschaftsmentalität in moderner und antiker Deutung", *Münstersche Beiträge zur antiken Handelsgeschichte* 2, 2, pp. 65–90.

1984, "Überlegungen zum Problem senatorischer Handelsaktivitäten. Teil 2. Zwischen 'otium' und 'negotium': Gelegenheitsunternehmungen und domestizierte Wirtschaft", *Münstersche Beiträge zur antiken Handelsgeschichte* 3, 1, pp. 37–76.

Schmidt-Colinet, A., Stauffer, A. and Al-As'ad, Khaled 2000, *Die Textilien aus Palmyra*, Mainz.

Schneider, H. 1990, "Die Bücher-Meyer Kontroverse", in Calder and Demandt, pp. 417–445.

Schneider, Jane. 1977, "Was there a Pre-capitalist World System?", *Peasant Studies* 6, 1, pp. 30–39.

Schneider, Jürgen 1986, "The Significance of Large Fairs, Money Markets and Precious Metals in the Evolution of a World Market from the Middle Ages to the First Half of the Nineteenth Century", in Fischer, McInnis and Schneider, pp. 15–36.

Schwarz, H. 2001a, "Anmerkungen zu der Zollinschrift aus Myra", *Epigraphica Anatolica* 33, pp. 15–37.

2001b, *Die Finanzwirtschaft kleinasiatischer Städte in der römischen Kaiserzeit*, Bonn.

Schwarz, L. D. 1992, *London in the Age of Industrialization*, Cambridge.

Scullard, H. H. 1980, *A History of the Roman World 753 to 146*, 4th edn, London.

Seland, T. 1996, "Philo and the Clubs and Associations of Alexandria", in Kloppenborg and Wilson, pp. 110–127.

Serrao, F. 2000, "Impresa, mercato, diritto: riflessioni minime", in Lo Cascio 2000c, pp. 31–68.

Shanin, T. (ed.) 1987, *Peasants and Peasant Societies*, 2nd edn, Oxford.

Sharma, R. S. 1970, "The Ardha-Kathanak: A Neglected Source of Mughal History", *Indica* 7, pp. 49–73 and 106–120.

Sharp, M. 1998, *The Food Supply in Roman Egypt*, D. Phil. thesis, University of Oxford.

Shatzman, I. 1975, *Senatorial Wealth and Roman Politics*, Brussels.

Shaw, B. D. 1981, "Rural Markets in North Africa and the Political Economy of the Roman Empire", *Antiquitates Africanae* 17, pp. 37–83.

1984, "Bandits in the Roman Empire", *Past and Present* 105, pp. 3–52.

2001, "Challenging Braudel: A New Vision of the Mediterranean", *Journal of Roman Archaeology* 14, pp. 1–25.

Sherk, R. K. 1955, "The *Inermes Provinciae* of Asia Minor", *American Journal of Philology* 76, pp. 400–413.

1957, "Roman Imperial Troops in Macedonia and Achaea", *American Journal of Philology* 78, pp. 52–62.

(ed. and trans.) 1988, *The Roman Empire. Augustus to Hadrian*, Cambridge.

Sherwin-White, A. N. 1973a, *The Roman Citizenship*, 2nd edn, Oxford.

1973b, "The *Tabula* of Banasa and the *Constitutio Antoniniana*", *Journal of Roman Studies* 63, pp. 86–98.

Sijpestein, P. J. 1987, *Customs Duties in Graeco-Roman Egypt*. Studia Amsterdamensia ad Epigraphicam, Ius Antiquum et Papyrologicam Pertinentia 17, Zutphen.

Singh, C. 1988, "Centre and Periphery in the Mughal State: The Case of Seventeenth-century Panjab", *Modern Asian Studies* 22, pp. 299–318.

Singh, M. P. 1972, "Merchants and the Local Administration and Civic Life in Gujarat During the 17th Century", in *Medieval India. A Miscellany*, vol. 2, pp. 221–226, n.p.

1985, *Town, Market, Mint and Port in the Mughal Empire, 1556–1707*, New Delhi.

Sirks, B. 1991, *Food for Rome*, Amsterdam.

2002, "Sailing in the Off-Season with Reduced Financial Risk", in Aubert and Sirks, pp. 134–150.

Skinner, G. W. 1964, "Marketing and Social Structure in Rural China", *Journal of Asian Studies* 24, 1, pp. 3–43; 24, 2, pp. 195–228; and 24, 3, pp. 363–399.

Skocpol, T. 1979, *States and Social Revolutions. A Comparative Analysis of France, Russia and China*, Cambridge.

Skocpol, T. and Sommers, M. 1980, "The Uses of Comparative Historical Inquiry", *Comparative Studies in Society and History* 22, pp. 174–194.

Skydsgaard, J. E. 1976, "The Disintegration of the Roman Labour Market and the Clientela Theory", in K. Ascani *et al.*, *Studia Romana in Honorem Petri Krarup Septuagenarii*, Odense, pp. 44–48.

1997, "Theodor Mommsens romerske kejserhistorie", *Historisk Tidsskrift* 97, 2, pp. 305–312.

Smith, Adam 1976, *An Inquiry into the Nature and Causes of the Wealth of Nations*, Oxford.

Smith, Anthony, D. 1986, *The Ethnic Origin of Nations*, London.

Snell, R. 2005, "Confessions of a 17th-century Jain Merchant: The Ardhakathának of Banárasídás", *South Asia Research* 25, pp. 79–104.

Sombart, W. 1913, *Luxus und Kapitalismus*, Leipzig.

Sommer, M. 2005, *Roms orientalische Steppengrenze. Palmyra–Edessa–Dura–Europos–Hatra. Eine Kulturgeschichte von Pompeius bis Diocletian*, Wiesbaden.

Sørensen, G. 1994, "Hvad er udvikling?", *Den Jyske Historiker* 66, pp. 19–32.

Steensgaard, N. 1973a, *Carracks, Caravans and Companies. The Structural Crisis in the European Asian Trade in the Early 17th Century*, Odense.

1973b, "Universal History for Our Times", *Journal of Modern History* 45, pp. 72–82.

1980, "Asian Trade 15th 18th Centuries: Continuity and Discontinuities", *XVe Congrès International des Sciences Historiques Rapports II*, Bucharest, pp. 488–500.

1981, "Violence and the Rice of Capitalism: Frederic C. Lane's Theory of Protection and Tribute", *Review* 5, 2, pp. 247–273.

1984, "Set fra 1984. En model for nyere tids verdenshistorie", in *Tradition og Kritik. Festskrift til Svend Ellehøj den 8. september 1984*, Copenhagen, pp. 413–435.

1987, "The Indian Ocean Network and the Emerging World-Economy (c. 1550–1750)", in S. Chandra (ed.), *The Indian Ocean. Explorations in History, Commerce, and Politics*, New Delhi, pp. 125–150.

1990a, "The Growth and Composition of the Long-distance Trade of England and the Dutch Republic before 1750", in Tracy, pp. 102–152.

1990b, "Opdagelsernes plads i verdenshistorien. Varer, Ædelmetal og Tjenesteydelser i International Handel før 1750", *Historisk Tidsskrift* 90, pp. 221–246.

1990c, "The Seventeenth-Century Crisis and the Unity of Eurasian History", *Modern Asian Studies* 24, 4, pp. 683–697.

1991, "Emporia: Some Reflections", in Ptak and Rothermund, pp. 9–12.

Stein, A. 1927, *Der römische Ritterstand. Ein Beitrag zur social- und personengeschichte des römischens Reiches*, Munich.

Stein, B. 1985a, "State Formation and the Economy Reconsidered. Part 1", *Modern Asian Studies* 19, 3, pp. 387–413.

1985b, "Politics, Peasants and the Deconstruction of Feudalism in Medieval India", in Byres and Mukhia, pp. 54–86.

1998, *A History of India*, Oxford.

Stigler, G. J. and Sherwin, R. A. 1985, "The Extent of the Market", *Journal of Law and Economics* 28, pp. 554–577.

Stocking G. W., Jr 1995, *After Tylor. British Social Anthropology 1888–1951*, London.

Stoianovich, T. 1974, "Pour un modèle du commerce du Levant: économie concurrentielle et économie de Bazar 1500–1800", *Bulletin. Association Internationale d'Études du Sud-Est Européen* 12, 2, pp. 61–120.

1994, "Cities, Capital Accumulation, and the Ottoman Balkan Command Economy, 1500–1800", in Tilly and Blochmans, pp. 60–99.

Stuart, P. and Bogaers, J. E. (eds.) 1971, *Deae Nehalenniae. Gids Bij De Tentoonstelling Nehalennia de Zeeuwse Godin*, Leiden.

2001, *Nehalennia. Römische Steindenkmäler aus der Oosterschelde bei Colijnsplaat*, Leiden.

Subrahmaniam, L. 1999, "India's International Economy, 1500–1800", *Indian Historical Review* 25, 2, pp. 38–57.

Subrahmanyam, S. 1989, "State Formation and Transformation in Early Modern India and Southeast Asia", in P. J. Marshall *et al.* (eds.) *India and Indonesia during the Ancien Régime*, Leiden, pp. 91–109.

(ed.) 1990a, *Merchants, Markets and the State in Early Modern India*, Delhi.

1990b, *The Political Economy of Commerce*, Cambridge.

(ed.) 1994, *Money and the Market in India 1100–1700*, Delhi.

1995, "Of *Imârat* and *Tijârat*: Asian Merchants and State Power in the Western Indian Ocean, 1400 to 1750", *Comparative Studies in Society and History* 37, pp. 750–780.

(ed.) 1996, *Merchant Networks in the Early Modern World*, An Expanding World 8, Aldershot.

1998, "Hearing Voices: Vignettes of Early Modernity in South Asia, 1400–1750", *Daedalus* 127, 3, pp. 75–104.

Swain, S. 1996, *Hellenism and Empire. Language, Classicism, and Power in the Greek World, AD 50–250*, Oxford.

Syme, R. 1958, *Tacitus*, vols. 1–2, Oxford.

1977, "La richesse des aristocraties Bétique et de Narbonnaise", *Ktéma* 2, pp. 373–380.

Talamanca, M. 1955, "Contributi allo studio delle vendite all'asta nel mondo classico", *Atti della Accademia Nazionale dei Lincei* 6, pp. 35–251.

Talbert, R. J. A. 1984, *The Senate in Imperial Rome*, Princeton, NJ.

Tandrup, L. 1979, *Ravn*, vols. 1–2, Viborg.

Tate, G. 1992, *Les Campagnes de la Syrie du nord du IIe au VIIe siècle. Un exemple d'expansion démographique et économique à la fin de l'antiquité*, Paris.

Taubenschlag, R. 1955, *The Law of Greco-Roman Egypt in the Light of the Papyri (332 B.C.–A.D. 640)*, 2nd edn, Warsaw.

Tavernier, J. B. 1889, *Tavernier's Travels in India*, vols. 1–2, ed. and trans. V. Ball, London (original French edn 1676).

Tchernia, A. 1983, "Italian Wine in Gaul at the End of the Republic", in Garnsey, Hopkins and Whittaker, pp. 87–102.

  1986, *Le Vin de l'Italie romaine*, Paris.

  1989, "Encore sur les modèles économiques et les amphores", in *Amphores romaines et histoire économique. Dix ans de recherche*. Collection de l'École Française de Rome 114, Rome, pp. 529–536.

  1992, "Le dromadaire des Peticii et le commerce Oriental", *Mélanges de l'École Française de Rome. Antiquité* 104, pp. 293–301.

  1995, "Moussons et monnaies: les voies du commerce entre le monde Greco-Romain et l'Inde", *Annales. Histoire, Sciences Sociales* 50, pp. 991–1009.

  2000, "La vente du vin", in Lo Cascio 2000c, pp. 199–211.

  (ed.) 2005, *Autour de la rationalité antique*, in *Topoi. Orient-Occident* 12–13, pp. 259–314.

  2006, "La crise de L'Italie impériale et la concurrence des provinces", *Cahiers du Centre de Recherches Historiques* 37, pp. 137–156.

Teixidor, J. 1984, *Un Port romain du désert. Palmyre et son commerce d'Auguste à Caracalla*, Semitica 34, Paris.

Temin, P. 2001, "A Market Economy in the Early Roman Empire", *Journal of Roman Studies* 91, pp. 169–181.

  2006, "Estimating GDP in the Early Roman Empire", in E. Lo Cascio (ed.), *Innovazione tecnica e progresso economico nel mondo romano*, Bari, pp. 31–54.

Temin, P. and Kessler, D. 2007 "The Organization of the Grain Trade in the Early Roman Empire", *Economic History Review* 60, 2, pp. 313–332.

Thebert, Y. 1980, "Économie, société et politique aux deux dernières siècles de la république romaine", *Annales. Histoire, Sciences Sociales*, pp. 875–911.

Thompson, E. P. 1993, *Customs in Common. Studies in Traditional Popular Culture*, New York.

Thrupp, S. L. 1958, "Editorial", *Comparative Studies in Society and History* 1, pp. 1–4.

Tilly, C. 1984, *Big Structures, Large Processes, Huge Comparisons*, New York.

  1992, *Coercion, Capital and European States, A.D. 990–1992*, Oxford.

Tilly, C. and Blockmans, W. (eds.) 1994, *Cities and the Rise of States in Europe, A.D. 1000–1800*, Boulder, CO.

Tomber, R. 1993, "Quantitative Approaches to the Investigation of Long-Distance Exchange", *Journal of Roman Archaeology* 6, pp. 142–166.

Toner, J. P. 1995, *Leisure and Ancient Rome*, Cambridge.

Torri, M. 1998, "Mughal Nobles, Indian Merchants, and the Beginning of British Conquest in Western India: The Case of Surat 1756–59", *Modern Asian Studies* 32, 2, pp. 257–315.

Tracy, J. D. (ed.) 1990, *The Rise of Merchant Empires. Long-Distance Trade in the Early Modern World*, Cambridge.

(ed.) 1991, *The Political Economy of Merchant Empires*, Cambridge.

Treadgold, W. 1997, *A History of the Byzantine State and Society*, Stanford, CA.

Tylor, E. B. 1871, *Primitive Culture*, London.

Udovitch, A. L. 1962, "At the Origins of the Western *Commenda:* Islam, Israel, Byzantium", *Speculum* 37, pp. 198–207.

1970, *Partnership and Profit in Medieval Islam*, Princeton, NJ.

Veblen, T. 1899, *The Theory of the Leisure Class*, New York.

Vélissaropoulos, J. 1980, *Les Nauclères grecs*, Paris.

Vera, D. 1994, "L'Italia agraria nell'età imperiale: Fra crisi e transformazione", in *L'Italie d'Auguste à Dioclétien*, Collection de l'École Française de Rome 198, Rome, pp. 239–248.

Verboren, K. 2002, *The Economy of Friends. Economic Aspects of "Amicitia" and Patronage in the Late Republic*, Collection Latomus 269, Brussels.

Vernhet, A. 1991, *La Graufesenque céramiques gallo-romaines*, Millau.

Veyne, P. 1961, "Vie de Trimalchion", *Annales ESC* 16, pp. 213–247.

1971, *Comment on écrit l'histoire. Essai d'epistémologie*, Paris.

1976a *L'Inventaire des différences*, Paris.

1976b, *Le Pain et le cirque*, Paris. (Published in English, 1990.)

1979, "Rome devant la prétendue fuite de l'or: mercantilisme ou politique disciplinaire?", *Annales ESC*, pp. 211–241.

1990, *Bread and Circuses*, trans. B. Pearce, London.

Virlouvet, C. (ed.) 1997, *La Rome impériale. Démographie et logistique*, Rome.

Visscher, F. de 1940, *Les édits d'Auguste découverts à Cyrène*, Louvain.

Vittinghof, F. 1953, "Portorium", *Paulys Realencyclopädie der classischen Alter-tumswissenschaft*, 22, 1, cols. 346–399.

Voltaire, F. M. A. de 1963, *Essai sur les moeurs et l'esprit de nations et sur les principaux faits de l'histoire depuis Charlemagne jusqu'à Louis XIII*, 2 vols., Paris.

Vries, J. de 1976, *Economy of Europe in an Age of Crisis 1600–1750*, Cambridge.

1984, *European Urbanization, 1500–1800*, London.

1990, "Problems in the Measurement, Description, and Analysis of Historical Urbanization", in A. Woude, A. Hayomi and J. de Vries (eds.), *Urban-ization in History. A Process of Dynamic Interactions*, Oxford, pp. 43–60.

Vries, J. de and Woude, A. 1997, *The First Modern Economy. Success, Failure and Perseverance of the Dutch Economy, 1500–1800*, Cambridge.

Wacke, A. 1993, "Gallisch, Punisch, Syrisch oder Griechisch statt latein? Zur Schrittweisen Gleichberechtigung der Geschäftssprachen im römischen

Reich", *Zeitschrift der Savigny-Stiftung für Rechtsgeschichte. Romanistische Abteilung* 110, pp. 14–59.

1994, "Die adjektivischen Klagen im Überblick, I: Von der Reeder- und der Betriebsleiterklage zur direkten Stellvertretung", *Zeitschrift der Savigny-Stiftung für Rechtsgeschichte. Romanistische Abteilung* 111, pp. 280–362.

Wagner, D. 2001, "The Administration of the Iron Industry in Eleventh Century China", *Journal of the Social and Economic History of the Orient* 44, 2, pp. 175–197.

Wallace-Hadrill, A. (ed.) 1989, *Patronage in Ancient Society*, London and New York.

1991, "Elites and Trade in the Roman Town", in Rich and Wallace-Hadrill 1991, pp. 241–272.

1994, *Houses and Society in Pompeii and Herculaneum*, Princeton, NJ.

Wallerstein, I. 1974a, *The Modern World-System*, vol. 1, San Diego, CA.

1974b, "The Rise and Future Demise of the World Capitalist System: Concepts for Comparative Analysis", *Comparative Studies in Society and History* 16, pp. 387–415.

1979, "The Ottoman Empire and the Capitalist World-Economy: Some Questions for Research", *Review* 2, 3, pp. 389–398.

Waltzing, J. P. 1895–1900, *Étude historique sur les corporations professionelles chez les Romains*, vols. 1–4, Louvain.

Watson, A. 1992. *The Evolution of International Society. A Comparative Historical Analysis*, London.

Weber, M. 1920a, "Die protestantische Ethik und der Geist des Kapitalismus", *Gesammelte Aufsätze zur Religionssoziologie*, vol. 1, Tübingen.

1920b, 'Vorwort' in M. Weber, *Gesammelte Aufsätze zur Religionssoziologie* vol. 1, Tübingen.

1922, *Gesammelte Aufsätze zur Wissenschaftslehre*, Tübingen.

1924a: "Agrarverhältnisse im Altertum", *Gesammelte Aufsätze zur Sozial- und Wirtschaftsgeschichte*, pp. 1–288, Tübingen.

1924b: "Die sozialen Gründe des Untergangs der antiken Kultur", *Gesammelte Aufsätze zur Sozial- und Wirtschaftsgeschichte*, pp. 289–311, Tübingen.

1924c: "Zur Geschichte der Handelsgesellschaften im Mittelalter", *Gesammelte Aufsätze zur Sozial- und Wirtschaftsgeschichte*, Tübingen, pp. 312–443.

1972, *Wirtschaft und Gesellschaft*, Tübingen.

Wee, C. J. 1997, "Framing the New East Asia", in R. Salim (ed.), *"The Clash of Civilizations?" Asian Responses*, Karachi, Oxford and New York, chapter 5.

Weeber, K.-W. 2003, *Luxus im alten Rom. Die Schwelgerei, das süsse Gift*, Darmstadt.

2006, *Luxus im alten Rom. Die öffentliche Pracht*, Darmstadt.

Whitbread, I. K. 1995, *Greek Transport Amphorae. A Petrological and Archaeological Study*, Athens.

Whittaker, C. R. 1985, "Trade and the Aristocracy in the Roman Empire", *Opus, International Journal for Social and Economic History of Antiquity* 4, pp. 49–75.

1989, "Amphorae and Trade", in *Amphores romaines et histoire économique. Dix ans de recherche.* Collection de l'École Française de Rome 114, Rome, pp. 537–539.

1993, *Land, City and Trade in the Roman Empire*, Aldershot.

1994a, *Frontiers of the Roman Empire. A Social and Economic Study*, Baltimore, MD.

1994b, "The Politics of Power: The Cities of Italy", in *L'Italie d'Auguste à Dioclétien*, Collection de l'École Française de Rome 198, Rome, pp. 127–143.

1995, "Do Theories of the Ancient City Matter?", in Cornell and Lomas, pp. 9–26.

2002, "Proto-industrialization in Roman Gaul", in Karen Ascani *et al.* (eds.), *Ancient History Matters. Studies Presented to Jens Erik Skydsgaard on His Seventieth Birthday, Analecta Romana Instituti Danici* Suppl. 30, pp. 11–22.

Wickham, C. 1984, "The Other Transition: From the Ancient World to Feudalism", *Past and Present* 103, pp. 3–36.

1985, "The Uniqueness of the East", *Journal of Peasant Studies* 12, pp. 167–196.

1988, "Marx, Sherlock Holmes and Late Roman Commerce", *Journal of Roman Studies* 78, pp. 183–193.

2005, *Framing the Early Middle Ages*, Oxford.

Wierschowski, L. 1995, *Die Regionale Mobilität in Gallien nach dem Inschriften des I.–3. Jahrhunderts n. Chr.*, Historia Einzelschriften 91, Stuttgart.

Will, E. 1957, "Marchands et chefs de caravannes à Palmyre", *Syria* 34, pp. 262–277.

1992, *Les Palmyréniens. La Venise des sables (Ier siécle avant – IIIéme siécle aprés J.C.)*, Paris.

Wills, J. E., Jr. 1993, "Maritime Asia, 1500–1800: The Interactive Emergence of European Domination", *American Historical Review* 98, pp. 83–105.

Wilson, A. 2001, "Timgad and Textile Production", in Mattingly and Salmon, pp. 271–296.

2002, "Machines, Power and the Ancient Economy", *Journal of Roman Studies* 92, pp. 1–32.

Wink, A. 1989, " 'Al-Hind' India and Indonesia in the Islamic World-Economy, ca. 700–1800", in P. J. Marshall *et al.*, *India and Indonesia during the Ancien Regime*, Leiden, pp. 33–72.

Wittfogel, K. A. 1957, *Oriental Despotism: A Comparative Study of Total Power*, New Haven, CT.

Wolf, E. 1966, *Peasants*, Englewood Cliffs, NJ.

1982, *Europe and the People Without History*, Berkeley and Los Angeles.

Wolff, C. 2003, *Les Brigands en orient sous le haut-empire romain*, Rome.

Wolff, H. J. *et al.* 1978, *Handbuch der Altertumswissenschaft*, 10.5.2: Das Recht der griechischen Papyri Ägyptens in der Zeit der Ptolemaeer und des Prinzipats, Munich.

1980, "Römisches Provinzialrecht in der Provinz Arabia", *Aufstieg und Niedergang der Römischen Welt* 2, 13, pp. 763–806.

Wolters, R. 1999, *Nummi Signati. Untersuchungen zur römischen Münzprägung und Geldwirtschaft*, Munich.

Wong, R. B. 1997, *China Transformed*, Ithaca, NY.

Woolf, G. 1990, "World-systems Analysis and the Roman Empire", *Journal of Roman Archaeology* 6, pp. 44–58.

1992, "Imperialism, Empire and the Integration of the Roman Economy", *World Archaeology* 23, 3, pp. 282–293.

1993, "Roman Peace", in Rich and Shipley, pp. 171–194.

1997, "The Roman Urbanization of the East", in Alcock 1997a, pp. 1–14.

1998, *Becoming Roman. The Origins of Provincial Civilization in Gaul*, Cambridge.

2001, "Regional Productions in Early Roman Gaul", in Mattingly and Salmon, pp. 49–65.

Wrigley, E. A. 1987, *Peoples, Cities and Wealth. The Transformation of Traditional Society*, Oxford.

1988, *Continuity, Chance and Change. The Character of the Industrial Revolution in England*, Cambridge.

Yang, A. A. 1998, *Bazaar India. Markets, Society, and the Colonial State in Gangetic Bihar*, Berkeley, Los Angeles and London.

Yaron, R. 1964 "Reichsrecht, Volksrecht and Talmud", *Revue Internationale des Droits de l'Antiquité*, 3rd ser. 2, pp. 281–298.

Yon, J.-B. 2002, *Les Notables de Palmyre*, Beirut.

Young, G. 2001, *Rome's Eastern Trade. International Commerce and Imperial Policy, 31 BC–AD 305*, London.

Zaccagnini, C. (ed.) 2003, *Mercanti e politica nel mondo antico*, Rome.

Zanker, P. 1987, *Augustus und die Macht der Bilder*, Munich (English translation by A. Shapiro, Ann Arbor, MI, 1988.)

Zelener, Yan 2006, "Between Technology and Productivity", in E. Lo Cascio (ed.), *Innovazione tecnica e progresso economico nel mondo romano*, Bari, pp. 303–18.

Zevi, F. 1989, "Introduzione", in *Amphores romaines et histoire économique. Dix ans de recherche*. Collection de l'École Française de Rome 114, Rome, pp. 3–19.

Ziche, H. 2006, "Integrating Late Roman Cities, Countryside and Trade", in Bang, Ikeguchi and Ziche, pp. 255–276.

Ziegler, K.-H. 1971, *Das private Schiedsgericht im antiken römischen Recht*, Munich.

Zimmermann, R. 1990, *The Law of Obligations. Roman Foundations of the Civilian Tradition*, Cape Town.

Ørsted, P. 1985, *Roman Imperial Economy and Romanization*, Copenhagen.

2000, "Roman State Intervention? The Case of Mining in the Roman Empire", in Lo Cascio and Rathbone, pp. 70–76.

Ørsted, P., Carlsen, J., Ladjimi Sebai, L. and Ben Hassen, H. (eds.) 2000, *Africa Proconsularis. Regional Studies in the Segermes Valley of Northern Tunisia*, vol. 3: *Historical Conclusions*, Aarhus.

Østergård, U. 1973, "Den Antikke Produktionsmåde. Oversigt over historieskrivningen om forholdet mellem økonomi og samfund i Antikken", *Den Jyske Historiker* 5–6, pp. 4–42.

1976, "Studiet af førkapitalistiske samfundsforhold – Mulighed og relevans. Teoretiske og metodiske problemer", *Den Jyske Historiker* 6, pp. 52–135.

1996, "The Meaning of Europe – Empire, Nation-states, Civilization", *Arbejdspapirer fra Center for Kulturforskning, Aarhus Universitet* 29, Aarhus.

1997, "Hvad nu hvis . . . Kontrafaktiske hypoteser og "åbne" situationer i historie og historieforskning", *Arbejdspapirer fra Center for Kulturforskning, Aarhus Universitet 46*, Aarhus.

INDEX

Mughal Empire (*cont.*)
    and old world Eurasian trade 304–6
    promoting corporate
        associations 246–8
    as tributary systems 110–21
Murecine wax tablets *see* Sulpicii
    archive/bankers
Muziris 281, 283–4

Navigation Act 56
Needham, Joseph 43
Nehalenia 131, 261
Nero (attempt to curb abusive conduct of
    publicans) 207
Nerva 98
networks of trade,
    compartmentalised 287–9
Nile, River 155, 281
North, Douglass 49, 140
    see also Akerlof; transaction costs

Obasanjo, Olusegun 38
Obeysekere, Gananath 37
Oenoanda 109–10
olive oil 73–6, 289
    see also Monte Testaccio
Opium Wars 58
Opramoas of Rhodiapolis 106–9
Orient/Orientalism 1–2, 44
    and classics 17
Oriental luxury goods 121, 258, 281,
    305–6
    and customs dues 214–15, 228
Ostia
    Piazzale delle Corporazioni 250–3
"otherness", the politics of 6, 23, 32–3,
    37–40, 43–4, 46
Oxyrhynchus 166, 248

Palmyra 151, 196, 221–2, 228, 230–1,
    283–4, 305
    customs law of 224
    merchant community of 253–4,
        257
Pamuk, Orhan 40
Panopolis 68–9, 79
partnership 270, 273–6
    see also *commenda*
Parthian Empire 18

Paul (the Roman jurist) 278
Pax Romana 29, 70
    peace dividend 235
    quality of protection offered by 228–9,
        238
peculium 276
    and limited liability 277–80
    see also *commenda*; credit
pedlar-market 196–7
    see also bazaar
Peking *see* Beijing
Pelsaert, Francisco 145, 199
    see also chartered joint stock
        companies
pepper 146
Pergamon 216
Petronius 132, 264–5, 301
Philo 245
Piraeus 151
pirates 131, 203, 230–2, 237
Pisa 288
    see also *terra sigillata*
Plato 262
Plautus 277
Pliny (the Elder) 134, 135, 202, 302
Pliny (the Younger) 99, 139, 240
Plutarch 103, 105
Pol Pot 24
Polanyi, Karl 23, 49, 67, 119
    see also anthropology; Finley; Geertz;
        Malinowski; primitivism–
        modernism; redistribution;
        Sahlins
Pollux 202–3
Pompeii 121
population size 86, 124
predation 12, 13, 62, 66, 83, 122, 150–1,
    204–12, 226, 235, 239
primitivism–modernism 1, 12, 19–36,
    291–2
    parallel debates 8, 37–45
private (aristocratic) property 97–110
production, decentralised 30, 74–6
productivity gains 122–3, 125
protection 13, 200–1
    costs of 233–4
    locally organised 230–2, 234
    and predation 203–4
    see also *Pax Romana*

INDEX

provisioning policies *see* consumer
city/interests
publicans (*publicani*) 121, 204
weak state constraints on 206–12
Puteoli 253, 272, 283–4
Tyrians in 254

Rabirius Postumus, Caius 142
Red Sea 254, 281
redistribution 67–9, 72–3, 119–21,
125–7
revenues, prebendal 96–7, 125
Rhodes 231
Rhodian Sea Law 191
Rhone–Saône–Rhine arterial route 71,
127
Ricardo, David 72
see also economic integration
risk and uncertainty 4, 13
in trade 132
and the bazaar 199, 240–1, 269,
287
risk, diversification of 195–201, 275
Rodinson, Maxime 43
Romaia Sebasta, festival of 216
Rome (the imperial capital) 2, 9, 142,
222, 247, 254, 280
compared to London 47
concentration of consumption in 47,
66, 127
the grain supply of 176–8, 273
Rostovtzeff, M. I. 21, 29–55, 74, 75, 258,
291

Sabora 223
Sahlins, Marshall 37, 290, 302
see also anthropology; "otherness", the
politics of
Said, Edward 44
Sardis 248
Sartre, Jean-Paul 24
Scaevola 280
Seleucia 254
Seneca 101
seviri Augustales 259
Shahjahan 80
Sidonius 143
silver, American 306
slavery 274, 276–80

Smith, Adam 51, 62, 147, 152, 240
Smithian dynamics 45, 48, 291
see also agrarianate society; economic
integration; markets
societas 275–6
and *commenda* 276
see also partnership
Sombart, Werner 299
Song dynasty 43
sources *see* evidence
Spain 73
Spasinou Charax 253
spices 302
state
segmentary 111
size of Mughal 83–4, 93–4
size of Roman 69–70, 92–3, 115–16
state-system, European 55–6
Stein, Burton 111
stock exchanges 50
Sulpicii archive/bankers 187–8, 267–8,
272, 279, 283–4
Surat 57, 196, 243, 244, 247
surplus extraction 78–9
see also taxes and trade
Syria 66

Tacitus 98, 99, 207
Taj Mahal 80, 296–8
Tarsus 248
Tavernier, J.-B. 96
tax-farmers
see publicans
taxation
and price records 155–6
Roman and Mughal 79
see also custom dues; tribute
taxes and trade 8, 12, 47–50, 62, 83,
113–21, 291, 293–4
Tebtunis 170
temple of Bel 254, 257
terra sigillata 30, 74, 288–9, 304
Tertullian 245
theory
see conceptualisation
third world, the 6
Timur Lenk 79
Titus 103
tonnage, ships 136

357

For EU product safety concerns, contact us at Calle de José Abascal, 56–1°, 28003 Madrid, Spain or eugpsr@cambridge.org.

 www.ingramcontent.com/pod-product-compliance
Ingram Content Group UK Ltd.
Pitfield, Milton Keynes, MK11 3LW, UK
UKHW012156180425
457623UK00018B/214